TECHNICAL WRITING IN A CORPORATE CULTURE:

A Study of the Nature of Information

Writing Research

Multidisciplinary Inquiries into the Nature of Writing

edited by Marcia Farr, University of Illinois at Chicago

Arthur N. Applebee, *Contexts for Learning to Write: Studies of Secondary School Instruction*

Christine Barabas, *Technical Writing in a Corporate Culture: A Study of the Nature of Information*

Barbara Couture, *Functional Approaches to Writing*

Carole Edelsky, *Writing in a Bilingual Program: Habia Una Vez*

Lester Faigley, Roger Cherry, David Jolliffe, and Anna Skinner, *Assessing Writers' Knowledge and Processes of Composing*

Marcia Farr (ed.), *Advances in Writing Research, Volume One: Children's Early Writing Development*

Sarah W. Freedman (ed.), *The Acquisition of Written Language: Response and Revision*

George H. Jensen and John K. DiTiberio, *Personality and the Teaching of Composition*

David A. Jolliffe (ed.), *Advances in Writing Research, Volume Two: Writing in Academic Disciplines*

Judith Langer, *Children Reading and Writing: Structures and Strategies*

Bennett A. Rafoth and Donald L. Rubin (eds.), *The Social Construction of Written Communication*

Leo Ruth and Sandra Murphy, *Designing Writing Tasks for the Assessment of Writing*

Jana Staton, Roger Shuy, Joy Kreeft, and Leslie Reed, *Dialogue Journal Communication: Classroom, Linguistic, Social, and Cognitive Views*

William Teale and Elizabeth Sulzby (eds.), *Emergent Literacy: Writing and Reading*

IN PREPARATION

Robert Gundlach, *Children and Writing in American Education*

Elizabeth Sulzby, *Emergent Writing and Reading in 5–6 Year Olds: A Longitudinal Study*

TECHNICAL WRITING IN A CORPORATE CULTURE:

A Study of the Nature of Information

Christine Barabas

Northern Illinois University
Barabas & Associates

ABLEX PUBLISHING CORPORATION
NORWOOD, NEW JERSEY

Second Printing 1995

Printed in the United States of America

Library of Congress Cataloging-in-Publication Data

Barabas, Christine Peterson.
    Technical writing in a corporate culture : a study of the nature
of information / Christine Peterson Barabas.
       p. cm. — (Writing research)
    Includes bibliographical references (p.).
    ISBN 0-89391-603-X. — ISBN 0-89391-664-1 (pbk.)
    1. Technical writing. I. Title. II. Series: Writing research
(Norwood, N.J.)
    T11.B346 1990
    808'.0666—dc20   90-32194
                                                        CIP

Ablex Publishing Corporation
355 Chestnut Street
Norwood, New Jersey 07648
P

CONTENTS

PART III A STUDY OF PROGRESS REPORTS IN AN R&D ORGANIZATION: WRITER INTENTIONS, TEXTS, AND READER EXPECTATIONS

List of Tables

List of Appendices and Figures

Acknowledgments

First and foremost, I wish to thank those dearest to me who, during the last few years as I worked on this volume evenings, weekends, and vacations, gave me the love, support, and understanding I needed to persevere. To Robert, my husband, and Jason, my son, I owe more than words can express. Together, they helped keep me sane throughout this endeavor. When I complained, they comforted; when I was discouraged, they encouraged. To Mary Ryba, my friend and business partner for more than the last decade, I am forever indebted. Without her wisdom, love, compassion, and endless tolerance, I could not have finished this volume.

To my other relatives and friends who have remained at my side and cheered me along the way, I am also very grateful: especially my mom and dad, my mother-in-law Josephine, Kris and Harold, Casey and Judy, Dan, and all my other friends for being understanding when my work on this project prevented me from being with them. I wish to thank them all for allowing me to put them on hold for so long and for always being there at my convenience.

Finally, I want to acknowledge the several individuals who were directly involved in this work at some point during its long evolution. The idea for this study began several years ago, in 1982, when I was a doctoral student at the University of Illinois at Chicago. To the chairman of my dissertation committee—Martin Steinmann, Jr., the best mentor and editor one could hope for—and to the other members—Chadwick Hansen, Marcia Farr, and John Mellon—go my thanks for being so receptive to my research proposal and for giving me both the guidance and the latitude I needed to pursue my research. I benefited greatly from their good suggestions and thorough critiques.

Since 1984 when my dissertation was completed, I have expanded the scope of my study to incorporate recent research in the field of real-world writing. Marcia Farr, the editor of this series, was a motivating force behind that effort, as she was the one who early on suggested that at the heart of my dissertation study lay the important issue of what it meant to write well in an academic versus a corporate setting. As a result, I added Part I and Part II to my original dissertation, which, though considerably expanded, is reported in Part III of this volume.

In addition to Marcia Farr, two other individuals were especially helpful in reviewing my early drafts. Apart from the person whom I contracted to run the statistical tests on my data, my friend and former colleague, David Workman, reviewed Part III for its use of statistics and patiently gave me tutorials in plain, simple English. This work has also profited greatly from the painstaking comments of an anonymous reviewer who critiqued an early version of this work, and who, like David Workman, expressed some reservations about the use of t tests for small numbers of subjects such as those involved in Phase 3 of my study. Both the reviewer and David indicated, too, however, that if anything my conclusions are conservative. That reassures me somewhat, for at least I have not erred on the side of exaggeration. As for whatever problems may remain in this work, I take full responsibility.

Last, but certainly not least, I wish to express my appreciation to those at the R&D organization at which I conducted this study for being so cooperative and friendly as I repeatedly interrupted their research so that I could do mine. In addition to the directors, supervisors, and researchers who gave freely of their time and from whom I learned so much, I want to thank the vice president of R&D for agreeing to allow me to conduct this on-site study. My special thanks go to the manager of personnel and his secretary for handling the many arrangements and details that the study reported in Part III of this volume entailed.

About the Author

Christine Barabas is Associate Professor of English at Northern Illinois University where she teaches undergraduate and graduate courses in technical writing. In addition, she is president of Barabas & Associates, a training and consulting firm in business and technical communication. Before joining the faculty at Northern Illinois University, she served as Assistant Professor of English and Director of Composition at George Williams College for ten years, and later as partner of Barabas, Ryba and Associates, Ltd.

Dr. Barabas received her B.A. in English and Secondary Education from the University of Illinois at Urbana-Champaign, her M.A. in English from Northwestern University, and her Ph.D. in English, with a specialization in rhetoric and composition, from the University of Illinois at Chicago.

WRITING RESEARCH:
Multidisciplinary Inquiries into the Nature of Writing

Marcia Farr, series editor
University of Illinois at Chicago

SERIES PREFACE

This series of volumes presents the results of scholarly inquiry into the nature of writing. The research presented comes from various disciplines, those which have emerged as significant within the last several decades in the burgeoning field of research on writing. These primarily include linguistics, anthropology, psychology, literary theory, philosophy, rhetoric, and education. In this series, research on writing is viewed as constituting a field, rather than a discipline. A field is seen as a multidisciplinary entity focused on a set of significant questions about a central concern (e.g., American Studies, or literacy), whereas a discipline is seen as sharing theoretical and methodological approaches which have a substantial tradition behind them. If research on writing evolves into a more unified discipline, rather than remaining a multifaceted field, much will be lost from the rich multiplicity of traditions which now contribute to it.

The history of this particular field is unique. Much early work, a great deal of which has been reported in this series, was conceptualized at and funded by the National Institute of Education, formerly of the U.S. Department of Education. Following a planning conference in June, 1977, a program of basic research on the learning and teaching of writing was developed and funded annually. During the 1980s, in spite of considerably reduced government support, this field flourished and expanded. New Ph.D. programs were created, primarily within English and education departments. At the same time, scholars from yet other disciplines (notably social historians) turned their attention to writing and literacy. The interest in literacy, in fact, reflected a growing awareness of the inter-relatedness of writing with other aspects of language, culture, and society. Simultaneously with the scholarly expansion, a serious concern for the apparent failure to achieve mass literacy in our educational institutions grew and deepened.

As we near the 21st century, unprecedented demographic changes in the United States (in which European-origin whites will become a minority) urge us to press on in this work. Scholarly grounding in a variety of disciplines continues to be of paramount importance, but no less so than grounding the scholarship in the concerns of mass literacy. What this literacy will consist of, and how it will be used in educational, work, and other institutional and personal domains remains, of course, to be determined. All scholarly work within the boundaries of these concerns continues to be invited for submission to this series.

Introduction

since feeling is first
who pays any attention
to the syntax of things
will never wholly kiss you

opening stanza of a poem
by e.e. cummings

Two recent and related developments in the research and teaching of writing are beginning to have significant effects upon our discipline: One is the growing interest being shown in real-world writing (or what academicians call "nonacademic" writing) and the other is the increased importance being attached to the particular contexts within which texts are written, read, and used. As a result of these developments, we have begun to question almost everything we thought we knew about writing. Moreover, we have begun to ask some very basic questions that have been overlooked in most of our previous studies. One of the most fundamental and important of these questions is, "What is good writing?"

Despite the interest in real-world writing, however, very little is known about this field as yet. The main reason is that, for the most part, the study of writing during the last 25 years has been synonymous with the study of composition. Almost everything that we, as researchers and teachers, know about writing has been based upon primarily one context: the writing that students do in school, especially essay writing as it is taught and practiced in our college composition courses. While we now know more than ever before about the features that distinguish good essays from poor ones, and about the composing strategies of our most proficient versus our least proficient student writers, we know very little about whether the composition skills we teach and study in academic settings have anything to do with the written communication skills that students will need later in their careers. As Boice (1985) has suggested:

> The prescriptions of composition researchers seem to apply only to the context in which they typically do their research and theorizing—the classroom within an academic semester or, more often, within a few sessions of writing. In my experience, the same people who had excelled in writing classes may

not have learned to write in other settings—where guidelines are ambiguous, where writing is easily put off, and where the consequences of writing include promotion and tenure. (p. 473)

Furthermore, we know little about whether the criteria that teachers and researchers use to evaluate writing in school are at all related to the criteria that managers use to evaluate their employees' writing. There is, however, some evidence to suggest that what those in academe regard as good writing may be different from what those in the real world regard as good writing.

For example, in a study that examined how different audiences evaluate the same text, Bogdanowicz (1983) found that English teachers, as well as engineering faculty, based their evaluations primarily upon microlevel features of texts such as sentence structure and word choice whereas managers based their evaluations primarily upon macrolevel features of texts such as content and layout. Her findings are not surprising since, traditionally, composition teachers and researchers have not been as concerned with the information or ideas contained in student essays as they have been with such things as the essay's method of organization, means of development, syntactic versatility, cohesiveness, and grammatical correctness—in other words with form rather than content, with *how* something is said rather than with *what* is said or *why* it is being said. Often, the writing topic is contrived solely as a vehicle for the student to learn that week's pattern of exposition. As Dillon (1981) notes, "It is not clear to many students what the purpose of their themes is, except to practice their 'writing,' which is to say that themes have no communicative purpose" (p. xii). The result is that students become very adept at what Roberts (1980) calls, in an article of the same title, "How to Say Nothing in Five Hundred Words." In short, students know, and the teacher knows, that the purpose of the assignment, even when it calls for a response to a hypothetical "real-world" situation and reader, is not really to communicate but rather to demonstrate that the students have whatever writing skills the teacher considers important.

Typically those skills are the conventions of the five-paragraph theme genre. As Rubin and Rafoth (1986) found in their study, teachers give the highest ratings to essays that conform to this genre, and student writers, recognizing this, "depend on the five-paragraph theme pattern as a safe, formulaic approach" (p. 19), regardless of the writing task. Students, in other words, equate proficiency in writing with the arbitrary standards of college writing as established, taught, tested, and validated primarily by composition teachers—standards that typically emphasize the structure rather than the substance of texts. So pervasive are these standards that, as Rubin and Rafoth speculate, many instances of exposition composed by professional writers and appearing in commercial publications probably would not fare well against the rating criteria (namely, holistic scoring) that teachers commonly use to evaluate writing. And, indeed, this is precisely what Freedman (1984) found in her study.

Freedman examined how composition teachers, using an adaptation of Diederich's holistic rating scale (1974), evaluated essays written by students versus those written by professionals. She found that the teachers (who assumed that the professional writers' essays had also been written by students) rated the professionals' essays lower than they did the students' essays. Although the professionals' essays received higher scores on voice, sentence structure, word choice, and usage, the essays received lower scores on development and organization, the two traits in holistic scoring that Freedman, in earlier studies (1977, 1979a, 1979b), found most significant in influencing the teachers' overall holistic scores.

As one explanation for the lower ratings given to the professional writers' essays, Freedman suggests that the teachers may have responded negatively because the organization and development of the professional writers' essays were unconventional and thus violated the teachers' own preconceptions of what an essay should be and should sound like. As support for this view, Freedman refers to the distinction made by Searle (1969) and Horner (1979) between "real questions"—in which writers assume they are being asked to give information to readers—and "exam questions"—in which writers assume they are being asked to demonstrate to readers that they know what the readers expect them to know. Freedman speculates that the students in her study approached the essay assignment as they would an "exam" question, and thus they assumed that their purpose was not to convey what they knew but rather to demonstrate to the teacher/rater that they knew how to write. The professionals, on the other hand, approached their writing task as if it were an occasion for genuine communication in which a real reader had posed a real question that required real thought and response. As a result, the professionals' responses, when compared with those of the students, did not conform to the usual conventions of the traditional five-paragraph essay. Rather, the professionals took a less contrived and less formal approach to the writing task, one that conveyed a more deliberate, spontaneous, and assertive tone. Freedman further suggests that the teachers may have interpreted this tone as inappropriate, and perhaps even offensive, since they are accustomed to a more deferential, passive, and rhetorically lukewarm stance on the part of student writers. The students, in other words, were much more aware than were the professionals of the artificiality of the writing task. They realized what the professionals did not: that the teacher-raters were not as interested in communication as they were in composition skills, with how ideas are expressed rather than with what those ideas are.

The above studies point to a major shortcoming in most composition research and instruction: our traditional emphasis upon the structure rather than the substance of texts, upon their form and expression rather than their content and function. As will be discussed in Part One, our almost single-mindedly attention to the "syntax of things" has fostered the notion, amongst ourselves and our students, that good writing is good writing—that there exist some universal, objective criteria that govern the quality of written texts, regardless of their specific purposes and audiences. It is not surprising, therefore, that frequently many real-world writers, especially those just out of the university, mistakenly assume that the requirements and standards of real-world writing are the same as those of academic writing, and that what their former professors considered a good essay, lab report, or research paper is the same as that which their managers consider a good report. Perhaps what is most ironic is that by teaching students to become good academic writers we may inadvertently be teaching them to become poor real-world writers. For, as many composition-teachers-turned-writing-consultants soon learn, it is often this failure to distinguish between the aims of academic writing and those of corporate writing that accounts for many of the problems experienced by real-world writers.

Support for this view is provided by Paradis, Dobrin, and Miller (1985), who, in their study of writing at Exxon ITD (the Intermediates Technology Division of Exxon's R&D, Research & Development, organization), discovered that even scientists and engineers who had taken college courses in technical writing find the transition from academic writing to corporate writing difficult. As Paradis et al. (p. 300) point out, many writers, especially the youngest and the newest to the company, tend to equate (and assume that their readers equate) the quality of their writing with the quality of their effort, "a holdover attitude from the college environment." As a result, their reports are often laborious chronicles of their research, with major emphasis upon their methods, procedures, and findings. According to Paradis et al., what such writers fail to realize is that, whereas college professors are most interested in *how* students get results (see also Barton and Barton, 1981), R&D supervisors in industry "want *results* and *recommendations*—save the logic for later." Further evidence that this is the case is provided by Souther, who, in his Westinghouse study (summarized in Souther and White, 1977), found that, while researchers (scientists and engineers) often reproduce in their reports their problem-solving process, neither do managers want such a review nor do they usually expect an extensive account of the findings. Rather, what they do want is information that will help them make decisions, which in turn will help achieve organizational goals.

Albert Einstein once said, "Our age is characterized by the perfection of means and the confusion of goals." He may well have been characterizing not only the main problem of the real-world writers referred to above, but also the history of composition research and instruction to date. For until quite recently, we have been obsessed, in our research and teaching of composition, with writing as though it were a means and end unto itself. We have neglected the fact that, except perhaps for school writing, most of the writing that people do has genuine communicative aims and that to teach or study either writing or writers without taking these aims into account is, as Beach and Bridwell (1984) put it, "a little like studying animal life by visiting zoo cages" (p. 6).

In order to teach, evaluate, or investigate writing, as opposed to composition, we need to get out of our own academic cages. We need to look at the functions and the goals that writing, as a means of communication, serves beyond our classroom walls. If, as Odell and Goswami (1982) have suggested, the contexts and consequences of real-world writing are quite different from those of academic writing, then we need to explore in what ways these two contexts differ and, upon the basis of our findings, to develop theories and models that reflect what, why, and how people in real-world settings write. We need, perhaps most of all, to set aside our academic, English-teachery notions of good writing and to discover what other people who neither read, write, nor teach essays as a living, regard as good writing.

The present work is an effort in that direction.

THE IMPETUS FOR MY RESEARCH

A common theory about the source of creativity and inquiry is that it is rooted in a feeling of dissonance—that unease we experience when the pieces do not quite seem to fit. It is this same sense of dissonance or anomaly that according to Kuhn (1970) inspires researchers to seek new explanations of phenomena for which current theories or models are somehow inadequate. And it is this same sense of uneasiness, "the seed from which subsequent investigation grows," that Young, Becker, and Pike in *Rhetoric: Discovery and Change* (1970, p. 91) suggest is the motivation for writing.

In my own case, the seeds for the study reported in Part Three were sown out of the feelings of dissonance I experienced some years ago when I was concurrently a director of a college composition program and an assistant professor of English, a business and technical writing consultant and trainer in corporations, and a doctoral student in a composition and rhetoric program. It was, in short, a dissonance-rich environment. One of the things that increasingly disturbed me was that writing, as I was teaching it and studying it within the college and university setting, was quite different from writing as I was observing it in the corporate world. While the questions that concerned the real-world writers seemed to be the same as those of my student writers, questions such as what to say and how best to say it, the answers to those questions were not quite as simple or as clear-cut as they appeared in the classroom, textbooks, and scholarly literature. Neither the process nor the product models of writing typically espoused by the teachers and researchers of writing adequately described or addressed the needs of real-world writers. Indeed, the more I attempted to adapt such approaches to the teaching of business and technical writing within organizations, the more convinced I became of the limitations of academic models and theories, and the more I questioned their usefulness. At worst, I began to suspect that the rhetorical and pedagogical baggage I had carried with me from academia and into my corporate teaching and consulting was hindering more than helping the development of the adult writers with whom I worked. For, increasingly, it seemed to me that the real problem with many of their reports, letters, and memoranda was *not* that their texts did not conform to the prescriptives of good writing as typically promulgated by writing teachers and researchers, but rather that their texts *did*.

Where I felt particularly vulnerable and handicapped was in evaluating their texts out of context, with little more knowledge about the texts' audiences, purposes, and functions than what the writers themselves were able to intuit. I say "intuit" because, as I later discovered when I had occasions to talk to others within the organizations (particularly the intended readers of the texts), the writers sometimes had either inaccurate or vague notions about why they were writing and to whom.

It was out of a similar experience involving the apparent disparity between writer intentions and reader expectations that the idea for my research was conceived. I was teaching a technical writing course for researchers (scientists and engineers) at the R&D organization of a major corporation when one day in class the group was critiquing each others' monthly progress reports. The ensuing discussion became lively as the researchers debated the appropriateness of including this or that type of information in a progress report. At the heart of the discussion, I realized, were not only their conflicting ideas about what constituted a good progress report, but also their quite different notions about the criteria of effective writing and, beyond that, their very concepts of "progress" itself. Since I was the hired expert on writing, the researchers turned to me for the definitive answers that would resolve their debate.

Like a typical consultant-teacher, I took the "I'll-check-into-it" tack. It seemed only natural to me then that the first place to turn to for answers would be to the authoritative sources in the field, in this case to the technical writing textbook we were using in class. When that provided little help, I checked numerous other technical writing textbooks to see what they had to say about progress reports. But few of them, I found, contained much more than a passing reference to progress reports, and in the rest of the textbooks the advice and models were often either so contradictory or so general as to be useless. Thus, as a last resort, I decided to find out from the researchers' supervisors and directors themselves what they thought a progress report should be.

It was during a meeting of R&D supervisors and directors of the same company that I broached the subject of progress reports and recounted their researchers' confusion about what constituted a good progress report. Their initial reaction was shock: "Certainly," they exclaimed, "our people must know why they're writing progress reports!" "They're the lifeblood of our work here." "They write them all the time." "Why, a few years ago I think we even published something or another on progress reports and distributed it, didn't we, Henry? Where is it? Let's dig it out and circulate it again." And so forth. Whatever consensus there initially appeared to be, however, soon turned to dissension as the supervisors and directors began describing their specific ideas about what a progress report should and should not include:

"Well," said one, "I just want to know what they've done during the past month and what they're going to do next month."

"I don't care what they've done," retorted another, "so much as what they've found out." To which someone else interjected:

"More damn data and graphs, you mean? I'm drowning in it already. Let them just tell me what all the gibberish means."

"*Means?*" inquired yet another, "What do you mean *means*? How can they can possibly know when they're in the midst of it all? Besides, isn't that what we're supposed to do, figure out what it all adds up to?"

"Hell no!" burst a fifth person, and then tempered it with, "Well, yes, of course at some level we're the ones with the big picture and all, but they've got to be doing more for their pay than running tests and generating data, otherwise we can get rid of the lot of them and just rely exclusively on robotics. I want to see some evidence of *thinking* in their progress reports— speculations and conclusions, however tentative."

"That's fine, George, except you're forgetting one thing: the distribution list. We're not the only ones who get these reports. How about corporate headquarters? What happens when they run wild with our speculations and assume they're conclusive, and then three or eight months down the line they get another report from us that contradicts our earlier ones? We'll lose credibility at R&D if we take those kind of leaps. To the VPs in New York we'll look like we've got our heads—"

"And I say," countered George, "that we might as well fold up R&D if that's our idea of progress, to wait until we're 100 percent proof positive every time we write, say, or do anything because that day is never going to come. The nature of research *is* uncertainty. We're forced to make conjectures at every point along the way. The progress report ought to be the person's best guess-timate as to the status of the project at that particular point in time, and, based on the evidence available, his projections about where it looks headed."

By the end of the meeting, about the only thing clear to me was the lack of agreement among the supervisors and directors, as well as their re-searchers, about what characterized good progress reports. I left the meeting without answers, but I left, too, convinced that here was a subject worth investigating. For beneath the apparent confusion lay some impor-tant questions about writing, progress, and the functions of information in an R&D organization that, to my knowledge, had gone unexplored in the research on writing.

At this point, lest my readers speculate that the situation described above is atypical of corporations or R&D organizations, I wish to point out that, based on my consulting and teaching experiences in corporations over the last 10 years and the findings of others (for example, Paradis et al., 1985), the lack of consensus regarding the nature and function of company docu-ments is not unusual nor is the confusion about what constitutes good writing restricted to only progress reports or even to technical writing per se. Few companies, including many prestigious corporations, have explicit policies, standards, or guidelines for written communication (see, for exam-ple, Gilsdorf, 1987). When they do, the guidelines tend to be either style pamphlets, with prescriptives lifted from English handbooks; format speci-fications more suitable for secretaries than for writers; instructions for com-pleting laboratory notebooks; or company protocols concerning such items as the distribution and release of proprietary information. Rarely do com-panies, as a matter of course, develop guidelines for writers that (a) describe the various types of reports required of employees, the audiences and pur-poses for the various reports, and the functions each serves each within and outside the organization; (b) illustrate positive and negative examples of each type of report; or (c) offer advice on how to approach various writing tasks in order to avoid the common pitfalls associated with each. To do so requires a major undertaking for which few individuals in an organization seldom have either the time, inclination, knowledge, or authority. At best, more modest attempts to develop such guidelines seem to be initiated at the department or division level by individual supervisors or managers who, for any number of reasons, feel compelled to improve the quality of written communication within their specific work units.

Even at that, however, such attempts seem to be the exception rather the rule. In most instances, as will be discussed in Chapter 1, employees receive little formalized training or guidance when it comes to writing, even though for most of them writing accounts for a substantial portion of their job responsibilities and is a significant factor in job performance and promotion. As the subjects in my study indicated, and as most writers with whom I have worked over the years repeatedly tell me, the typical way in which they learn what is expected of them as writers is by "trial and error," "osmosis," or "OJT" (on-the-job training). Even on individual writing tasks, writers rarely get much direction from their supervisors. As Paradis et al. (1985) found in their study of writing at the Exxon's ITD R&D facility:

> The most common source of conflict was the failure of supervisor and staff to discuss matters of organization, purpose, and audience before the document was written. . . . Managers sometimes assumed that the writing task was simple and straightforward, when, in fact, the writing task was unfocused and difficult. The opportunities for confusing motives in document preparation seemed endless. (p. 300)

One result of such "confusing motives" is that often a document, particularly if it is a formal report, is subjected to more rounds of critiquing, editing, and revising by managers, supervisors, and others involved in the project than normally would have been necessary had expectations been made clearer at the time the writing task was assigned. While the report-cycling process is common in most organizations, as Paradis, Dobrin, and Miller point out, many inexperienced writers are not aware that this editorial stage is a normal and important phase of document production within companies. Consequently, they tend to take criticism hard, especially after they have worked on a document for days, weeks, or months, earnestly trying to meet what they assume are their supervisors' expectations. Frequently writers become defensive and interpret their evaluators' comments or text changes as "mere editorial whims" rather than as differences of view based on managerial priorities and experience. Oftentimes, too, as will be discussed in Chapter 1, the manager's criticism is so nebulous as to be useless to the writer.

A CASE IN POINT

The following case demonstrates two of the problems alluded to in the foregoing discussion: (a) the failure of supervisors to make clear their expectations when they assign a writing task and when they critique a draft; and (b) in lieu of such guidelines or constructive criticism, the tendency among writers to rely upon academic criteria of good writing. The examples cited on the following pages are based on three iterations of the same document, a long technical report, the first two written by a researcher (a Ph.D. engineer) and the third written by his manager. Because of the length of these reports (each about 30 pages) and because of their proprietary nature, I am unable to reprint them in whole or part. Rather, what follows are doctored versions of the abstracts from these three reports. While I have changed all identifying information (for example, the company, location, type of reactor, and process parameters) to preserve confidentiality, I have maintained the character of each abstract in all other respects—the type of information included in it, its organization and development, and its syntax and style. In each example, the abstract is a fair representation of the structure, content, and emphasis of its respective report. Finally, while the examples are not, as is the subject of my study in Part Three, progress reports (since normally these are not subject to the same intensive cycling/revision as are formal reports), the types of problems manifested in these examples, as well as the situation that gave rise to the confusing motives, occur in the production and revision of many types of documents, including progress reports.

Situation

Watcom, Inc. operates a water filtration plant in Lester, Georgia. As part of its operations, the Lester plant has three anaerobic digesters, which transform raw sludge feed into carbon dioxide and methane, the latter of which is especially profitable for Watcom, Inc. since they use it or sell it as raw fuel.

On April 7, 1988, one of the digesters experiences a shutdown. Days pass, and still the operators at the Lester plant have been unable to identify or correct the problem. In the meantime, the situation has reached crisis proportions as the company is losing hundreds of thousands of dollars a day. As a result, a researcher and his team from Watcom R&D, who were instrumental in designing the digester, are delegated to examine the situation. The head researcher is told by his manager to take the next plane to Lester, Georgia in order to investigate the problem. The manager does not have time to say much more to the researcher except that he expects the researcher to have a full report on his desk by Monday morning.

Later that Monday, upon receiving the researcher's report, the manager complained that it read "too much like a detective story," that it was "too inflammatory," and that the "sentences were backwards." The manager handed the report back to the researcher and told him to revise it, which he promptly did. However, the manager was not satisfied with the researcher's revised report either, indicating that it was all too theoretical. And so, because the manager's deadline for submitting the report was drawing near, the manager decided to revise the report himself.

The following are the researcher's original abstract and his revised abstract, as well as the final abstract as written by his manager. Then, following the abstracts, is my analysis of how the researcher and his manager interpreted the purpose of the report differently, and how the researcher, without a clear sense of the report's intended audience and purpose, resorted to forms of writing typical of academic school-based writing.

Abstract #1
(Researcher's 1st Draft)

ABSTRACT

This report presents a study of the causes of an anaerobic digester shutdown that occurred at Watcom, Inc.'s water filtration plant at Lester, Georgia, on April 7, 1988. Included are the details both of what happened on that day and the significance of those events for the anaerobic digester process.

The claims about what happened on April 7 are based upon a site investigation that included personal interviews with operators, supervisors, and directors at the Lester plant, as well as readings of thirty-seven measuring devices that monitor the digester's operation variables on a regular basis. The Watcom research team, composed of both biochemists and mechanical engineers, was met at the airport by D. Peterson, who gave us a tour of the Lester plant. To help us interpret the readings, we also developed a computer-generated simulation of the digester under its April 7 operating conditions.

Results of these data indicate that the April 7 shutdown was due to an operator's failure to reduce the feed temperature and feed rate once the optimal bed conditions had been attained. This created a build-up of raw sludge feed and volatile acids, which, in turn, caused the bed to slump and the digester to plug. Initially, it was thought that the shutdown was due to runaway reactions in the digester; however, the data indicates that human error was the actual cause.

At normal operating conditions, the digester is not at steady state. In other words, the degree of alkalinity and amount of volatile acids will quickly rise if the rate of feed and temperature are not carefully monitored. When, as on April 7, the rate and temperature of feed increase beyond prescribed limits, the ebullating bed becomes vapor bound and the digester fails to operate. However, such problems can be easily avoided if operators promptly adjust the raw sludge feed rate and temperature.

The delay in adjusting the feed rate and temperature that caused the April 7 shutdown can be attributed only to operator failure. My investigation reveals that he was young and inexperienced, that he had received only minimal training, and that he was working the third shift, unsupervised. Most likely, this is an isolated incident that is not likely to recur. However, if it does, one effective emergency response would be to quickly reduce the feed rate and temperature as soon as the volatile acids begin to rise.

Abstract #2
(Researcher's 2nd Draft)

ABSTRACT

In an anaerobic digester, microorganisms transform raw sludge into digested sludge, a byproduct of which is methane gas, which Watcom, Inc. both uses and sells as fuel. The acid-forming microorganisms in the sludge transform the raw sludge into volatile acids, alcohols, and carbon dioxide. The volatile acids are organic carboxylic acids such as ascetic and propionic. This is the first of the two-step biological process which takes place in anaerobic digestion. At the same time, the methane-formers convert the acids and alcohols into carbon dioxide and methane.

The content of the feed sludge, the length of the detention time, and the temperature of the sludge feed are the main variables that affect how well the sludge is digested and how much methane is produced. In a properly operating digester, the gases usually consist of 60–65 percent methane and 35–40 percent carbon dioxide, with a couple percent of other gases. The production of methane is especially important since it can be used or sold as energy. A cubic foot of good digester gas will produce about 600–650 British Thermal Units (BTUs) of energy when burned. If the acid formers are accelerated, the carbon dioxide content will increase and there will be a decrease in the methane.

However, accelerating the acid formers by letting the temperature of the raw sludge feed rise can result in plugging the feed bed and thereby shut down the digester. This appears to be what happened at Watcom, Inc.'s Lester, Georgia filtration plant on April 7, 1988. Results of our investigation suggest that the digester was being operated at cryophilic rather than thermophilic temperatures, and hence this accounted for the sludge buildup, the reduction of methane production, and the eventual shut down of the digester.

Abstract #3
(Manager's Abstract)

ABSTRACT

One of the byproducts of the anaerobic digester process used at Watcom, Inc.'s Lester, Georgia, water filtration plant is methane, which Watcom uses or sells as raw fuel. During 1987, methane production at the Lester plant resulted in a combined fuel savings and sale of over fifteen million dollars.

On April 7, 1988, one of the anaerobic digesters at Lester, Georgia, the C–47, experienced a shutdown. Although the digester is now fully operational, the two-day shutdown cost Watcom nearly $750,000.

This report describes a study which used a computer simulation of the C–

47 digester, along with pilot plant data and interviews, to investigate the following:

1. The causes of the digester shutdown that occurred on April 7, 1988, and
2. Possible strategies for preventing a recurrence.

Results of this study indicate that:

1. Under normal operating conditions, the digester is inherently unstable— i.e., without manual controls, the amount of volatile acids will continue to rise, thereby creating a slump in the feed bed and a reduction in the amount of methane produced.
2. Although unstable, the digester is by no means either uncontrollable or unsafe.
3. The preferred parameters for process control are the raw sludge feed temperature and the sludge flowrate.

Several recommendations concerning the operating procedure for the C–47 digester, as well as the other anaerobic digesters at Lester, Georgia, are included.

Analysis of Abstract #1

The first abstract is a technical variation of the ubiquitous "What-I-did-on-my-summer-vacation" narrative essay typical in many writing classes. The researcher first errs in assuming that the key question the manager wants answered in the report is "What happened?" As a result, the researcher takes, quite literally, the manager's directive to "examine the situation," failing to realize (or intuit) that, while this may have been the intended purpose of the trip, it was not what the manager had in mind as the purpose of the report.[1]

Keeping in line with the narrative genre, the researcher adopts the stance of an investigative reporter, and the report, as the abstract suggests, is a detailed chronicle of his findings. Consequently, the abstract, and indeed much of the whole report, is presented like a detective story and is arranged

---

[1] As a side note, my consulting experiences indicate that this tendency among technical writers to confuse a *task purpose*—that is, the aim of the work, research, or project—with a *report purpose*—that is, the aim of the report or the reasons for which the intended readers need the information—is quite common. The reason, I suspect, is that researchers often become so immersed in the details of their work, they develop tunnel vision, so that when it comes to writing their reports, either they assume that what is important to them—their methodologies, procedures, findings, data, and so forth—is equally important to their readers, or they fail to recognize their readers' needs at all.

chronologically, with frequent time references to the events of April 7th. The reader is taken on an adventure, from the time the research team is greeted at the airport in Lester, Georgia, to the computer-generated simulation of the digester at its April 7th operation conditions, to the findings, and finally to the cause of the problem. The abstract, in short, reads like a "Whodunit" thriller and the writer's emphasis is on cracking the case.

Although the chronological organization of the report is problematic, the real problem is the writer's insensitivity to the politics of the situation. And it is this, I suspect, that the manager found most objectionable about the report and why he considered its content "inflammatory." For, whether or not the writer was explicitly told so, he should have realized that one of the main audiences for the report would be the managerial personnel at the Lester plant. The researcher's repeated emphasis on "human error" and "operator inexperience" (five such allusions in the abstract alone) is a clear indictment of the Lester plant personnel and its management's failure to properly train or oversee plant operators. While this may in fact have been the direct cause of the shutdown, the focus on blame is not likely to create goodwill between those at Watcom and those at the Lester plant. Rather, the result is more likely to be hard feelings and defensiveness on the part of Lester management.

The real problem with the researcher's first draft, then, is that it is problem-oriented rather than solution-oriented, and that it represents the situation in personal rather than objective terms. More than likely, the report, as the manager realized, would have led to conflict and dissension rather than to cooperation and resolution. The researcher, on the other hand, seems unaware of any audiences other than his immediate manager. And while the researcher's probable motives are laudable and understandable— to prove how thoroughly he conducted the investigation, to show he has gotten his facts straight, to demonstrate he has identified the problem, and, in short, to convince his manager of his worth—his first abstract (and report) lacks tact and foresight. When his manager remarked that the researcher's sentences were "backwards," perhaps what he really meant is that the researcher's *thinking* was backwards, for throughout the abstract and the report, the researcher is much more concerned with documenting the past than with explaining how similar crises can be prevented in the future.

Analysis of Abstract #2

The researcher's second abstract is the direct antithesis of his first. Whereas the first was a blow-by-blow account of the researcher's experiences and findings at Lester, the researcher's second abstract and report are primarily a theoretical, context-free account of the biological processes underlying anaerobic digestion. In this second abstract, in other words, the emphasis is not on the researcher and what he found but rather on the anaerobic digester process itself. The discussion is purely abstract, as one might find in an academic treatise, professional paper, textbook, or in a student research paper.[2]

In the second abstract, the researcher assumes that the question the manager wants answered is not "What happened?" but rather "How does it (the process) work?" Here, the story of the earlier version is replaced by a lecture. Narration is supplanted by exposition. So that what we have here is essentially a "paper," rather than a report. Except for the last two sentences of the abstract, the references to time, self, company, situation, problem, and other people that figured so prominently in the first abstract are expunged. Whereas the writer's stance in the first abstract is one of narrator/investigative reporter, here the stance is professorial, one of a pedant who assumes, or pretends to assume, that the audience is unknowledgeable— the same type of academic, erudite persona that college students often attempt to adopt when writing their essays.

And just as in the expository essays of students it is difficult to tell just who the intended audience is, here too the audience is amorphous. It cannot be the manager, for certainly he is aware of how the anaerobic digester works and the importance of methane production. Is the researcher then attempting to educate the Lester operators by writing a primer on anaerobic digestion? Perhaps, but if so, the technical report is the wrong format and medium. For if, as the researcher indicates in the first abstract, the operators are young, untrained, inexperienced, and unsupervised, they probably need something more (or rather something less) than an abstract, academic account of the process. What they probably need is a simple, down-to-earth operations manual.

My hunch is that the researcher, responding to his manager's vehement reaction to the first abstract and report as "inflammatory," decided in his revision to play it safe and to give the manager a neutral, toned-down report that was not likely to excite or offend anyone. But, unfortunately, the revision, while it does not create tension or ill will, neither informs nor

---

[2] My college teaching experiences convince me that this is the type of writing many students try to emulate because, having been subjected to it in their college textbooks and often rewarded for it by their teachers, they therefore think it sounds "impressive," a criterion of "good" writing that often lingers among real-world writers. I am reminded of an anecdote Mina Shaughnessy related at a conference several years ago: One day, a student came into her class, excited and waving a paper, exclaiming, "Ms. Shaughnessy, I've got it this time! This is finally an 'A' essay." Her curiosity piqued, Ms. Shaughnessy inquired, "Really, Susan? And what makes you think that this is an 'A' essay?" To which Susan responded, "Well, I gave it to my roommate and she couldn't understand a word of it!"

helps anyone. The discussion is elevated to such a theoretical plane that it is virtually removed from either organizational or human interest.

Analysis of Abstract #3

Compared with the researcher's two abstracts, the manager's abstract, beyond its improved layout, is a good example of a writer and manager fully cognizant of the nature of organizational communication, the complexities inherent in a particular rhetorical situation, and the probable effects upon his readers (and the eventual effects upon himself and his department) both of what he says and of how he says it. Whereas the researcher's two abstracts focused on either the immediate crisis and its immediate causes (abstract #1) or the principles governing the digester process (abstract #2), the manager's abstract focuses on the viability of the digester's design and its implications for future operations. The question his abstract (and report) addresses is not so much "What happened?" or "How does the digester operate?" but rather "What can be done to prevent a recurrence?" It is this shift from the past to the future, and from problem to solution, that most distinguishes the manager's abstract from the researcher's abstracts. These different points of view are what separate those who have what Young, Becker, and Pike (1970), drawing upon an analogy from particle physics, refer to as a "field" view versus those who have a "particle" or "wave" view.

Whereas in the researcher's second abstract, the "field" is defined academically—as a topic of scholarly interest—in the manager's abstract the "field" is defined organizationally—as an important issue of company concern. For example, the manager's abstract begins with a corporate context and goal that are missing from both of the researcher's abstracts. Immediately, the reader is reminded of the significance of the Lester plant's operations to the parent company, Watcom, Inc., and, from the first paragraph on, the reader, whether he is from Watcom headquarters or Lester, has a pragmatic interest in the subject and the report, and a reason for reading. Furthermore, the manager's abstract (and report) strikes a balance between, on the one hand, the problem recently experienced at the Lester plant, and, on the other hand, the inherent instability of the digester, which by virtue of its design necessitates careful monitoring and manual control. References to the problem and the solution are not personal; rather, they are presented as objective phenomena: "the digester," "the process," "the normal operating conditions," the "preferred parameters." Though later in the report, the manager does analyze the events of April 7th, nowhere in the abstract does the manager mention the operator error that figures so prominently in the researcher's first abstract. And yet, beneath the lines of the manager's abstract, the implication of operator error is subtly but clearly there. That it is conveyed in such a politic, palpable manner increases the likelihood that the report will lead toward constructive action and remediation. Finally, as indicated by the recommendations alluded to in the abstract's last paragraph, the manager's concern is not limited to remedying just the current problem with the one digester but extends to preventing future occurrences at the Lester plant's other digesters.

To summarize, the manager demonstrates an organizational awareness that the researcher lacks. In the first two abstracts, the researcher misjudges the audience and purpose of the report. In the first, he defines them too narrowly; and in the second he defines them too broadly. In both instances, he relies on typical forms of school-based writing: in the first, narration; in the second, exposition. Like students who have become accustomed to writing in a vacuum, the researcher regards his writing task as close-ended. He seems unaware of the dynamic function that communication serves within the organization, and of the report's probable effects—its "fallout." Rather, he construes his writing task, much as students do, as an assignment, and his report as a finished product, an artifact for the files. He fails to recognize that the report will have an afterlife and aftermath, which, in turn, will influence how the organization functions and how its members interact. By contrast, the manager seems acutely aware of rhetorical dimensions of writing within the company. Unfortunately, however, he was unable to convey this understanding to the researcher when he assigned the writing task and when he reviewed the researcher's first report.

In their study of writing in an R&D organization, Paradis, Dobrin, and Miller (1985) explain that writers rarely receive systematic guidance about how writing functions in the R&D environment "possibly because few people know how to articulate the process" (p. 302). Learning to write well within an organizational setting is largely a matter of socialization or enculturation—learning what it means to think, act, and be a member of that culture. When, as Purves and Purves (1986) point out, "an individual is transplanted from one culture to another culture [such as from the school setting to the corporate setting], the individual has a great deal to unlearn and to learn if he or she is to be accepted as a writer in that culture" (pp. 193–194). Perhaps the most difficult things to unlearn are the conventions, composing strategies, and criteria of academic writing, and perhaps the most difficult thing to learn is "the organizational savvy required to write successful documents," a savvy "that may take up to three or four years for a person to acquire" (Paradis, Dobrin, & Miller, 1985, p. 302). For researchers of writing, investigating that savvy can sometimes take just about as long.

OVERVIEW

This volume is about progress and about writing. Generally speaking, it is about the progress being made in the research and teaching of writing—

particularly how, within the last few years, our interest in real-world writing has led to new avenues of research that are beginning to challenge some of our most cherished assumptions about writing and good writing, and to make us more aware of the distinctions between writing in real-world versus academic settings. Such progress is the subject of Part One, which serves the contextual backdrop for the rest of this volume. The aims of these chapters are as follows:

Chapter 1 Traces the growing interest in real-world writing, the reasons for this interest, and the impact that it is having upon our discipline.

Chapter 2 Discusses current, academic views of writing and the assumptions about good writing underlying each. This chapter further suggests some of the limitations that the process and product views of writing particularly have for the study, teaching, and practice of real-world writing.

Chapter 3 Focuses on emerging views of writing as social activity and examines the interrelationship among culture, community, and communication, with emphasis upon corporate cultures and organizations as rhetorical contexts.

Chapter 4 Examines the role of written communication within organizations, specifically how writing both influences and is influenced by an organization's culture and its community.

More specifically, this volume is an inquiry into what it means to write well within a corporate setting, where oftentimes the functions of writing and the criteria used to evaluate writing are unclear or ambiguous. The focus of my investigation (in Part Three) is the informational content of progress reports in an R&D organization. In Part Two, which provides the theoretical and conceptual background for my study, I examine some of the research on scientific and technical writing, discuss traditional and emerging models of technical communication, and explore different theories about the nature of science, technology, knowledge, information, language, and progress. The chapters in Part Two are as follows:

Chapter 5 Discusses the research on scientific and technical writing, focusing especially on writing within research organizations. This chapter further explains the issues underlying my own study and illustrates the importance of progress reporting within organizations by discussing two major crises from our nation's recent past.

Chapter 6 Explores the relationship between science and technology and discusses theories of reality, knowledge, rhetoric, information, communication, and progress that underlie traditional models of technical writing.

Chapter 7 Suggests a conceptual framework for my study. This chapter explores modern theories of technical writing and models of communication, especially speech-act theory, upon which my study is based. Also discussed is the general nature of progress reports and information.

In Part Three, I describe the study itself, the main objective of which was to investigate what distinguishes good progress reports from poor progress reports, as judged by the intended readers of these reports. In brief, the study, which was conducted at the R&D organization of a major international corporation, is an examination of the match among the writer's intentions, the writer's text, and the readers' expectations: the type of information that researchers (engineers and scientists) *intend* to include in their reports; the type of information actually *contained* in the reports; and the type of information that intended readers *expect* in the reports.

One of the main assumptions underlying this study is that, contrary to traditional models of communication, good commmunication (and good writing) is more than conveying information clearly; in addition, it is conveying information appropriate for the readers' needs. One criterion of an effective progress report, then, is the extent to which there is a match among the writer's *intentions*, the *text*, and the intended readers' *expectations*. If this study is based on any hypothesis, it is that this three-way match ought to be closer for the writers of progress reports judged superior by their intended readers than for the writers of progress reports judged inferior by their intended readers.

In order to examine this three-way match, I employed a variety of research methodologies, including surveys, discourse-based interviews, text analysis, and context-based experimental studies. In scope, substance, and methodology, this study represents a departure from most studies within the field of composition research in that:

1. It focuses upon the interrelationships of writers, texts, and readers, rather than upon any one of these in isolation.
2. It examines the content of written texts rather than their structural or stylistic features.
3. It studies the dynamics of communication in a real–world rather than an academic setting.
4. It employs criteria of effective writing that the research subjects themselves identified as important within the particular context rather than any predetermined criteria superimposed from the outside.

The chapters in Part Three describe the objectives, subjects, methodology, and findings of each of the study's three main phases, as well as the major conclusions from this study. These chapters focus upon the following:

Chapter 8   Provides an overview of the study, its three phases, assumptions, and objectives, as well as its major findings.

Chapter 9   Explains Phase 1, the purposes of which were (a) to examine the general nature of progress reports as perceived by the writers and readers at this R&D organization—the functions that such reports serve within the organization and the types of information most preferred in these reports; and (b) as a result of these findings, to develop a classification scheme that could later be used to analyze the different types of information contained in progress reports.

Chapter 10   Explains Phase 2, the purpose of which was to analyze the progress reports of the previously identified good writers and poor writers in order to determine whether there were any significant differences in the types of information contained in the reports written by these two groups.

Chapter 11   Explains Phase 3, which consisted of two experimental tasks designed to investigate whether, when presented with the same progress report, the writer and his or her[3] supervisor/reader would similarly identify (a) the report's most important versus least important information, and (b) the report's data, results, and conclusions.

Chapter 12   Summarizes the main conclusions of this study and suggests the significance and implications that this study's findings may have for the understanding, teaching, study, and practice of real-world technical writing.

THE CHALLENGES OF RESEARCHING
REAL-WORLD WRITING

The study of writing in an organizational setting poses what Harrison (1987) has described as "a formidable research challenge," one that requires "an understanding of both composition theory and organization theory to formulate research questions that get at the interrelationship between organizational processes and writing processes" (p. 4). When the subject is

---

[3] To avoid prolixity, hereafter I use the pronoun "he" to refer to any individual, whether male or female.

technical report writing, the challenge is even greater because the researcher must also become acquainted with other disciplines tangential to the study of science and technology.

From a practical standpoint, the study of technical writing in an R&D organization is further complicated by the proprietary nature of in-house technical reports—especially in the case of progress reports that are based on highly confidential research that may not be disclosed to the public, much less to all in-company personnel, for weeks, months, or even years after a project has been completed. To obtain permission to investigate such reports at the time they are being produced and to take researchers, supervisors, and directors away from their work in order to interview the writers and readers of these reports are the first major obstacles in conducting such research.

This may one of the reasons that in the few studies that have investigated writing in R&D organizations (for example, Latour & Woolgar, 1979; Gilbert & Mulkay, 1984; and Knorr-Cetina, 1981), the texts that have been studied have invariably been the published, company-sanctioned works of researchers or the earlier drafts upon which these published works were based. Further, and more importantly, in most cases the texts have been scientific works (professional papers or scholarly articles) intended for academic audiences rather than for in-company audiences. As I will point out later, the difference is important insofar as the aims of scientific, academic writing are quite different from those of scientific and technical corporate writing.

Once the first obstacle is overcome (gaining permission to do the research), the next obstacle is abiding by the corporation's nondisclosure or confidentiality agreement while at the same time figuring out how to demonstrate concepts without actually citing examples from the company reports that are the subject of one's research. In a few instances in which the work was not proprietary, I was able to use the researchers' progress reports or excerpts from them. For the most part, however, the examples in this volume, like the abstracts created for the case study discussed previously, are based on information drawn either from other nonconfidential, published reports, or from government research reports. In the contrived examples, I have tried to represent, as faithfully as possible, the types of information contained in my subjects' original progress reports.

AUDIENCE

This work is intended for a heterogenous audience: for those in academe who are interested in either studying or teaching technical writing and for those in R&D organizations who either write or read technical reports.

Addressing such a mixed audience is a challenge that many researcher writers, including those in my study, confront daily. As Fahnestock (1986) notes, Einstein, in a foreword he wrote for Lincoln Barnett's (1968) popularization of the theory of relativity, defined the Scylla and Charybdis of attempting to explain scientific concepts to lay readers. Einstein's remarks, I think, also capture the dilemma writers face when attempting to address a diverse audience, some of whom are specialists and others of whom are nonspecialists:

> Anyone who has ever tried to present a rather abstract scientific subject in a popular manner knows the great difficulties of such an attempt. Either he succeeds in being intelligible by concealing the core of the problem and by offering to the reader only superficial aspects or vague allusions, thus deceiving the reader by arousing in him the deceptive illusion of comprehension; or else he gives an expert account of the problem, but in such a fashion that the untrained reader is unable to follow the exposition and becomes discouraged from reading any further. (Barnett, p. 9; quoted in Fahnestock, p. 276)

In writing this volume, I had a difficult time determining just who my specialist readers and who my nonspecialist readers would be. On the one hand, while it seemed to me that those in academe would have knowledge of rhetorical theory, I assumed that, for the most part, they probably lacked the practical experience of either reading or writing in-company technical reports. On the other hand, while it seemed to me that those in R&D organizations had plenty of real-world experience in reading and writing technical reports, I assumed that most of them were unfamiliar with composition research and rhetorical theory. By trying to accommodate both audiences, I have no doubt covered territory that to one audience will seem familiar and well-worn but that to the other audience will seem novel and untraveled. Such is the nature of trying to please all of the people all of the time: Inevitably, some will want more details, while others will want fewer. At best, all I can hope is that somewhere in the middle ground, each audience will find something in this work of value to them, whether they are researchers of writing or writers of research, or whether they are readers, writers, or teachers of technical writing.

I
Writing in Academic Versus Real-World Settings

1
The Growing Interest in Real-World Writing

Sometimes you have to go a long way out of your way to come back a short distance correctly.

from Edward Albee's play, *The Zoo Story*

Until recently, the study and teaching of writing have focused primarily upon one type of writing: academic writing, especially the writing that students do in school. As a result, the social function of writing has been obscured by debates about the function of writing courses within the school curriculum: whether, for instance, their purpose should be to teach students the conventions of standard written English, to develop their cognitive skills, to encourage self-expression and individuality, or even, as Marshall (1987) suggests, to promote ethical behavior. As will be discussed in the next chapter, the debate still rages, and the literature is filled with competing theories and models of writing and writing processes, each of which is based on different assumptions about what good writing is and how it is developed. Increasingly, however, some skeptics are beginning to wonder whether whatever skills are being taught in writing courses have any relevance beyond the classroom. And, interestingly, many of those skeptics are our students themselves, and our former students now in business and industry, either who, as writers, are having a difficult time making the transition from academic to corporate writing, or who, as managers, are having to contend with the poor writing of their subordinates.

While it would be lovely to think that the surging interest in real-world writing springs from scholarly motives—from our own intellectual desire to understand writing as a form of communication—such is not the case. Rather, just as in much scientific research, our motives have been primarily pragmatic and self-serving. If we suddenly have become interested in non-academic writing, it has not been because of any great progress within our discipline or because of any noble quest for knowledge, but rather because, in order to survive, we have had to become responsive to external demands and needs. Students are lining up by the droves to register for courses in business and technical writing, and a growing number of companies are instituting their own in-house writing programs to take up the slack left by the universities.

In the meantime, some teachers are retooling their composition courses to give them a more practical edge, as evidenced, for example, by all the writing-in-the-workplace textbooks on the market. What's more, composition teachers now find themselves teaching more and more business writing and technical writing courses, and most major universities have instituted or are currently developing new undergraduate and graduate programs in business and technical communication to meet the growing interest in real-world communication. In short, business is booming in the English department, and suddenly it's a bull market. But in many ways, the situation is like that of a company which unwittingly strikes a huge market without having done much upfront research and without having developed a solid product to sell.

For the problem is, as it so often is, that research has lagged behind instruction. There has been little inquiry into either business writing or technical writing, and as a result many of the present courses and textbooks are recycled and repackaged composition courses and textbooks—clones of the very pedagogies, models, and theories of writing that the new courses and programs should be redressing. In other words, to use an old adage, a case of old wine in new bottles. Furthermore, as will be discussed in this chapter, underlying many of the studies on real-world writing, especially the earlier ones, are the researchers' own a priori and academically-based assumptions about what constitutes good writing.

Gradually, however, the situation is changing as researchers and teachers are becoming more aware of the pragmatic and social functions that writing serves in organizational settings. From a historical standpoint, the current interest in real-world writing is interesting and ironic because in many ways it is bringing us back full circle to the nature of writing as it developed nearly ten millennia ago. If one theme pervades the research on the origins and evolution of writing, it is that the first forms of writing developed because of the needs of those in business to document and communicate information. As Schmandt-Besserat (1982) points out, the earliest precursors of writing were systems of recording or record keeping (at first tokens, then written symbols, and eventually complete texts) that enabled people to function more efficiently in an increasingly changing society.

If anything, the need to communicate effectively is far greater in today's society where the day-to-day operations and the very success of every business or organization depend upon managing, documenting, and conveying vast amounts of complex information. In the real world, the practical needs that fostered the development of writing are still alive. In the academic world, however, only recently has attention been paid to the pragmatic functions that writing serves beyond the classroom. As Schumacher (1986) argues, we need to recognize and revive the powerful role that communication played in originating writing and that it continues to play in nonacademic settings. We need, furthermore, to understand the important implications that the evolution of writing has for understanding and promoting the development of writing within individuals.

In our teaching and research of writing, we have gone a long way out of our way by ignoring the connection between writing and communication. But if the burgeoning interest in business and technical writing is any indication, we may well be on the track of coming back a short distance correctly by realizing that today, just as long ago, writing is a means of communication that is motivated by very real, practical social needs.

This chapter examines the growing interest in business and technical writing both within universities and within companies; suggests the main reasons for this interest and its impact; and reviews and critiques recent survey research in the field of real-world writing. As discussed below, a major shortcoming of such research as been the myopia engendered by our own limited knowledge and experience of real-world writing and writers. With little more than academic writers (students) and their writing (essays) as their reference points, many researchers of real-world writing have based their surveys upon the traditional criteria of academic, school-based writing. As I will discuss later in this chapter, these criteria may not be the same as those used in nonacademic, organizational settings.

RISING ENROLLMENTS IN BUSINESS AND TECHNICAL WRITING COURSES

Interest in real-world professional writing, as opposed to academic school-sponsored writing, is evident everywhere—in our textbooks, in our journals, and at our conferences. But nowhere is this interest more apparent than in the swelling enrollments in business writing and technical writing courses during the last few years. So heavy has been the demand that colleges and universities are having a difficult time providing enough courses to keep up with student requests. Houp and Pearsall (1984, p. v), for instance, have reported that, in technical writing courses alone, enrollments increased tenfold, from 25,000 in 1968 to more than a quarter of a million in 1982, a figure that undoubtedly is considerably higher today. Enrollments in business writing courses are also increasing at record pace. For example, in 1985 the University of Illinois at Urbana-Champaign offered 50 to 55 sections of business communication each semester and still was unable to meet the demand (Gieselman, 1985, p. 2). From all accounts, other universities and colleges are experiencing skyrocketing enrollments in both technical writing and business communication courses.

In addition to trying to meet the growing demand for more career-oriented writing courses, most English departments of major universities, which traditionally have offered graduate programs devoted primarily to the study of literature, either have recently instituted degree programs in business and technical communication, have such a program in the works, or are seriously considering one. Observing this trend in 1984, R. Eric Staley, the executive director of Associated Writing Programs, predicted:

> In the 1990's most master's programs for writers will lead to professional rather than fine-arts degrees. The new-style programs will emphasize business communications, technical writing, editing, and screenwriting rather than the writing of fiction, nonfiction, or poetry, and they will in general stress applied communication arts rather than fine arts. (Staley, 1984, p. 80)

Judging from the number of universities sending out promotional flyers advertising their new programs in business and technical communication, apparently that day is already here.

SOCIETAL INFLUENCES

At least two societal forces are responsible for this change of emphasis in writing courses and programs. The first is the transition from an industrial to an information society, and the second, related to this, is the growing importance, and almost reverence, with which our society regards science and technology.

At the beginning of this century, we experienced a shift from a predominantly agrarian society to an industrial society. With the popularization of computers in the 1960s, we experienced yet another and equally cataclysmic shift as we moved into the age of information. In his best seller, *The Third Wave*, Alvin Toffler (1980) warned that "an information bomb is exploding in our midst" (p. 156). In many ways, we are now dealing with the fallout triggered by that bomb, one effect of which has been to change the nature of many jobs. For instance, in another best seller, *Megatrends*, John Naisbitt (1984, p. 4) estimated that, whereas in 1950 only 17 percent of the work force was employed in information jobs, in 1984 the figure rose to 65 percent. Some current estimates put this figure at closer to 80 percent. With about three out of every four people now employed in occupations that in some way require them to retrieve, store, process, generate, and send information, the need for communication is greater than ever before.

While some interpret this as a need for more sophisticated computer hardware and software to access, manage, and manipulate information, an even greater need is for improved "humanware": (a) the thinking skills necessary to assimilate and evaluate information, and (b) the written and verbal communication skills necessary to provide other people with the information they need to do their jobs.

Related to the overwhelming importance of information in today's society, another reason for the demand for communication courses—business communication courses, and especially technical writing courses—is our society's increased emphasis upon science and technology. To a greater extent than ever before, business, industry, and government are investing heavily in R&D (research and development) as a means of securing their position in the world marketplace by continuing to improve current products and technologies, and as a means of garnering potential markets through the development of new (and patent-worthy) products and technologies. While communication is vital in any industry and any business, written communication and documentation are especially important in an R&D enterprise. As one vice president of the R&D division of a major corporation put it, "Our real product here is paper. Without the written report, our research, no matter how innovative and potentially profitable, simply does not exist." There are at least two reasons that written communication is especially important in R&D organizations.

One reason has to do with the external constraints imposed by state and federal legislative bodies, regulatory commissions, licensing agencies, and patent offices, as well as those imposed by professional, scientific, and engineering organizations. Each of these groups requires written evidence that the company's product, procedure, or process conforms to various standards and requirements. Whether the company is seeking a patent for a new technology or device, or defending itself in a court case, the future of the company may well hinge upon how well its researchers have documented their work. In some cases—as, for example, the recent controversial case in which a biogenetics company was awarded a patent for a gene splicing procedure that creates new forms of animal life—the company's lab notebooks and published research are essential in establishing legal proprietorship. In other cases—as, for example, the recent suit against Morton Thiokel, Inc., the engineering firm that designed the rocket boosters for the ill-fated Space Shuttle Challenger—internal status reports written by engineers may later become the evidence by which the company is prosecuted or acquitted.

In addition to providing a legal record of the research, another reason that writing plays such an important role in R&D organizations concerns the highly specialized and often esoteric nature of the research itself. Frequently, there are but a handful of people in the company who have the education, experience, and expertise necessary to understand fully the research being done. Typically, these are the scientists and engineers closest to a particular project. And while they may be able to communicate easily with their colleagues, oftentimes they speak of things that few others can understand and in esoteric terms that only other specialists in their area can comprehend. Thus, in order for management to make sense of their work—to determine the feasibility and profitability of their proposals, to assess the progress being made on present projects, and, in general, to have the information they need to plan and achieve corporate goals—it is important that researchers be able to communicate complex ideas in a way that nonspecialists can understand. In an address at the U.S. Senate's Science Policy Hearings in 1985, John Seely Brown, from the Intelligent Systems Laboratory of the Xerox Palo Alto Research Center, spoke of this need: "One of the crucial problems of increasing specialization in the sciences (and elsewhere) is the need for effective communication between individuals and subgroups and for preserving group knowledge over time and across projects" (p. 204).

Although some of this communication is informal and verbal, at some point all organizations require that it be documented in writing. First, the written record of the research makes it possible for others to trace the project's evolution, review the work, and if need be to replicate or revise it in the future. In addition, written reports, as opposed to oral reports, are generally a more practical, appropriate means of conveying scientific and technical information, which often includes supporting data, equations, graphs, figures, and the like. Such information is more easily comprehended if a person is reading rather than listening, for the written text enables one to think about, reread, and review the ideas, and later to discuss them with others. Finally, writing serves another function: It encourages researchers to think about what their findings mean. Several of the supervisors in my study (reported in Part Three) mentioned that researchers, and especially scientists working on long-range projects, often become so immersed in the details of their daily work that they lose sight of the project's relationship to larger corporate goals. As one supervisor put it, "Even if our company did not require written reports, I would still insist that my people write them, for the sheer act of writing (and knowing that their reports will be read by management) forces them to reflect upon the significance of what they are doing, and that is really the main reason they are hired—to think and solve problems."

As mentioned above, one effect of these societal changes has been the increased importance of communication skills in the workplace. It is the recognition of this fact that is perhaps the most compelling reason that students are flocking into university courses and programs in business and technical communication, and that researchers, in turn, have become more interested in investigating real-world writing.

IMPORTANCE OF COMMUNICATION SKILLS

Within the last 10 years, researchers have begun to learn more about the importance, frequency, and types of writing being done within various organizations. In the most extensive review of this research to date, Anderson (1985) summarizes the findings of his own study and 50 others that questioned people about the writing they do at work. The following highlights the results of these studies, as well as others, and in addition examines a couple of studies in detail in order to point out the typical problems and inherent academic biases often associated with this type of research.

Speaking and Writing

In virtually every study that has investigated the qualities that employers most desire in their employees, good communication skills, both verbal and written, rank high among the top priorities of those in business and industry. For example, Hildebrandt, Bond, Miller, and Swinyard (1982) surveyed business executives to find out which of 13 college courses they considered the best preparation for business leadership. Oral and written business communication was selected as "very important" more often than any of the other courses. In a similar study that focused on technical communication skills, Kimel and Monsees (1979) interviewed employers from nationally known companies, asking them to evaluate recent engineering graduates and to indicate among 13 areas of competence (most of them technical) the ones they regarded as most important for their engineers. The employers ranked speaking and writing as the *most important* area of competence in both civil engineering and electrical engineering, and second most important in mechanical engineering. Of further interest is that in all three engineering fields the employers identified writing and speaking as the areas in which their recent engineering graduates were *most deficient.*

Evidence that communication skills have become even more important in the last several years is provided by Bennett and Olney (1986) in their survey of vice-president executives in 100 randomly selected *Fortune 500* companies. Among their findings is that 97.7 percent of the executives attribute their advancement to a top executive position to good communication skills, a figure that is up 13 percentage points from the 84 percent that Bennett (1971) reported in a similar study conducted 15 years earlier.

Writing

Studies that have focused upon writing in the workplace reveal that the ability to write well is essential in all professions, that it is a factor in promotion, and that courses in business and technical writing consistently head the list of those college courses that employees regard as having been most beneficial in preparing them for their careers.

In a major study that examined the importance of writing skills to college graduates, Anderson (1985) surveyed 1052 alumni from Miami University (Ohio) and found that 93 percent of his respondents said that the ability to write well is at least of "some importance," while 57 percent said that it is of "great" or "critical" importance. In an earlier survey of 837 business graduates from the same university, Storms (1983) obtained similar results when he asked the graduates to evaluate how important writing well would be for someone who wanted to perform their jobs. Of the respondents, 74 percent indicated that writing well would be at least "very important," and 30 percent indicated that it would be "critically important." As Anderson (1985) notes in his literature review, the results from the Storm's study, as well those from his own study, corroborate the results earlier obtained by other researchers: Davis (1977), Bataille (1982), and Flatley (1982).

Researchers who have surveyed employees in both business and technical fields have found that a person's ability to write well often enhances his prospects for promotion. For example, in the Storms (1983) study cited above, 88 percent of the respondents said that the ability to write well has at least "some effect" on advancement, 54 percent said it has at least a "great effect," and 14 percent said it is essential to advancement. As noted by Anderson (1985), several other researchers who have examined the relationship between writing proficiency and promotion report similar findings: Belohlov, Popp, and Porte (1974); Cox (1976); Hetherington (1982); Stine and Skarzenski (1979); and Van Dyck (1980). Likewise, those researchers who have surveyed people in technical fields have discovered a close relationship between a person's writing skills and his chances for advancement. For example, Davis (1977), in his survey of 245 people listed in *Engineers of Distinction*, found that 96 percent of his respondents said that their writing ability had "helped" their own advancement, and 89 percent said that writing well was usually an "important" or "critical" consideration when others were being considered for advancement. Comparable results were obtained in two other studies: Spretnak's (1982) survey of 595 graduates who had graduated from the College of Engineering at Berkeley during the last 30 years, and Barnum and Fischer's (1984) survey of 305 graduates from Southern Technical Institute during the last 15 years.

Finally, research indicates that college-educated workers consider their previous courses in business and technical writing as among the most beneficial in preparing them for their job responsibilities. Simonds (1960), for example, in his survey of 133 upper-level managers, found that about 80 percent of his respondents put business writing at the top of a list of some 62 college courses. Similar results were obtained by Traweek (reported in Penrose, 1976), who found that business writing was rated as the second most important course (next to accounting) by business administration alumni who had graduated from the University of Texas between 1917 and

1954. In the field of engineering, the importance of technical writing courses has also been documented. In a survey of 4,057 engineers (reported in Middendorf, 1980), the American Society for Engineering Education asked the engineers to identify those subjects most needed for professional careers in industry. While the respondents identified management practices as the most helpful, they ranked technical writing above all other subjects.

Frequency of Writing

One reason that writing is important in the workplace is simply because it represents a substantial portion of the college-educated employee's workday. As Anderson (1985) notes, the more than 20 studies that have examined this matter report that employees spend, on an average, approximately 20 percent of their workday writing, or, in other words, the equivalent of one full work day per week. Other studies cited above (Spretnak, 1982; Storms, 1983; and Cox, 1976) have reported higher averages of 25 percent. Furthermore, as Paradis, Dobrin, and Miller (1985) found in their study at one R&D organization, writing may account for as much as 33 to 50 percent of a person's job-related time. One problem with such percentages, however, is that in most studies the definition of *writing* is left up to the research subjects themselves. Hence, some may interpret *writing* to mean only recording words on a page or screen, while others may interpret it to mean, in addition, all the thinking, discussion, worrying, reading, and revising that go into creating a final document.

Of further interest are some studies that have examined the relationship between the amount of time spent writing and either the writer's job category or level in the organization. For example, Faigley, Miller, Meyer, and Witte (1981) found that professional and technical employees spend 29 percent of their time writing, while college-educated blue collar workers spend only 4 percent. Other surveys of engineers (Davis, 1977; Spretnak, 1982; and Barnum & Fischer, 1984) reveal that 69–79 percent of the respondents indicate that, as they advanced in their careers and assumed greater responsibilities, the amount of writing and the amount of time they spent writing also increased.

Functions and Forms of Writing

Given the importance with which employees and employers regard writing and given the portion of their workday that is devoted to writing, two questions naturally arise: (a) Why are they writing? and (b) What are they writing? According to Anderson (1985), only one study, that by Paradis, Dobrin, and Bower (1984), has asked respondents about the functions that their writing serves at work. In their survey, Paradis et al. (1984) asked 265 professional employees at 20 R&D organizations to indicate the importance of each of 10 functions that their writing serves within their organization. Table 1.1 lists the percentages of respondents who identified various functions as "vitally important":

Table 1.1.   Most Important Functions That Writing Serves.

Percentage of Respondents	Function of Writing
69	1. providing answers to specific questions
60	2. keeping others informed about major activities
52	3. helping plan and coordinate the activities of the individual and the organization
49	4. objectifying a situation so that its essential elements and interrelationships can be analyzed
47	5. instructing others
45	6. enabling individuals to make contact with others who are higher up in the organization or on the outside
38	7. establishing accountability

While the above suggests the wide range of functions that writing serves within R&D organizations, almost all of these functions, with the possible exceptions of the last two, have in common the communication of information for the use of others: whether that information is an answer (item 1), an evaluation of progress (item 2), a plan of action (item 3), an analysis (item 4), or instructions (item 5). Items 6 and 7 have social functions beyond that of simply conveying information. These functions, as will be discussed in Chapters 4 and 5, concern the organization's structure, culture, and community.

As Anderson notes, one limitation of the Paradis et al. study, as with many other surveys, is that it presented respondents with a predetermined list of items from which to choose, in this case only the functions of writing that Paradis et al. considered the likely options. Had the question been open-ended, it is possible that the respondents might have indicated additional functions that writing serves within their R&D organizations, functions that may have revealed persuasive as well as informational aims, such as establishing the researcher's credibility or worth, justifying budget expenditures, rationalizing setbacks or losses, obtaining approval for a proposal, being awarded a patent, winning a law suit, and so on. (As for whether aim of writing is ever strictly informational is something I will address in subsequent chapters.)

It should be noted, too, that the Paradis et al. study focused upon only R&D organizations and primarily the functions that writing serves *within* these organizations. Without further surveys investigating the functions of business writing in non-R&D organizations, it is difficult to determine whether the above findings, which pertain primarily to internal technical writing, reflect the functions that business writing serves within and outside other organizations not engaged in scientific and technological pursuits.

As for the kinds of writing being done within organizations (R&D and otherwise), most studies indicate that the most frequent forms are letters, memoranda, and reports. In a survey of top executives from 58 California-based companies that are among the *Fortune 500* largest U.S. corporations, Bennett and Olney (1986) found that the forms of business communication most frequently used by the respondents were memoranda (95.6 percent), letters (95.6 percent), analytical reports (80.4 percent), and informational reports (71.8 percent). In other studies, Faigley et al. (1981), Storms (1983), and Anderson (1985) report that the majority of college-educated employees surveyed indicate that they "sometimes" write as many as seven or eight different types of letters, memoranda, and reports. For instance, Faigley et al., in their study of 200 workers from a cross-section of job categories, found that their respondents write, on an average, 8.5 different types of letters, memoranda, and reports per week. However, while this suggests great diversity and frequency of writing, it says little about the relative importance of these forms of writing. In fact, some researchers have found that those forms of writing that are written most frequently are not necessarily the ones regarded as most important.

For example, in the Faigley et al. study referred to above, respondents indicated that, of the eight forms of writing addressed to readers outside the organization, they most frequently write letters in response to inquiries but that they regard as most important their sales letters, which they write far less frequently. Similarly, Paradis, Dobrin, and Bower (1984) found that, while researchers in R&D organizations spend more time writing progress reports than they do several other forms of writing, the writers do not consider their progress reports as important as their other forms of writing.

However, what was not investigated in either the Faigley et al. or the Paradis et al. study (or any other study of which I am aware), and what may be both more illuminating and interesting, is whether the writers and their intended readers have similar notions about which forms of writing are most important. In the case of progress reports at least, my own study suggests that not only may writers and readers disagree about the importance of progress reports, but they may also have quite different notions about what constitutes "progress."

Quality of Writing

Many surveys have asked supervisors and managers about the general quality of their employees' writing and about the skills they consider most essential in job performance. In a word, the majority of executives surveyed indicate that the overall quality of their employees' writing is dismal. In a survey that Anderson (1985, p. 64) calls "one of the most favorable views of writing in the workplace," Rainey (1972) found that, among the 50 executives from firms listed in the *Thomas Directory of American Manufacturers,* 38 percent said that the writing in their companies was "outstandingly good," while a greater percentage, 40 percent, said it was so poor that it was costing their companies a tremendous amount of money in lost sales or contracts. Other studies (Faigley et al., 1981; Andrews & Sigband, 1984; Kimel & Monsees, 1979; Cox, 1976; and numerous others—nearly 50 as Anderson notes), report that the majority of their respondents regard deficiencies in writing skills as a significant problem in the workplace. In the Cox study, for instance, respondents indicated that poor writing is an even greater problem than inefficiency and absenteeism. In the Faigley et al. study, 51 percent said that poor writing was a "real problem," while another 27 percent said it was a "severe problem." When asked what they regarded as the effects of this problem, they indicated, as reported by Anderson (p. 65), "misunderstanding (58 percent); loss of time (49 percent); and bad public image (40 percent)." Other effects mentioned were "lack of impact (23 percent); loss of business (17 percent), and 'impedes professional advancement' (10 percent)."

Given the negative effects that poor writing skills have upon company productivity and profit, Cox, in his 1976 study, further asked his subjects (150 people who had taken his business communication class in the previous 15 years and had earned an A or B in it) why managers are not doing something about the problem. The respondents cited two main reasons: lack of time and lack of knowledge. The majority, 61 percent of the respondents, said that managers simply do not have the time necessary to supervise revisions of their subordinates' writing; and another 37 percent said that, although managers can recognize poor writing, they are unable to identify its faults, much less able to explain to writers how to remedy those faults. The latter finding is especially noteworthy since it implies that even if the managers *did* have the time to oversee revisions, many would not be able to do so because they lack the knowledge and terminology needed to analyze and evaluate written texts, and to help their employees improve their writing.

Although the Cox study was conducted more than 10 years ago, my consulting experiences convince me that his findings are as valid today as they were a decade ago. For example, frequently I am called upon in situations in which a manager has reached an impasse in his attempts to explain to a subordinate how to revise an important document for distribution to others. Sometimes, a manager might read the document and simply tell the writer, "This won't do. Rewrite it!" Other times, a manager might write extensive comments in the document's margins, comments such as, "unclear," "confusing," "needs work," "illogical," "choppy," or "?." And still other times, usually at about the third draft, a manager might vent his frustration and resort to such epithets as "garbage!" or, as I recently read in the margin of one researcher's report, "bullshit!"

Without constructive criticism, however, the writer is invariably at a loss as to precisely what the problems are and, more importantly, how to correct them to the manager's satisfaction. If something, for instance, is marked "confusing," the writer often has no way of intuiting why it is confusing. Is it a problem of organization? Content? Sentence structure? Word choice? Layout? Or some combination of these? Frequently, it is only by persistently probing the manager (something that writers, by virtue of their subordinate position, may be hesitant to do) that it is possible to identify the root of the problem. And even in situations in which the manager might be able to explain, for instance, that the confusion is due to organization, for the writer that still leaves unanswered just what exactly is wrong with the organization.

In their on-the-job-training, if not in their college courses, managers are usually prepared for most of their supervisory responsibilities. Many have taken managerial courses in such skills as leadership, conflict resolution, time management, and team building. Few, however, are prepared to supervise their employees' writing, even though this is often an important part of their daily supervisory responsibilities. As a result, it is not unusual to find managers critiquing their employees' writing in much the same way that many of their former English teachers once critiqued their college essays: that is, by scrutinizing and marking errors and problems. The effect upon writers is often as demoralizing and counterproductive as it is when students get back their essays bathed in red ink and looking as though they had been butchered. In fact, I have had writers confide that the more their managers massacre and edit their initial drafts, the less inclined they (the writers) are to submit polished work. As one researcher put it, "Why should I waste my time laboring over my first draft when he [the supervisor] is only going to rip it apart anyway?" Other writers tell me that they are convinced that their managers are displaced or closet English teachers who take perverse delight in wielding a red pen.

But perhaps what is most frustrating for writers is that sometimes the problems that the manager identifies are not at all, as it later turns out, the real problems with the document. For example, I have seen several instances in which a writer, at his manager's request, has significantly improved the clarity or organization of a report, only to discover that it is still unsatisfactory because the content, approach, or wording is inappropriate for the particular situation. The fault, I think, is not that the managers are careless (or, as their employees sometimes think, sadistic) but that they, like the people whom they supervise, have quite naturally derived their criteria, as well as their methods, for evaluating texts from those that were used in their college writing courses. In most of those courses, the criteria for good writing usually had to do with how clear, coherent, well organized, and developed an essay was; thus, these are the features that managers tend to look for in their employees' writing. Such criteria, however, as was demonstrated in the Introduction to this volume, do not account for how well the information contained in the text suits its intended purpose and audience. Yet, it is these other context-governed criteria that are often what, in real-world writing, ultimately determine a document's effectiveness.

In the next chapter, I will illustrate the kinds of problems that writers (as well as readers) have when they mistakenly assume that the conventions and criteria of academic, school-sponsored writing are the same as those of real-world writing. For now, however, let us examine the kinds of writing skills that have been identified as most important to college-educated workers and the kinds of problems typically associated with their writing.

Specific Skills and Deficiencies

Although several studies have asked people about the writing skills that they regard as most important for their jobs, in the vast majority of these studies the researchers have provided the respondents with close-ended lists of skills that the researchers themselves have predetermined as important. Since, invariably, the researchers are English teachers, the lists usually contain those skills most often emphasized in college writing courses. "Consequently," as Anderson (1985) notes, "some items that the respondents think very important will escape notice until (and if) some other researcher thinks to include them in another study" (p. 55).

With that caveat in mind, then, the five skills that respondents ranked the highest in surveys by Stine and Skarzenski (1979), Storms (1983), Barnum and Fischer (1984), and Bennett and Olney (1986) are clarity, conciseness, organization, grammar, and spelling. However, when other less traditional skills were included on the list, respondents sometimes ranked them higher than these other five skills. For example, in the Storms survey, the respondents ranked "clearly stating your purpose" as the second most important writing skill, a skill that was not listed in other surveys. Also, in a study by Green and Nolan (1984), which surveyed 181 people who had earned associate degrees from Cincinnati Technical College, 79 percent of the respondents or their supervisors indicated the importance of using graphic and visual aids.

In addition to identifying the skills most essential for real-world writing, some researchers have also examined the kinds of deficiencies most often observed in real-world writing. Not surprisingly, there is a close connection between the skills needed and the problems noted. For example, in the Stine and Skarzenski survey cited above, executives of 83 businesses in Iowa were presented with a list of 20 writing problems and asked to indicate how often they see these problems in the correspondence sent to them. The problems most frequently noted by the respondents were (in order): wordiness, grammar, sentence structure, spelling, clarity, and organization.

Similar results have been obtained more recently by Goodin and Swerdlow (1987) in a study that I will examine more closely not only because its findings suggest the same kinds of writing problems mentioned in the previous studies but moreover because the researchers' criteria and methodology for evaluating writing are symptomatic of many of the problems inherent in the study and teaching of real-world writing.

The aim of the Goodin and Swerdlow study, as the researchers themselves assert, was to assess the current quality of written correspondence in a cross-section of 13 different types of industries and organizations. They did so, not by surveying the writers or readers within these industries and organizations, but by collecting and analyzing nearly 800 letters and memoranda according to a list of criteria consisting of 43 writing deficiencies. These criteria, which the researchers say they drew from business communication textbooks, as well as from their teaching and consulting experiences, were then sorted into five categories: form, grammar, content, sequencing, and style.

Among Goodin and Swerdlow's findings is that, across industries, the letters they analyzed most often contained errors in the categories of grammar, style, and form ("form" referring to the "appearance" of a letter, such as its date, inside address, subject line, signature line, spacing, typos/spelling, and so forth). Specifically, they found that the letters contained, on an average, the highest percentages of errors in the following: word usage (52 percent), sentence construction (45 percent), punctuation (44 percent), overused terminology (38 percent), wordiness (36 percent), and salutation (33 percent). On the other hand, Goodin and Swerdlow found comparatively few errors in the letters' content (only 1 percent) and sequencing (9 percent). What may be more interesting and significant than these findings, however, is what the criteria scheme reveals about the researchers' priorities.

There is an old saying that goes something like this: To a man with a hammer, everything is a nail. In this case, as well as in many other studies, the researchers' heavy emphasis upon certain criteria may have blinded them to the importance of other criteria. For instance, of the 43 deficiencies that Goodin and Swerdlow identify as their criteria for evaluating writing quality, they include 41 of these within the categories of either form (which contains 10 deficiencies), grammar (which contains 16 deficiencies), or style

(which contains 15 deficiencies). The two remaining deficiencies are identified as single-item categories, with "content" referring only to "inappropriate information," and "sequencing" referring only to "inappropriate sequencing of information" (p. 13). (What's more, for some unexplained
reason, they list "misleading information" as a deficiency in their "style"
category.)

Apart from Goodin and Swerdlow's lopsided emphasis upon deficiencies
of form, grammar, and style, there remains the more important issue of just
how the researchers could have evaluated the "appropriateness" of the 800
letters' content and sequencing (much less their style) when they had no idea
of why or to whom the letters were sent. My suspicion is that they probably
found relatively few errors in these two categories not because the letters'
information and organization were necessarily "appropriate," but because
the researchers lacked the contextual knowledge necessary to make such a
judgment. While Goodin and Swerdlow maintain that their "editorial analysis followed basic, strict business communication rules of form, grammar,
content, sequence, and style" (p. 12), they do not explain what these rules
are, especially with regard to the slippery matter of "appropriateness."
What they fail to realize is that appropriateness (whether of content, organization, or style) is not subject to the same kind of "basic, strict rules" that
govern correctness (tense, subject-verb agreement, capitalization, and so
forth). To blur that distinction and to imply that one can as easily detect an
error in punctuation as an "error" in content, or that the two are problems
of the same ilk and magnitude, creates a distorted view of writing and
writing "quality." As I will argue elsewhere in this volume, it is this view,
essentially reductionist in nature, that underlies much of what we study and
teach as writing and that, in turn, accounts for many of the preconceptions
and problems that adults later have in their job-related writing. Up until
recently, the unquestioned, unexamined criteria of good writing have been
established and promulgated primarily by those in academe who teach and
study writing rather than by those in the real world. Thus, even when they
assess the quality of writing outside academe, researchers are often using
and reaffirming nothing more than their own predetermined standards of
writing.

In the Goodin and Swerdlow study, for example, the researchers explain
that in order to evaluate the wide variation in the errors they detected, "a
benchmark had to be developed to determine a level of acceptability" (p.
13). Of the 13 industries and organizations represented in their study,
whom do they choose as their benchmark but those within education (academe) because, as Goodin and Swerdlow explain, the letters written by
people within this group "consistently had the lowest average percentage of
letters with mistakes." One wonders, however, whether such "exemplary
performance," as Goodin and Swerdlow praise it, would have won equally
high acclaim had the letters been assessed by criteria other than those estab-

lished by educators themselves and instead by people outside academe, who, if asked to list their 43 criteria for writing, might not have placed as much emphasis on form, grammar, and style.

Since few studies have used open-ended questions to examine what real-world writers and readers regard as the main problems with writing, and since few studies have inquired about the skills most needed for technical writing, I would like at this point to report some of my own informal findings, based upon my experiences in teaching technical writing in R&D organizations. During the last 10 years or so, I have made it a practice in these courses to ask the participants (scientists and engineers, some of whom are supervisors, managers, and directors) what they consider the major problems with the company correspondence they read (namely, reports, letters, and memoranda). While I have not kept exact figures of the total number of participants over these years (I estimate the number at well over 500) or the percentages of those who indicated this or that as being most problematic, Table 1.2 lists, in order of severity, the major weaknesses as identified and described by these writers and readers.

Table 1.2. Major Weaknesses of In-company Technical Writing.

1. *Unclear purpose*
   "I don't know why I'm reading the report."
2. *Lack of conclusions*
   "The emphasis is invariably upon what the person did and how it was done; I want to know what all of this means for me and what I do. Often, conclusions are missing or at best only hinted at. Readers shouldn't have to be mind readers."
3. *Insufficient contextual background*
   "Nothing is worse than being plunged into a report without having been given a clear idea of the problem, situation, or need that motivated the report or the work in the first place. Writers assume too much. Even when it's something I'm supposedly familiar with, I need some brief reminder at the beginning of the report."
4. *Muddled sentences, garbled expression*
   "At the very least, I expect writing that is clear. I don't want to have to struggle to decipher meaning. I don't have the time or the patience."
5. *Too much or not enough detail*
   "On the one hand are writers who swamp you with unnecessary details and data until you're ready to cry for mercy—'Get to the point!' On the other hand are those writers who fill their reports with one glowing generalization after another so that all you're left with are questions and a craving for particulars. The first group of writers unnerves me; the second group makes me suspicious."
6. *Unclear relationship among ideas*
   "Trying to figure out how idea A is connected to ideas B, C, and D is frustrating. Sometimes writers expect readers to read between the lines and provide the logical connections. Most readers, however, aren't going to expend the effort, or, if they do, they just might make the wrong connections."
7. *Unexplained jargon*
   "While it is true that every field or discipline has its own specialized terms, to inflict these upon the unknowing and unsuspecting reader is not only unfair, but also rude."

Before commenting on this list, I should mention that, while some of these items appear to be more problematic in technical writing than in business writing (especially items 2, 5, and 7), the problems listed above are not unique to technical writing. When participants in my company business writing courses are asked the same question (i.e., "What do you regard as the main weaknesses in the reports you read?"), they usually generate a similar list. Thus, the main distinction I want to make in the following discussion is not between the writing skills needed for technical writing as opposed to those needed for business writing, but rather the distinction between the skills that those who write and read real-world writing (business or technical) regard as important as opposed to the skills that many of those who survey real-world writers and readers assume are important.

One of the most interesting things about the list in Table 1.2 is that, while the respondents indicate concern for conventional problems of syntactic and lexical clarity (items 4 and 7) and organization and continuity (item 6), they are even more concerned with problems of content (items 1, 2, 3, 5). As the respondents' explanations suggest, they attribute many of the weaknesses in the reports they read to the writer's limited understanding of his rhetorical task, that is, to his failure to consider the needs of his readers, to clarify his purpose, and to provide his readers with information appropriate for their use. These problems are not due to a lack of specific *writing* skills per se, such as the ability to write clear, concise, correct sentences, or even the ability to organize ideas logically and coherently. Rather, these problems are due to a lack of general *communication* skills, such as the ability to analyze one's audience and purpose to determine what information is most appropriate to include and how best to convey that information. That ability, in turn, depends upon the individual's awareness of the communicative function that writing serves within particular contexts; an awareness, in other words, that writing is not an end in itself but rather a means toward an end.

Until quite recently, the theoretical experts in the field of writing, the teachers and researchers of writing, have lacked such awareness. For example, in the surveys discussed earlier, the writing skills (and the writing deficiencies) that the researchers predetermine as important, and thus that are included in their close-ended lists, typically are those language skills that pertain to *how* something is said (matters of expression and correctness) rather than those communication skills that pertain to *what* is said and *why* (matters of content, function, and appropriateness). Similarly, in most college writing courses the traditional emphasis has been upon writing as both a means and an end in itself, upon writing as process (for instance, strategies for generating ideas and planning texts) and writing as product (for instance, patterns of organization, methods of development, and features of clarity, conciseness, correctness, and so forth). While such instruction may help students write papers that meet the criteria set by their professors, what is often overlooked in many courses is the interrelationship of process and product (the connection between how one approaches a writing task and what one writes), and, more importantly, how these two are influenced by specific contextual constraints, functions, and criteria that govern writing in nonacademic settings. So long as the writing skills that are typically the focus of many research studies and college writing courses (even upper-level courses in business writing and technical writing) concern primarily academic, school-sponsored writing, the real deficiencies may not be in our students' writing skills but in our own skill and knowledge in researching and teaching real-world writing.

THE GROWTH OF CORPORATE TRAINING PROGRAMS

Evidence that education may not be preparing students for the knowledge and skills later required of them in business and industry is provided by the recent growth of corporate training programs. As reported in the 1985 Carnegie Foundation study, *Corporate Classrooms: The Learning Business* (Eurich, 1985), companies at that time were investing over $40 billion a year on their own in-house training programs, a figure that came close to the annual expenditure of all four-year colleges and graduate universities in the United States. Furthermore, in 1985, enrollment in corporate education programs was nearly 8 million people, nearly equal that of all college and university enrollments.

While that training covers a wide range of topics—including orientation sessions on company policies, practices, and procedures; managerial development seminars; and technical courses—a good share of that training is increasingly devoted to improving employee writing skills. Noting the trend in 1979, an article in *U.S. News and World Report* ("Why Business Takes Education into Own Hands") suggested that "Behind the moves by business into education and training is dissatisfaction with the performance of conventional schools in teaching the basics. . . ." (p. 70). In the following year, William Blundell (1980) substantiated this statement by reporting that many businesses were developing their own writing programs because universities were turning out students who lacked the appropriate business writing skills. According to a study by Meister and Reinsch (1978), 42 percent of the training directors at 261 Illinois manufacturing firms said that their new trainees are deficient in writing. The effect of this deficiency was best summed up by Robert L. Craig in 1980: "Poor writing," he maintained, "is a significant factor in the whole drop in growth of American productivity" (cited in Leslie, 1986, p. 51).

As Leslie (1986) points out, many companies are taking matters into their own hands and no longer relying upon universities to provide instruction in written communication aimed at meeting managerial needs. General Motors, for example, now has an accredited engineering and business college that includes in its curricula courses in oral and written communication; other major corporations, such as Xerox, Dow Chemical, and Amoco, as well as many other companies, have instituted their own in-house courses in writing. Still other firms, such as Arthur Anderson and nonprofit organizations such as the American Management Association, now run mini-colleges for business people, with courses in management, finance, accounting, and computers, as well as courses in written and oral communication.

The field of training has itself become big business as many companies increasingly hire professional consultants and trainers. For example, Denton (1979), who surveyed training managers for 316 employers listed in the *College Placement Annual,* found that, while 36 percent of company-sponsored writing courses are taught by members of the company's training staff, 19 percent are taught by college faculty hired as consultants, and 10 percent are taught by professional consultants, with the remaining courses either taught by a combination of company staff and outside trainers or handled in some other way. As for the types of courses covered, the most common is the "general course in writing skills" (31 percent), followed by technical-report writing (20 percent), business-letter writing (19 percent), and proposal writing (6 percent). Finally, as testimony to the need for such courses, 86 percent of the respondents in Denton's survey projected that in the following five years their organizations would experience an increased demand for writing courses.

That forecast was made in 1979. In the decade since then, the number of writing courses sponsored by companies and taught by outside consultants has grown considerably. However, whether or not such in-company courses are effective in meeting the needs of real-world writers may be another matter. For example, in surveys that have asked workers what most helped them develop their writing skills (Paradis, Dobrin, & Bower, 1984; and Bataille, 1982), the majority of respondents (71 percent in the Paradis study) attributed their improvement to on-the-job experience, or practice, rather than to either their college writing courses or even their company-sponsored writing courses. One reason, I suspect, is that because company courses are frequently taught by moonlighting English or composition teachers, the courses are therefore based on the same assumptions, principles, and criteria governing academic writing. What all too often has been missing—in our academic courses, in corporate courses, and in our survey studies of real-world writing—has been an awareness of writing as a means of communication.

Fortunately, the situation has begun to change as some researchers are on the track of coming back, as the character Jerry in Albee's play *The Zoo Story* says, "a short distance correctly." Since the early 1980s especially, some researchers have begun exploring the social and pragmatic functions writing serves within real-world, nonacademic settings. In Chapters 3 and 4, I will discuss that journey by examining some views of writing that are beginning to challenge academic notions of good writing and by reviewing some studies that have increased our understanding of writing within organizational settings. For the time being, however, it is important to take a look at where we have been and how it is that we have gone such "a long way out of our way" to ignore the connection between writing and communication. As I will discuss in the next chapter, as yet much of our teaching and research is still based primarily upon three academic views of writing, none of which accurately describes how, what, or why real-world writers write, much less, according to many critics, how, what, or why even students write. As I will furthermore illustrate in the next chapter, many times our students later get into trouble by applying these same academic views of writing to their real-world writing and by assuming that the criteria of "good" writing instilled in them in our writing courses also extend to their nonacademic writing.

2

Academic Views of Writing: Product, Process, and Context

Form follows function.

Lewis Sullivan

As discussed in the last chapter, one of the effects of the growing interest in real-world writing has been to make us reconsider whether what we teach and study as effective writing in school has anything to do with what those in nonacademic settings regard as effective writing. In the past, we have often operated under the assumption that writing is writing, without taking into consideration the various forms and functions of writing beyond the classroom. The result, as indicated by the surveys discussed previously, is that we have graduated students who, while they may be able to write a good essay or term paper, often have difficulty writing a business letter or technical report that meets organizational standards and expectations. Those surveys further suggest that in many cases even those individuals who have taken university courses in business and technical writing are inadequately prepared for the demands of real-world writing.

Such charges are not new to English teachers. They and the courses they teach have often been the target of national criticism. In the early 1970s, the media was filled with stories about "Why Johnnie Can't Read" and "Why Johnnie Can't Write." The cry then was for a return to the "basics," which essentially meant a heavier dose of the rules of grammar, usage, and mechanics, and more emphasis upon sentence structure and the conventions of the five-paragraph essay. The panacea, in other words, was more attention to form.

Today, the crisis is more pervasive but the solutions less apparent. Johnnie (or Jane) has grown up, taken a job as a corporate executive, engineer, or research scientist, and yet his writing is still deficient in many ways. The problem, as we are beginning to realize, is not primarily one of form, nor one that the basics could have cured. In fact, it is not even a writing problem per se (as "writing" is commonly defined), but rather a communication problem: a failure to understand the pragmatic functions that writing serves in a social context and the ways in which those functions, in turn, influence the social context.

The concept of organicism that revolutionized American architecture, art, and literature at the turn of this century—that form follows function— has only recently begun to influence the way in which we teach and study writing. Increasingly, we are beginning to discover what our colleagues in psychology and speech departments have known for years: that meaning is context-dependent and that it is impossible to interpret or evaluate any phenomenon, including a written text, apart from the situation in which it exists. More than ever before, we are realizing that academic, school-sponsored writing is only one type of writing for one type of audience, and that the conventions and criteria of academic writing may not be transferable to other discourse situations. Call this increased awareness a major breakthrough, paradigm shift, revolution, pre-paradigmatic dissonance, or simply a return to the real basics—whatever, it is beginning to alter the ways in which we think about, teach, and study writing.

Much has been written lately about the role that context plays in influencing not only how texts are interpreted, used, and evaluated, but also what real-world writers write and how they approach their writing tasks. However, while acknowledging the importance of context, few researchers have actually investigated writing in real-world settings. Rather, the emphasis of our research and instruction has been upon academic, school-sponsored writing, and, as a result, most of our theories and models of writing have been based upon this one context alone. Since this context has itself rarely been the subject of close scrutiny and critical investigation, we run the risk, in our study and teaching of real-world writing, of assuming that it is governed by the same kinds of constraints and criteria as those of academic writing. What may be worse, as suggested in my Introduction, is that by making such assumptions we may be turning out students who are handicapped in their real-world writing because they fail to distinguish between the nature of academic writing and that of real-world organizational writing. Yet, if our students fail to make that distinction, it is partly because we ourselves, as teachers and researchers of writing, often fail to do so. As Anderson (1986) notes, "All too often composition researchers have focused on the *how* and *what* of writing at the expense of *why*. This is true both for traditional classroom rhetoric, with its emphasis on written products and surface grammatical detail, and for the new 'cognitive' rhetoric, with its emphasis on the individual thinker-writer and the *structure* of thinking-writing processes" (p. 736).

Lately, many theorists, researchers, and teachers of writing are growing disenchanted with current models and theories of writing. As Applebee (1986) has pointed out, "Many scholars and teachers question whether research has any relevance to practice at all" (p. 5). One of the most renowned educators in our field, Edward J. Corbett, candidly admits in an article in *College Composition and Communication* (1987), "After all these years of teaching writing, I am beginning to ask myself whether I have done any of my students any good. . . . I do not turn my good writers into excellent writers, and I do not detect that my bad writers are any less bad at the end of the term" (p. 452). Similarly, in a review of national writing programs and projects, Applebee (1986) concludes that, though "seemingly sensible," each of them "has failed to achieve widespread reform of educational practice," and he suggests that the overall failure of such reform movements is that "we have allowed our understanding of teaching and learning to focus on what we do when we teach—the activities and the curriculum—rather than on why we do it" (p. 6). In what is perhaps the most succinct and dire indictment of our discipline, Bruffee (1986) contends that "What was a bad dream has become a profession" (p. 794).

Many others in the field of composition, noting our tendency to confuse the means of writing with the goals of writing, have begun to criticize the myopia of composition research. Steinmann (1982), for example, has pointed out that the separation of process from product and purpose makes little sense. "How," he asks, "can researchers investigate a means without knowing what end it is a means to?" (p. 297). In the same vein, Shuy (1981) has emphasized the need for a holistic approach to the teaching of language arts, a constructivist approach that includes communicative competence in both the forms and the functions of language. Shuy's main point is that in the way children naturally learn language, function always precedes form, whereas in the schools (and I would add, in research studies) the emphasis is primarily on form alone.

In the early 1980s some researchers, many of them from outside the mainstream of composition research, began to investigate writing in non-academic settings in order to study writing as it is naturally used. Heath (1981), for instance, in her study of writing in rural communities of North and South Carolina, demonstrated how the writing of students dramatically improves when they have real versus classroom or hypothetical reasons for writing. Furthermore, Scribner and Cole (1981), in their study of writing among the Vai, a traditional West African society, refuted the notion, common among composition researchers, that there is a necessary correlation between writing skills and thinking skills by proving that those who have no written language can think as analytically and as "well" as those who have developed a written language.

Increasingly, teachers and researchers are beginning to realize that writing cannot be taught or studied apart from its social settings and that writing is a means of communication. As a result, they are questioning, as never before, the value of the last 30 years of composition research and instruction and its relevance to writing beyond the classroom. While there has been a tendency in the past to clone one study after another (witness, for example, the numerous sentence-combining studies of the 1970s or the protocol anal-

tention but is SELF-LIMITING writing (for example, feature articles in magazines; student research reports, technical papers, and laboratory reports; and other "content-limited" types of government and business writing such as "progress reports, program analyses, explanations of budgets, and reports on marketing research").

3. Extended REFLECTIVE writing in which the writer discovers much of his or her thought during the writing process (for example, "scholarly writing, speculative or exploratory articles, and reflective philosophical writing").

While Kinneavy and Hairston maintain that the aim of discourse determines its form or mode, D'Angelo (1975, p. 34) contends that patterns of discourse are conceptual patterns of thought, and he identifies the following patterns: "description, narration, classification, comparison, contrast, analogy, cause and effect, partition, and enumeration." These patterns, he further claims, "are embedded in sentences, in paragraphs, and in longer units of discourse. . . . When they are embedded in sentences, we call them aspects of style. When they are embedded in paragraphs and extended units of discourse, we call them aspects of structure." Earlier, Christensen (1965) had proposed a "generative rhetoric" of paragraph structure based on the coordinate-subordinate syntactic and semantic relationships of the sentences within a paragraph, beginning with the topic sentence. This topic sentence, as Christensen and Christensen (1976, p. 154) later explained, serves as the central thought or "plumb line" that controls the development of the paragraph. Out of Christensen's work came the idea of the essay as "a kind of macroparagraph" (D'Angelo, 1975, p. 61), with thesis statement, major supports, and minor supports—a structure that has become popularly known as the five-paragraph essay. Christensen's early work also inspired a legion of sentence-combining enthusiasts (for example, Mellon, 1969; Hunt, 1970; and O'Hare, 1973) and other researchers (for example, Daiker, Kerek, & Morenberg, 1978; Kerek, Daiker, & Morenberg, 1979, 1980; and Morenberg, Daiker, & Kerek, 1978) whose studies of sentence-combining pedagogies and syntactic versatility led to the conclusion that proficiency in writing (and hence the quality of a text) could be measured by the number, type, and length of syntactic units in a text. Since then, other researchers (for example, Halliday & Hasan, 1976; Collins & Williamson, 1984; and Kintsch, 1974) have attempted to equate the quality of writing with the semantic features of texts, such as their cohesive ties or propositions.

The product approach to writing is also evident in textbooks on technical writing, many of which are thinly disguised composition textbooks. In many of these textbooks (for example, those by Mills and Walter, 1978; Lannon, 1982; Houp & Pearsall, 1984; Pauley & Riordan, 1987; Emerson, 1987; and Markel, 1988) chapters are arranged by patterns of discourse—for instance, definition, description, classification, comparison/contrast, and partition—and by generic modes, or structural models, of technical writing—typically, letters, memoranda, informal reports, proposals, and formal reports.

A common argument for the product approach to writing, and one espoused by many of the theorists discussed above, is that form serves a heuristic function for writers; that is, that the modes and structural models help writers shape information into acceptable and generally recognizable formats. While that is true to some extent, there are at least two problems with this argument. First, the product approach, as Winkler (1983) has pointed out, does not account for how writers generate the information that is supposed to be shaped to fit the form. Winkler, like Dillon (1981), challenges the notion that writers are teeming with information and need only a form in which to express it. "Composing," he emphasizes, "does not begin with the process of arranging data into specific patterns. . . . The content is not 'given'; it is the result of an investigation and is shaped by rhetorical considerations" (p. 115). To put it another way, "The main point to bear in mind," says Dillon, "is that form is not something we pour a plastic content into" (p. 55). Second, the little research that has investigated writing in organizational settings suggests that (a) individual companies develop their own formats for reports, memos, and proposals, (b) these formats vary considerably from company to company, and (c) learning to write well within a particular organization is partly a matter of learning the local, idiosyncratic conventions governing what is and is not acceptable in a particular document. For example, Freed and Broadhead (1987) in their study of proposals written by two consulting firms, find that the differences in content, structure, and emphasis of each company's proposals can be explained by differences in each firm's image, reputation, services, and target markets. Faigley (1986), paraphrasing Bakhtin (1981), points out that "Words carry with them the places where they have been" (p. 535). As will be discussed in Chapters 3 and 4, reports also carry with them the places the company is or wants to be.

Another problem with the form approach to writing is that, in the real world at least, texts usually have several purposes and usually include a combination of modes. Rarely, for instance, is the aim of a text ever strictly expressive, referential, literary, or persuasive. Even within Kinneavy's subdivision of referential writing, many technical documents may combine scientific, informative, and exploratory aims. Similarly, Hairston's taxonomy of aims oversimplifies the complexities of real-world writing by forcing all texts into only one of three categories. In reality, however, rarely does anyone, as Hairston suggests, simply convey messages ("only information"), write purely "self-limiting" and "content-limited" reports, or engage strictly in extended "reflective" writing geared toward discovery and speculation. Almost any real-world writing, including progress reports (which Hairston includes as an example of her second category, Self-Limiting writing), defies the boundaries of aim she and Kinneavy propose. Rather, real-world writers usually have multiple aims and often multiple audiences. In addition, seldom are the patterns of organization and modes of development employed in real-world texts restricted to one type, such as definition, comparison/contrast, partition/division, description, or process analysis; more typically, these modes are used in combination. Furthermore, their use is guided not, as D'Angelo maintains, by tapping a mental reservoir of preexistent cognitive strategies but rather by attending to the functions that writing serves within a particular context. As Beach and Bridwell (1984) point out, researchers are recognizing "the limitations of their own definitions of writing genres" and that "the distinctions among concepts such as 'expository' and 'descriptive' were [are] arbitrary and vague" (pp. 4–5).

Perhaps the most serious objection to the product view of writing is the assumption that texts—and the aims of discourse—somehow exist as objective entities apart from the contexts within which they are produced, read, and used, and that, therefore, texts can be evaluated purely on the basis of form or aim alone. In the teaching of composition this separation of text from context has created the notion among students that the structural or syntactic features of a text determine its quality; that, in other words, form is everything. When transferred to their real-world writing, the product view of writing often makes writers obsessed with the surface features of their texts and thus blinds them to the importance of the extra-textual or contextual elements of their texts, elements such as audience, purpose, and situation that ought to inform their decisions about structure, content, and style. I find, for instance, that many writers in business and R&D settings are sometimes more concerned with matters of correctness and form than they are with content. For some writers, their greatest worry seems to be whether or not it is appropriate to split an infinitive, to begin a sentence with a conjunction, or to end a sentence with a preposition. Others still assume, as they did in school, that the longer their reports, the better they will be; the more polysyllabic words and Latinate expressions they use, the more impressive sounding their writing; or the more syntactically complex their sentences, the more erudite they will appear. In my company courses, for example, there are always a few individuals who initially resist using strategies to write more clearly and concisely because, as they explain, that's not the way they learned to write and that's not what they were rewarded for in their school writing. Others fear that by saying what they mean in plain, simple English they will not sound, as one participant put it, "business like." They have become so accustomed to reading sentences like, "We can optimize our profit potential by maximizing our productivity in the realm of time management" that it is a challenge to convince them to write instead, "Profits will increase once we learn to use our time more wisely."

In addition to fostering misguided notions about effective, real-world writing, the product view of writing also encourages a blind adherence to various prescriptives learned in school. When asked what they remember most about their college writing courses, many people will cite lexical and syntactic rules, rules that continue to guide them as writers but which for various reasons often cause confusion in their real-world texts. While some writers may sense that the same rules which worked well for them in their school essays (and which helped them earn high grades) are not serving them quite as well in their business or technical writing, many continue to follow them. Why? Simply because they assume that the rules are the rules. (After all, they learned them from English teachers who, if anybody, ought to know best, right?) Besides, in lieu of these rules, what other, better, more formalized rules are there to guide writers? Few. Thus it is, that for many writers their former teachers remain the arbiters of good writing, and their former college handbooks the authoritative sources to which they turn when they want definitive answers to stylistic issues.

By way of illustration, the following identifies only a few of the prescriptives that frequently mislead real-world writers. These are the "rules" that writers most often recite to me when, during my consulting sessions with them, I point to a confusing passage and ask them to explain why they chose certain words or decided to structure certain sentences in a particular way. The examples below are based on business and technical reports written within organizations. After each "rule" (or principle) and example is a brief explanation of why that particular rule is problematic.

Rule #1:   *Vary your word choices. Don't keep using the same words to refer to the same things. It creates monotony.*

Example: Take the sample and pipette 100 ml of the catalyst into a 100 ml vial. Add 25 ml of solvent to the compound and stir 1 min to dissolve the xylene.

Discussion: In teaching students to vary their word choices, teachers often place the criterion of variety over the criterion of clarity. In doing so, they encourage the kind of elegant variation illustrated in the above example, in which the words *sample*, *catalyst*, and *compound* have the same referent and in which the words *solvent* and *xylene* have the same referent.

While variation of word choice may be a virtue in literary writing, in technical writing it is not only confusing but potentially dangerous. Readers, for example, may misinterpret instructions and hence mix the wrong chemicals or attach the wrong parts of an instrument. In the case of assembling a bicycle, the result may be only an unrideable bike and a skinned knee. However, in the case of mistakenly mixing volatile chemicals or incorrectly attaching bolts to the pylon of a jet airliner, the results may be much more disastrous.

Rule #2: *Vary your sentence structure. Don't keep using the same syntactic structure. It creates a "Dick-and-Jane" monotony.*

Example: The final test rating is lowered by one grade in the presence of blisters. A reduction of bond strength reduces the final test rating by two letter grades. At least one grade is lowered when excessive holidays are observed.

Discussion: The problem with this rule is similar to the problem with Rule #1: It sacrifices clarity for variety. It also violates another principle of good writing, and one that is particularly important in technical writing: parallelism. Unless similar ideas are expressed in similar grammatical form, readers will have a hard time comprehending the text. While syntactic variety and flexibility are often touted as the hallmark of good, "mature" student writing, in real-world writing syntactic versatility can impede meaning.

Rule #3: *Avoid the passive voice; instead, use the active voice. It is more concise, direct, and action oriented.*

Example: In our analyses, we found that the baseline worked extremely well, although we did have a problem with an unknown peak. After investigating the situation thoroughly, I discovered that there were impurities in the air at UniForm Corporation. As a consequence, I reran the tests, and I detected the true composition of the samples submitted.

Discussion: Many teachers of writing and most textbooks on writing nowadays—either those concerned with academic, business, or technical writing—advocate the use of the active voice. While there are several problems with this rule, two of the main ones in technical writing, as illustrated by the above example, are that for many writers it blurs the distinction between what I will call the "animate" and the "inanimate" use of the active voice, and it fosters the notion that the active voice is always better than the passive voice regardless of emphasis or context.

To many writers, like the one who wrote the above example, using the active voice simply means constructing a sentence in which the grammatical subject is the agent or doer of the action. In technical writing especially, however, seldom is the animate active voice appropriate since rarely does it make any difference who did what. For if the methodology is sound, any researcher ought to obtain the same results, and, therefore, the agent of the action becomes irrelevant. Furthermore, since research in organizations is usually a collaborative effort, personal references to one's self ("I") or group ("we") are usually considered out of place, if not narcissistic and self-aggrandizing.

Few writers realize that they can still use the active voice without references to person, that is, the inanimate active voice. That, for example, instead of writing the passive, "An illustration of how the SEG effect is produced by the Z-rays is shown in Figure 6," they can write the active, "Figure 6 shows how Z-rays produce the SEG effect." Even at this, however, while the active construction is more concise and perhaps more "readable," there may be good reasons for choosing the first version (the passive) over the second (the active). For the difference between the two constructions really goes beyond the passive and the active voice and beyond the syntax of a single sentence itself. Rather, the difference involves a matter of emphasis that cuts across syntactic boundaries and establishes semantic interrelationships among sentences. If, for instance, the main topic of the passage is the SEG effect, then the first version (the passive) is appropriate; but if, on the other hand, the main topic and emphasis is Figure 6, then the second version (the active) is more appropriate.

While many writers (especially, it seems, scientists and engineers, who are accustomed to dealing with mathematical symbols, formulas, and algorithms) crave hard and fast rules for constructing "good" sentences, what they often fail to realize is that, contrary to the impression given them in their writing classes, syntax is often a matter of choice rather than rule—of what, in a given text and context, best achieves the writer's intended emphasis, purpose, and meaning. That there is no single syntactic structure that by itself is inherently and universally "good" is unsettling to many writers. Their first instinct is skepticism, as they pull out a textbook and point to some rule. In the face of such "authoritative" evidence and their years of schooling, sometimes it is not easy to convince them that form follows function.

Beyond the above types of local-level problems that occur when real-world writers adhere to the lexical and syntactic rules of writing they learned in school, sometimes writers approach their job-related writing tasks as though they were essay assignments or exam topics, and thus they structure their texts accordingly. They rely, in short, upon the typical modes and patterns of exposition they learned in their college writing courses. In the Introduction to this volume, for example, I illustrated how one writer, in composing a technical report, first employed a narrative format and, when this proved unsatisfactory to his manager, then resorted to an expository format in the second draft of his report, which, as it turned out, was even more unsatisfactory to his manager. The tendency among real-world writers to write in an academic, essay mode and to assume that their real-world writing will be evaluated according to the same criteria as their school-based writing, tends to be especially common among inexperienced real-world writers. Take, for example, the following internal report written by a young engineer just out of college. The report is reprinted below in its entirety, with only the company name and the engineering specification IDs changed to protect confidentiality.

August 24, 1988

Use of Subsurface Foam Injection as Fire Protection for Polar Liquids

Nitex Engineering Specification 480C–2, Welded Carbon Steel Storage Tanks (Open Top Tanks with and without Floating Roofs, Section 3.7) deals with the applications of foam for the fire protection of flammable liquids stored in an open floating roof tank. This Nitex engineering specification prohibits the application of subsurface foam nozzles to polar liquid additives such as ethanol, methanol, t-butyl, alcohol, ether, etc.

There are two general classes of flammable liquids: hydrocarbons and polar solvents. Hydrocarbons are classified as nonwater miscible products, e.g., crude oil, gasoline, hexane, naphtha, diesel oil, etc. Polar solvents are organic liquids having chemical molecules with a functional radical at one end. Such liquids are easily mixable with water, hence its molecules have the tendency to become firmly attached to the foam molecules.

Furthermore, there are two generic types of foams available on the market, protein and synthetic (Universal) base types. Protein foams are used for hydrocarbon liquids, whereas the synthetic type is recommended for polar liquids. Synthetic foams cost about $14 versus $8.50 per gallon for protein foams. The improper application of a subsurface foam in a polar liquid would result in the foam dissolving itself into the polar liquid before it could reach the surface, thus preventing the formation of a protective fire shield.

In conclusion, the use of subsurface foam nozzles on polar liquid solvents is inadequate. For such a service, a synthetic type foam should be considered. For best field performance, synthetic foam should be applied onto the surface of the polar type liquid under controlled conditions.

While this example might be quite appropriate in an essay on the nature of subsurface foam injection, the audience and purpose for this report are illusive at best. Like many student essays, the report lacks a contextual reference. No mention is made as to the reasons for either the writer's investigation into the subject or the readers' need to know or use such information. Rather, the report begins, as do many essays, *in medias res*. It is an academic foray into a topic, the result of some obscure "assignment" that lies beyond the text itself. And while a good, academic treatment of the subject, the report is nonetheless an essay—something that would be more suitable in a research paper or a magazine article in which unsolicited, gratuitous information is the norm. The text is not appropriate for organizational readers who, presumably, are picking up the report expecting information that addresses some previously identified problem. The structure of the report, too, is clearly influenced by the typical five-paragraph essay genre. (Though here there are only four paragraphs, interestingly the writer confided that he thought one weakness of the report might be that it was missing a fifth paragraph.) The body paragraphs (paragraphs 2 and 3) are models of academic, expository writing. Each begins with a clear topic sentence based on the generic pattern of classification, predictably developed by a discussion of the first category and then the second category. Also, the last paragraph employs the traditional, hackneyed phrase often used in student essays to signal its conclusion: "In conclusion. . . ." In terms of the text's structure, there is little to fault the writer. Were it an essay, it probably would have gotten a high mark, for its form is exemplary. But as an organizational memorandum, the text is less than satisfactory. For while the report is easy to follow (the paragraphs and sentences are clear and readable), it violates one of the main criteria of good real-world writing: functionality. At best, just why the report was written or what the reader is supposed to think or do upon reading it is only hinted at between the lines of the concluding paragraph. Though even at that, there is considerable room for interpretation (and misinterpretation) on the part of the reader. "In conclusion," the writer, by relying upon an academic genre of writing and by focusing his attention upon the structure of his text, seems to have been diverted away from a genuine consideration of his audience's needs and his reasons for writing. In this case, whatever heuristic function form ideally serves for a writer has evidently backfired.

As illustrated in the above report, the problem with the patterns or modes approach, as Blyler (1986) and others have observed, is that "the individuality of each writing task, as influenced by audience, purpose, and context, is overlooked in favor of applying a generic form" (p. 103). In the classroom, students often learn to manipulate forms—common modes of thinking or cognition, as D'Angelo describes them—as a means and end unto themselves rather than as strategies that can be used as tools to produce texts that fulfill communicative functions. The result, as some scholars (for example, Odell, Goswami, & Quick, 1983; Knoblauch & Brannon, 1983; Cooper et al., 1984; and Herrington, 1985) stress is that students are not being encouraged to think and to shape content and style to suit a particular rhetorical situation. As Cooper et al. (1984) report, even the best students seem unaccustomed to writing with readers in mind and rely upon flimsy logic and sweeping generalizations. The problem, according to Herrington (1985), is that "students are often asked to write for limited purposes, to no other audience than the teacher-as-examiner or expert, and in circumstances that do not lead them to think critically" (p. 333). Composition assignments that require students, for example, to compare and contrast the advantages and disadvantages of attending a large university versus a small college, to recount their most embarrassing experiences, to describe their dorm rooms, or to argue the pros and cons of capital punishment may help students practice patterns and modes but such assignments do not develop the kinds of thinking and writing skills students will later need to communicate effectively with anyone other than perhaps more teachers in graduate school.

Until recently, the product view of writing that has dominated the study of composition has also influenced studies of technical and scientific writing. In the few early studies, researchers were interested primarily in the structural features of texts apart from the natural contexts in which they were produced and intended to be read. For example, Davis (1968), Witt (1976), Frase (1981), and Faigley and Witte (1983) analyzed the effects that stylistic variables have upon the readability of technical texts, but in their studies college students were used as the reader-subjects and excerpted or dummy passages as the experimental texts. In short, the studies created artificial contexts; they focused upon the form of writing (for example, the text's organizational, syntactic, or lexical features) apart from its communicative function and effectiveness in a real-world setting.

Similarly, most studies of scientific and technical texts have focused upon the analysis of scholarly articles published by and for the academic community rather than upon the texts produced by and used within research organizations. Huddleson (1971) and Gopnik (1972), for example, have analyzed the syntactic structures of scientific articles, and de Beaugrande (1977) has examined how grammatical features guide the focus of given versus new information in technical articles. In all of these studies, the emphasis is on writing as a text—a product—rather than upon writing as a dynamic, social interaction between writer and readers. Thus, whatever conclusions can be drawn from studying technical or scientific texts for the public or for the academic community cannot necessarily be applied to writing in organizations where the audiences and purposes for writing are quite different.

The major shortcoming of these studies is that they are based on the product view of writing, namely the assumptions that form, content, meaning, and function are separable and that the effectiveness of a text, paragraph, or sentence can be determined apart from its specific context. What is often overlooked in such studies and in many writing courses is that in good writing, as in good architecture, form follows function. That is, the quality of a text can no more be judged by its structural features alone than can the quality of a building. The product is always more than the sum total of its parts. To neglect the importance of context in influencing the production, interpretation, and evaluation of texts is to foster the notion that writing is simply a matter of construction—arranging parts—and that there exist some prefabricated forms into which content can be laid. The result is that teachers, students, researchers of writing, and real-world writers come to regard writing, not as a means of communication, but as a end in itself. They furthermore come to believe that for each aim and mode of writing there are some predetermined, objective criteria of good writing that apply regardless of the situation.

PROCESS VIEWS OF WRITING

Within the last several years, some scholars, having grown disenchanted with the product view of writing, have gone the opposite direction by embracing the process view of writing. According to this view, the single-most important aspect of writing is not the text (or the final product) but rather the act of composing itself. The fervor with which process devotees preach their view often comes close to evangelism. As Faigley (1986) notes, the process movement has even been heralded in our journals by Richard Young (1978) and Maxine Hairston (1982) as a Kuhnian paradigm shift in our discipline. While such claims are now considered by some as hyperbolic, "it is evident," as Faigley further points out, "that many teachers in grade schools, high schools, and colleges have internalized process assumptions. . . . nearly everyone seems to agree that writing as a process is good and 'current-traditional rhetoric' is bad" (p. 527). Well, not everyone. Hagge (1987), for instance, lambastes the process movement as a religion based on views of "mental mysticism" and "antinomianism" that encourage solipsistic thinking and writing (p. 100). However, before discussing the limitations of the process approach to writing and its influence on students and real-world writers, let us examine some of the assumptions underlying the process view of writing and the criteria of writing implicit in this view.

As Faigley (1986) notes, definitions of process vary from theorist to theorist. However, the two views of composing that have most dominated writing instruction and research are the expressive view and the cognitive view. The following describes each of these, and the implications and limitations each has for the studying, teaching, and evaluation of writing both within schools and within organizational settings.

The Expressive View

The expressive view of writing is essentially a vestige of the let-it-all-hang-out 1960s, a reaction against conformity and conventions (be they of dress, mores, or writing) and an exultation of individuality, creativity, and self-expression. Based on the literary and romantic school of writing, the expressive view holds that it is the journey itself—the act of writing—and not necessarily the destination—the product or text—that matters most. "Process" from the expressive view does not mean a formalized method for composing. Quite the contrary, the "method," if it can be called that, is no method at all but rather an uncharted process in which, ideally, the individual discovers meaning while writing.

Among the many apostles of this view are Ken Macrorie (1968), William Coles (1969), Donald Stewart (1969), Peter Elbow (1973), Donald Murray (1978), Ann Berthoff (1982), and C. H. Knoblauch and Lil Brannon (1984). In their work, organic metaphors of writing abound (for example, writing as growing, writing as cooking); the student, to use Hagge's description (1987, p. 99), is regarded as a "sensitive plant"; and the role of the teacher is essentially one of nurturer, muse, or therapist. Rohman (1965), for example, maintains that "teachers must recognize and use, as the psychologists do in therapy, a person's desire to actualize himself" (p. 108). As Emig (1967) defines it, teaching becomes "intervention," either by the "proffering of freedoms" or by "the establishing of constraints" (p. 128), the latter of which, she cautions, can lead to a "dangerously truncated, irresponsible, and anti-humanistic" view of teaching (p. 129). Needless to say, few process proponents, as Hairston (1986) and Hagge (1987) note, have much use for traditional rhetoric, nor are they very concerned with matters of form, correctness, mechanics, or grammatical rules—all of which presumably only stifle creativity and inhibit the students' spontaneity as they compose (Emig, 1971, pp. 16, 53; Perl, 1979, pp. 324–28; Perl, 1980, pp. 368–69; Sommers, 1980, p. 383; and Knoblauch & Brannon, 1984).

According to the expressive view, the main purpose of writing is to help students discover what they know and feel. The underlying assumption, as Hairston (1986) explains, is that students "cannot know what to write or how to write it until they actually begin writing" (p. 442). Thus, the implication is that students cannot really be *taught* how to write; rather, by engaging in the process itself, they get an experience of, or a feel for, writing. Writing, in short, is a "trip," both in the normal sense of the word and in its 1960s sense. That trip is perhaps best captured by Henry Miller in a passage that Knoblauch and Brannon (1984, p. 62) quote as a description of what writing is *really* like:

> I begin in absolute chaos and darkness, in a bog or swamp of ideas and emotions and experiences. . . . I am a man telling the story of his life, a process which appears more and more inexhaustible as I go on. Like the world-evolution it is endless. It is a turning inside out, a voyaging through X dimensions, with the result that somewhere along the way one discovers that what one has to tell is not nearly so important as the telling itself. . . . From

the very beginning almost I was deeply aware that there is no goal. I never hope to embrace the whole, but merely to give in each separate fragment, each work, the feeling of the world as I go on, because I am digging deeper and deeper into life, deeper and deeper into past and future. (cited in Lynn, 1987, p. 907)

For creative writers, perhaps, Miller's account rings true. But to suggest, as some process proponents do, that this ought to be a model for all composing seems a bit farfetched. Imagine, for example, a research scientist or engineer who has been called into his manager's office:

Manager: Tom, this technical report you wrote is a bit confusing and hard to follow. Maybe we ought to rethink its content and structure. Tell me, just what did you have in mind as you wrote it? As we say around here, what was your "master plan"?

Tom: Well, I began in absolute chaos and darkness, in a bog or swamp of ideas and emotions and experiences. . . I am a man telling the story of his research, a process which I found more and more inexhaustible as I went on. . . .

From the expressive point of view, the criteria of good writing, as summarized by Faigley (1986), are integrity, spontaneity, and originality. Both Rohman (1965) and Stewart (1969) emphasize the need for students to write with integrity and authenticity—to discover the "combination of words which allows a person the integrity to dominate his subject matter with a pattern both fresh and original" (Rohman, p. 197), and above all for students to *believe* what they are saying (Stewart, p. 225). The second quality of writing, spontaneity, is best expressed by free-writing guru Ken Macrorie and by *Writing without Teachers* advocate, Peter Elbow (1973). Both feel that good writing is not the result of following rules but rather the result of following the inner workings of one's imagination, in other words, of stepping to the beat of one's own drummer, or "going with the flow." Finally, the third criterion, originality, as Faigley (1986, p. 531) explains, stresses the individual's creativity—his need for self-actualization. Writing aids self-development, and self-development, in turn, aids writing.

One obvious limitation of the expressive view of writing is that it makes the study and evaluation of writing virtually impossible. Upon what basis, for instance, does one assess the writer's sincerity, integrity, spontaneity, or originality? If writing becomes mimetic of the writer's evolving thought processes and emergent feelings—that is, if the text reflects a psychological rather than a rhetorical organization—we are left only with the writer's effusive, fragmentary, and illusive meanderings. Interpreting and evaluating texts then becomes something akin to deciphering a Rorschach test. But what may be worse is that the expressive-process approach encourages among writers a narrow, egocentric, and esoteric view of writing, which, though it may be fine for composing personal or literary works (for example, diaries, poetry, or novels) is inappropriate for professional academic writing and certainly all organizational writing.

In real-world professional writing there is little room for the expressive-process view of writing. As Lynn (1987) warns, "Students who really view all writing as expressive, 'open-ended,' and 'eternally renovative' surely encounter serious problems in many situations—writing business letters, progress reports, legal briefs, technical instructions, and many other projects requiring a reasonable subservience to form and content" (p. 908). While writing can itself serve a heuristic function and be the pathway to discovery—"a way of knowing" (Nystrand, 1982)—and while writing can provide a cheap means of therapy, considerate and enlightened writers would no more subject their readers to such early, rough drafts than they would bore their guests with a long evening of home videos.

For obvious reasons, the expressive view of writing has gotten little coverage in business and technical writing courses and textbooks. Still and all, there are some real-world writers, who perhaps because they were influenced in their college writing courses by teachers who advocated the expressive view of writing, or who, for whatever other reasons (bad manners, bad mood, inflated egos, or sheer naivete) seem bent on unloading their minds and emotions on their unsuspecting readers. Consider, for example, the following excerpt from a "self-actualizing" real-world writer, one who clearly believes what he says, writes off the cuff, and feels (as he told me in interview) that his strengths as a writer are that he is forthright and does not mince words. As brief background, this memorandum was precipitated by an EPA visit to the company's waste disposal site. After his visit, the EPA official recommended revisions in the company's procedures for drilling core samples of hazardous waste. In this internal company memorandum, the writer is responding to the EPA official's recommendations and revisions. The writer's primary audience is his immediate director, and his secondary audiences are others within the company. The writer also indicated, however, that in such situations copies of internal memoranda are included as appendixes to their correspondence with the EPA regions. (I have changed the name of the permit writer and the number of the EPA region.)

> We scrutinized in detail each page of the EPA Region 15 revisions and developed some comments that were at all of issue or concern to anyone involved. It appears that the permit writer for Region 15, Joel Wrightman, either is incapable of understanding or refuses to accept the fact that the material we are talking about has been fully characterized by the company that generated the waste. As is our normal, stringent procedure, a certified representative sample

of the generator's waste stream was analyzed and evaluated. Furthermore, his incoming waste stream is continually being sampled to ensure that it matches the generator's characterization.

Apparently, however, Mr. Wrightman persists in believing that generators are not to be trusted and that they are covertly getting rid of some suspect material at their own site, especially when it comes to solid drums or truck loads, by loading the bottom of drums and trucks with toxic material and then covering it up with acceptable material. Accordingly, Mr. Wrightman, operating under this delusion, insists that every drum or truck of solids which are sampled be cored right down through the whole entire vertical length. Such a procedure is not only unnecessarily time-consuming and costly but downright ridiculous. By requiring such excessive and extraordinary sampling procedures, Wrightman and the EPA, we believe, do not have a legal leg to stand on. This appears to be but another attempt at harassment and a power play on Wrightman's part to stall our permit. It is time for us to take a firm stand.

Compared with most technical memoranda, this one evinces a refreshing candor; however, that candor is at the expense of professional tact and diplomacy. When I questioned the writer about his tone, he staunchly defended it by citing the long-standing adversarial relationship between his company and EPA Region 15. "These people," he said, "don't understand a thing about our operations. They continually treat us as though we're the enemy and try to throw up roadblocks wherever they can. And so we're forced to deal with them in this way." As the writer himself admitted, his memorandum served as a cathartic release, a chance to let off steam and "put these guys in their place, otherwise they'll just walk all over us."

Rarely, unless perhaps it is a case of life and death (and we will see an example of such a case later in Chapter 5) is emotive language appropriate in technical or business writing. Part of the professional ethos expected of real-world writers is that of a calm, reasonable person who forms judgments on the basis of facts and deliberation rather than on emotions, who has the wisdom and foresight to anticipate the consequences of what he says and does, and who is understanding of another's position, even when—and especially when—he personally disagrees with it. To write well in real-world situations means to communicate well, and that in turn means being attentive to the pragmatic functions writing serves within a social context. A major problem with the expressive view of writing is that it makes writers insensitive to the communicative functions of writing. It makes writing an essentially private act and encourages among writers an inflated sense of self-importance and a disregard for anything other than their own opinions and feelings. In short, the expressive view, when transferred to nonacademic contexts for writing, fosters an unhealthy egocentrism and lack of responsibility which are counterproductive to effective communication.

The Cognitive View

The cognitive view of process, unlike the expressive view, is based on the assumption that there is a method—a series of mental operations—that writers use while composing. From this point of view, writing is neither an emotional purging or outpouring, nor a discovery of one's own personal world of meaning. Rather, the writing process is a deliberate problem-solving activity. As Faigley (1986) points out, the cognitive view of composing developed as a reaction against the expressive view and was influenced, in part, by cognitive developmental psychology. Adapting Jean Piaget's concept of *egocentrism*, theorists in the late 1960s and 1970s (for example, Moffett, 1968; Britton, Burgess, Martin, McLeod, & Rosen, 1975; Kroll, 1978; and Lunsford, 1980) argued that emphasis on expressive writing inhibited the student's ability to *decenter*—to imagine audiences and perspectives for writing other than their own. One consequence, as some observed, was that on writing tasks calling for abstract thinking, students tended to lapse into personal narrative. Noting a similar phenomenon, Flower (1979) made the useful distinction between writer-based prose and reader-based prose and concluded from her own study that proficient writers are more aware of their audiences than are nonproficient writers.

Unlike the expressive view, which holds that writing is a mystical, organic process (beginning in chaos and darkness and eventually, through the act of writing itself, emerging in occasional glimmerings of meaning), the cognitive view is based on an essentially mechanistic approach to writing. Underlying most cognitive models are two assumptions: (a) that writing consists of a series of steps or stages, and (b) that it is possible both to study and to teach these. While cognitive theorists disagree about what these stages are, most of them, despite their protestations to the contrary, seem to agree that there is indeed "*a* process." One of the earliest and most cited models was that proposed by Rohman and Wlecke (1964). They advocated a linear three-stage model: *Pre-Writing, Writing,* and *Re-Writing.* In the last 25 years, other researchers, influenced by cognitive psychology, have refined and redefined their model. Recently, for example, Kellogg (1987) proposed a three-phase model of "product development," including *prewriting, composing a first draft,* and *reworking subsequent drafts,"* seemingly a clone of Rohman and Wlecke's model but which Kellogg insists does *not* refer to writing processes. Rather, the term *writing process,* he claims, "refers to collecting information, planning ideas, translating ideas into text, and reviewing ideas and text" (p. 271), subprocesses that can occur during any of the three phases of product development, phases which are themselves recursive.

But the researchers who put the cognitive process of writing on the map and who mapped what presumably goes on in the mind as people write were Flower and Hayes (1980b, 1981). Borrowing theories and models from cognitive psychology and from information processing, they proposed a three-stage model of composing: planning, translating, and reviewing. In essence, it is an updated version of Rohman and Wlecke's pre-writing, writing, and re-writing model—though, actually, both of these models (that of Flower and Hayes and that of Rohman and Wlecke) are modern renditions of classical (Quintilian) rhetoric, with its emphasis on invention, arrangement, and style. (As a sidenote to the uninitiated—my real-world, nonacademic readers—it should be obvious by now that composition theorists have a religious penchant for triadic models, which apparently goes back to Aristotle.) Where Flower and Hayes differed, however, was in attempting to lend scientific credibility to their model by characterizing the mind as something akin to the central operating unit or motherboard of a computer. Thus, they represent the subprocesses of composing (planning, translating, and reviewing) as a schematic similar to a computer flowchart, with numerous boxes and arrows and loops that supposedly reflect the mind's circuitry during composing. The idea that the brain, like a computer, is composed of a memory bank and an information processing unit presupposes that, at some prior point in time, somehow and somewhere there was "input." Flower and Hayes, however, do not account for how the goals and plans, which figure so prominently in their model and which turn the cognitive gears, are derived. That is one problem with their model.

Another problem is the assumption that there is one process that governs all writing, regardless of a text's audience and purpose. While cognitive theorists repeatedly emphasize that there is no single process, that "writing is a dynamic activity" (Kellogg, 1987, p. 271), and that "the stages can be highly flexible and their characteristics vary greatly" (Hairston, 1986, p. 24), they nonetheless talk about "*the* process," "*the* stages," and "*the* phases" (for example, Kellogg, 1987, pp. 270–71; Hairston, 1986, p. 24). Accordingly, many researchers have tried to study *the* cognitive processes of proficient versus nonproficient writers. For the most part, however, the studies have focused on the writing of college students, with "proficiency" predefined as conformance to the researcher's or teacher's predetermined criteria of "good" writing, as for instance in the Kellogg study (1987, p. 280), in which quality of writing was assessed by "language usage, coherency, idea development, effectiveness, and mechanics." In other cognitive-based studies (for example, Matsuhashi, 1981, 1982), researchers have examined the eye movements and pen pauses of students as they compose, in the hopes that from these outward signs researchers might divine the writers' inner mental machinations.

The research technique, however, that the cognitive-process theorists are most fond of is the "think-aloud" protocol analysis (as popularized by

Hayes and Flower, 1983) or variations of it, such as Kellogg's (1987) "directed introspection." Whatever its nomenclature or guise, protocol analysis is based on several dubious assumptions: that (a) the student is aware of and can describe his composing process, either during or after composing; (b) the protocol analysis itself, when it interrupts writing, does not significantly alter the writing process; and, most of all, (c) the experimental situation, with its contrived assignment, time limit, and hypothetical audience and purpose for writing, is somehow representative of what, how, or why students, or anyone else for that matter, write. Criticizing the artificiality of the writing tasks and situations in process-based studies, Brandt (1986) contends that the "writers' texts seem to keep subjects merely occupied while their cognitive or scribal processes are documented. As a result, the act of writing itself tends to be perceived as an autonomous mental process and described without reference to public context or to the interplay of writer and text" (p. 140).

To take a short detour here, I have often wondered, while reading such studies, what the results would have been if, at the end of the experiment, the researchers had asked their subjects two more questions:

1. In the writing assignment as presented, did you feel a genuine need to communicate information either to the hypothetical audience as defined, to the researcher, or to anyone else?
2. If you were actually writing to a real audience, do you think you would have approached your writing task in the same manner? If so, how? If not, why not?

My intuition is that students, sensing the seriousness with which we investigate their writing, are often inclined to go along with the rules of the game as we define them because they trust that we, after all, must know what we are doing even if to them what we do and the rules we make them play by may seem illogical. (See, for example, Sperling & Freedman, 1987, "A Good Girl Writes Like a Good Girl," for an interesting account of how students revise their texts to comply with their teachers' expectations even though the students neither understand nor agree with their teachers' criticisms.) I suspect, too, that given half the chance and the conviction that we are truly interested in their opinion, our students, even our most deficient—and perhaps our most deficient because we have not yet converted them—would admit that our research experiments, not to mention our classroom writing assignments, strike them as a bit artificial, if not downright bizarre.

That we, as presumably bright, educated people, could put so much credence—not to mention time and energy—into researching the writing efforts of students who are in our classes because they lack the very skills we are supposed to be teaching them is an anomaly I have yet to understand.

What other skill-related disciplines, I wonder, have developed theories of proficiency by studying the aberrant behavior of students? Yet we often go about our research as though our students, many of whom have been placed in our composition courses because they did not do well on the university's entrance exam in writing, can reveal to us the mysteries of the composing process or that by analyzing their essays we can refine our criteria for good writing. Perhaps we have been guided in our research, not by lofty, scholarly motives, but by sheer ease. As Beach and Bridwell (1984, p. 227) point out, college students "are a captive pool of 'subjects,'" a cheap, compliant, and unending reservoir of guinea pigs. They don't complain, they don't question, they don't resist. No matter how obscure the assignment, they try to do it. For, how can they object when those doing the research are often their own teachers? This further raises the incestuous, self-perpetuating nature of studies in which the individuals conducting the research are often the teachers of the very subjects whom they study, and these teachers are invariably also the ones to judge what is and is not "good" writing. With the odds so stacked in the researchers' favor, it is probably a wonder that there is any debate at all about what constitutes effective writing. But enough of my expressivist diatribe; let us return to the discussion of the cognitive-process view of writing.

As Hagge (1987) points out, process models have little application in real-world business or technical writing because such writing is often dictated by exigencies specific to a particular company or situation. Nevertheless, there are many real-world writers, who by virtue of their schooling, have been indoctrinated with cognitivist assumptions about writing. What happens then, for instance, when they attempt to write technical reports? Sometimes the obsession with the cognitive process itself results in reports that detail the writer's mental processes. For instance, according to some researcher-writers with whom I have worked (especially scientists engaged in basic research), their main purpose in writing is to demonstrate in their reports the soundness of their procedures, findings, conclusions, or recommendations by retracing every step along their mental route. Frequently, such writers mistakenly assume that their readers cannot fully understand or appreciate their conclusions unless they (their readers) are subjected to a blow-by-blow description of the project and are taken on a vicarious, cognitive journey. Paradis, Dobrin, and Miller (1985) also note this phenomenon in their study of writing in an R&D organization. They describe the case of a young engineer whose technical report was considered unsatisfactory by his supervisor and manager because its main findings and recommendations came toward the end of the report. The author, according to Paradis et al. (p. 301), "vigorously defended his document, because it *showed* the logic leading up to his decision. In this way, his reasoning could be reviewed, he said: the logic was as important to him as the recommendation itself." By demonstrating to his superiors the thinking underlying his conclusions, the writer was also trying to get them to share in the accountability for those conclusions. However, as Paradis et al. point out, neither the supervisor nor the manager "felt the academic urge—nor did they have the time—to review the fine points of the author's reasoning." While such writers often interpret their superiors' criticism as a lack of interest in the details of their work, the real problem is usually the writers' failure to understand their responsibility within the research effort, their superiors' expectations, and the function their reports serve in helping achieve organizational rather than personal goals.

The above case also illustrates the main limitations of the cognitive-process view of writing. Often, writers who approach composing as primarily a problem-solving activity produce reports that have problems in both organization and content: Invariably, their reports are arranged inductively and include a lot of extraneous information. They assume, in short, that good writing is good thinking, and that the purpose of a report is to validate one's own cognitive prowess.

Both the expressive and the cognitive views of process are based on the assumption that meaning is a product of internal representations, whether it is, as in the expressive view, discovering the significance within oneself, or, as in the cognitive view, arriving at logical conclusions by applying problem-solving strategies. The result is that, in both views, writing remains an essentially private, egocentric matter: writing as a form of communing with oneself rather than communicating with others. Most of all, both views fail to account for how social contexts influence meaning and affect both how one approaches a writing task (the process) and what one writes (the product). The danger, Hagge (1987) notes, is that emphasis on process alone directs students and researchers "away from language as an essentially interpersonal, social act that always takes place in a concrete situational context" (p. 110). Recognizing the limitations of the expressive and cognitive views of process, some theorists have proposed yet another view of writing—the contextual.

THE CONTEXT VIEW OF WRITING

Based on traditional rhetorical theory, the context view of writing is hardly new to the field of composition. What is new, however, as will be discussed later, are recent attempts to broaden the concept of context to include writing in nonacademic settings. While there are many strands of the context view of writing, all of them to some extent emphasize that the writer's awareness of audience and purpose influences both what and how he writes. Today, almost every composition textbook, or technical writing or business writing textbook, is based on the assumption that writing is a rhetorical activity; hence, preliminary chapters of such textbooks invariably include advice for analyzing one's audience and purpose. Typically, such advice consists of a list of demographic questions for audience analysis (for instance, questions about the reader's age, position, knowledge, experience, attitudes, etc.), and a list of generic purposes for writing (for example, to inform, persuade, justify, analyze, instruct). In many instances of school-based writing, however, either the student is given only a topic and is expected to invent an audience and purpose, or the student is given a hypothetical case that explicitly defines a narrow audience and purpose. Neither situation realistically reflects real-world situations for writing in which writers often must address heterogeneous audiences, in which their texts often must achieve multiple purposes, and in which composing is as much a matter of analyzing the organizational culture as it is analyzing a specific rhetorical situation.

Though "context" is a common buzzword in many textbooks, classrooms, and articles, our understanding of it is as yet superficial. The reason, as I speculated earlier, is that our research and teaching have been restricted to primarily one context for writing, the academic. As Brandt (1986) points out, "Although widely acknowledged, context in composition remains largely unexplored. It remains in the background of most investigations of writing and writing processes, as a dark stage upon which writer's plans and thoughts and language are played out" (pp. 140–41). Precisely what the role of context is in shaping discourse has become a topic of much recent debate. Harrison (1987) proposes two views of context: one based on traditional rhetorical theory, and the other based on modern rhetorical theory. As discussed below, the first view of context, the traditional view, has served as the mainstay of composition research and instruction for several years and continues to influence what we study and teach as good writing. The section following this one explores another, broader view of context, one that considers rhetorical situations for writing within the larger framework of organizational communication.

According to traditional rhetorical theory, context, as defined by Bitzer (1968), is the situation or occasion that motivates discourse. Three elements constitute a rhetorical situation—audience, exigence, and constraints—all of which determine a rhetorical response to fit the particular situation. An important assumption in this view is that the situation is objective and external to the rhetor; that the rhetor, in other words, stands outside the context. The writer is presented with a rhetorical problem, and, by carefully assessing the demands of the situation, determines an appropriate response or solution. Or, to use the classical Aristotelian definition, writing is a matter of finding the available means of persuasion appropriate for a given occasion.

While many researchers have attempted to study how writers respond to rhetorical situations, typically the subjects of such studies have been college students, who have little experience addressing real-world audiences and situations. In studies that have used "expert" writers as subjects, usually the experts, as Faigley et al. (1985) observe, are "either upper division college students, journalists, fiction writers, or English teachers" (p. 57) rather than adult writers in organizational settings. Furthermore, usually the writing tasks used in experimental studies, like the assignments in many composition courses, are artificially contrived and depict situations that for the writers lack any sense of immediacy or concern. For example, the writing task in a Flower and Hayes study (1980a) required the subjects (in this case, both expert and novice writers) to "write about your job for the readers of *Seventeen* magazine, 13–14 year-old girls" (p. 23). The difficulty with such an assignment, MacDonald (1987) observes, is that it "contains no pre-defined problem—neither a publicly defined problem others have recognized nor a problem generalizable to another writing situation. So the assignment requires the writer to create the problem in order to solve it" (p. 327). In other writing tasks which attempt to define both a problem and a context, the situation is often so complicated and intellectually demanding that writers can spend more time and effort trying to untangle and decipher it than they do actually solving it. (For an exception see Couture and Goldstein's *Cases for Technical and Professional Writing*, 1984).

In an academic context, trying to create meaningful nonacademic contexts for student writers is no easy task. Sometimes writing tasks based on hypothetical situations create only even greater obstacles for the writers, as when for instance the situation and topic are far removed from the writers' experience, knowledge, or interest. Other times writers, recognizing the artificiality of the writing task and its mythical context within a real, academic context, are presented with a rhetorical conundrum of audiences within audiences and purposes within purposes. Should the writers analyze the real audience—the teachers or researchers—and try to second-guess this audience's real purposes in giving the hypothetical task, and then approach the writing task to meet whatever they think are these readers' expectations? Or should the writers forget about these and instead try to analyze the mythical context as if it were a real occasion for writing, even though in their analysis of the hypothetical audience and purpose they have to fictionalize the context further since the writing task gives them only minimal clues? Or should the writers try to accommodate both sets of audiences and purposes? As discussed in the Introduction to this volume, specifically in reference to Rubin and Rafoth's (1986) findings, students typically take the first tack; that is, regardless of the writing task, they try to conform to what they think the teacher or the researcher wants. But when they do so, this can present problems for us as evaluators, especially in experimental situations in which we assume the students are responding genuinely to a hypothetical situation for writing. It can skew our results by making us think that what the students say (write) they think is really what they think, and that how they write is representative of how they would normally write were the hypothetical context for writing actually real. The problem is exacerbated when the wording of the writing task sends students conflicting messages about whom their "real" audience should be and what their "real" purpose in writing should be. To illustrate, the following examines Cooper et al.'s (1984) study of the writing quality of incoming freshmen at the State University of New York (SUNY).

As explained in the Cooper et al. study, entering freshmen at SUNY were given the task of writing an essay to a fictitious board of directors of a fictitious company, arguing either for or against hiring a woman candidate when two other male applicants for the same job were better qualified. According to the researchers, most revealing among the study's findings is that even the best writers (those whose essays received the highest ratings as judged by general impression, holistic scoring) resorted to stereotypical arguments and failed to consider the facts or the situation in any depth. Commenting upon their findings, Cooper et al. express surprise and dismay that the students "didn't seem accustomed to writing with readers in mind" (p. 43) and that they seemed incapable of carefully analyzing data. All of which, Cooper et al. speculate, bodes ill for the students' potential to think and write critically in other situations: "Reading and rereading the papers," they remark, "we came to feel that this tendency to ignore the facts not only was detrimental to analysis of abstract ideas such as would be encouraged in the humanities or social sciences, but was likely also to extend to analysis of hard data in engineering and the sciences" (p. 45). As an explanation for their findings, Cooper et al. offer the following:

> It appears that these students were being taught to think alike, in their high schools, from their parents, and—we suspected—most importantly, from their television sets. The uniformity and naivete of these essays persuaded us that these students had been actively taught to fear and shun complexity, and especially to deny moral and legal ambiguity. (p. 47)

Such speculations, while hardly novel in themselves, are nonetheless sobering and another reminder of the school's responsibility to teach students to think critically. Yet, for Cooper et al. to blame the problems in the students' essays on parents, educators, and television strikes me as too easy and glib an explanation for their findings—in fact, quite similar to the kind of uncritical, sweeping generalizations that they found so objectionable in the students' essays. My own speculation is that, had they more carefully analyzed the rhetorical situation of the SUNY writing task itself, as well as their own assumptions about what entering college freshmen ought to know, they might have discovered other possible explanations for their findings.

First, if Piaget and other cognitive psychologists are correct in their conclusions that individuals do not develop higher-order reasoning skills until their middle or late teens, it may have been unrealistic for Cooper et al. to expect graduating high school students (even the top 12 percent who comprised the sample in their study) to already possess the refined analytical thinking skills that a college education is supposed to help them develop. We are, after all, talking about youngsters who are but 13 to 14 years old. Furthermore, when one considers the time constraints of the writing task (a limit of 90 minutes), the sophisticated subject with which the students were expected to deal (affirmative action), and the pressure upon the students to perform, it is curious that Cooper et al. should have been so surprised by their findings.

More important, however, are the problems inherent in the way the writing task was presented to these entering freshmen. As Cooper et al. describe it, the sheet the students received was entitled, "A Test of Writing Ability," and the opening sentence of the instructions was as follows: "Your performance on this essay test will enable us to make specific recommendations about writing courses you might take" (p. 22). My suspicion is that, despite the hypothetical writing task that followed this statement, the student writers understood very well the *real* rhetorical situation. They clearly knew to whom they were writing and why—namely, to English teachers whose assessments of their writing skills would determine whether or not the students had to take extra writing courses as part of their college requirements. Thus, while the writing task tried to engage the students in a game of rhetorical make-believe, and while the students, in turn, tried to play along by the rules as they interpreted them, I suspect that most of them recognized that the hypothetical writing task was simply a ploy—that is, that their purpose in writing was not to respond honestly to the contrived rhetorical situation but rather to conform to what they assumed were their evaluator's criteria of good writing.

As an alternative explanation for Cooper et al.'s findings, then, I would contend that the students, like many real-world writers, were actually quite sensitive to their real audiences (English teachers), and that, for the most part, they were motivated by very practical, understandable concerns. If they relied upon stereotypical arguments, it may have been because they regarded these as the most conventional and therefore the safest—those premises and means of persuasion that conformed most to popular beliefs. Thus, they attended to what they assumed would be the criteria by which their essays would be evaluated: namely form as opposed to content. And though I have doubts about whether young college undergraduates, much less high school graduates, are mature enough to grapple deeply with such complex and abstract issues such as affirmative action, abortion, and capital punishment, I wonder, too, what the results would have been had the examiners made clear to the students the criteria by which their essays would be judged. For example, would Cooper et al.'s findings have been the same if the writing task were presented as follows: "In this writing task, we will be evaluating your essay, not only upon the basis of how well organized and clearly developed your ideas are, but moreover upon the basis of how carefully you have examined the facts as presented and to what extent your conclusions are based on original rather than stereotypical thinking."

Except for the Smith and Combs (1980) study, in which students were explicitly told that their essays would be evaluated primarily upon the basis of syntactic complexity—and in which the students who had had no instruction in sentence combining exercises wrote essays as syntactically versatile as those students who had had weeks of such instruction—I know of no other study in which the researchers made explicit the criteria they would be using to evaluate the writers' texts. Rather, writers are often left in the lurch—of figuring out, on the one hand, some amorphous, hypothetical criteria for an amorphous, hypothetical writing task, and of intuiting, on the other hand, the criteria they think their teachers will be using to evaluate the quality of their essays and thereby the quality of their thinking. If, as Cooper et al. conclude in their study, students "did not show any capacity for considering the larger context of the problem" (p. 45), perhaps their capacity would have been enlarged had the context as described in the writing task been extended to include the criteria by which the students' essays would be assessed.

As will be discussed in Chapter 4 and in my study in Part Three, the situation is seldom any better in real-world situations for writing. Even there, writers often encounter ambiguous contexts for writing and have the same difficulty with inexplicit company standards and vague expectations on the part of those assigning the writing tasks. In lieu of clearly defined contexts and criteria for writing, real-world writers often resort to the traditional view of context they learned in school. As a result, the writer focuses upon his immediate audience and purpose. By doing so, however, the writer may overlook the larger organizational context within which his text exists. According to Harrison (1987), this is the main limitation of the traditional rhetorical view of writing: "The rhetorical situation places contextual boundaries around singular events and thus focuses our attention at an analytic level below that of 'organization'" (p. 6). To interpret context at simply a local, personal level is to overlook the broader implications and ripple effects of communication within an organizational context.

For example, to refer again to the abstracts cited in my Introduction, in the first one the researcher defined his rhetorical situation very narrowly: To him, his audience was simply his manager and his purpose for writing the report was merely to investigate the cause of the digester's shutdown. As the writer's manager recognized, had the original version of the report been issued, it would have strained rather than facilitated communication between the R&D facility and the pilot plant because of its emphasis on fault finding. The writer failed to realize that the report, and the situation that motivated it, were part of a larger organizational context: that, for instance, beyond his manager, there would be several other, more important audiences for the report, and that many of these audiences would not interpret the researcher's thoroughness as good investigative work but as a witch-hunt. In many ways, the writer approached his task as a student would in responding to a research paper or lab report assignment or exam question—as a terminal text (something simply to be "handed in"), with no purpose other than demonstrating to the manager the writer's industriousness and ability to arrive at the correct answer. Implicit in the report is the writer's assumption that the facts would speak for themselves. To his mind, it was a simple open and shut case: The reactor malfunctioned because the operator failed to monitor the feed temperature. When the manager suggested that the report was "inflammatory," the writer was perplexed, for, from his perspective, he had been totally objective: He had simply reported what had happened and why, which is what he assumed he had been assigned to do. The writer seemed totally unaware that the true "meaning" of the report lay beyond the text itself: in the way others, depending on their roles and responsibilities at R&D or at the pilot plant, would interpret the report. As the manager no doubt realized, the report, while strictly factual, was in effect a scathing indictment of the quality of training and supervision at the pilot plant—a message, in short, that the plant was being mismanaged. And, while that indeed may have been the case, the manager knew, as the writer apparently did not know, that for one manager to blatantly point the finger of blame at another manager is not just bad communication but bad politics. Whereas the writer defines his rhetorical task upon the basis of a single event (the April 7th shutdown) and assumes a narrow audience (his manager) and purpose (to document and inform), the manager, in his revision, defines the rhetorical situation from a much broader, organizational perspective—one that foresees the probable impact of the report upon himself and others, that downplays past failings, that emphasizes positive measures for preventing similar occurrences in the future, and that, overall, encourages continued cooperation and communication among those throughout the company.

As many have pointed out (for example, Driskill & Goldstein, 1986; Brandt, 1986; Lutz, 1986; Harrison, 1987; and Faigley, 1986), the traditional models of audience analysis taught in school—"a set of all-purpose questions to be tacked on to an assignment to help students invent and identify an audience" (Park, 1986, p. 486)—are inadequate for writers in non-academic, real-world settings. At best, such questions are too cumbersome, time consuming, and simplistic for practical purposes. In the final analysis, creating a detailed, demographic profile of each potential reader may not yield the kind of information the writer needs to decide what to include in a report. For such decisions, according to Driskill and Goldstein (1986), depend less upon analyzing the characteristics of readers and more upon the writer's awareness of the organizational context. Writers need to understand the interrelationship among individual, departmental, and corporate goals, and which of these, given the document's intended readers, most need to be addressed. As Driskill and Goldstein put it, "What is most crucial for the writer to supply is what the reader must know but does not know, must feel but does not feel, must believe but may not believe. In this gap lies the definition of the document's necessary content and persuasive challenge" (p. 44).

But to discover what knowledge their readers most need, writers must first have knowledge of the social context within which discourse functions. As Park (1986) stresses, "To identify an audience means identifying a situation" (p. 486)—identifying not simply, as in the traditional view of context, the given rhetorical situation or occasion for writing, but moreover the particular organizational situation: for instance, which audiences within the organization need which information, which events pose exigencies, and which factors constrain action. As Harrison (1987) maintains, to understand a rhetorical situation, writers need "detailed knowledge of the understandings that make up everyday life within a given organization," and to explain this kind of knowledge one needs an expanded view of context, "one that incorporates the idea of organizations as communities of meaning forming contexts for rhetoric" (p. 7).

EMERGING CONCEPTS OF WRITING AS SOCIAL ACTIVITY

Recent research on writing in organizational settings suggests that as writers compose they are attuned to much more than simply the text's immediate audience and purpose. Beyond these local considerations, they are aware of such things as how their texts convey an appropriate image of themselves and their department or company; how what they say and the manner in which they say it will influence their readers; and how their texts help further individual, departmental, and corporate goals. Such knowledge constitutes an organizational understanding that cannot be attained solely by traditional rhetorical analysis and that some (for example, Lutz, 1986) maintain cannot be learned in school but only by slowly becoming socialized or immersed within a particular organizational culture.

The idea of organizations as cultures, as meaning-bearing and meaning-producing social milieux, underlies many approaches to modern or contemporary rhetorical theory, or, as Berlin (1982) calls it, the "New Rhetoric." Central to this view is the idea of context as community, and the premise that knowledge and language (including writing) cannot be understood from the perspective of an individual but only from the perspective of a society. Whereas traditional rhetorical theory is predicated on the notion of an external, objective reality existing independently of the knower, modern rhetorical theory assumes that whatever we call "reality," "knowledge," and "truth" are subjective, social constructs, and that therefore it is impossible to separate the knower from the known (Miller, 1979), or the dancer from the dance. As Gregg (1984) contends, "context determines what we are willing to accept as knowledge" (p. 136). *Context* in this sense includes more than the traditional rhetorical elements characterizing a specific rhetorical situation; context, moreover, embodies a particular way of perceiving those elements and the rest of the world—"a set of assumptions that give meaning to stimuli and enable individuals to define experience" (Harrison, 1987, p. 8). Finally, whereas the traditional view of rhetoric is based upon the assumption that good writing, like truth and knowledge, is governed by objective, universal criteria, modern views of rhetoric are based upon the assumption that the criteria of good writing are themselves determined by the particular social context.

As will be explored in Chapter 6, modern rhetorical theory, as influenced by recent scholarship in the philosophy and sociology of science, has implications not only for what is accepted as fact and knowledge in science and technology but also for how writers of research reports (such as progress reports) define their rhetorical tasks. For the present, let us examine more closely the idea of communication within social and cultural contexts.

3
Culture, Community, and Communication

All inquiry is motivated.

Umberto Eco (1976)

Within the last few years, explorations into the nature of real-world writing have made researchers aware of the limitations of academic views of writing. Increasingly, our journals are filled with articles criticizing traditional, academic approaches to the study and teaching of writing and calling for research that investigates writing within natural, social contexts. While some scholars (for example, Witte, 1987) maintain that we can make progress within our discipline simply by refining our existing methodologies, and while others (for example, Gieselman, 1986) argue that academic theories of writing ought to dictate practice, still others (for example, Connors, 1983, and Anderson, 1986) suggest that (a) the real problem is not necessarily with *how* we study writing but rather with *what* we study and *why* we study it; and (b) practice ought to inform theory rather than the other way around.

As discussed in the last chapter, composition researchers have spent a lot of time trying to analyze the writing processes and products of good versus poor student writers, and as a result have developed theories and models of writing based on the distinctions of these two groups of writers and their texts. In many cases, however, the studies have been governed by the teacher-researchers' own conceptions of good writing. Until recently, few researchers have questioned whether such conceptions have any basis beyond the academic contexts within which they teach and study writing. Nor have they had to, for there have been few to challenge their assumptions. Their subjects, mainly college students, have been in no position to criticize either what their teachers are teaching or what the researchers (usually their teachers) are investigating. Similarly, their colleagues, other like-minded teachers and researchers, typically have been motivated by the same pragmatic interests—namely tenure and the need to publish or perish—and by the same need to conform to pedagogical and research conventions. Thus, for the most part, their efforts have been restricted to embellishing, confirming, and justifying what they already know: to find-ing new ways of keeping alive old debates about such matters as whether we ought to be studying cohesion or coherence; counting a sentence's clauses, T-units, idea-units, chunks, or propositional units; or employing ethnographic versus experimental research methodologies. Few researchers or teachers have stopped to consider that maybe what they ought to be doing is questioning the very assumptions about writing upon which their studies and courses are based. One of the first questions they might ask themselves, as some researchers have recently begun to do, is whether what they regard as good writing is at all related to what those in real-world settings regard as good writing.

To begin to answer that question, however, often requires a herculean effort. First, the researcher/teacher has to go outside the academic institu-tion in order to find willing research subjects. And that is no easy task, especially when many of those in academe may have limited access to those in government, business, or industry and when those within such organiza-tions may be reluctant to admit the researchers because they are either too busy or too suspicious of "academic types." Unless the researcher has con-tacts and can convince key people within the organization that there is likely to be some benefit or payoff to them or the organization, the researcher is likely to encounter resistance. Second, and oftentimes a greater obstacle, is the researcher's own lack of incentive and inertia. With the majority of his colleagues conducting studies with college students, the researcher may have little motivation to go outside the college or university. After all, why should we go to the trouble of leaving comfortable, familiar surroundings when we can stay home and do our research there? But the physical effort may be minor when compared with the intellectual effort. The more en-trenched in academe our theories of writing have become, the more difficult it has become to look at them objectively and critically, much less to aban-don them. It is not only a lot easier but much safer to build upon existing theory than to question that theory, for in doing so one risks the criticism of one's peers, which in turn could jeopardize one's reputation and job se-curity.

In reference to scientific breakthroughs, Kuhn (1970) observed that the theories which have revolutionized science have come not from those with-in the established community of science but rather from those on the out-side, those least indoctrinated and least constrained by conventional think-ing. Similarly, emerging views of writing as a social phenomenon—views that counter the theories established during the last several decades of com-position research and pedagogy—normally have come not from those within the ranks of composition scholarship but rather from those either on the fringe or in other disciplines. Furthermore, seldom have those who should most be able to contribute to our understanding of real-world writing—those readers and writers within organizational settings—been involved in research on writing (except occasionally as research subjects), participated in our professional organizations, or served on the editorial boards of our journals. To illustrate how tightly knit and closed our academic community is, the following table is a brief survey of the constituency of the editors and editorial boards of the major journals in our field in 1987:

Table 3.1.   Constituency of Editorial Boards for Journals: Members from Academe vs. Business.

Journal	Editors or Members of Editorial Boards	
	Number from universities (including institutes)	Number from business
College English	22	0
College Composition and Communication	12	0
Research in the Teaching of English	15	1
Written Communication	34	3
Technical Writing Teacher	17	0
The Journal of Business Communication	11	1

In summary, of the 111 editors and members serving on the editorial boards for these journals, only 5 were from outside academe—a mere 4.5 percent. Since four out the six journals cited above include either "teaching" or "college" in their titles, it may be argued that these journals are geared specifically toward academic writing, pedagogy, and scholarship, and that therefore they need not be concerned with nonacademic writing nor include on their editorial boards members from outside the academic enclave. However, as I have argued in the previous chapters, such insularity and xenophobia lie at the heart of our problems as a discipline.

This chapter and the next one take a look at a view of writing that has recently emerged in our literature—a view of writing unlike those described in the previous chapter and one derived from the cross-fertilization among such diverse disciplines as science, sociology, anthropology, philosophy, psychology, and linguistics, and from hybrids of these disciplines, for example, the philosophy and sociology of science, and psycholinguistics. It is a view of writing predicated on the assumption that writing is essentially a social act and that, therefore, in order to study, teach, or practice writing as a means of communication, one must be aware of context from a much broader frame of reference than simply the immediate rhetorical situation. As discussed below, the major premises underlying a social view of writing are that language is itself a social construct and that all meaning is context-determinant. This chapter extends this view of writing further by exploring the idea of organizations as cultures and as rhetorical contexts. The next chapter then examines the role writing plays in both shaping and projecting an organization's culture.

The epigram to this chapter, Umberto Eco's observation that "all inquiry is motivated," encapsulates both our pragmatic need as a discipline to explore writing beyond the classroom, as discussed in Chapter 1, and the need of real-world writers and researchers to understand the personal, social, and organizational exigencies that influence written texts and that ultimately determine what characterizes effective communication.

AN INTRODUCTION TO SOCIAL THEORIES OF LANGUAGE AND COMMUNICATION

As alluded to in the last chapter, and as expounded by Bruffee (1986), modern rhetorical theory goes by many rubrics—"New Rhetoric," "social construction," "new pragmatism," "dialogism," or just plain "Kuhn." While there are many variations of the social theory of language and communication, underlying most of them are two basic assumptions:

1. That what we know and how we know it are influenced by the particular time, place, and culture in which we live.
2. That meaning is context-dependent.

These assumptions will be examined more fully in Chapter 6, which focuses on theories of scientific and technical communication. In the meantime, however, it is impossible to talk about a social theory of organizational communication without some understanding of these concepts. The following, therefore, is a brief summary of each of the above assumptions, as well as examples of their application in real-world texts and situations.

Knowledge and Knowing as Culturally Determined

More than anyone else, Thomas Kuhn is regarded as the father of social constructionism, a philosophy which has influenced modern theories of communication. Among Kuhn's contributions to epistemological thought is the idea that scientific knowledge, as he puts it toward the end of his book, *The Structure of Scientific Revolutions* (1970), is "intrinsically the common property of a group or else nothing at all" (p. 201). Rorty, in *Philosophy and the Mirror of Nature* (1979), expands Kuhn's thesis and integrates the theories of Dewey, Heidegger, and Wittgenstein to support his thesis that all knowledge, not just scientific knowledge, is socially based. One implication of this social constructionist position, as Bruffee (1986, p. 774) explains, is that in any discipline "entities we normally call reality, knowledge, thought, facts, texts, selves, and so on are constructs generated by communities of like-minded peers." These constructs are in turn "symbolic entities that define or 'constitute' the communities that generate them, much as the language of the *United States Constitution*, the *Declaration of Independence*, and the 'Gettysburg Address' in part constitutes the political, the legal, and to some extent the cultural community of Americans."

This social constructionist theory of knowledge helps explain both why we have clung to our own academically-oriented views of writing and why these views, when transferred to the study of writing in other contexts or communities, often fail to reveal the true nature of the discourse under investigation. For to study writing in another context, we must know what counts as knowledge and knowing to those who live there; we must learn their "language," their way of perceiving. This is not a position that many teachers/researchers are used to, for within their own academic community and their own classrooms they have become accustomed to the role of authority. They determine what is good writing and poor writing, who passes and who fails, who has to take remedial courses and who does not, which features of texts indicate quality and which do not, and so forth. It was Eldridge Cleaver, I believe, who said, "Those who define master." In academe, we have been the ones to define the contexts for writing, the criteria for writing, and even the methods for assessing our own criteria. In our own academic culture we are the unchallenged masters; we are on safe ground; in short, we live in a community of "like-minded peers."

Bruffee suggests that social constructionist thought offers a "strikingly fruitful alternative to the way we normally think and talk about what we do" (p. 776). Typically, as he points out, the language that we, as scholars, researchers, and teachers, use to talk about our work is cognitive in derivation and based on positivist premises of traditional—mainly Cartesian—epistemology, which has influenced academic scholarship since at least the seventeenth century. Like Rorty, Bruffee notes that even the visual metaphors we commonly use to describe what we know reveal our cognitive assumptions about the nature of reality and knowing: namely that there is some external, objective reality, which is "perceived" and "reflected" by our mind's inner "eye." Even the term *theory*, as Bruffee "observes," has the same etymological root as *theater*, implying a "viewing." We "contemplate," "imagine," and talk about our "insights," sharing our "point of view" in a "clear," "lucid" manner, hoping others will "get the picture." If they do not, they are probably "blind" to reason, and lack "vision" and "foresight." (Do you "see" what I mean?) As I will "speculate" in Chapter 7, the way in which we talk about and "envision" progress also "reveals" similar notions of a cognitive journey toward some objective truth.

By contrast, the social constructionist "view" is based on the assumption that what we know lies neither in the mind nor in nature as mirrored in the mind, but rather resides within a particular community of knowledgeable peers. Thus, there is no universal foundation for knowledge, only the agreement and consensus of the community. As Bruffee puts it, "Concepts, ideas, theories, the world, reality, and facts are all language constructs generated by knowledge communities and used by them to maintain community coherence" (p. 777). One of these theories, and one that underlies the bulk of composition research, is that there exist some universal, objective, and even measurable mental processes. Hence, we talk about "cognitive processes," "higher order reasoning," and "intellectual development" as though these terms somehow refer to preexistent (innate? God-given?) entities rather than to social constructs of our own making. According to social constructionist thought, our theories about how the mind works are simply conversations about another conversation: "talk about talk" (Bruffee, p. 777). Thus, for instance, when researchers attempt to investigate the cognitive processes of writers, what they are studying in effect are simply their own constructs of how they *think* thinking operates. Similarly, when researchers study written texts, they do so, not upon the basis of some universally recognized criteria of good writing, but rather upon the basis of criteria developed by colleagues with whom they share the same theories of writing.

Finally, the social constructionist view challenges the cognitive notion, common among composition teachers and researchers, that language (and writing) can be reduced to a set of "skills" for conveying information and ideas. From the social constructionist position, knowledge and language—what we know and how we convey it—are inseparable; furthermore, and most importantly, both of these are shaped by the discourse community either within which we are members or to which we aspire to become accepted members.

The social constructionist view has several important implications for the study and teaching of writing. First, it reminds us that our knowledge and theories about writing are essentially our own fabrications, and that what we regard as effective writing may be different from what those in other, nonacademic discourse communities regard as effective writing. Second, it underscores the need for researchers and teachers of writing to make clear the theories and assumptions underlying their investigation or instruction. In few studies of writing, for instance, are the researchers' own biases and preconceptions made explicit; rather, they seem to be treated as "givens," as the article plunges into the perfunctory review of the literature, methodologies, findings, conclusions, and the ever ubiquitous need-for-further-research. As will be discussed in the Chapter 5, the conventions of scholarly works are based on cognitivist assumptions about reality and perpetuate the guise of objectivity, discouraging researchers from reporting the true, subjective circumstances that influenced their resear   a   colored their findings. In the writing classroom, too, instructor   ly acknowledge that what they are teaching and how they are evaluating essays are simply what English teachers have agreed are the skills students need and that these skills and criteria for "good" writing may have little to do with communicating successfully beyond the classroom.

Finally, the social constructionist view of knowledge has implications for how we study writing in nonacademic settings. As researchers, we have to realize that as soon as we leave own academic community, we become aliens in a strange land. We cannot assume, for instance, that writers or readers in organizations share our assumptions about writing. Perhaps the most difficult adjustment we must make is to realize that, on their turf and in their camp, we may not be the experts and final authorities on writing.

In recent years, the social, constructionist view of writing has led researchers to anthropological and ethnographic approaches to investigating real-world writing. In these studies, researchers attempt to come unarmed with preconceived ideas about the phenomena they are observing and to get down in the trenches alongside writers to understand what, why, and how they write. More than ever before, researchers are beginning to view themselves as archaeologists out on a dig and to examine texts as cultural artifacts. As Doheny-Farina and Odell (1985) note, ethnographic research has become increasingly popular. It promises to contribute substantially to our present knowledge of composing processes and products and to fill gaps in our understanding of the ways in which readers, other than composition teachers or researchers, interpret, use, and evaluate written texts. The results of such research may have important implications for composition theory and pedagogy, the most significant of which may be a reconsideration of what we regard as good writing and a long overdue look at writing as a means of communication within social settings.

As discussed in the last chapter, the focus of our research and teaching has been upon writing as process or product. Only recently have we paid attention to the content of texts. The following section examines the importance of context in shaping the meaning of texts and the knowledge writers need to write effectively within organizational settings.

Meaning as Context Dependent

Two major tenets of a social view of language concern (a) the interrelationship between language and culture, and (b) the indeterminacy of meaning apart from context. Linguists point out how language reflects culture and how culture influences language. For instance, whereas in English we have only a few nouns to refer to cows, in Hindustani languages, because to

Hindus cows are sacred, there are as many as 30 words to differentiate between different types of cows. Similarly, as Clark and Clark (1977) note, Eskimos, whose daily existence depends on weather, have in their language four words to make distinctions among snow conditions whereas in English we have only one word, *snow*—unless we are expert skiers, in which case we may have many, such as *powder, corn, ice,* and the like. Even within the same culture and language, the words we use to describe similar phenomena reflect and influence our thinking. Szasz (1973), for instance, cites several examples of linguistic variation within our culture: "If General Motors sells cars, it's called advertising; if the National Institute of Mental Health sells psychiatry, it's called education; if a streetwalker sells sex, it's called soliciting; if a street urchin sells heroin, it's called pushing dope" (reprinted in Eschholz, Rosa, & Clark, 1974, p. 40). In his "Semantic Parable of Town A and Town B," Hayakawa (1980) illustrates how using different words to refer to the same phenomenon influences different attitudes and behaviors. He would contend, as would most linguists, that a rose by any other name would not smell as sweet. Ignatieff (1984) further maintains that as language and communities change, and as words either drop out of language or become clichés, human needs "do not simply pass out of speech: they may cease to be felt" (p. 138). According to Bruffee (1986), "Lacking the language, we tend to lack the feelings as well" (p. 782). As will be further illustrated in Chapter 6, what we call reality and knowledge is largely a social construct of language, and language, in turn, is constructed of our cultural beliefs, values, and mores.

As psychologists have demonstrated, however, the primacy of cultural context lies deeper than language itself; it goes straight to the core of how we perceive and interpret the world. Schumacher (1986) notes, for instance, the extensive interest among psychologists on how context influences such areas as perception, cognition, and problem solving. For example, Wason and Johnson-Laird (1972) have shown that subjects regard tasks involving reasoning as very easy or difficult, depending on the particular context in which the task is set. Similarly, Anderson, Reynolds, Schallert, and Goetz (1977) have demonstrated that subjects will interpret a passage to mean one thing in one context but will interpret the same passage to mean quite different things in other contexts. In summary, context, as Harrison (1987) puts it, embodies "a particular way of seeing. . . a set of assumptions that give meaning to stimuli and enable individuals to define experience" (p. 8).

An interesting explanation of this view as applied to written texts is contained in George L. Dillon's *Constructing Texts* (1981). Dillon maintains that it is impossible to determine the meaning of a text from simply from the words on the page. "Readers," he stresses, "always go beyond what is explicitly stated, drawing inferences, enriching the text with pieces of personal knowledge, evaluating and interpreting it in terms of personal beliefs and values, interests and purposes" (p. xi). He further points out that the notion of reading as a matter of extracting or decoding propositional content from a text corresponds to the notion of writing as a matter of transmitting or encoding propositional content into words and sentences. Such models of reading and writing, Dillon maintains, woefully impoverish "the notion of *discourse* as a human communicative act" (p. 15). Wherein, then, lies the "meaning" of a text? Dillon argues that it resides within the minds of the writer's intended readers: "To say that the reader actively constructs texts," Dillon explains, "is to say that the text is completed in the mind of the reader, and, since readers will differ in the actual constructions they make, there is no one fully determinate, publicly accessible text" (p. xiv). Inevitably, our knowledge, experience, and frame of reference influence how we make meaning of texts.

By way of illustration, in my technical writing courses I often use the following passage from a technical report to demonstrate that "meaning" and "readability" are not simply a matter of comprehensible words and well constructed sentences. Normally, I tell the course participants to close their eyes, and then I read aloud to them this paragraph:

> The deteriorating condition of the seals continues to be a concern. Our preliminary scientific investigations reveal that the situation is becoming acute. Specifically, the seals are being exposed to severe atmospheric changes that jeopardize their life expectancy. We therefore ask that, if you see these seals in the field, you collect and identify them, and immediately ship them in appropriate containers to our research laboratory in Nevada.

I next ask them what they envisioned as I was reading this passage: in other words, what did they assume the text referred to? Some say they see animal seals in the Antarctic, while others say they see gasket-type seals, such as those on pipe joints and fittings. One of the most interesting aspects of this exercise is the adamancy with which individuals defend their own interpretation as the "right" one, and, later, when they realize there are other equally plausible interpretations, their sense of surprise and disorientation.

Traditionally, our colleagues in speech have always assumed that the content, organization, and style of discourse depend on the specific situation or rhetorical context. In the past, writing was viewed as different from oral discourse in that it was "decontextualized"—that it leaned less heavily on immediate context (see, for instance, Goody, 1977, and Olson, 1977). Other, more recent theorists (for example, Hirsch, 1977; Prince, 1981; Tannen, 1982; and Rogoff, Gouvain, & Ellis, 1984), however, suggest just the opposite: that writers, *because* they are removed from the situation in which a text is read, have to create a context within the text to help ensure that the meaning the reader derives is the one the writer intends. As Dillon puts it,

"The trick for the writer is to get these processes [how readers interpret and evaluate texts] to go in the direction they [the writers] intend or at least ones not notably at variance with the ones they do intend" (p. xi). But just how writers accomplish this, and how readers recognize writer intentions, have not been the subject of much investigation. Rather, the emphasis has been upon theories of reading, especially upon what psycholinguists refer to as *discourse processing.*

One of these theories from psycholinguistic research is that readers comprehend texts by matching up the text with what Smith (1978) calls "the theory of the world in our head" (p. 57). As Brandt (1986) explains, this view of reading holds that "readers bring to a text stores of prior knowledge about the world and about the nature of discourse that allow them to fill in the inferences and make predictions that are necessary for comprehension" (p. 151). By bringing to the text their stored knowledge about settings, episodes, roles, and the like, readers fit the text to their *domain of reference* (Sanford & Garrod, 1981)—in much the same way as my course participants interpreted the above seals paragraph in different ways according to their personal domains of reference. And that is just the problem with this view: It is a static rather than a dynamic explanation of reading. It accounts only for how readers use their prior experience and knowledge to comprehend texts, but not for how the unfolding text also directs, modifies, and contributes to that knowledge.

Brandt (p. 150), drawing upon the work of language sociologist Rolf Kjolseth (1971), phenomenologist Alfred Schultz (1962), and others, points out that communication involves several "grounds" of knowledge by which meaning is constituted. Kjolseth labels two of these grounds *background* knowledge ("What *anybody* knows is *always* relevant *anywhere* and *anytime*") and *foreground* knowledge ("What *anybody* knows is *categorically* relevant *for the duration of this setting*"). Background knowledge includes knowledge of such things as a culture's commonly held values, beliefs, and routines, while foreground knowledge includes knowledge of conventions that allows us to distinguish between, for instance, a party and a lecture, or a novel and a scholarly work. While both grounds are essential to interpreting texts, they represent only static forms of knowledge. In addition to these, Kjolseth contends that two other grounds of knowledge are necessary in order to either produce or comprehend discourse. One of these, as Brandt points out, is the *emergent* ground, "what *we* know is *specifically* relevant *here and now.*" Included in this are the exigencies and constraints of a particular rhetorical situation. The other is the *transcendent* ground, "the knowledge necessary to anticipate potential meaning, the ability to look backwards and forwards to interpret incomplete patterns and their possible significance" (Brandt, p. 151). This ability to look behind and ahead at the same time, to be able to synthesize what Young, Becker, and Pike (1970) call particle, wave, and field views, or, as the poet Blake put it, "to behold the world in a grain of sand," is similar to what Kjolseth (1971, pp. 70–71), in reference to discourse, calls *situationally competent imagination*, which he considers essential to communicative competence.

These last two grounds of knowledge, the emergent and the transcendent, are useful distinctions for writers to make when analyzing their audiences and purposes for writing and when determining the kinds of information necessary to include in their texts. If the emergent ground—the knowledge of here and now—is related to the writer's immediate rhetorical context (that is, the specific writing task, its audiences, and purposes), then the transcendent ground—the knowledge and ability to infer and speculate, to go beyond "here and now knowledge"—is related to the broader organizational context within which the writer and the text exist. As will be discussed in my study in Part Three, a common problem writers have in their technical reports is interpreting their writing task from primarily an emergent ground. Compared with poorer writers, better writers are more apt to consider the transcendent ground and to include in their reports, not only data, observations and findings, but also evaluations, implications, and speculations. They do not leave to their readers' imaginations, as oftentimes the poorer writers do, the significance their research findings have for helping readers make decisions concerning the department's or the organization's goals. They fill in the gaps for their readers.

The case of the anaerobic digester reports discussed in the Introduction to this volume clearly demonstrates the importance of attending to both the emergent and transcendent grounds. In the first two versions of the abstract, the researcher-writer was insensitive to how his readers would be likely to interpret his report. To the writer, the meaning of his report lay upon the page, and he construed his rhetorical task narrowly. However, as his manager realized, the real meaning of the text lay in all the inferences and implications that other readers would make based on their own particular involvement in the plant shutdown. The manager was aware of a much broader and dynamic context than the specific incident that triggered the report. In short, he was aware, as the researcher was not, of the transcendent ground for the report.

As some studies have indicated (for example, Mathes & Stevenson, 1976, pp. 18–19; and Hays, 1984, pp. 16–20;), such awareness of audience and context is a key factor in successful business and technical communication. However, as Paradis, Dobrin, and Miller (1985) observed in their study at Exxon, the knowledge needed to transcend the immediate rhetorical situation and the foresight needed to sidestep political snares are usually acquired only as one gains experience and moves up the administrative ladder. New and inexperienced employees especially have a difficult time as writers, trying to maneuver their way through a report without in some way detonating a land mine—for example, setting off someone who they did not realize would be receiving their report; using words or phases that connote to their readers an entirely different meaning than that which the writers intended; or in some way inadvertently insulting the readers' competence or overstepping the organization's uncharted territorial lines. In their interviews with researchers at Exxon ITD, Paradis et al. (1985) noted that "a frequent complaint from younger staff members was that their documents had to be political—that is, shrewdly tailored to the social environment, in which many unknown interests were competing" (p. 303).

While it is impossible ever to control with absolute certainty how readers will comprehend and respond to texts, the more writers are aware of not only their readers' knowledge and experience (their background and foreground knowledge), but also their readers' immediate interests and needs (their emergent knowledge and their transcendent knowledge), the more writers can shape texts in which their intentions match their readers' expectations. As will be discussed later in Part Two, speech-act theory helps explain the interrelationship between writer intentions and reader expectations and the pragmatic nature of communication upon which my study is based. For now, however, let us examine in the following sections how an awareness of culture and community—whether that of a country or an organization—helps inform our understanding of communication.

WRITTEN COMMUNICATION, COMMUNITIES, AND CULTURE

Increasingly, many scholars within the field of composition research are beginning to realize what some cultural anthropologists have long since recognized: that rhetoric becomes meaningful only within the context of a particular community and culture. One of the most interesting examples of the ways in which people interpret texts according to their own culture is contained in an essay by cultural anthropologist Laura Bohannan, entitled "Shakespeare in the Bush" (1980), in which she amusingly recounts how, one night over a campfire, she attempted to tell the story of *Hamlet* to the natives of the Tiv tribe in Western Africa. In her essay, Bohannan describes how the Tiv elders, because of their own tribal mores governing such matters as marriage, family relations, duty, law, morality, vengeance, religion, and the afterlife, construed the plot and the characters' motivations in a way totally at odds with mainstream Shakespearean scholarship in the Western world. And yet, given their culture, their exegesis of the play was entirely logical. To cite only a few of what we would call "misreadings," from the perspective of the Tiv natives Claudius and Gertrude behaved in the best possible manner, especially since Claudius, as a chief, did not have, as he should have had, several other wives; Laertes killed his sister Ophelia by witchcraft because he needed money quickly to pay off fines for his fights and his gambling debts, and because he knew no one else would want to marry his sister, a woman desired by the son of a chief (i.e., Hamlet); and Hamlet, far from being a tragic figure, was simply a fool, totally undeserving of sympathy, for he naively believed the vision of a zombie (what he thought was the ghost of his father) when instead he should have known enough to consult with his tribal elders, who could have read the omen correctly and quickly settled the matter. Though this example is based upon literature (which many would say is by nature subject to variable interpretations anyway), as I will discuss in Chapter 6, the tendency to perceive and interpret facts and events in light of our own cultural biases and beliefs is as common in the "hard" sciences as it is in literature or in any of the "soft" sciences (for example, psychology, sociology, or history).

Just as in interpreting texts people make meaning according to their own cultural biases, so too in writing most people attempt to shape their texts according to whatever they intuit are the prevailing assumptions, beliefs, and knowledge that make up their particular culture and that govern that discourse community's standards and expectations regarding effective communication. As Miller (1979) points out, for instance, "to write well is to understand the conditions of one's participation—the concepts, values, traditions, and style [in other words, the culture] which permit identification with that community and determine the success or failure of communication" (p. 617). Others, such as Harrison (1987), emphasize the reciprocal relationship between rhetoric and culture, one in which writing, among other symbols, both influences and is influenced by an organization's particular community, culture, and character.

The following explores the relationship between culture and communication, examining first the influence that national cultures have upon written communication; second, the concept of organizations as rhetorical contexts; and, third, some of the symbolic patterns of discourse important within organizational cultures. The next chapter takes a closer look at how one of these symbols—writing—shapes and reflects an organization's image, structure, and direction.

The Influence of National Culture upon Communication

Frequently, the rites, rituals, and conventions governing organizational communication are national in origin, reflecting the broader culture of a particular country. Advances in modern technology and the growing importance of international business relationships make it imperative that we recognize and understand how communication practices are steeped within a country's values and culture. To remain competitive in today's international marketplace, we are going to have to become more aware of the conventions governing communication in countries other than our own. In the past, perhaps, we could afford to be oblivious to such cultural differences because we were the world's uncontested political and economic superpower. But today the situation is rapidly changing.

The most compelling example comes from Japan, the land of the rising sun, a country that has also risen as a serious contender in international business and a major threat not only to the American economy but to the world economy as well. Increasingly, our nation's newspapers, magazines, professional journals, and television programs are filled with stories about how Japan, despite (and because of) the ravages of World War II, has become a leader in world finance, surpassing even the United States. According to a recent news broadcast, whereas ten years ago seven of the ten world's largest banks were American-owned, today nine of the world's top ten banks are Japanese-owned, with only one of them American-owned, and that one holding on by a thread. In our high schools and universities, students of Japanese and Eastern-Asian descent are consistently outperforming other students, to the extent that some colleges and universities are being accused of practicing reverse-discrimination quotas by restricting the number of Asians admitted to their institutions. Our nation's graduate schools of business, as well as our nation's major corporations, are more and more turning to Japanese concepts of business practices in the hopes of bolstering our country's sagging productivity. Whether it is finance, food, or fashions, America is beginning to feel the influence of Japanese culture.

Even as I write, our nation's public broadcasting system is televising a series on Japan, hosted by Jane Seymour and depicting the ways in which, despite all odds, this tiny country, virtually leveled by bombing during World War II and possessing no natural resources to speak of, has managed to become a world power by salvaging the best of its culture heritage: an abiding sense of community, a belief in the importance of hard work, and a commitment to quality. All of which, ironically, are—or at least used to be—the very values of American culture.

An intriguing feature of this television series is the importance of communication rituals within the Japanese culture, rituals which, in the past, American visitors regarded as merely charming oddities but which nowadays have become social necessities if they expect to be accepted by the Japanese and to do business with them, rituals such as observing the depth of one's bow upon meeting another person (the deeper one's bow, the more one pays deference to the other's higher social position). As a friend of mine who frequently does business with Japan told me, at minimum one needs to have a business card printed in both English and Japanese. (In my case, however, he advised me not to waste my money since in Japan there are still strict cultural biases against "women businessmen.")

In an interesting article in the *Bulletin* from the Association for Business Communication, Varner (1987) stresses the importance of teaching students to become aware of the cultural differences inherent in international business communications. She explains, for instance, the limitations of our notions of sentence structure and paragraph structure when applied to the lexicon and syntactic structures of other languages such as German, Japanese, and Chinese. This becomes especially apparent when attempting to apply American readability formulas, such as the Gunning Fog Index, to other languages. As Varner notes, "If we go outside Western languages, the counting of syllables does not make any sense at all" (p. 9). (Though just how much sense readability formulas make in assessing the readability of texts written in English is doubtful given the discussion of context and meaning in the previous section.) Dense, periodic sentences, with numerous modifiers and appositives, are the norm in German and, while they may be difficult for us to comprehend easily, the Germans apparently have few problems reading them. (As a side note, however, such sentences may not be pragmatic. According to an anecdote, it was because of the syntax of their language that the Germans lost World War II. Supposedly a German general at the front lines of battle received a telegram from his field marshall at German headquarters consisting of one long, convoluted, imperative sentence which ended with the verb, "charge!" However, as the story goes, by the time the general reached the end of the sentence, his troops had already been attacked and captured.) Varner further points out that our concepts of readability with regard to paragraph structure have no application to non-Western languages, such as Japanese and Chinese, in which neither sentences nor paragraphs, as we know them, exist.

Even when business communications are written in English, oftentimes the organization, content, style, and tone of written texts are influenced by the particular country's culture, as are other routine business practices. To illustrate the latter, Varner explains that in Latin America, where businessmen do not watch the clock, American managers often have to set deadlines far in advance of when they actually need to receive reports. By contrast, in Germany timeliness and accuracy are of utmost importance. Thus, for instance, when dealing with German banks, Americans need to account for the last penny, though in dealing with Italian banks, they can expect far looser and lenient regulations.

Varner further illustrates how the conventions governing the openings and closings of business correspondence vary considerably from culture to culture, even when the texts are written in English. In Japan, for example, apparently it is considered impolite and bad form to begin a letter by baldly announcing its purpose. Rather, it is customary to approach the topic on tiptoe by initially making innocuous references to the weather, crops, health, or personal circumstances. For instance, Varner (p. 10) cites the following as a perfectly acceptable and traditional opening for a Japanese business letter:

> The season for cherry blossoms is here with us and
> everybody is beginning to feel refreshed. We
> sincerely congratulate you on becoming more
> prosperous in your business. (from Haneda & Shima,
> 1982, p. 29; paragraphing and indentation are those
> of Haneda and Shima)

By contrast, openings of German business letters, while they also tend to be circuitous by American standards, are less personal and more formal, as illustrated by Manekeller (1980, p. 53):

> Referring to your kind inquiry from the 31st of this month, we take the
> liberty to remind you with this letter. . .

German business reports, according to Hildebrandt (1973) often start with "Adam and Eve" openers, with extensive background information, whereas French reports begin with abstractions and theories before eventually suggesting their practical applications. All of these approaches are likely to seem odd and frustrating, if not "wrong," to Americans, who typically prefer a much more direct and pragmatic way of beginning and ending a business report or letter. On the other hand, the Japanese, French, and German business people, as well as those from other countries, may consider as inappropriate the usual way in which American business letters and reports are organized: that is, the proverbial "Tell 'em what you're going to tell 'em, tell 'em, and tell 'em what you told 'em." From their perspective, we probably seem rude, dull-witted, and uninterested in anything but the bottom line.

In the closings of business correspondence, too, there are also notable cultural differences. Varner observes that German endings, for example, tend to be formal and aloof and that, unlike American endings, are not nearly as positive or as action- and future-oriented. From beginning to end, however, there is a consistency of tone and style in German business letters and reports. The same consistency is exemplified in Japanese letters, which usually end, as they begin, with the same kind of references to weather and the same polite, formal well wishes for good fortune, as in the following example from an article in *Japanese Communication* (volume 29), cited by Varner (p. 10):

> The summer heat is still lingering, but we hope that you
> are prosperous as ever and we thank you very much
> for your constant patronage.

> It will be some time before autumn cool. I pray that you
> take good care of yourself.

Given the influence that Western culture has had upon the music, fashions, food, and political ideologies of other countries, and given the predominance of English as the standard language of international business, perhaps such cultural differences in the organization, content, and style of communication may disappear before the end of this century so that we need not concern ourselves with them. It is possible, too, that such standardization may happen even more rapidly, and that by the time this volume is published the examples referred to above may seem anachronistic; that, for instance, the KISS principle of business communication so popular in American business correspondence nowadays (and variously interpreted as KEEP IT SIMPLE and SUCCINCT, or KEEP IT SIMPLE, STUPID) may have taken over world business communications with the same lightning speed as McDonald's franchises have sprung up across the globe. On the other hand, if Japan continues to exert as powerful an influence on American business communications as it has upon our economy and our graduate schools of business, it is equally possible that in the future, in addition to acquiring a taste for sushi and to becoming more skillful with chopsticks, I may have to refrain from starting my business letters with:

> Thank you for your recent inquiry regarding our customized courses in business communication. As you requested, I have enclosed. . .

and instead begin them with:

> The blustery winter of Chicago has now subsided. What
> snow the city's plow trucks did not carry away has begun
> to melt, and the crocuses are peeking their heads above
> the sun-thawed ground. We hope that the green promise
> and prosperity symbolized by spring find you in good
> spirits and yield fruitful abundance for you and
> yours. . . .

Is one version "better" than the other? It is a moot question, for the question, like the texts, has no meaning apart from its cultural context. But for the time being, when I am writing to clients, I will continue to use variations of the first introduction—unless, that is, those clients happen to be located in Japan, in which case I will need to brush up on the climate and the flora and fauna of Japan.

ORGANIZATIONS AS RHETORICAL CONTEXTS

While it is important, for the purposes of international business, to understand the ways in which communication practices vary from country to
country, we are as yet a long way from understanding the role that communication plays even within the business organizations of our own culture. To repeat the recurrent refrain of this volume, our concepts of writing
and our criteria of good writing have been influenced primarily by our
notions of academic or school-sponsored writing, and these may have limited application when it comes to communicating well within a nonacademic or real-world environment. What we need are models and theories of communication that explain the knowledge individuals need in order
to communicate effectively within organizational settings.

One of the most potentially useful of these theories is that organizations,
as Huff (1983) and as Harrison (1987) point out, themselves provide a
rhetorical context for communication. Referring to the work of Smircich
(1983), Harrison describes two strains of thought that have emerged from a
cultural analysis of organizations and that are relevant to the study and
practice of writing within organizational settings. The first is the concept of
organizations as cognitive systems of knowledge, and the second is the
concept of organizations as patterns of symbolic discourse.

How Organizational Culture Produces and Shapes Knowledge

As systems of knowledge, organizational cultures "are constituted in part
because its members share in a potentially unique worldview embodied by
the idiosyncratic content and structure of its knowledge system" (Harrison,
1987, p. 11). It is, in other words, the community, or the individuals within
an organization, who, by interacting with each other within a particular
environment, generate and sustain the organizational culture. Two comple-
mentary perspectives on knowledge construction pertain here: the evolutionary model of Weick (1979) and the social information processing model
of Salanick and Pfeffer (1978).

The evolutionary model emphasizes how knowledge is constructed and
interpreted at the organizational level. According to this model, environmental cues within the organization stimulate individuals to enact, select,
and retain certain information. These environmental cues, or "cognitive
maps" (see Johnson, 1977), are stored in the organization's "memory" in the
form of legends, stories, myths, operations procedures, employee manuals,
and the like. These furthermore serve as a basis for guiding, interpreting,
and evaluating the appropriateness of one's behavior.

By contrast, the social information processing model emphasizes how an
organization's social environment shapes the knowledge, beliefs, and atti-

tudes of its members, and in so doing, influences those of the organization. Through social interaction, individuals begin to perceive and structure experience in similar ways, and this sense of "group think" or community in turn gives rise to organizational culture: to commonly held views of the organization's image, shared assumptions, goals, and means of achieving of them. This system of evolutionary knowledge acquired by community consensus is what Pfeffer (1981) and Kuhn (1970) have called a "paradigm."

According to Harrison (1987), "a fundamental assumption of the cognitive or knowledge-based approach to organizational culture [as espoused by Smircich, 1983] is that thinking is linked to action" (p. 12), and that what members of an organization do is related to what and how they think. Or, in other words, that the organizational culture is influenced by the beliefs and actions of its community. For instance, some researchers (for example, Kiesler & Sproull, 1982, and Meyer, 1982) have suggested that managers notice and perceive problems related to organizational change according to their own world views and belief systems, views and beliefs which are often shaped by the organization's culture.

If all of this sounds a bit circular, it is. Starbuck (1982, p. 3), for instance, contends that organizations are comprised of "logically integrated clusters of beliefs, values, rituals, and symbols" that define organizational expectations and determine the probable success of alternative actions. In turn, organizations use these ideologies to justify why a preferred course of action, as opposed to other possible actions, is necessary. (For a discussion of the ways in which researchers in R&D similarly justify their findings, see Chapter 5.)

As Harrison observes, as convincing as such cognitive theories of organizational behavior are, to date no one has been able to describe the rules (formal, implicit, or otherwise) that individuals use either to translate organizational knowledge into behavior or to shape organizational knowledge by individual behavior. At the same time, however, cognitive psychologists (for example, Luria, 1976, and Rogoff, 1984) have demonstrated the extent to which our thinking is governed by our environment—how the content, form, and processes of cognition are influenced by contextual factors. Similarly, Scribner (1984) has shown how familiarity with an organization breeds knowledge and competence. She explains, for instance, how, due to their specialized knowledge and problem-solving strategies, industrial plant employees far outperformed nonemployees on two types of organizational tasks. According to Scribner, "on-the-job experience makes for different ways of solving problems or, to put it another way, the problem-solving process is restructured by the knowledge and strategy repertoire available to the expert in comparison to the novice" (p. 38).

How Symbolic Patterns of Discourse Reflect Organizational Culture

Another view of organizational cultures, but one that complements the view of organizations as cognitive systems of knowledge, is that the culture of an organization manifests itself through its symbols and patterns of discourse. Researchers following this tack contend that often an organization's culture—its character, beliefs, and values—is expressed through the company's logo, sayings and jingles, legends and stories, heroes, specialized language, or other identifying signs and symbols. As Harrison (1987) points out, like the cognitive perspective, the symbolic perspective is also based on the assumption that organizational cultures are made up of shared systems of meaning—except that, in this case, the emphasis is upon "the symbolic means by through which knowledge and meaning are expressed" (p. 12). In the past few years several theorists and researchers have stressed the important role that slogans, metaphors, and symbols play in influencing organizational thought, behavior, and discourse.

SLOGANS

Deal and Kennedy (1982, 1983) provide several examples of how company slogans communicate to employees and to the public the essence of an organization's philosophy and ethos. For instance, DuPont's slogan, "Better things for better living through chemistry," expresses the company's most distinctive value: the belief that product innovation arises out of chemical engineering; Continental Bank's slogan, "We'll find a better way," captures the bank's commitment to meeting customer needs; Tandem's slogan, "It takes two to Tandem," emphasizes the importance Tandem places upon people, creativity, and fun; and Avis's slogan, "We try harder because we're #2," stresses the company's belief in service and hard work, a slogan so successful in recent years that it is difficult to recall who is, or used to be, #1 in the rental car industry.

To illustrate how a company's slogan infuses managerial policies and employee attitudes, Deal and Kennedy (1982) cite the example of Delta Airlines, whose slogan, "The Delta Family Feeling," expresses the importance with which the company regards people (both its own employees and its customers) and explains in a nutshell the reason this airline has managed to be so successful when many other airlines have been plagued by labor strikes and FAA violations in recent years. During the recession beginning in the early 1980s, Delta, unlike many other carriers, did not lay off its employees, and its employees and shareholders accepted cutbacks and decreased dividends much more readily than did the employees of other competing airlines. The reason? According to Deal and Kennedy, "Shared values are what has made [and make] Delta great" (1982, p. 32). Over a long period of time the company has communicated to its members the sanctity of this value of "family"; they believed in the Delta slogan. My own experiences in flying Delta convince me that they still believe in it, as well as in Delta's newer slogan, "We love to fly and it shows."

Recently, some companies—in order to try to change their image and to forge a new cultural/organizational identity—have adopted new slogans, which, ironically, often attempt to capitalize on the firm's Achilles' heel. For instance, to use another example from the airline industry, Continental Airlines recently launched a new television advertising campaign in which they freely confess the problems they have had in the past with poor service. The gist of their new slogan is that they promise to do better in the future to earn the faith (that is, the business) of the American public. Coming on the heels of the Jimmy Bakker and James Swaggart scandals in evangelistic ministry, Continental's marketing strategy might be termed the "born-again," "forgive-me-for-I-have-sinned" advertising ploy. Many other companies that have been the target of the media and environmentalist groups—especially oil companies, chemical companies, and hazardous waste companies—have taken a similar but more subtle tack, call it the Calvinistic "but-look-at-all-my-good-deeds" ploy. Rather than recounting their sins and promising atonement, they have created ads, many of them cleverly disguised as public service announcements, aimed at neutralizing their negative images by emphasizing all the good works they are doing voluntarily in the name of health, safety, and the environment. They have learned that ethics, or at least the appearance of ethics, pays.

Finally, in response to the widespread conviction that American goods, especially cars and electronic/computer devices, are shoddy compared with foreign goods, many American companies are jumping on the Japanese "quality" bandwagon (or rickshaw), trying to convince consumers that their products are as good or better than those manufactured abroad. To cite only a couple of examples of the "quality" craze in American companies today, Ford's new slogan is, "Where Quality is Job 1," and Zenith's new slogan is, "The Quality Goes In Before the Name Goes On." Whether such slogans are only that—just slogans—or whether they symbolize the spirit of a new managerial philosophy and business ethic that has infused the attitudes and behavior of its workers and that, most importantly, has resulted in superior products remains to be seen. For, beyond being catchy words, a slogan must be a symbol of the organization's living philosophy and values, and the organization's members must believe in it and pay allegiance to it if it is to inform organizational life and have any lasting impact upon the company's success.

METAPHORS

Other researchers have shown how metaphors and images reveal an organization's character, its activities, and its decision-making processes. Koch and Deetz (1981), for instance, have illustrated how employees rely upon the company's dominant images and metaphors to understand the nature of the organization, to help them interpret organizational activities, and to guide their own behavior. Some organizations, for example, are based upon mechanistic metaphors (the company as machine), in which everything is reduced to timing, logic, rules, and quantitative results; other organizations are based upon organic metaphors (the company as plant), in which growth and success evolve out of inspiration, creativity, and innovation; and still other organizations are based upon team metaphors (the company as community), in which emphasis is upon dialogue, cooperation, and consensus. As will be discussed further in the next section, problems can occur when there is a mismatch between an employee's character and that of the company, as for instance, when individuals who are by nature or experience rational, regimented, and mechanistic find themselves in an organization where inspiration, creativity, and innovation are the prevailing values—or vice versa. Or when individuals who work best alone and independently are in a situation where they are expected to work collaboratively—or, again, vice versa.

Another study, by Hirsch and Andrews (1983), has demonstrated how the metaphors used to describe corporate takeovers reflect the company's character and mode of operations. They point out, for example, how the processes of acquisition and merger, as well as the roles of the participants and their behavior, are guided by whether the company typically views such a situation as one of courtship, warfare, or Western, and whether, in turn, they are apt to think of themselves as either suitors, conquerors, or cowboys.

Whether it is on a grand scale, as in the case of dramatic and well-publicized corporate takeovers, or whether it is on a more mundane basis, as in the case of the daily life and operations of the organization, metaphors play an important part in helping define and direct organizational behavior and culture. In short, metaphors shape and reflect the organization's ethos. Sometimes, the metaphors are evident only by the company's actions and reputation. Other times, the metaphors are intertwined with the company's slogans, symbols, or logos.

SYMBOLS

Symbols can serve as an efficient, effective means of metaphorically expressing and conveying the organization's character, its values and beliefs, either to the public and/or to members within the organizational community. Many of the symbols with which the public is most familiar are simple pictorial logo-symbols or logotypes that identify the company, for instance, McDonald's golden arches and the specific typeface used to print the name McDonald's. Other times, however, ordinary language may serve symbolic functions, as for instance when words become imbued with specialized meanings—meanings, which, while they are well understood by those within the organizational culture, for the most part remain obscure to outsiders. In the first case, logo-symbols are important in that they (a) project and advertise the organization's image to consumers, while at the same time they (b) help further an organization's sense of community and purpose by providing a central image with which members can identify. In the second case, the specialized and symbolic use of language serves a more private, local, esoteric, and internal function within an organization: namely, to foster the community's exclusivity and to nurture among members their allegiance to whatever it is that makes their group unique and gives it cohesiveness. The following briefly discusses both of these types of symbols.

Logos, in the form of imagistic symbols or logotypes, are the trademarks of most organizations and for the public provide immediate name recognition and company identity. Imagistic symbols often represent the values or image the company wishes to project to the public, such as Allstate Insurance Company's logo of the cupped hands and its accompanying slogan, "You're in good hands with Allstate," or John Deere's logo of a deer in flight and its accompanying slogan, "Nothing runs like a Deere." In the first case, Allstate's logo conveys a sense of protection, care, and personal concern, or quality service. In the second case, Deere's logo, along with its slogan, conveys the speed and dependability of its equipment, or quality products. As another example, sometimes company names are themselves symbolic, as in the case of Apple computers (and its trademark logo the bitten apple), the apple traditionally symbolizing education. Other times, company logos are simply logotypes, that is, special typefaces or fonts used to spell out the company name, as for instance in the case of Mobil, CocaCola, or IBM. The logotype in itself does not symbolize anything unique about the company's character; however, as the company becomes successful, in time the public begins to identify that particular logotype with the company.

In between these two types of logos are what I will call "symboltype" logos, that is, logos that use stylized letters of the company's initials to symbolically represent either the company's product or business, or its character. Many times, these symboltype logos are very subtle and subliminal, and even the company's employees may not see the symbol in the letters until someone points it out to them. An example of the first type, letters which simply symbolize the company's product or business, is the logo of the now-defunct International Harvester, with the "I" superimposed on the "H" to symbolize a farmer on a tractor, the dot on the "I" representing the farmer's head, and the two vertical lines of the "H" representing the tractor tires. An example of the second type, letters which symbolize the company's character, is Waste Management's symboltype of the left-slanted "W" stacked on top of the right-slanted "M," which looks like a speeding arrow. As in the case of International Harvester's logo, part of its effectiveness is its subtlety. Waste Management's symboltype subconsciously conveys metaphoric images of the company's modernity, swiftness, and responsiveness, images consistent with both this company's fast-paced growth and with the youthful, aggressive spirit that characterizes this firm (where, I am told, in the mid–1980s the average age of its employees was 28). Interestingly, too, whether by intent or coincidence, this image is further conveyed in the lobby of the company's international headquarters where the artwork focuses on American-Indian and cowboy paintings and sculptures. The metaphor upon which the company is based is one of conquests and new horizons: unbridled American opportunism, reminiscent of the early West. The company's independent, pioneering spirit, as conveyed by its symboltype, is further evident in its organizational structure, managerial style, and policies, as well as in its written communications—the format, content, and style of which are largely left up to the individual writer.

Finally, organizations and cultures develop other types of symbols that help sustain group identity and solidarity. Sometimes these symbols may take the form of special colors, hand signals, attire, or certain practices—red, white, and blue for America; the "V" hand sign for the peace movement; black leather jackets for the Hell's Angels motorcycle gang; an earring in the right ear to symbolize male homosexuality and availability; and so on. Other times, the symbols are verbal, that is, a specialized use of words or phrases that only those who are members of the group or subculture share. Unlike logos, the main purpose of these types of symbols is not to advertise or to solicit membership, but rather to create group identity and exclusivity. To cite some examples of verbal symbols, every generation of teenagers has certain slang words which have helped galvanize the teen subculture—for example, everything in the 1950s was *keen* or *hip*; in the 1960s, *outta sight* and *far out*; in the 1970s, *groovy* and *neat*; and in the 1980s *bad* and *awesome*. Evered (1983) notes that the ability to understand and use Navy jargon is a sign of group membership and an indication of a shared world view. In some subcultures, not only words but also syntactic structures become symbolic of a subculture, such as "Val Speak," which started among the teenage "Valley Girls" in California's San Fernando Valley.

The above examples illustrate the importance of nonverbal and verbal symbols in creating and sustaining organizational and cultural identity. In the next chapter, I explore how written texts often serve the same purposes. Before doing so, however, let us examine the nature of organizational cultures and communities, and the interrelationship between communication and corporate culture.

COMMUNICATION AND THE CORPORATE CULTURE

Borrowing heavily from the sociology of knowledge, particularly social constructionism, and from anthropology, recent theories of organizational communication and behavior (see Huff, 1983, for example) suggest:

1. Organizations are both culture-forming and "culture-bearing milieux" (Louis, 1983).
2. Written and oral communication play an important role in shaping and maintaining an organization's sense of community and culture.

This section focuses on the first—on organizational culture, and specifically on the concept of corporate culture. It further examines the importance of corporate communication policies and illustrates the kinds of communication dysfunctions that can occur when writers are unaware of the corporate culture and the conventions governing communication within their particular organization.

The Importance of Corporate Culture

Increasingly, the literature on organizational communication is filled with references to the importance of "corporate culture." Quoting from Webster's *New Collegiate Dictionary*, Deal and Kennedy (1982), authors of *Corporate Cultures: The Rites and Rituals of Corporate Life*, maintain that corporate culture, like any other culture, is defined by "the integrated pattern of human behavior that includes thought, speech, action, and artifacts and depends on man's capacity for learning and transmitting knowledge to succeeding generations" (p. 4). A more informal, operational definition of corporate culture is that offered by Marvin Bower, for years the managing director of McKinsey & Company and author of *The Will to Manage* (1966). Bower's definition of corporate culture is simply, "the way we do things around here."

In their study of nearly 80 major corporations, Deal and Kennedy (1982) examined the ways these corporations do things. Their main finding was that the most successful corporations (those that are consistently "high performers") are those with strong corporate cultures, those with "a cohesion of values, myths, heroes, and symbols that has come to mean a great deal to the people who work there" (p. 4). Conversely, they found that the least successful corporations are those with weak cultures, in which "employees waste a good deal of time just trying to figure out what they should do and how they should do it" (p. 15). Deal and Kennedy found great diversity among the corporate cultures of even the most successful companies. As they observed, the only thing that the early leaders of such corporations shared was a belief "that the lives and productivity of their employees were shaped by where they worked"; and that their role as managers was to create an environment—in effect, a culture and a community—in which employees felt the loyalty and security necessary to make the business a success. Interestingly, despite all the competing philosophies and theories of management propounded within today's MBA programs and within organizational literature, Deal and Kennedy note that the early leaders and builders of corporations, just as those of today, "had no magic formulas"; rather, they "discovered how to shape their company's culture by trial and error," and they paid "almost fanatical attention to the culture of their companies" (p. 5), to creating and sustaining a sense of corporate community and identity.

Deal and Kennedy further point out two ways in which a strong culture motivates employees to do their jobs a little better. The first is by making the culture apparent. A strong culture, Deal and Kennedy maintain, is "a system of informal rules that spells out how people are to behave most of the time" (p. 15). Despite this statement's apparent oxymoron (that is, can the rules be "informal" if they are "spelled out"?), in a weak culture, not only are the rules not spelled out (however informally) but often they are nonexistent. Yet even in the most successful corporations individuals usually have to learn the rules and the ropes in the same way as most corporate cultures evolve: through trial and error. One of the main differences between the weak and the strong cultures, however, is that in the strong ones the amount of trial and error is minimized through better orientation and training programs. In successful companies, managers take an active interest in the professional development of their employees and help them become assimilated into the corporate community and culture by serving as mentors and by clarifying company goals and expectations. Related to this is the second way in which corporations with strong corporate cultures motivate their employees: by enabling "people to feel better about what they do, so they are more likely to work harder." A strong corporate culture nourishes job satisfaction and reduces the degree of uncertainty among employees by providing "structure and standards and a value system in which to operate" (p. 16). Nevertheless, problems may arise when those structures, standards, and value systems conflict with those of the individual's.

While many people starting their careers may think of a job as just a job, sooner or later they realize the importance of understanding what makes their particular company's corporate culture tick. For it is the culture, as Deal and Kennedy further explain, that "shapes their responses in a strong, but subtle way," making them, for instance, fast or slow workers, tough or friendly managers, team players or individuals. At Xerox, for example, where employees are expected to maintain "a near frenetic pace" in order to succeed (or to survive), competition among peers is keen, and emphasis is on productivity. By contrast, at General Electric the pace is slow-moving and success depends more upon "a strong sense of peer group respect, considerable deference for authority, and a sense of deliberateness." As Deal and Kennedy speculate, if bright and successful GE employees were to leave that company and go to Xerox, they could "quickly fizzle out at Xerox— and never understand why," even though they continued to work as hard, or even harder, at Xerox (pp. 16–17). Which is to say that corporate cultures are unique and that being successful in one organization does not guarantee success in another organization.

When individuals make the transition from an academic to a corporate environment, or when they leave one company and go to another, they often experience culture shock. If they fail within the new organization, frequently it is not necessarily because they are not doing their jobs but because either they fail to read the corporate culture correctly, or they fail to adapt to it smoothly. The latter occurs especially when there is a misfit between the organization's character, values, and goals and those of the individual. For example, a research scientist working on a long-range project may find it frustrating to work in an organization governed by a "results management" philosophy, in which the emphasis is upon productivity and profitability and in which employees are evaluated upon the basis of their short-term rather than their long-term achievements. Conversely, if an engineer thrives on seeing his solutions to technical problems put into immediate action, he may have difficulty working in a company where the main value is on research and product quality. Whenever individuals are out of step with the prevailing organizational culture, chances are they are going to have problems—unless the culture itself is in a state of revolutionary change and they are in a position to help shape the new culture.

Corporate Communication Policies

One of the most important ways in which a corporate culture evolves and endures is through the company's communication policies and practices. Twenty years ago, Norman B. Sigband, in an article entitled, "Needed: Corporate Policies on Communication," urged organizations to establish clear guidelines for written and oral communication (Sigband, 1969). Such policies, he maintained, if practiced from the president on down, would foster open, constructive communication at all levels of the organization and thus would help the firm achieve its goals. In recent years, the need for such policies, as Gilsdorf (1987) points out, has intensified due to the "information explosion," the rapid growth and diversity of many of today's corporations, and the increasing use of computers to accomplish many of the communicative functions in business. However, while many organizational theorists (for example, Wildavsky, 1983) have detailed the problems associated with the sheer bulk of information that companies must now contend with, few researchers have investigated whether organizations have adopted communication policies to address these problems. Nonetheless, there seems to be widespread agreement, at least among the organizational theorists themselves, if not the managers within the organizations, that such policies are beneficial. The case for corporate communication policies is best summed up by Gilsdorf (1987):

> At the highest and most inclusive level, communication policy states a firm's chief communication values. Ideally, the policy integrates mission and goals with the communication function. It conveys a sense of 'who we are' as a corporation, and offers some guidance for communicators so that the desired corporate identity comes through in all a firm's communications. (p. 36)

The key word here is *ideally*. As Gilsdorf discovered in her search of the literature, few corporations seem to have explicit (written) company-wide communication policies. In their survey of corporate communication directors, Hellweg and Phillips (1983) reported that 53 percent of their 98 *Fortune 500* respondents said they had an established corporate communication policy statement. However, as Gilsdorf notes, the study's findings are conclusive for only the 20 percent of the firms who returned the survey, firms which may have been more likely to respond because they have a stronger communication orientation than do the 80 percent of the nonresponding firms. Furthermore, in the Hellweg and Phillips study, the respondents were not asked to indicate whether their firms' policies were written or oral, or whether they existed as high-level, company-wide policies or as low-level, departmental procedures.

In her own study of the communication policies of 28 companies, Gilsdorf concludes that "few organizations set inclusive, high-level written policy to ensure that all who represent the organization will communicate effectively and project the organization's chosen values, goals, and image" (p. 51). Rather, most organizations take a compartmentalized view of communication, one in which the responsibility for various aspects of communication is assumed to be the purview of a particular department or individual. For example, as alluded to earlier, in some organizations, for example, secretaries determine format and layout, the legal department determines what information is proprietary, the systems department determines how information is loaded, stored, and retrieved, and the public relations department determines what information is made available to the public.

As for why communications within an organization are not viewed more systemically and systematically, Gilsdorf speculates that the reason is that in some firms the word *communication* appears to mean almost every imaginable activity within the organization, while in other firms the word seems to refer only to a small number of restricted activities, such as routine messages to customers. Part of the problem, then, is the term *communication* itself, which can include a wide range of organizational activities: for instance, the format, organization, content, or style of company documents; the mode of communication (e.g., when and when not to put something in writing, when verbal communication is more appropriate than written communication); the flow of communication within the organization (e.g., when to send something up, down, or across hierarchical lines); filing procedures (e.g., what to file, why, how, and for how long); computerized communication and electronic mail (e.g., accessing, storing, retrieving, and editing of databases); security measures for safeguarding sensitive, proprietary information; public relations; or information systems.

Beyond the fact that communication is difficult to define and even more difficult to formalize and implement throughout an organization, there are other reasons why many companies have not developed high-level, inclusive written policies on communication. As some of the managers and executives in Gilsdorf's survey explained, sometimes the problem is simply inertia, due to either a failure to recognize the importance of communication, a lack of time because managers are too busy "fighting fires," or the inability of managers to agree on anything, since each of them invariably has quite different ideas on how to handle things. Among the other reasons cited were that "the concept was too idealistic," that no one would follow it, and that CEOs are convinced that "'anybody can communicate' and that therefore communication is supposed to take care of itself" (p. 49).

But perhaps the most interesting and compelling reason of all is that in some corporations the very effort to standardize and prescribe communication is regarded as antithetical to the corporate culture itself. One respondent in the Gilsdorf survey, for instance, claimed that his firm did not need a written policy because "we accomplish the same goal with a strong, positive corporate culture." Another indicated, "At this point our firm is moving away from written policy. Today we are trying hard to hire carefully, direct new hires on customer orientation and a service attitude, and *trust* them to represent us well." And still another suggested that a communication policy "could be intimidating," adding that "People who are good at their jobs should be able to make their communication decisions without always checking against a manual" (p. 49). Thus, in some companies— particularly young, aggressive firms that put a premium on creativity, innovation, and individuality—the idea of legislating communication practices may be regarded as a threat to the very qualities the company tries to nurture among their employees.

My own consulting experiences corroborate Gilsdorf's findings: namely, that the desire for communication policies is greater at the lower and middle levels of an organization than at the higher levels. That is, while individual managers or supervisors may be interested in instituting communication policies or procedures for their particular departments or work units, that interest tends to wane when the issue becomes extending policy throughout the entire organization. For instance, I have encountered several cases in which upper management was less than eager to develop company-wide, much less department-wide, guidelines and formats for written documents, even though others in the company were appealing to me on the side to try to encourage upper management to implement some minimal standards and procedures concerning company reports. The case of one company especially comes to mind, in which employees typically spend their evenings and weekends creating, from scratch, lengthy client proposals. When, in my conversations with the vice president, I noted that there appeared to be no consistent procedure, organization, content, or style for generating these proposals, he interpreted my observations as a compliment. "Good," he beamed. "I'm glad to hear that. I'd hate to think I had a bunch of automatons working for me. Every proposal needs to be unique."

In another similar case, my business partner and I became members of a company's project team, staying up round the clock for two days without going home or changing clothes in order to help writers produce an important proposal and meet an impending deadline. From what the employees confided, this was the typical modus operandi at the company. While upper management (most of whom were divorced or never married) seemed to thrive on these late night brainstorming sessions, many others in the firm were on the brink of burnout. Despite the fact that morale was low and turnover high, management was convinced that such sessions produced a synergy that could not otherwise be achieved by following a routine procedure or by working during normal business hours. Every proposal, as one employee put it, was a matter of "reinventing the wheel." But for the president and vice presidents at least, the real thrill seemed to be the process itself—immersing themselves into a project, the men rolling up their shirt sleeves, the women slipping off their shoes, the secretaries ordering out pizza at 2:00 a.m. The scene was reminiscent of my college days, staying up all night with dorm friends to cram for final exams the next day. And maybe it was something of that spirit of community or family that the upper managers sought. For when my partner and I suggested that, through better planning and a more systematized approach to creating client proposals, they might produce better proposals in less time, the president was nonplussed. "And give all this up?!" he exclaimed, waving his arm to encompass all the bleary-eyed employees huddled over desks, feverishly writing in collaboration, running back and forth to the computers, printers, and copying machines, and to other offices where similar teams were hustling and bustling to create other parts of the proposal. For whatever reasons (I leave that to psychologists to figure out), upper management seemed to revel in the spontaneity, intensity, and overdrive characteristic of these all-night sessions. These were dominant features of this firm's corporate culture.

Perceptions of Culture and Communication

In order for any corporate culture to endure, its members must recognize and, at some level, subscribe to the culture, if not in belief than at least in behavior. As discussed previously, in strong corporate cultures, the members constitute a community of believers and doers—people whose values and goals shape and are shaped by those of the corporation and whose actions are consistent with those values and goals. In the cases described above, however, many of the employees, while they did what was expected of them, did so begrudgingly, though many of them were reluctant to express this to upper management for fear their performance evaluations would suffer or their very jobs would be jeopardized. It does not take experience in the real world to learn this lesson of survival. As Sperling and Freedman (1987) observed in "A Good Girl Writes Like a Good Girl," students in our composition classes early on learn how to conform to their teachers' expectations and standards, even when these conflict with the students' personal preferences and judgments.

Such discrepancies between belief and action raise questions about the relationship between community and culture, and about the very definition of a corporate culture itself. Organizational theorists seem to be divided along two lines, as Glaser, Zamanou, and Hacker (1987, pp. 173–174) point out in their review of the literature. On the one hand are those (Pettigrew, 1979, and Smircich, 1981, 1983) who maintain that an organizational culture is defined by *shared meaning*—"patterns of belief, symbols, rituals, and myths that evolve over time and function as the glue that holds the organization together." On the other hand, are those (Schwartz & Davis, 1981; Silverzweig & Allen, 1976; and Van Maanen & Barley, 1984) "who have adopted a normative definition of culture by emphasizing an organization's *shared expectations* for consensually approved behavior." According to the first school of thought, culture exists because the members of the community share certain beliefs; according to the second school of thought, culture exists because the members share certain expectations about what is and is not acceptable behavior, regardless of whether they also believe in what they are expected to do. In a strong organizational culture, such distinctions are not apparent because there is a close match between the organization's values and those of its members, and between these values and the organization's expectations and the members' actions. In such organizations, as Deal and Kennedy (1982) found, employees experience greater job satisfaction, the turnover rate is lower, and the company's productivity and profitability are higher. Moreover, in such organizations, the quality of communication at all levels is invariably high, and the members, in addition to "speaking the same language," perceive and interpret the culture in much the same way.

Increasingly, there is evidence to suggest that in weak organizational cultures, values and expectations are either nonexistent, vague, or not shared (either not communicated or not subscribed to) throughout the organization. In one way or another, often an organization's problems—whether they are poor management, lack of teamwork, personnel conflicts, disgruntled clients, shoddy quality control, or declining profits—can be traced to failures in communication.

While researchers have developed theories for discussing and describing organizational cultures, until recently there have been few empirical studies aimed at assessing culture in an organizational setting. Glaser et al. (1987), however, have developed an Organizational Culture Survey (OCS) that examines six components of organizational culture, which have been identified in nearly 30 studies from both management and communication research: teamwork–conflict, climate–morale, information flow, involvement, supervision, and meetings. Glaser et al. administered their OCS to 195 employees of a governmental agency. Chief among their findings is that upper-level managers and lower-level employees have significantly different perceptions of their organization's culture. Compared with the line supervisors, clerical staff, and the line workers, top management (a) perceive a significantly more positive climate, (b) feel significantly more involved in the organization, (c) perceive communication to be significantly stronger, and (d) perceive supervision to be significantly more effective. In short, as Glaser et al. note, "What emerges from the analyses of OCS scores and S/D ratios is an organization with dissatisfied employees at all but the top management level. Employees are experiencing low morale and are dissatisfied with their organization's level of teamwork, information flow, supervision, and involvement" (p. 185).

Based upon interviews with their subjects, Glaser et al. suggest that the organization's problems are due primarily to poor communication within the organization. They identify five main themes that emerged from their subjects' comments, themes that should be familiar to anyone who has done consulting in organizations and that should be of interest to all managers concerned with promoting effective communication within their organizations. These themes, as listed by Glaser et al. (p. 186), are as follows:

1. Top management and supervisors do not listen to or value the ideas and opinions of their employees.
2. Limited interaction between department and divisions causes misunderstanding and confusion.
3. Meetings are too often only informational and do not involve enough interaction and decision making.
4. Employees are often unclear about what they should be doing and where the organization itself is headed.
5. Supervisors are deficient in providing feedback to their employees, and giving recognition for good work and suggestions.

The influence of communication on organizational culture is a subject that merits further study. My experiences as a consultant convince me that the findings from the above study are not unique to this one organization, or even to governmental agencies in particular, though in the past the communication problems inherent in governmental bureaucracies have been well publicized. Rather, the problems are more common than would be expected even in some of the largest, most successful, and supposedly best run corporations in our country. Indeed, the larger the corporation, the more difficult it becomes for top management to keep in touch with the spreading ganglia of divisions and departments. While some companies view this as the need for increased centralization and for greater standardization throughout the organization, other companies view this as the need for decentralization and for more autonomy and accountability at the regional or divisional levels. Deal and Kennedy (1982) speculate that the trend in corporate cultures is toward the latter. Glaser et al. similarly suggest that "organizations are generally composed of subcultures rather one guiding mega-culture." If so, then high-level corporate communication policies become even more important if top management has particular cultural values, expectations, and standards that they expect subcultures to share throughout the organization.

Communication Dysfunctions

Rarely do beginning organizations establish full-blown communication policies and procedures as part of their start-up operations. For one, there are too many other, seemingly more important matters to attend to when launching a new business. And for another, there is simply no way of knowing, except by experience and by trial and error, what the organization's communication needs will actually be. As the organizational culture evolves, so do communication practices and patterns. At some point, however—usually through error—someone realizes the necessity of clarifying and formulating expectations concerning the nature, flow, storage, or security of information. For new employees especially, knowing who gets what information when, why, where, and how is as important to performing their jobs satisfactorily as is possessing the right kind of technical knowledge and skill.

In companies that have either vague or nonexistent guidelines regarding oral and written communication, the possibilities for communication dysfunctions are endless. Consider, for instance, the following situations:

- A technician of an analytical services division has a suggestion for reducing the turnaround time of client samples by 30 percent. He writes up a proposal and sends it to his supervisor, but the proposal dies and never reaches the division manager because for the last several months the supervisor has been building a case for dismissing the technician.
- A newly hired systems conversion analyst goes out on a client call with her supervisor. The analyst, eager to serve the client, makes the mistake of saying to the client that their new computer system "can be up and running within three weeks." The analyst's supervisor is flabbergasted for he knows that it normally takes at least twice as long to complete such a conversion. Nonetheless, the analyst has made a verbal promise that the supervisor is now going to have to find a way to keep.
- During a social gathering at a national conference on lasers, a vice president overhears one of his company's research scientists spilling proprietary information about a new laser technology that the company has spent millions of dollars developing but which it has not patented as yet.
- An account executive for a bank tells a major customer that the bank cannot extend his line of credit beyond the limits prescribed by bank policy. As a result, the customer closes all of his accounts and takes his sizable business elsewhere. When the bank president learns of this, he calls the account executive onto the carpet. The account executive attempts to justify his action by explaining that he was only following bank policy. To which the president responds, "And you should have known that our unwritten policy is always to consider making exceptions for our most valuable customers." The account executive is demoted and put on probation.
- A documentation specialist is working for a communication consulting firm that has been subcontracted by Company A to write a computer

manual for their client, Company B. At Company A's request, the specialist submits a rough and incomplete draft of the manual to Company A for their preliminary review, without, however, marking the text "rough draft" or attaching a cover letter explaining the revisions and additions the specialist intends to make in the final draft. Unbeknownst to the specialist, Company A sends the rough draft manual to their client, Company B, again without appending any explanations. The managers at Company B read the manual and are alarmed since they assume the manual is in its final or near-final form. Company B fires Company A, who in turn fires the consulting firm, who in turn fires the specialist.

- A chemical engineer working for a toxic waste disposal company has completed a preliminary investigation that suggests that the company's underground storage tanks are leaching hazardous chemicals into the soil at one of the company's waste sites. Since the engineer suspects that the leaching is being caused by faulty tank liners, he decides to send a copy of his internal report to the company that manufactures the tank liners so that they can promptly initiate their own studies. When the engineer's manager sees that the report has been distributed externally, he is furious. From his point of view, not only has the engineer overstepped bounds by issuing the report outside the company but the engineer, upon the basis of only his preliminary investigation, has publicly and prematurely exposed the company to possible litigation.

To a large extent, the problems cited in the above examples could have been avoided if the company had established policies concerning the nature, flow, distribution, and disclosure of company communications. But even in lieu of formalized policies and procedures, such problems could have been prevented had the managers provided their subordinates with better guidance, been clearer about their expectations, and created an atmosphere in which their subordinates would have felt more comfortable discussing their assignments and asking questions before they made faulty assumptions. For, at its roots, the quality of communication within an organization depends primarily upon the quality of interpersonal communication between management and their subordinates: people talking to people. An organization's administrative structure can facilitate open channels of communication, but whether or not individuals actually use those channels may be another matter. As will be discussed in Chapter 5, two cases in our nation's recent history have dramatically demonstrated the consequences of communication dysfunction: the circumstances surrounding the crash of the Space Shuttle Challenger in 1986 and those of the Iran–contra affair of 1987. Both cases clearly illustrate what happens when the channels of communication are either weak or circumvented. In both cases, the presidential commissions appointed to study these crises attributed them mainly to failures in communication.

This chapter, despite its length, has provided only a glimpse at the symbiotic interrelationship of culture, community, and communication. To summarize briefly, we have seen how cultures shape how their members think and communicate, and how communities in turn shape culture. With respect to organizations, we have seen also how slogans, metaphors, and symbols help define and sustain a sense of community and corporate culture. And, finally, we have seen some of the communication dysfunctions that can occur when employees are unaware of their company's or their supervisor's expectations and standards governing verbal or written communication.

Underlying this chapter and this entire volume is the belief that communication and meaning are inseparable from the particular culture and community within which discourse exists. For writers, one of the major implications of a social theory of communication, as discussed early in this chapter, is that they must understand their rhetorical contexts from an organizational, cultural perspective rather than from simply the narrow perspective of their text's immediate audience and purpose. Finally, this chapter has explored how organizations are both culture-forming and culture-bearing milieux. The next chapter examines the role that written communication plays in shaping and maintaining organizational community and culture.

4
Written Communication and Organizational Culture

It is the culture, finally, [that] establishes standards for "good writing."
Purves & Purves (1986, p. 193)

Before turning at last to the ways in which writing both shapes and reflects organizational culture, it may be appropriate at this point to gather up some loose ends and to suggest what bearing the previous three chapters have upon this chapter, and how the issues discussed in those chapters provide a general framework for the rest of this volume.

As I indicated in the Introduction, while the focus of my own study (reported in Part Three) is upon technical writing in an R&D setting, and specifically upon the nature of information in progress reports, the fundamental question with which I began my inquiry was quite simply, "What is good writing?" Within the context of the R&D organization at which I conducted my research, that broad question was narrowed to, "What is a good progress report?" or, more accurately, "Within this particular R&D organization, what do the writers and intended readers of progress reports consider a good progress report?"

The previous chapters in Part One have addressed the broader question ("What is good writing?") from several angles, focusing primarily upon the differences between school writing and real-world writing. In these chapters I have attempted to set my work within the context of current research and theory in the fields of both academic writing and organizational communication.

In Chapter 1, I began with the challenge confronting us as teachers and researchers of writing: namely, that the writing skills of those in business and industry are, according to numerous surveys, woefully inadequate and that the universities need to do a better job of preparing students for the types of writing required of them beyond school. Accordingly, the main purposes of Chapter 1 were to examine the importance of writing in non-academic, business settings and to underscore the very real and practical reasons we have for learning more about what, why, and how real-world writers write. To those outside our discipline, the fact that we have done so little research on real-world writing often comes as a surprise. One of my colleagues from another discipline, for instance, was quite nonplussed when a few years ago I described my study of real-world writing as something of a departure from the mainstream of research in the field of composition. "But if you folks haven't been studying what it means to write well in the real world," he asked, "then upon what basis have you developed your theories of good writing? If you haven't been studying proficient writing and proficient writers, then just what have you been studying?"

Some of the answers to that question were explored in Chapter 2, which examined the main assumptions underlying the research and teaching of writing in academic settings. In that chapter, I discussed the limitations of the process, product, and context views of writing and pointed out some of the problems real-world writers often have when they assume that the conventions and standards of business or technical writing are the same as those of academic writing.

Finally, having reviewed what have been the major concerns of our discipline in the past, I next turned, in Chapter 3, to emerging views of writing that are beginning to inform our understanding of writing as a means of communication within nonacademic, real-world settings. Among the main concepts discussed in that chapter was the importance of viewing writing from the perspective of the particular culture within which it exists. In that chapter, I explored the interrelationships among culture, community, and communication, emphasizing primarily the nature of corporate cultures and the ways in which organizations manifest their cultures; and the important role communication policies and clear supervisor expectations can play in helping individuals become socialized into the corporate community, in preventing communication dysfunctions within the organization, and in ensuring that writers project an image consistent with organizational values and goals. The major premise of that chapter was that culture and community exert a powerful influence on everything we know and do, including the way we communicate.

This chapter examines the latter, specifically the ways in which writing reflects and shapes organizational culture. To the extent that organizations differ, and to the extent that even communities or subcultures with the organization may differ, so too will the standards and expectations regarding written communication. There is, in other words, no easy, simple answer to the broad question, "What is good writing?" At best, all we can give is the kind of generic answer provided by Purves and Purves (1986, p. 193): that "It is the culture, finally, [that] establishes standards for 'good writing.'"

Within their own academic culture and community, composition researchers and teachers have come a long way toward identifying, formalizing, and analyzing the standards they have established for good academic writing. However, with the recent interest in real-world writing, many researchers, teachers, and consultants are beginning to realize that they cannot impose their own academic notions of effective writing onto individuals within other cultures, but rather that they need to find ways of investigating what it means to write well within organizational settings outside academe. Within the last few years, some researchers have been attempting to do just that.

HOW ORGANIZATIONAL CULTURE INFLUENCES WRITING

As discussed in the last chapter, every organization is unique: each has its own character and image, its own goals, and its own ways of achieving those goals. The ethos of an organization is promulgated in many ways—through, for instance, its leaders, heroes, legends, myths, slogans, and policies—and is manifested through such things as its organizational structure, floor plans, office decor, stationery and brochures, marketing and advertising—right down to such matters as the number of conference rooms and overhead projectors available, who eats where and with whom, and who gets which offices.

One of the most important and revealing ways in which an organization conveys and sustains its character is through its written communications. As Dobrin (1983, p. 248) notes, "The way they handle technical writing at Kodak is very different from the way they do at Corning, and each way is tied up with the corporation's organization, its self-image, its decisions about what is acceptable behavior, its valuations of judgment and knowledge, and so on." Although Dobrin is referring to technical writing specifically, the same applies to business writing as well. Broadhead and Freed (1986, p. 12), for instance, maintain that every company, profession, discipline, or the like has its own institutional norms, whether formal or informal, that govern both the writing process—"the writer's overall environment for thinking, composing, and revising," and the product—the text's layout, organization, content, style, and tone. Freed and Broadhead (1987, p. 157), further point out that even in companies within the same industry—for example, IBM, Digital, Hewlett Packard, and Apple—the rules and standards for effective writing vary considerably because each constitutes a different culture. Since the rules of the game are apt to change depending on a particular organization's norms, and since even these norms are not always apparent to those inside the organization nor always consistently applied across departments or even within the same department, we can see how difficult it is not only for writers to acquire the knowledge they need to write effectively on the job, but also for researchers of writing to study writing within nonacademic settings. Nevertheless, a few researchers are making the effort.

Doheny-Farina (1984), for example, has investigated how the contingencies specific to an organization shape the rhetorical purposes of organizational documents. Similarly, in a study of technical writing, Debs (1985) has reported how writers attend to not simply the constraints of their subject matter but also the idiosyncratic constraints imposed by their organizations. Investigating the latter, Freed and Broadhead (1987) have analyzed the differences between the organizational cultures of two major consulting firms—one a management consulting firm and the other an auditing firm. In their study, they examine how these differences, in turn, are reflected by the different strategies and styles representative of each firm's proposals to clients. For example, in the one firm, the management firm, the proposals tend to emphasize the reputations of the specific individuals assigned to the project team and what the particular team can do for the client. Thus, the tone of their proposals is typically informal and the content stresses the abilities of the consultants and the "chemistry" they will bring to the project. By contrast, in the other firm, the auditing firm, the proposals tend to be more formal and the content stresses the firm's reputation rather than that of its individual auditors (each of whom, presumably, is as good as another auditor, otherwise none of them would be working for the firm). Accordingly, the auditing firm's proposals focus on skills and procedures—on what the firm (not the individual consultants) can do for the client and what the key steps and responsibilities are for both the firm's and the client's participation. Throughout the management firm's proposals, on the other hand, the focus is on the firm's individualized approach and the concept of "value-added," or the benefits the client can expect from engaging the firm's management team. Among the common themes in their proposals are those of "commonality, equality, and partnership," stressing "joint goals, processes, and teamwork" (p. 160), or, in other words, mainly intangibles not subject to quantification. In the auditing firm's proposals, however, benefits are de-emphasized, primarily because the firm realizes the dangers of making promises to clients which later the firm may not be able to keep. Their proposals, therefore, avoid telling clients that they can save a certain amount of money or make a certain profit as a result of using the firm's services.

Beyond the different features of these two firm's proposals, one of the more interesting aspects of organizational writing, as Freed and Broadhead note in their study, is how thoroughly each firm knows its niche in the marketplace and how well each firm tailors its proposals to a specific audience—which is to say that these firms are probably successful in part because they are keenly aware of the importance of rhetoric (in the best sense of the word) and have been able to communicate to their employees the standards and expectations concerning that particular firm's written communications.

In many organizations, however, the rules and norms governing company documents are not made explicit. As discussed in Chapter 3, for example, few corporations have communication policies and in many cases when such policies do exist they rarely address the kinds of questions that typically plague most writers—general questions such as the audience and purpose of particular types of company documents, and, related to a specific document, more difficult and troublesome questions such as what information to include, how much detail is appropriate, and how to achieve a style and tone consistent with the image the firm wishes to project. How do writers, especially those newly hired, learn these things? How, as Lutz (1986, p. 188) puts it, do they "learn the way the organization does things, the way it wishes to speak, and the way it wishes its writers to speak for it"? More often than not such training is informal and on-the-job. While most companies have orientation programs and manuals for new employees, seldom do these specifically address the kinds of writing required within the organization. Rather, as is usually the case, employees learn the conventions regarding written documents by studying similar documents written by others in the organization or department and by having their work reviewed and critiqued by their superiors. In other words, mainly by practice and trial and error.

In what have been the most frequently cited studies of real-world writing to date, Odell and his colleagues have examined how experienced writers in governmental agencies use their tacit knowledge of organizational culture to help them make rhetorical decisions (Odell & Goswami, 1982; and Odell, Goswami, Herrington, & Quick, 1983).

The first of these studies is acclaimed by Beach and Bridwell in their volume, *New Directions in Composition Research* (1984, p. 227), as representing great strides in the research of writing in nonacademic settings in two ways: (a) Unlike most studies within the field of composition, it is not based on a contrived context for writing, and (b) It examines in depth the reasons writers themselves give for the substantive and stylistic choices they make. For other researchers of writing, one of the more interesting aspects of this study and the others discussed below are the methodologies Odell and his colleagues have developed and refined over the last few years in order to investigate how an organizational culture influences a writer's rhetorical choices. The following, therefore, summarizes not only the key findings of these studies but also the studies' methodologies.

In this first study, Odell and Goswami (1982, 1984) conducted interviews of administrators and two groups of caseworkers in a Department of Social Services agency and analyzed their memos and letters in order to examine the reasons writers give for substantive or stylistic choices in their texts, whether the writers vary certain linguistic features of their texts according to different rhetorical contexts (i.e., different audiences and purposes), and whether their judgments about acceptable style vary from one type of writing to another. Among their findings are that all subjects in the study were sensitive to the rhetorical context for their writing, and that the administrators varied several linguistic features according to the type of writing they were doing. Furthermore, when the subjects were presented with alternative ways of expressing the same thing, both administrators and caseworkers demonstrated a complex awareness of audience, self, and subject in the justifications they gave for preferring one version of a text over another.

As for the subjects' judgments about the acceptability of style, however, their preferences varied only slightly according to the subject's job position. When given variations of texts written by others, all groups preferred passive constructions regardless of the type of writing (letter or memo). Commenting on this anomalous finding, Odell and Goswami speculate that, perhaps because the subjects were given no specific information about the audience and purpose of the texts presented to them, they may not have been influenced by the same criteria they would normally use to guide stylistic choices in their own texts. Certainly this is a plausible explanation. But as for just what criteria writers *do* use when they are presented with texts for which they are given no background or context, Odell and Goswami do not further speculate. My suspicion, however, based on the discussion and examples in Chapter 2, is that, in the absence of knowing the rhetorical situation within which a text was produced, writers often resort to the criteria of effective writing they learned in school. Thus, in this case, maybe the writers said that they preferred the passive constructions to the active constructions because the passives most conformed to the traditional notions many people have about writing style—namely, the need to avoid references to self; to create a seemingly more objective, businesslike stance and tone; and, in general, to sound more impressive.

Whatever the reasons for the subjects' preferences, the point is that it makes little sense to study writing apart from the specific contexts within which texts are created, read, and used. For to do so is to take an absolutist, reductionist view of writing, one based on the assumption that there are some universal criteria of effective writing that apply in all situations, cultures, and communities, regardless of one's specific aims and audiences. As has been discussed throughout the previous chapters, it has been this assumption among researchers of writing that has underlain the majority of our studies; that has blinded us to the social aspects of writing as a form of communication; that has pervaded our teaching of writing; that has fostered among our students these same academic, rigid notions about writing; and that later, as the students enter the workforce, often creates problems for them when the standards of writing they learned in school conflict with those being used to evaluate their job-related writing. To their credit, Odell and Goswami recognized this limitation in their study, for in their discussion section they suggest the need for different lines of inquiry to investigate writers' sense of "acceptable" style. One of the questions that they suggested needs consideration is, "What stylistic preferences would workers exhibit if they were asked to judge alternative versions of pieces that the workers themselves had written?" (p. 256). The next study was designed in part to examine answers to that question.

In the second study, Odell, Goswami, Herrington, and Quick (1983) used discourse-based interviews to examine the reasons writers (workers in a state Department of Labor) have for preferring a particular choice of content or style in their *own* memos and letters. (For a more complete description of the discourse-course based interview procedure, see Odell, Goswami, & Herrington, 1983.) Prior to the interviews, the researchers read and analyzed a number of samples of the subjects' writing and identified the following five types of variations (p. 26):

1. Form used in expressing a command or a request (e.g., "Please do X" versus "You must do X").
2. Form used in referring to oneself (e.g., "I" versus "we").
3. Use (or lack thereof) of an introductory, context-setting statement.
4. Use of informative detail (e.g., abstract statements followed by elaboration or example).
5. Justification of assertions (e.g., rationale for conclusions, as in clauses beginning with "because" or "since").

During the tape-recorded interviews, the researchers used these types of variations as the basis for framing questions about why the writer, in one of his own memos or letters, had decided to use this or that form, or to include this or that information. In addition, the researchers presented the writers with alternative versions of the writers' own texts and asked them whether the alternative versions would be equally acceptable. Once the taped interviews were transcribed, the researchers then analyzed the writers' statements and "assigned the writers' statements to one or more of the following categories of reasons for accepting or rejecting a particular alternative" (p. 27): audience-focused reasons, writer-focused reasons, subject-focused reasons, or text-focused reasons.

Among the major findings of their study are that the types of choices writers made were heavily influenced by their awareness of the particular rhetorical context and by the *persona* they wished to create (or avoid), and that the writers' experience and status within the organization influenced the types of reasons they gave for making certain choices of content and style. All of the writers, for instance, were especially concerned about their audiences: "They frequently mentioned some prior contact with their readers, remarked upon the characteristics of their audience, and speculated upon ways their readers might respond to a particular choice" (p. 30). However, as would be expected, compared with the inexperienced writers, the administrators and the more experienced workers within the organization revealed a deeper understanding of their readers' knowledge, attitudes, biases, and needs. Furthermore, the administrators, to a greater extent than both the experienced and inexperienced workers, were more likely to refer to audience characteristics when explaining why they preferred a particular way of expressing a command or request, and were more likely to refer to the need for accuracy of information when explaining why they would or would not include some informative detail. By contrast, the inexperienced writers were more likely to refer to writer-based or subject-based reasons when justifying, for example, their choices to use a certain form of expression, to include contextual background, or to use informative detail.

One of the unstated implications of the above study's findings seems to be that the longer one has been with an organization and the higher one's position in the organization, the greater one's understanding of the need to view a rhetorical task within the context of the organizational setting and to write in a manner consistent with the organization's rather than the individual's *persona*. To some extent, Odell must have sensed this and must have recognized, too, that researchers studying writing, like the writers themselves, also need to take into consideration the organizational context within which texts are produced. For in the next study, Odell (1985) employed the same procedure of discourse-based interviews he had used in earlier studies, but this time to explore how the culture of an organization influences what, why, and how writers write.

In this study, Odell interviewed and observed a small group of supervisors and administrative analysts working in the same office of a state bureaucracy in order to discover how their writing is influenced by their interactions with each other and by their awareness of their organization's culture—"its widely shared attitudes, knowledge, and ways of operating" (p. 250). Among Odell's major findings are that, according to the analysts, the content of their letters, memos, and reports are based on their familiarity with the culture in which they work. As Odell (p. 252) notes, the writers frequently referred to the following types of knowledge as being most influential in their writing:

1. Widely shared attitudes or values, in their own office or in other branches of the agency (e.g., anticipating reader reactions to certain content upon the basis of what the writer knows will or will not influence the reader).

2. Prior actions or previously held attitudes (e.g., being familiar with what has or hasn't worked in the past, and why or why not).
3. Ways in which the agency functions (e.g., a knowledge of how things work, what the formal and informal procedures are, and how long they will take).

Of further interest, Odell also found that often the writers' perception of audience seemed to be based not so much upon their personal knowledge of their intended readers or their experiences with them, but rather upon an understanding of the immediate organizational context in which the analysts do their writing. For example, "Even when the analysts referred to the audience's knowledge of the subject at hand," Odell explains, "they rarely talked about what the reader actually did know. Rather, they usually spoke about what the reader *might* or *should* know (or not know) about the subject at hand" (p. 257). As a clue to why these findings may seem paradoxical given the results of Odell's earlier studies described above, almost half of the writers in this study indicated that, regardless of who their readers might be, they still needed to justify why they were recommending a certain action. In short, as Odell notes, "All the analysts had a very definite sense of the questions their readers might ask" (p. 270)—whether those readers were their intended primary or secondary readers, or even some unknown, unintended readers. I would add, too, that the rhetorical and political savvy required to write an effective letter, memo, or report comes not from simply analyzing its particular audience and purpose but moreover from recognizing how well the text addresses larger, organizational concerns. For, as has been demonstrated countless times—most notably in the hearings from the Watergate scandal, the Iran-contra affair, and the Space Shuttle Challenger accident—one never really knows when, where, why, and by whom even the most personal and confidential memos and letters might be read. One of the most important things, and alas sometimes the last thing, a writer within an organization learns is the necessity of what seasoned real-world writers commonly refer to as "CYA" (Cover Your Ass). To my knowledge, this rule is not discussed in any technical or business writing textbook, article, or course. And yet, as I read the reasons that many of Odell's subjects gave for their choices of content and style, it is obvious that many of these writers are sensitive to the potential consequences of what they write, not only for their readers or for them personally but also for their particular department and for the entire organization. In short, they view their rhetorical task from a much broader perspective than simply their immediate audience and purpose. They have vision. They have what was described in the last chapter as "transcendent knowledge," or "situationally competent imagination." They know the culture and community within which they work and write, and they know, moreover, that their fate and that of the organization are intrinsically intertwined.

HOW WRITING INFLUENCES ORGANIZATIONAL CULTURE

In his work on organizational communication, Karl E. Weick (1979) pointed out 20 years ago that not only do organizations influence people but also that "people play an important role in creating the environments around them" (p. 5) and in helping shape an organization's culture. While we are beginning to gain a better understanding of how organizational contexts influence writing and the functions that writing serves within particular organizations (see, for example, Paradis, Dobrin, and Miller, 1985), as yet we know little about the role writing plays in defining and shaping an organization.

Some recent theorists, however, contend that writing serves more than a pragmatic function within organizations. According to Harrison (1987), "Writing in organizations is more than just an activity for accomplishing organizational tasks; it may additionally be seen as a discourse process fundamental to the creation of organized activity" (p. 17). Harrison's view that writing, as a social process, creates and maintains organizations is similar to Farrell's (1976) earlier idea that social communities are formed by rhetorical action. Unfortunately, however, few studies to date have investigated how writing helps define an organization's character, culture, or community.

To anyone who has started a business, the importance of the company's written communications in helping to create and to convey its organizational ethos soon becomes apparent. Whether it is as seemingly simple a matter as deciding the company name or its logo, or whether it is the more complicated matter of developing the company's promotional literature, both entail addressing the most fundamental questions confronting all businesses, small or large, new or old: Who are we? What do we do? How do we do it? Why do we do it? And, where are we headed? For instance, the first time the president or partners of a fledgling firm sit down to write their company's brochure, they inevitably find themselves engaging in a lot of organizational soul searching. What image should we project? (Staid, traditional, and conservative? Or progressive, modern, and avant garde?) What services or products should we emphasize? (A wide gamut or a select few?) What makes us different from our competitors? (Range of services? Quality? Price?) What look do we want to project through our promotional materials? Do we need to market our services, or should we rely on word-of-mouth? Can we work out of our homes, or do we need a plush office with an administrative staff, a reception area, conference room, production area, storage room, and sophisticated phone system? Can we do our own tax returns, or do we need to hire bookkeepers, accountants, and lawyers? And so on. In many cases, answers to such questions may well determine not just how their company is perceived but also the company's direction. And that, in turn, will influence whom they hire, what they do, how they structure the business, where they locate their offices, the floorplan and layout of their offices, the kinds of equipment and furniture they buy, their employees' attire, and so forth and so on. "But aren't all of these things," one might ask, "decided well before one writes a brochure? Don't you first think, plan, and then write?" Rarely, or at least not nearly that systematically. More often than not, the writing and the organizational planning go hand in hand. It is an ever-evolving process in which the writing feeds the culture, and the culture the writing. And this typically occurs, whether it is in a *Fortune 500* corporation or a one-person law practice, and whether it is presidents and CEOs formulating a five-year plan or a committee of administrative assistants developing an office procedures manual. In short, while some written documents serve primarily to reflect and to help preserve a culture that is already well rooted, in other cases written documents help create and promulgate the culture. In many instances, as for example in the case of the *United States Constitution*, a document serves both purposes.

One of the most important functions of writing within an organization is that often it is a way of crystallizing an issue and of making people come face to face with hard questions about what they are doing or ought to be doing and why. Someone once said, "How can I know what I think until I write it"? Similarly, for most people, the very act of writing, of having to commit something to paper, forces them to think, to reassess, to define, and to evaluate. As discussed later in Part Three, one supervisor in my study, in talking about the importance of writing progress reports, commented that even if the company did not require progress reports, he would still insist that his researchers write them because the sheer act of writing forced them to make sense of their work and in so doing helped guide the department's future work. And so it is with many other types of company documents—proposals, policy statements, procedure manuals, formal reports. That is, beyond the content of the document itself, the very writing of it has a heuristic value. As Paradis, Dobrin, and Miller found in their study (1985, p. 293), writing helps "develop a kind of social consciousness of the organizational environment." For whenever writers write, they are to a large extent interpreting, testing, and formulating the very values, beliefs, knowledge, and attitudes that make up the organizational community and its culture.

In an ethnographic study of an emerging computer company, Doheny-Farina (1986) examined this phenomenon. Specifically, he looked at how four vice presidents collaborated on the writing of the company's new business plan and how, through this writing process, the structure, goals, and nature of the organization itself changed. As Doheny-Farina notes, and as the vice presidents who were writing the new business plan soon realized, "Whoever had power to establish the company's goals had a large measure of control over the evolution of the company" (p. 166).

During the company's first year-and-a-half, it was the president who had wielded that power. He had written the company's first business plan and had tightly controlled the company by making all the decisions himself according to his own promotional, entrepreneurial perspective. During that time, however, the company was not generating any sales revenues; far from making a profit, the company was, in fact, on the brink of bankruptcy. Consequently, the company, at the board's behest, hired a consultant to help improve the company's production system. He proposed a system whereby the various segments of the company—programming, quality control, marketing, and finance—would be integrated, and he further recommended that the vice presidents work as a team, with the president monitoring overall operation. But because this system could not be implemented in time to save the company, the president and the vice presidents decided that the quickest way to attract investors would be to write a new business plan, one that would explain the company's history, purpose, and goals for the next five years.

The president assumed he would be writing the new plan, just as he had written the original one. However, shortly after starting it, he had to leave for a week-long business trip. In his absence, the vice presidents decided to work on the plan together. Doheny-Farina (p. 167) points out that two significant things happened during this collaborative effort:

1. For the first time ever, the vice presidents made large-scale company decisions without the approval of the president.
2. The vice presidents came to believe that the financial crisis occurred not only because the company had suffered from a previously unorganized production system, but also because the president had seriously mismanaged the company's finances.

Once the company's board of directors learned of this revelation, they decreed that the president's authoritarian rule had to end. Thus, the process of writing influenced not only the substance of the business plan but an entire change in the company's corporate structure, as well as its very culture.

A couple of other cases drawn from my consulting experiences further illustrate the effects writing can have on a department or company. In one analytical division of an R&D organization, the manager challenged the technicians of the various work units to think of "ways we can work smarter." One group of technicians decided they needed to standardize their analytical methods in order to improve the training and cross-training of technicians in their work area. To meet that need, they proposed to develop Technicians Reference Manuals for each laboratory, manuals which would include, among other things, written procedures for the various analytical tests they performed. In addition to providing better training, the manuals in turn led to a massive clean-up and reorganization of the laboratories, to better quality control standards and procedures, and eventually to reduced turn-around-time of client samples. The division benefited because clients were being better served—and that made the manager happy. The work unit benefited because, during the writing of the test procedures and manuals, their self-esteem, enthusiasm, and team spirit were bolstered as they worked jointly on a project they themselves had conceived and planned—and that made both the work unit and their supervisor happy. Finally, the technicians benefited because they acquired writing skills that enhanced their prospects for promotion—and that, of course, made many individuals very happy. Recently, the same work unit has completed a video training tape of one their more complicated analytical test procedures, and this video is now serving as a pilot for future training videos in the company's other divisions and subsidiaries.

In another R&D organization of a major corporation, researchers are required to submit one "idea paper" per year. The function these serve within the organization is similar to an R&D suggestion box—a relatively risk-free way for researchers to evaluate existing technologies or products, or to propose new ones, whether or not the ideas relate to the researchers' own work areas. Unlike the routine types of work-related reports and memos the researchers normally submit, the idea papers do not have to conform to a prescribed format nor are they screened or revised by the researchers' immediate supervisors. Rather, they are submitted directly to upper management. Sometimes the idea papers die on the manager's desk and nothing ever becomes of them. But other times, it can be a short idea paper that shakes up an organization and alters its course of research or even gives birth to a whole new company.

Take, for example, the case of one young researcher who in an idea paper questioned why the company for the last several years had been using a particular refining process. As a result of his idea paper, management began to critically assess their commitment to this particular process, and they confirmed what the researcher had proposed: that the process was indeed antiquated. As their inquiries revealed, whatever reasons had originally justified using the process were no longer valid given state-of-the-art technology. Moreover, projections indicated that, if the company continued to use the current process, it would lose its share of the market and profits would quickly decline.

As for why this information had not surfaced earlier, investigations suggested that over the years those working on the project had developed tunnel vision. Few people, when pressed, could recollect the rationale for what they were doing. Most simply recalled that, as far back as they could remember, the project had always existed and that "this is simply how things have always been done." Until the researcher's idea paper, no one had stopped to ask the simple question, "Why?" or to consider new, alternative technologies. The fact that no one prior to this had been asking "Why?" led upper management to assess the quality and flow of its internal communications. Of special relevance to the study reported in Part Three of this volume is their finding that one of the major pitfalls in communication was the nature of information typically contained in the organization's progress reports. The very format of the progress report, with two headings—*Work Accomplished* and *Future Work*—did little to encourage critical thinking among the researchers. Rather, the format engendered, as one manager put it, "a time-clock and anthill mentality" by conveying to researchers the impression that what mattered most was that they got their work done according to schedule, never mind whether the work was worth continuing or contributed to the company's goals. In the next part of this volume, I will examine in greater detail the importance of progress reports in organizational settings and the notions of progress inherent in different types of progress reports. For now, however, I want to take a slight detour to briefly address a question that is probably in the minds of my readers at this point, and that is how, in a successful, multibillion dollar corporation (and in the corporation's R&D organization at that), those at the helm could not foresee that they were headed for troubled waters.

Newton's Third Law of Thermodynamics states that an object in motion tends to stay in motion. Often a similar law applies in organizations, and the bigger the organization, the more it seems to apply. Given the enormous investment of time, money, and human resources it takes to launch and propel a major project, and given the personal, vested interests that individuals working on the project have in keeping the project afloat, sometimes projects can remain in motion far beyond their usefulness to the company and far longer than even common sense alone would normally allow. In R&D organizations especially, where basic research is not expected to yield an immediate payoff, the more time and money that have been expended, the more difficult it becomes to bail out. Since setbacks are not unusual, it becomes easier in these circumstances to justify negative findings and attribute them to simply the nature of scientific research rather than to a fundamental flaw in concept or design. After all, after investing millions of dollars in a project and working on it for years, it is not easy to admit that the project lacks promise. Many times it takes a force far greater than that which originally set the project in motion to finally still it. Sometimes, as is often the case, it takes an organizational shakeup or an infusion of new managerial blood—top-level executives hired from outside the company—to clear the decks and put the company back on course or to chart new courses.

To switch metaphors, other times, as in the case of the researcher's idea paper, it takes only a tiny spark to ignite and fuel a massive reorganization and redirection of the company's research efforts. In this case, the company phased out the old refining process and developed a new process, all because of a four-page idea paper written by a young, inexperienced, low-level researcher. As for the researcher himself, he received a substantial promotion.

The studies and the examples discussed in this chapter attest to the important role writing serves within organizations—how it both reflects and influences organizational cultures and communities. As Harrison (1987) stresses, "It is important to recognize that the relationship between rhetoric and the community in which it occurs is reciprocal. Communities of thought render rhetoric comprehensible and meaningful. Conversely, however, rhetorical activity builds communities that subsequently give meaning to rhetorical action" (p. 9). To date, most of what we know about the interrelationship between written communication and organizational culture has been based upon only a handful of studies, upon anecdotes, or upon our observations and experiences as teachers, consultants, or practitioners of writing in business and industry.

THE NEED FOR RESEARCH ON
REAL-WORLD WRITING

In his study, Doheny-Farina (1986) laments the fact that there have been so few studies investigating the social aspects of writing in real-world settings. As Doheny-Farina and as Paradis, Dobrin, and Miller (1985) note, one consequence of the dearth of such research is that we have little understanding of the significance, functions, and complexity of in-house organizational writing. Referring specifically to technical writing within industrial settings, Paradis, Dobrin, and Miller suggest that it has been the attitudes among teachers, researchers, and even the practitioners of real-world writing themselves that have retarded such research:

> Writing is commonly viewed as a pragmatic routine of transferring and archiving information. . . . Staff engineers and scientists often do not appreciate that their writing is part of a larger social process by which they create and maintain significant professional relationships with colleagues. . . . [or that their writing] can deeply influence the inner workings and success of their organizations. (pp. 281–282)

As we have seen in the chapters in Part One of this volume, those attitudes seem to be changing. Increasingly, many theorists and researchers are beginning to realize the need to view writing as a social activity. As discussed in Chapter 1, for very practical reasons of their own (namely survival), university English departments are now beginning to take seriously (though still somewhat begrudgingly in some instances) the subject of real-world writing. As Freed and Broadhead (1987) point out, "In its quest to become a discipline, our profession. . . has fostered a desire to study social and cultural systems through and by which writing takes place" (p. 155). We are realizing, in short, that, with our emphasis on school-sponsored writing during the last 30 or so years, we have focused almost exclusively upon our own narrow academic discourse community, one that we ourselves have defined and circumscribed within the educational system. By restricting our studies to primarily the composing processes and products of our own students, as discussed in Chapter 2, we have been a bit shortsighted, even narcissistic or egocentric, in our research and teaching. Or maybe we have been simply naive, misjudging our educational responsibility by thinking that all we needed to do to help students become good writers was to familiarize them with the conventions and standards governing writing within our own academic community. However, as Bizzell (1982) observes, we have not done an adequate job of even that, for, as she argues, a major cause of students' writing problems is that they lack an understanding of our own academic discourse community.

Others (Reither, 1985; Bruffee, 1986; and Cooper, 1986) have underscored the need to make students aware of the importance of viewing writing within the context of various other discourse communities, and to familiarize them with the types of knowledge, conventions, and strategies governing writing in nonacademic settings. Cooper (1986), for instance, emphasizes the necessity of understanding the dialectic underlying the relationship between discourse and community—one in which each acts upon the other and changes the other. This interrelationship between written communication and the organizational culture and community, which has been the focus of the this chapter, is best summarized in Cooper's definition of writing:

> Writing is an activity through which a person is continually engaged with a variety of socially constituted. . . systems: all the characteristics of any individual writer or piece of writing both determine and are determined by the characteristics of all the other writers and writings in the system. (pp. 367–368)

To return to this chapter's epigram, if, as Purves and Purves maintain, it is the culture that finally determines the standards of good writing, then we need to understand how those within cultures and communities other than our own learn and apply those standards, and what criteria that they, as opposed to we in academe, use to evaluate writing.

As preface to the study in Part Three of this volume, the next chapters in

Part Two focus upon the field of technical and scientific writing—the major theories and assumptions of science and technology that underlie our notions about knowledge, information, and progress, and that have led to our models of technical writing. A major premise of the chapters in Part Two is that scientific technical writing, like other forms of writing, is an essentially social activity and that its conventions and criteria are determined by the particular contexts and discourse communities within which it exists.

II
Explorations in Science, Technology, and Communication

Scientific and Technical Writing: What We Know and What We Need To Know

Where is the wisdom we have lost in the knowledge?
Where is the knowledge we have lost in the information?
Where is the information we have lost in the data?

John Seely Brown (1985)

In a twist to a well-known poem by T.S. Eliot, John Seely Brown, of the Intelligent Systems Laboratory of Xerox's Palo Alto Research Center, provides a timely reminder of the real purposes of scientific research and technological innovation. With the increasing specialization in the sciences (and elsewhere), we run the risk, he claims, of losing sight of the reasons we are doing what we are doing and of becoming victims of our own technologies. A century and a half ago, in *Walden*, Thoreau, observing the spread of the intercontinental railroad and the coming of industrialism, similarly warned those of his age that, "We do not ride upon the rails; they ride upon us." Were he writing today (assuming he could find a woods unspoiled enough from which to serenely contemplate civilization's follies), Thoreau might say, "We do not run our computers; they run us." The irony is that, while in our stride toward progress we have gained much, at the same time we have lost much. Most of all, we are losing our sight, both literally and figuratively speaking.

Optometrists (Carr & Francke, 1976) have demonstrated that a society's culture affects how its members see. Other researchers (according to optometrist R. Barabas, 1988, personal conversation) report that, as a nation, Americans have become increasingly more near-sighted during the last 100 years, and especially the last 50 years, due primarily to the nature of jobs that require us to work at close range for extended periods of time. Of all work, the most strenuous on the eyesight is staring at CRTs all day long. Fortunately, we have the technology to correct for myopia so that we can still have the 20–20 vision necessary to see at a distance. But there is no technology in the world that can correct our failing intellectual and moral vision. Indeed, as Brown suggests in his poem, it is the increasing data and information produced by advanced technology that may be blinding us to the knowledge and wisdom we most desperately need to meet today's challenges. Commenting upon today's age of science and technology, Einstein similarly remarked that it is "characterized by the perfection of means and the confusion of goals." As never before in the history of the world, we have the means to amass vast amounts of data and information, but whether all of this has made us any more intelligent or wise is debatable.

James Burke, in his 1978 book and more recent television series, *Connections*, contends that it has not, as he cynically comments on the so-called progress of our times: "Never before," he says, "have so many known so much about so little." Were Burke familiar with the history of composition research during the last 30 years, he might say much the same. In the field of research on scientific and technical writing, however, the opposite is the case: That is, never before have so few known so little about so much.

This chapter briefly explores the relationship between language and science and technology, discusses some studies that have investigated scientific and technical writing within research organizations, explains the situation and the issues that motivated my own study of technical writing within an R&D organization, and discusses the important role that progress reports play in providing decision makers with the information they need to act intelligently and responsibly.

LITERACY IN AN AGE OF TECHNOLOGY

Robert J. Connors (1985) has predicted that, with the increasing emphasis in our society upon information, science, and technology, the new rhetoric of the future will be explanatory rhetoric. "Explanation," Connors notes, "is becoming as important as persuasion in our increasingly complex and intermediated world" (p. 69). While our interest in and understanding of persuasion can be traced to classical rhetoric nearly 2000 years ago, we have only recently within the last 200 years paid much attention to explanation. Until the 1960s, with the rise of composition studies, expository writing had second-class status within English departments. Despite swelling enrollments in business and technical writing courses, functional, explanatory discourse is still regarded as suspect in many traditional English departments—as careerism, or as Smith (1986) puts it, "vocational training for mindless drones: how to fill out job application forms" (p. 570).

One of the reasons for the antipathy toward technology and technical communication, as Smith suggests, has been the attitude among English teachers that literature in the personalistic mode is superior to instrumental

language. As Marx (1964) has shown, a common theme in American literature itself—for example, in the works of Cooper, Thoreau, Melville,
Faulkner, Frost, and Hemingway—has been the evils of technology. According to Smith, teachers who take this literary stance foster in students
the notion that "a curled lip toward technology is a prerequisite for refinement" (p. 569). For technical students especially, this attitude may teach
them a kind of self-hatred. But what this attitude does most of all, as
Professors Mary Coney, Judith Ramey, and James Souther (1984) point
out, is to reveal our own intellectual myopia and xenophobia, our own lack
of understanding and appreciation for disciplines other than ours:

> Whatever the source, this lack of rapport [between the traditional English
> teacher and the contemporary college student] manifests itself as an inability
> to delight in the problems and methodologies that the students grapple with in
> their fields of major study, an unwillingness to perceive the mastery involved
> in successfully communicating information in ways appropriate to their fields,
> and, in the grossest cases, even distaste or contempt for the disciplines that the
> students study. (p. 41)

Smith interestingly observes that, while the study of literature in this
country was originally intended as a means of democratically spreading
literacy among the middle classes, that same belletristic model "now
hampers democracy by impeding the flow of information, and alienates
students from the writing process by making language study seem irrelevant or even obstructive to instrumental goals—elitist, anachronistic, and
impractical" (p. 570). Robinson (1985) further contends that the belletristic
stance is a major obstacle to literacy in today's world—a world in which, as
Smith points out, "the most influential examples of discourse come from
other fields of endeavor, such as politics and technology, and in other forms
than novels or poems, such as televised speeches and interviews and technical reports" (p. 569). What we need to recognize, as Nunberg (1983) points
out, is that literature no longer has the kind of public importance it once did
in the eighteenth and nineteenth centuries when "Men like Johnson and
Arnold hoped that the refinement of English would lead to the perfection of
literature and culture" (p. 40).

This is not to suggest, however, that literature study ought to be aban-
doned in favor of functional discourse. On the contrary, as Smith (p. 568),
using Kenneth Burke's terms, stresses, both modes—the "personalistic"
and the "instrumental"—are technological uses of language, though each
has a different aim:

> We use the technology of language in the personalistic mode to create mythol-
> ogy (including literature), and with it, personal and group identity. We use

the technology of language in the instrumental mode to create all other technologies, thereby materially sustaining—even creating—the selves we identify personalistically. (Smith's personal correspondence with Burke, 1986)

The traditional emphasis upon language as myth making (that is, upon literature) has created, in Smith's words, a "dysfunctional literacy" (p. 568) which handicaps students by giving them the impression that language in its highest form and best use is primarily expressive and literary. An equally important use of language, however, and one that is gaining attention, is its instrumental functions in a world where literacy increasingly means the ability to access, interpret, use, and convey information. Along with this change, Grice (1988) notes that within many companies (for example, IBM) the responsibilities of technical writers have grown to include "information development," and that this expanded view of technical writing has implications for both teachers of technical communication and technical communicators. (For a discussion of the differences between "information development" and traditional "technical writing," see Saar, 1986.).

LANGUAGE, INFORMATION, AND TECHNOLOGY

According to popular lore, the main distinction between literature and technical communication is that in literature a text is viewed an artifact that has intrinsic value in its own right. By contrast, technical communication, as Halloran (1984, p. 44) notes, "views a text as a tool rather than as an artifact, as a means toward some end rather than as a thing of intrinsic value." Smith (1986), however, contends that all texts, whether they are literary or instrumental, ultimately serve some end, even if it is a personalistic one. "The idea of a piece of discourse being good in the abstract, divorced from the context which gives it meaning, is," as Smith claims, "nonsense, like the idea of an elegant machine that does nothing but spin, disengaged" (p. 572).

Justifying the functional aims of literature, however, has always been problematic. In the late 1960s, for instance, I was part of a National Institute of Education federal grant project, the purpose of which was to have English teachers write behavioral objectives for the study of literature—objectives that would specify, in quantitative terms, what students would be able to think or do as a result of reading, for example, Shakespeare's *Hamlet*. Imagine, if you will, trying to reduce to multiple choice items a student's enjoyment or appreciation of literature, and you will get some idea of the impossibility of that project.

In technical communication, the relationship between language and action is more apparent. In the introduction to this chapter, I suggested that the fast pace with which today's technology is advancing makes it increasingly more difficult for us to control it and that, as a result, we run the risk, as Thoreau warned, of becoming "the tools of our tools." One of the ways we lose control of technology, Smith contends, "is by losing control of the language about technology—the vocabulary, the rhetorical forms, the patterns of information storage, retrieval, and exchange" (p. 567). As Russell and Russell (1977) have observed, information is central to our notions of democracy—it "enables the recipient to behave more freely, to have a greater range of choice and decision" (p. 48). To a large extent, progress, and the very quality of our lives, is determined by the quality of our information. Gordon Gecko, the main character in the movie, *Wall Street*, perhaps best summed up the utility of information when he said, "The most valuable commodity I know of is information." As I will discuss later in this chapter in reference to progress reports, sometimes what we regard as failures in technology or failures within an organizational structure are really failures in communication, as for instance in the cases of the Space Shuttle Challenger and the Iran-contra affair, in which decision makers, for different reasons, did not have access to the information they needed to act intelligently. Other times, as in the recent case of the Navy ship, the USS *Vincennes*, which in 1988 shot down an Iranian commercial airliner because it mistook it for an enemy jet, our technology can be so sophisticated that it forces us to make snap decisions on the basis of limited information.

Another example dramatically attests to the important interrelationship between language and technology: the disaster that occurred at the Three Mile Island nuclear power plant nearly ten years ago. According to Mathes (1980), the incident at Three Mile Island was presaged by a memo that warned of the possibility of a meltdown. However, while the memo was grammatically correct and technically accurate, it was apparently unintelligible to those who received it. Testifying before the presidential commission investigating the accident, company officials said that, while they had indeed received and even read the memo, they neither understood it as a warning nor could ascertain from it whose responsibility it was to act. This example, as Smith (1986) notes, illustrates how a failure in communication, in this case the clarity of language, contributed to a failure in technology that had dire human consequences.

While some theorists have attempted to defend the study of technical communication upon humanistic grounds (see, for example; Carolyn Miller's (1979) frequently cited article, "A Humanistic Rationale for Technical Writing"), such appeals, as Dobrin (1985) and Smith (1986) note, often strike a defensive, apologistic tone, one that attempts to claim for technical writing the same lofty, abstract, humanistic aims as those typically ascribed to literature. Such attempts, Smith contends, are futile and ill-founded. A good poem or novel may lift our spirits and souls, and though that in itself is worthy justification enough for literature, it is not going to cure cancer or

AIDS, clean up our hazardous waste, promote world peace, or prevent the greenhouse effect from melting the polar cap and eventually destroying the planet until there is no one left to read or write great literature. In short, even those who cling to abstract notions of literature have, or ought to have, very practical, self-serving reasons for becoming interested in functional, technological communication.

RESEARCH ON SCIENTIFIC AND TECHNICAL WRITING: AN OVERVIEW

Until quite recently, few people have studied scientific and technical writing. The field of technical writing is especially barren of research, partially because, as Anderson, Brockmann, and Miller (1983) explain, technical writing lacks an academic home. The engineering or science departments do not want to adopt it because writing is not their area of expertise, and besides they cannot squeeze it into their curriculum because they have too many other, more important, required courses for their majors to take. The English departments accept it as a foundling that comes with a good dowry (the likelihood of packed courses in technical writing), but they are not quite sure of what to do with it either. Thus, most of our notions about technical writing, as represented in textbooks, journal articles, and the classroom, are based primarily upon what we know about composition; that is, primarily matters of form, such as patterns of exposition and methods of development—those matters about which we know the most and feel the most comfortable. Dobrin (1985b, p. 156) notes that, except in rare cases, "we are not the masters" when it comes to technical writing. Most people teaching it have little knowledge or experience with technical writing, especially as it exists in business and industry. For many of them, technical writing is another "service course" that has been foisted upon the English department; as Hairston (1986, p. 451) notes, "understandably, most of us have little enthusiasm for that kind of teaching." The attitude that functional writing is a less challenging, less respectable, and less noble enterprise than, say, literary, persuasive, or creative writing helps explain why there has been so little research on explanatory discourse. As Hairston further notes, "What we need to realize is that because a certain kind of writing is useful, that [sic] doesn't mean we're teaching it as a service"—though why else we should be teaching it, Hairston does not explain. Thus, contrary to her protestations, to Hairston, writing that is functional and "serviceable" is still inferior to other types of writing.

In research organizations, the attitude that technical writing is merely the transferring of information, "the afterthought of serious research activity" (Paradis, Dobrin, & Miller, 1985, p. 281), persists even among researchers themselves. Rarely is writing recognized as part of the research activity itself, as a social process that creates knowledge and that influences an organization's direction and success. Yet, in their interviews with researchers at Exxon, Paradis, Dobrin, and Miller (1985) found that writing was important in all of these respects and that it figured prominently throughout a project's development.

While a few researchers, such as Paradis et al., have begun to investigate technical writing within organizational settings, the majority of studies on technical writing have focused on readability, layout, and teaching strategies. Gieselman (1980), for instance, in his examination of articles in technical writing journals, found that most articles, such as those in the Society for Technical Communication's journal *Technical Communication*, have been devoted to either the efficiency or effectiveness of written and graphic materials: "A good example of the concern one finds here," he notes, "is the argument that has been carried on for several issues about justified versus unjustified type" (p. 8). Another major journal, *Technical Writing Teacher*, as the name suggests, has focused almost exclusively on pedagogy. Though recent articles have strived for a more theoretical basis, the emphasis of the journal's articles is still upon teaching tips based upon classroom practices rather than upon research findings. The result, as Gieselman (p. 14) points out, is that

> there is a dearth of information on how writers make choices—linguistic, stylistic, or substantive. Nor is there evidence, as King puts it, on how choices (strategies) "will vary according to the writer, according to context (and the expectations the writer brings to his writing), according to the writer's purpose, and according to the audience he has in mind." (King, 1978, p. 199)

Of the few studies that have examined scientific and technical texts, many of them suffer from the same limitations of most composition studies: the failure to examine real texts written in real settings for real communicative purposes. As discussed in Chapter 2, while some studies (e.g., Davis, 1968; Witt, 1976; Frase, 1981; and Faigley & Witte, 1983) have analyzed the effects that stylistic variables have upon the readability of technical texts, the reader-subjects have been college students and the texts either excerpts or dummy passages created for the sole purposes of the experiment. In other studies which have analyzed scientific and technical texts (e.g., Huddleson, 1971; Gopnik, 1972; and de Beaugrande, 1977), the emphasis has been upon the syntactic and grammatical features of scholarly articles published by and for the academic community. While such studies may further refine our understanding of academic, scholarly writing, their relevance to either the teaching or practice of technical and scientific writing in nonacademic settings is doubtful. At best, I suppose, we learn from such studies how those within the academic discourse community can write clearer research articles; how, in other words, we can communicate with each other better. At worst, the emphasis in all of these studies upon form may only further perpetuate the attitude, discussed above, that effective writing is simply a matter of transmitting and documenting information in a readable fashion. The main problem with such studies, in short, is that they analyze structural features of texts *qua* texts without consideration of how those features relate to genuine contexts for communication.

Perhaps the most noted, if not notable, research to date on the nature of real-world technical writing has been that sponsored by the National Institute of Education's Document Design Project. Over the last several years, the Project has produced numerous studies analyzing the readability and usability of public documents, such as tax forms, government regulations, and insurance policies, and, upon the basis of these studies, the Document Design Project (1981) has published guidelines for simplifying technical information for public consumption. In addition to conducting research and publishing a newsletter, *Simply Stated*, the Project, now under the auspices of the American Institutes for Research, has begun to develop, revise, and pilot test technical documents, such as forms, instructions, procedures, and manuals. What began as a research-oriented project that focused primarily on the generic features contributing to a document's readability—its organization, style, and layout—has expanded to include consulting services that examine how well a specific document meets the needs of its intended readers.

Increasingly, researchers are beginning to realize the futility of attempting to examine writing apart from the contexts within which texts are written, read, and used. The recent flurry of interest in scientific and technical writing has led some researchers to study writing within nonacademic organizations. For instance, the study at Exxon ITD by Paradis, Dobrin, and Miller has already been discussed at length in this and previous chapters. The following section examines some other studies that have investigated the nature of scientific and technical writing within R&D settings.

RESEARCH ON SCIENTIFIC AND TECHNICAL WRITING IN R&D ORGANIZATIONS

Lipson (1988) has noted that, "While the public writing of science has been subjected to careful scrutiny, the writing of industrial science has not" (p. 18). As for why so little research has been done on real-world technical writing, Allen (1977) explains that until recently the activities of R&D organizations themselves have seldom been a subject of interest even among the nation's top schools of management. Of the studies that have concerned communication within R&D organizations, most have examined either the sources of information that managers use to solve problems (for example, Fischer, 1979) or that scientists rely upon to generate ideas and to conduct their research (for example, Shotwell, 1970). Within the last decade, however, some individuals interested in the sociology and anthropology of science have investigated the ways in which scientists within organizations transform their research into written reports. (For an excellent review of the literature of the sociology of science, see Bazerman, 1983). A common theme in many of these studies, as discussed below, is the discrepancy between the way in which research evolves and the way in which it is reported.

Latour and Woolgar (1979), studying the activities in a biochemical laboratory, find that in their scientific papers researchers use numerous strategies to mask the circumstances of their discoveries in order to make their work appear more credible. As Bazerman (1983, pp. 168–169) notes, Latour and Woolgar (1979) regard the scientific papers as tactical moves in a chess game that the researchers play in order to establish their credibility, gain credit, and better position themselves to continue the game. In particular, Latour and Woolgar examined two features of texts. First, they analyzed statements for how closely the work, as reported, revealed the actual circumstances of discovery within a specific laboratory. By and large, as Latour and Woolgar found, such circumstantial particulars were avoided because the scientists knew that to include them would make their findings appear less factlike, less generally true, and hence less scientifically credible. Second, Latour and Woolgar examined the texts to reveal how, as part of the research game, scientists are apt to change the rules of the game in their favor and, in effect, raise the ante for competitors. For example, chief among the typical strategies scientists use in their research reports is to discredit the work of others by redefining the grounds for acceptability, while at the same time introducing new criteria to establish the credibility and superiority of the work presently being reported. In their analysis of the research literature on thyrotropin releasing factor (TRF), Latour and Woolgar examine the tactics that research teams use to advance the credibility of their work.

In another study, Gilbert and Mulkay, in their book, *Opening Pandora's Box: A Sociological Analysis of Scientists' Discourse* (1984), also examine the discrepancies between what goes on in the research laboratory and what is reported to the scientific community. Pandora's box, Gilbert and Mulkay explain, "is a metaphor for the remarkably diverse accounts of action and belief" (p. 1) that they found when they interviewed 34 English and American biochemists involved in a chemosmotic controversy, a controversy which for one of the scientists eventually led to the Nobel Prize. Gilbert and Mulkay divide the scientists' discourse into two categories: one, the "empiricist repertoire," and the other, the "contingent repertoire." In their formal scientific articles, scientists use an empiricist repertoire to stress the impersonality and objectivity of their experimental results, or in other words, to make their work appear more credible, just as the scientists in the Latour and Woolgar study attempted to do. However, as Gilbert and Mulkay discovered in their interviews, in their informal conversations about their research, scientists typically use a contingent repertoire, which acknowledges the social factors inherent in their work. As Latour and Woolgar also found in their study, when speaking "off the record," scientists often freely admit the subjective, particular circumstances of their work, though in their published works, few traces of these remain. In their examination of the introductions to scientific articles, Gilbert and Mulkay further show how scientists use the contingent repertoire to point out the deficiencies in other scientists' work, while they use the empiricist repertoire to justify their own work. Finally, Gilbert and Mulkay note that the tension between the empiricist repertoire and the contingent repertoire is not new nor has it gone unnoticed by scientists themselves. In fact, it is often the source of humor among even scientists themselves, as in the widely circulated joke definitions of typical phrases from scientific literature, such as "Three of the samples were chosen for detailed study," which in essence means, "The results of the others didn't make sense and were ignored" (p. 176).

As Knorr-Cetina (1981, p. 95) points out, the discrepancies between what is done in a laboratory and what is reported in a scientific paper have long been noted. She mentions that Robert Merton traces the issue back to Bacon and Leibniz, and she quotes Medawar (1969, p. 169), famous for his observation that the conventions of the research paper not only "conceal but actively misrepresent what happens in the laboratory." In her own study of the research activities of a laboratory investigating plant protein, Knorr-Cetina shows how scientific papers are purged of "the personal interests and situational contingencies" of research and are "inserted into a new framework of reason; in which, quite literally, the work is recontextualised" (p. 99). In the final version of the paper, explanations of why certain methods or materials were employed are expunged, leaving the impression that what was done was all that possibly could be done. Furthermore, and of especial relevance to my study in Part Three, Knorr-Cetina notes that the organizational format of scientific papers perpetuates the myth that the conclusions of research are somehow independent of how the research was conducted. She observes, for instance, that while in scientific research "such distinctions as 'methods,' 'results' and 'discussion' are hopelessly intermingled" (p. 122), in the scientific paper they are cleanly separated by section headings giving the appearance of autonomy.

THE FETISH OF OBJECTIVITY

The above studies raise an important issue for all researchers, regardless of their discipline, and that is to what extent, in our need to appear scientific, objective, infallible, and "scholarly," we are actually thwarting our own attempts to make progress by compromising the very reasons for our doing research in the first place. As Seely Brown suggests in the epigram to this chapter, something inevitably gets lost in the journey from data to information, information to knowledge, and knowledge to wisdom. The conventions of academic, scholarly writing put a high premium on data, information, and knowledge. But what often gets bypassed is wisdom. The difficulty of mediating between the facts as we know them and the facts as we report them to others can present an epistemological stumbling block, if not a moral dilemma. For instance, in the short term, while it may be practical, politic, and self-serving to perpetuate a fictive, idealistic account of reality—or, as Emily Dickinson more eloquently put it in a poem, to "tell the truth, but tell it slant"—in the long term, we run the risk of being proven wrong and discredited, unless of course we are very good at pulling the wool over our colleagues' eyes, or our colleagues are exceptionally dull-witted, or we die young. In other instances, as for example the memoranda written by the Morton Thiokel engineers to upper management before the launch of the Space Shuttle Challenger, there are ethical reasons, involving life and death, for telling the whole truth and nothing but the truth. Thus, whether it is from a pragmatic or moral standpoint, there may be good reasons for remaining true to the facts as we know them.

Referring to the dilemma confronting researchers, in this case researchers of writing, Dobrin (1987) notes that, "The facticity of every writing situation poses a terrible problem for those of us who would publish. If we write an article about a specific situation, it has no generality. But if we enunciate general principles, we are being vapid, for in every specific situation, the principles are overwhelmed by the facts" (p. 6). In a candid critique of the Exxon study he and his colleagues had published a few years earlier, Dobrin further observes:

> It was an attempt to provide disciplinary knowledge. It contained generalizations, tables, a certain veneer of jargon. It may have even proved useful to some people. But I'm afraid that it proved useful only for the reasons that certain mediocre fictions are useful. They present a story about the world which is more manageable and irresistible than fact. (p. 7)

Speaking of the report that, now in retrospect, he wishes he had written, Dobrin says that it would have been "one more true to the facts," a report that would have been nothing more than an intelligent, knowledgeable account of the situation there [at Exxon], one that was both true to the complexities and removed from the quotidian. The interest of such a report would not be that it contributed new specialized knowledge to a discipline. The interest would be anecdotal. The writing of such a report, if it were to have general applicability, would be as difficult as the writing of good fiction. And it would be successful only if, like good fiction, it allowed people to recognize themselves it in. (p. 7)

In an essay entitled, "Left and Right Hands," Jerome Bruner (1973), like Dobrin and the other researchers whose studies are discussed above, comments on the efforts of researchers to make their published work appear scholarly and scientific, and he suggests that such efforts may conceal sources of inquiry which, if revealed, might inspire other ideas for research:

Our articles, submitted properly to the appropriate psychological journals, have about them an aseptic quality designed to proclaim the intellectual purity of our psychological enterprise. Perhaps this is well, though it is not enough.

It is well, perhaps, because it is economical to report the products of research and not the endless process that constitutes the research itself. But it is not enough in the deeper sense that we may be concealing some of the most fruitful sources of our ideas from one another. I have felt that the self-imposed fetish of objectivity has kept us from developing a needed genre of psychological writing—call it proto-psychological writing if you will—the preparatory intellectual and emotional labors on which our later, more formalized efforts are based. (pp. 13–14)

My present aim in the following section is not to forge that new genre of proto-psychological writing that Bruner calls for, but to describe the context within which the seeds for my investigation were sown. These, I hope, will give the reader a better understanding of the concerns and issues that provided the very real and practical grounds for my later theoretical excursions into the nature of science and technology and that helped shape the design of my study.

WHY I WENT TO THE WOODS

To refer once again to *Walden*, early in that work Thoreau states, "I went to the woods because I wished to live deliberately, to front only the essential facts of life, and see if I could not learn what it had to teach, and not, when I came to die, discover that I had not lived." I wish I could say that the motivations for my research were as pure and lofty (and that I had had the luxury of writing this while cloistered in a quiet woods somewhere). Still and all, when I decided to go off to the "woods"—that is, into a corporate R&D setting to study real-world technical writing—it was out of a similar Thoreauean need to try to confront and figure out in my own mind some apparent contradictions between writing, as I understood it from the perspectives of a student and teacher of writing, and writing as I was observing it as a consultant in business and industry.

Generally speaking, composition teachers, like composition researchers, are unaccustomed to dealing with content; their forte is organization and style. Occasionally, they might also introduce some heuristic strategies of invention, if only to offset the students' bewilderment over how to generate ideas for an essay that has no real audience or purpose other than the hypothetical ones contrived for a classroom assignment. By and large, however, composition teachers, whether by inclination or training, usually are not interested in communication but rather in the skills needed to write essays.

Thus, when I began teaching technical writing in R&D departments of corporations, I brought with me the composition teacher's orientation: that is, I focused upon the planning, organization, and style of technical reports—the usual prewriting, writing, rewriting scenario. The matter of content was summarily discussed as the result of an individual's analysis of a specific audience and purpose; identify those and the content problem is solved.

Pretty sound advice, except that it became increasingly clear to me during the researchers' discussions that they had very conflicting notions about the kind of information that their supervisors expected in their progress reports. When I later brought this up at a meeting of the supervisors and directors, they were nonplussed; certainly, they said, their researchers must know what kind of information to include. However, in the ensuing discussion, it became obvious that the supervisors and directors themselves did not agree about the information that ought, or ought not, to be included in their researchers' progress reports.

Poor communication? Poor training? Unspecified expectations? Perhaps. But I suspected that part of the problem was the vague term *information*. All, for instance, could agree that the purpose of the progress report was to inform, but just what the nature of that information should be was a source of disagreement among them. Even the common terms used to describe information and to organize sections of the technical reports, terms such as *data*, *result*, and *conclusion*—terms that everyone thought they knew the meaning of—seemed to blur and to connote different things to different individuals.

This apparent source of dissonance between and among the writers and readers led me to consider other important issues related to the progress report. First was the whole notion of progress suggested by the term *prog-*

ress report itself. Progress concerning what? What the researcher had done during the time period covered by the report? What results the researcher had gotten during that period? What those results meant as related to the objectives of the research project? Or what the researcher thought that the results implied both for the direction of his future work and that of the research project? Some combination of these? Or all of the above?

Clearly, each of these interpretations of progress implies a different sort of report containing different sorts of information that for the writers fulfill different aims and that for the readers serve different ends—ranging from the narrative this-is-what-I did progress report designed to convince management that the researcher is busy and earning his salary, to the speculative or evaluative progress report designed to help management determine the present value and future direction of the project.

Given the purpose of an R&D organization, it would seem likely that readers of progress reports would want the latter kind of progress report. However, such a report carries with it a relatively high degree of risk for the researcher writer when compared with the low-risk of the narrative report of work accomplished. One must keep in mind, too, that progress reports, unlike formal reports written at the completion of a project, are written *in medias res*. Thus, researchers may not know for sure the long-range significance of results that in the short term may appear either significant or insignificant. They may be loathe to stick their necks out for fear of jumping to conclusions that later may turn out to be wrong and that hence might reflect upon them poorly. Furthermore, since researchers often lack the broader perspective of their readers, they may not even see it as their responsibility, much less be able, to second-guess the implications of their work for the project's and the group's larger research goals.

Complicating the issue further is the possibility that, in the different departments and groups of the R&D organization, the nature of progress reports (and thus notions of progress and information) may vary depending upon the nature of the research conducted within a given department or group. Indeed, it is conceivable too that even within work units various research projects may necessitate different kinds of progress reports. Scientists involved in basic research, for instance, normally are not expected to come up with immediate results for application; and, hence, in the majority of their progress reports, they may not be expected to speculate about the significance of their findings. By contrast, engineers working on problems of immediate significance—for example, problems in the daily operation of equipment in a processing plant—may be expected in their progress reports to draw immediate conclusions regarding their research.

This raises another issue concerning the diverse makeup of the individuals within the R&D organization. Some of the researchers are scientists and others are engineers. If, as will be discussed later, these two groups differ significantly in their backgrounds, education, and research activities, then it is possible that they may have different concepts of progress and thus view the goals of R&D quite differently. If so, then the type of information that these two groups emphasize in their progress reports may also differ.

Finally, another issue that I thought might be important in my investigation was the extent to which the stage of a research project might affect the nature of information contained in a progress report. It would seem likely that progress reports written right after a project has been inaugurated might contain quite different types of information than progress reports written in the middle or toward the end of the same research project. Common sense seems to dictate that the earlier the stage of the project, the less likely one would find conclusions in a progress report, and vice versa. However, because of the investment in time, money, and personnel involved in a project's continuance, it seems equally reasonable to assume that the sooner that management knows the likelihood of the eventual success or failure involved in pursuing a particular avenue of research, the better it can make business decisions affecting not only the fate of a particular research project but also the future of R&D and that of the entire corporation.

Researchers, as writers of progress reports, are caught in the dilemma of, on the one hand, maintaining their integrity as scientists and engineers (not to mention maintaining their job security) by withholding evaluation of their research findings until they can make relatively sound, safe conclusions and, on the other hand, providing management with the information they need to assess not only the progress of the ongoing research projects but also the progress of the researchers themselves.

These, then, were the many issues that confronted me as I considered answers to the question that most often plagues writers of progress reports (and, indeed, all writers): What should I include?

THE SIGNIFICANCE OF PROGRESS REPORTS

As mentioned previously in this chapter, although researchers are beginning to explore the nature of technical writing in organizational settings, to date they have studied only the final, published reports of scientists. A more frequent and equally important form of technical writing in an R&D organization, yet one which, to my knowledge, has not been investigated thus far, is the progress report.

The significance of progress reports to the daily operations of a research organization cannot be underestimated, for it is only through the ongoing communication of the results of the departments' various research projects that management can make intelligent decisions regarding the present and future processes and products of the parent corporation. Since progress reports are a primary means by which management keeps its finger upon the pulse of research, a vital sign of the health of an R&D organization is how clearly and effectively researchers—both scientists and engineers—can communicate upwards the information that middle and upper management needs to evaluate the status and progress of a department's projects. The informational content of these reports, then, is of paramount importance, and one measure of an effective progress report is the extent to which researchers are aware of and able to convey the information that management both expects and needs.

This, in a nutshell, is the focus of my study as reported in Part Three. In Chapter 7, which explains the conceptual framework for my study, I will have more to say about both progress and information. For now, however, I would like to conclude this chapter with a couple of cases that clearly illustrate the importance of progress reports.

COMMUNICATION, INFORMATION, AND PROGRESS

Two prominent events in our nation's recent history underscore the importance of good communication and the disastrous consequences when upper management is not kept regularly informed of the work of their subordinates. The first involves the crash of the Space Shuttle Challenger on January 28, 1986, and the second involves the 1985–1986 Iran-contra (also known as Iranscam or Irangate) scandal in President Reagan's administration. In both cases, the presidential commissions appointed to investigate these incidents concluded that failures in human communication were directly responsible for the events that in the first case led to the loss of the space shuttle and the deaths of the seven astronauts, and that in the second case led to the illegal arms-for-hostages deal and the covert funneling of funds to the Nicaraguan contras.

Although these incidents may seem far removed from the present study of progress reports in a corporate setting, they dramatically demonstrate the need for clearly defined channels of communication in any organization, whether it is the highest branch of the federal government, NASA, or a corporation such as Morton Thiokel (the engineering firm that designed and tested the solid rocket boosters on the Challenger). Furthermore, and of greater relevance to the present study, these cases underscore the need for periodic progress reports that provide upper management with the information they need to assess current projects and to make reasoned judgments about the projects' status and future direction. When, as in these two cases, there is a great gulf in the organization's chain of command between those who make the decisions and those who carry out the project, the need not only for regular reporting but also for good reporting is especially crucial.

With that, then, I would like to briefly discuss these cases in order to suggest the ethical and practical issues of internal organizational communication that each case raises, particularly with reference to progress reports and the kinds of information they contain. My reasons for beginning with these cases are as follows: (a) My readers are no doubt familiar with both events; (b) the cases have intrinsic interest; and, most importantly, (c) both cases reveal the subtle relationship between managerial style (or corporate culture) and the quality of an organization's internal communications.

The Case of the Space Shuttle Challenger

The crash of the Space Shuttle Challenger on January 28, 1986, which claimed the lives of its seven crew members, shocked the nation in many ways. First, the launch was televised in schools across the nation, and children witnessed in living color the disastrous consequences of space exploration gone awry. For some of these children, it was their own teacher, S. Christa McAuliffe, who perished in the accident. For most other children, as well as adults, the accident represented a loss of faith in American aerospace technology. In the wake of the accident remained one looming question: Why? Why had it happened? Investigations into that question have created a shock wave nearly as great and as alarming as that of the accident itself. One of the lessons learned from this tragedy has been the importance of open lines of communication and the need to take seriously the progress reports of those most closely associated with research.

Among the major findings in the *Report of the Presidential Commission on the Space Shuttle Challenger Accident* (1986) is that, while the immediate cause of the crash was a failure in the O-ring seals of the shuttle's right solid rocket booster, the primary cause was a failure in communication between the engineers at Morton Thiokel, Inc. (MTI)—the firm that designed the shuttle's rocket boosters—and the NASA officials directly responsible for giving the launch the go-ahead. The main problem, according to the Presidential Commission's study, was that there was no direct line of communication between the MTI engineers who had worked on the shuttle booster's design, tested its safety, and knew of flaws in its O-ring seals, and NASA top management who had the final authority on whether and when to launch the shuttle.

In this case, the MTI engineers' progress reports had little impact, simply because the audience for their reports was limited to MTI management and did not include top NASA officials. Interestingly, and prophetically, several months before the launch, some MTI engineers had tried, unsuccessfully, to persuade their MTI superiors that the O-ring seals of the solid rocket booster might not withstand climatic conditions beyond those of test conditions. One engineer in particular, Roger Boisjoly, was especially vociferous in warning his MTI superiors about the potential hazards of the O-ring erosion problem. In a July 31, 1985, five-paragraph interoffice memo directed to MTI's vice president of engineering, R. K. Lund, and copied to other MTI managers, Boisjoly begins by making clear his aim:

> This letter is written to insure that management is fully aware of the seriousness of the current O-Ring erosion problem in the SRM [solid rocket motor] joints from an engineering standpoint.

Later in the memorandum, after summarizing the erosion problem, Boisjoly twice warns of the consequences of management's "mistakenly accepted position" that they could "fly [the shuttle] without fear of failure." In the third paragraph Boisjoly states that "the result would be a catastrophe of the highest order." His last paragraph underscores his genuine concern:

> It is my honest and very real fear that if we do not take immediate action to dedicate a team to solve the problem, with the field joint having the number one priority, then we stand in jeopardy of losing a flight along with all the launch pad facilities.

In a progress report a couple of months later, on October 1, 1985, another MTI engineer registered even greater frustration and alarm by beginning the Executive Summary of his report with a dramatic, one-word SOS: "HELP!" and concluding his report with this paragraph:

> The allegiance to the o-ring investigation task force is very limited to a group of engineers numbering 8–10. Our assigned people in manufacturing and quality have the desire, but are encumbered with other significant work. Others in manufacturing, quality, procurement who are not involved directly, but whose help we need, are generating plenty of resistance. We are creating more instructional paper than engineering data. We wish we could get action by verbal request but such is not the case. This is a red flag.

Had these reports (which are reprinted along with others in the appendixes to the *Report of the Presidential Commission on the Space Shuttle Challenger Accident*, 1986) been read by NASA officials, it is doubtful that the January 28 launch would have taken place. As it was, however, while MTI managers knew of their engineers' concerns, they did not heed the warnings nor did they convey this information to NASA officials. As for why they failed to do so, in their report the Presidential Commission speculates that it may have been because of the mounting public and political pressures to launch the shuttle since it had already been postponed twice due to inclement weather.

As a sidenote to this episode, while one might think that, after the shuttle's crash and after the Presidential Commission's findings, MTI might have made Roger Boisjoly a hero and promoted him, such was not case. Quite the contrary, Boisjoly was made a *persona non grata* and expeditiously transferred to some desolate place in Utah where he had only a desk and no responsibilities—a safe, remote place from which, presumably, he would cause MTI no further embarrassments. For the worst thing, next to being wrong, is being right, especially when your company, though wrong, persists in thinking it is right. Which goes to show, I guess, that being forthright in progress reports requires a great deal of integrity and risk. In the end, however, the media—if not justice—sometimes prevails. Shortly after the Presidential Commission's study was published, the case of Roger Boisjoly captured national attention and, according to the last news report I read, he was being touted as the unsung hero of the Shuttle disaster. I doubt whether he is still sitting in Utah. Rather, I suspect he has gone on to much greener pastures—that he has been head-hunted by another company offering him triple his former MTI salary, or that he is lying on a beach somewhere writing his memoirs, the rights to which probably have been purchased by Hollywood for a television docudrama mini series. I hope so, for that indeed would be some measure of progress and would prove that sometimes there is justice in this world. And speaking of justice, as for Morton Thiokel, Inc., I last read in the newspapers that the company was filing for bankruptcy due to all the lawsuits filed by the families of the Challenger victims.

Among the lessons to be learned from this case are three: the first for the readers of progress reports; the second for the writers of progress reports; and the third for teachers of technical writing. First, if an organization is going to have researchers go to the trouble of writing progress reports, then readers need to take seriously the information contained in these reports, especially when, as in this case, writers clearly spell out the implications of their findings; otherwise, the very purpose of progress reports is defeated. At Morton Thiokel, management's reluctance to heed the engineers' warnings suggests further problems with the organization's managerial style and its culture. Second, writers of progress reports, despite whatever resistance they might encounter and despite the potential risks to their own job security, need to remain true to themselves and to the facts as they know them. The idea, common among some writers, that they should tell their readers what they (the readers) want to hear, does a disservice to their profession, themselves, and ultimately the company for which they work. As Thoreau in *Civil Disobedience* remarked, "It is truly enough said that a corporation has no conscience; but a corporation of conscientious men is a corporation *with* a conscience." At Morton Thiokel, unfortunately, such conscientiousness stopped short of upper management. This leads me to the third lesson of this case, that for teachers of technical writing. The notion, as discussed previously, that technical writing is simply functional writing—writing that helps get things done—encourages among students a narrow, utilitarian view of writing in which clarity, objectivity, and expediency become the main criteria of effective writing. Inherent in this view is the idea that technical writing is merely the transfer of information, and that the information being transferred somehow exists apart from the writer—that the writer is simply a conduit. Such a view absolves writers of their ethical responsibilities. The case of Roger Boisjoly convincingly demonstrates the need for writers to critically assess the implications of their research and to accept their moral obligation to give readers the information they need to act intelligently and responsibility, even if, as in this case, their readers choose to act irresponsibly.

The Case of the Iran-contra Affair

The Iran-contra affair is quite a different case, one in which the channels of communication were in place but, for whatever reasons, simply were not used. Unlike the Shuttle case in which those at the forefront repeatedly wrote progress reports to try to communicate with and influence top decision makers, in the Iran-contra case apparently few if any individuals directly involved in the arms-for-hostages deal attempted to make known to top decision makers, either verbally or in writing, the nature of their activities.

At the time I am writing this, the investigation of Iran-contra affair is as yet incomplete. By the time this volume is published, perhaps more of the facts surrounding the case will have been established. For now, however, the preliminary investigation by the presidentially-appointed Tower Commission has issued its report, and it is to this report (Tower, Muskie, & Scowcroft, 1987) that I refer.

The issue of President Reagan's managerial style became the focal point of the Tower Commission, which conducted the preliminary investigation into the Iran-contra affair. On February 26, 1987, the Tower Commission made public its report. From its findings, the commission concluded that it was flaws in President Reagan's managerial style—a style based upon the delegation of responsibility—that was primarily responsible for the fiasco. Ironically, at the same time that members of his administration were involved in covert operations, President Reagan's managerial style was being touted publicly as a model for corporate America. *Fortune* magazine, for example, put Reagan on their September 15, 1986 cover, headlining their feature story, "What Managers Can Learn from Manager Reagan" (Dowd, 1986), with this capsule quote from Reagan: "Surround yourself with the best people you can find, delegate authority, and don't interfere." On the cover of the magazine, Reagan looks casual, relaxed, and very much a man in control, just as he usually looks on the six o'clock news.

As the commission revealed, however, Reagan was far from in control of the Iran-contra events. In fact, he may not have even known about the operation at the time, or, if indeed he had been informed of the plan in advance, he later claimed failing memory. As reported on the CBS news (February 26, 1987), President Reagan attempted to lay to rest all of his own conflicting testimonies about what-he-knew-when by issuing the simple statement, "I do not remember, period."

It was the judgment of the Tower Commission that the president probably was telling the truth and that he was not involved in the affair, nor was he, unlike others in his administration, engaged in a coverup. Rather, he was, according to commission, simply "unaware of what was going on." And the reason he was unaware, as John Tower, chairman of the Tower Commission, indicated at the February 26, 1987 televised press conference, was because of his managerial style.

That style, which previously had seemed to work so well, was to decentralize authority by delegating responsibility to key individuals within the administration; in other words, not to hamstring people with red tape and an administrative maze but to let them "do their own thing." While such an approach makes good sense insofar as it encourages people to use their expertise, creativity, and judgment to the fullest extent in order to expedite action and cut through the administrative layers of approval, its success depends a system of review and reporting. The looser the hold a manager has upon the reins of his subordinates' activities, the greater the need for him to be kept informed of their plans, projects, and progress. Otherwise, as the saying goes, the right hand will not know what the left hand is doing. And this, evidently, was the case in the Iran-contra affair.

According to the Tower Commission, the procedure for review was there; it just was not being followed. Quoting from the commission's report during the February 26, 1987 press conference, Brent Scowcroft, a member of the commission, said, "The problem at the heart was one of people, not process. It was not that the structure was faulty; the structure wasn't used." People within the administration failed to brief the president. They did not make use of the existing channels of communication. But the fact that they did not, suggests that there was apparently no pressure upon them to do so. They did not feel that it was an expectation.

Thus, the real fault lay with the president himself. According to Edmund Muskie, another member of the commission, the president "should have followed up more. He did not demand accountability from his subordinates." As was further pointed out, at meetings with his cabinet the president rarely asked questions of any sort of anyone. Some probably interpreted his silence as complete understanding, others as total confidence in them, and still others, perhaps, as signs of creeping senility or utter apathy. Whatever the true cause, evidently it was not part of Reagan's usual style either to expect or to enter into substantive communication (oral or written) with his administration.

At the same press conference alluded to above, a reporter asked John Tower what he regarded as the biggest failing of the president. Tower responded, "not insisting on periodic reviews." Whether those periodic reviews might have been in the form of meetings or written progress or status reports, Tower's implication and that of the commission is clearly that such ongoing communication might have prevented the Iran-contra scandal. As the commission noted, people made decisions indiscriminately and unthinkingly, without regard to the potential consequences of their actions. They could do this only so long as they knew they their scheme would not be subject to scrutiny. If nothing else, better reporting would have encouraged discussion and deliberation. More than likely, the perpetrators of the Iran-contra operation would have been more reluctant to even suggest the plan had they felt they were expected to defend it in writing or in committee for the review of others. Covert operations, by definition, are possible only when information can be concealed.

Democracy is founded upon the belief that our freedom is dependent upon communication: the free flow of ideas and information. That same principle is at work not only in government but in private enterprise as well, though the motivation of the latter is more often profit rather than liberty. Nonetheless, corporations are learning the value of fostering communication between upper management and staff. The current popularity of Westernized versions of the Japanese management style in American corporations attests to a new breed of management that realizes the need to listen to the ideas of those working at the front lines of research, production, marketing, and sales. Managerial decisions that used to be made unilaterally, from the top down, are now giving way to decisions being made upon the basis of input from those at various levels of the organization. And not just because communication is, in and of itself, good, but because it makes good business sense.

In the process, the importance of communication has grown considerably. Unless the channels are there and unless people are expected to use them regularly, the corporation, while it may not face a crisis that approximates the dimensions of the Iran-contra case, may subvert its very own goals. The new management style makes progress reports more important than ever before. Not only that, but the nature of the information contained in progress reports also seems to be changing.

Traditionally, progress reports used to be little more than timecards, reports of work done and work to be accomplished. The more industrious the employee appeared to be, the better the report and presumably the greater the "progress." Today, however, managers need to know more than what someone is doing or will be doing. They need to know the value of the work. They need more than facts; they need assessments, speculations, and judgments to help guide them in their decision making. They need, in short, what Reagan did not get and what he did not insist upon getting. In some corporations in which I have worked, managers, in an attempt to reduce the amount of paperwork generated internally, have eliminated progress reports entirely. That strikes me a dangerous and ineffective way to address the problem of information overload. For when you eliminate progress reports, you may be eliminating progress itself. The result may be the same kind of chaotic, misguided behavior and myopic thinking that the Tower Commission said characterized the Iran-contra affair. You get people who push buttons, fill orders, and make deals for their personal, short-sighted aims. As Seely Brown in the epigram to this chapter notes, somewhere amidst the data and the information, wisdom gets lost.

As I mentioned previously, some of the supervisors in my study said that they would insist upon progress reports if for no other reason than that they periodically forced their people to take stock of their accomplishments and to draw conclusions, however tentative, about the potential significance and implications of their work. Progress reporting, in other words, can help encourage people to think. Certainly President Reagan could have learned a lesson from these supervisors.

The two chapters that follow provide a theoretical and conceptual backdrop for my own study of progress reports. In these chapters, I take a look at the progress that has been made in the fields of science, technology, language, and communication. Then, in the first two chapters of Part Three, I outline the specific objectives and corresponding phases that guided my study of progress reports in an R&D organization.

6
Theoretical Background

*In 1963, the authors of an NCTE [National Council of Teachers of English] report,
Research in Written Composition, openly lamented the state of research in that field:
they found research in composition in the same state as "chemical research as it emerged
from the period of alchemy."*

Introduction to *New Essays in Technical and
Scientific Communication: Research, Theory,
Practice* (Anderson, Brockmann, & Miller, 1983)

One of the problems of a study of real-world technical writing is that on the
one hand there simply is not as yet much research upon which to build.
Studies from the field of composition, as we have seen in Chapter 2, are
seldom concerned with real-world contexts for writing or with writing as a
means of genuine communication. Furthermore, while some researchers
have investigated the importance of writing on the job, for the most part
their studies, as reviewed in Chapter 2, have been limited to surveys based
upon the researchers' own academic standards of school-based writing. On
the other hand, there is a growing body of literature, influenced primarily
by sociology, anthropology, and organizational behavior, that has led some
theorists to explore written communication as a social activity, influenced
by a particular culture and community. In recent years, this social constructionist view of writing, discussed in Chapter 3, has kindled an interest in
studying writing within organizational settings. Some of these studies, reviewed in Chapter 4, have demonstrated how writing both influences and is
influenced by organizational culture.

The previous chapter examined some of the research in the field of
scientific and technical writing, described the circumstances and issues that
initially motivated my study, and discussed two cases that dramatically
illustrate the importance of progress reporting within a large corporation
and within the highest branches of federal government. To understand the
issues underlying my study in Part Three, it is necessary to look to still
other fields of inquiry tangential to the study of technical writing. This
chapter, therefore, is an amalgam of theories on the nature of technical
writing, communication, rhetoric, science, and technology.

Since trying to forge some unity amidst such diversity is a bit like practicing alchemy, let me suggest at the onset two ways in which the following theoretical discussion may help to ground my later investigation.

First, it seems likely that writers of progress reports might share some of the assumptions about technical writing that pervade textbooks and articles on the subject. Perhaps the main assumption is that technical writing, because it deals with scientific matters (or treats a subject scientifically), is thereby objective. Since a belief in this assumption implies other assumptions about the purpose, informational content, and style of a technical report—not to mention assumptions about the nature of communication, language, reality, and knowing—it is important to examine this assumption in detail, as it relates to both technical writing and science itself.

Second, because an R&D organization is a heterogeneous mix of managers, scientists, and engineers assembled for the diverse goals of science, technology, and business, communication among them may be problematic. Each of these groups may have different perspectives, backgrounds, and notions of progress. What's more, when writers of progress reports must address these different audiences within the same report, they may have difficulty determining what or how much information to include. Theoretical distinctions between the aims of science, technology, and business, and between scientists, engineers, and managers, may help us to understand the challenges of communicating within an R&D organization and the potential problems that confront writers within that context.

THE CONVENTIONAL DEFINITION OF TECHNICAL WRITING

> The single purpose of a technical report is to convey a set of facts from the mind of the writer to that of the reader.
> *Technical Report Writing* (Rhodes, 1941)

Since technical progress reports are a form of technical writing, perhaps the best way to launch the upcoming theoretical discussion of the above issues is to examine common notions of technical writing as contained in some of the most popular technical writing textbooks on the market during the last several years.

Although Rhodes' definition in the above epigram is over 40 years old, until recently most definitions of technical writing have not changed substantially. For the most part, technical writing through the 1970s was still distinguished from other types of writing by its supposedly objective (often synonymous with *scientific*) purpose, style, and content. Consider, for example, the following definitions:

Technical communication has one certain clear purpose: to convey information and ideas accurately and efficiently. (Ulman & Gould, 1972, p. 5)

Technical writing is expected to be objective, scientifically impartial, utterly clear, and unemotional. . . . Technical writing is concerned with facts and the careful, honest interpretation of these facts. (Pearsall, 1975, p. 1)

Because the focus is on an object or a process, the language is utilitarian, emphasizing exactness rather than elegance. . . . Technical writing is direct and to the point. (Brusaw, Alred, & Oliu, 1976, p. 475)

Since technical writing is by definition a method of communicating facts it is absolutely imperative to be clear. . . . The point of view should be scientific: objective, impartial, and unemotional. (Mills & Walter, 1978, p. 7)

Most notable about these definitions is the absence of any apparent concern for either the context or the purpose of the report. In the next chapter, I will suggest some other, more recent definitions of technical writing that attempt to account for these elements, but for now let us examine the theoretical assumptions about communication and about language, reality, and knowing upon which the prevailing view of technical writing is based.

THE TRANSMISSION MODEL OF COMMUNICATION

Rhodes' definition of technical writing as the conveyance of "a set of facts from the mind of the writer to that of the reader" is a capsule description of the transmission model of communication that for decades has dominated not only technical writing but business communication and composition theory as well. The model, which was developed around the same time as Rhodes' textbook was published, is derived from the work on information theory by Shannon and Weaver (1949). It is a familiar, simple model that when illustrated often resembles two tin cans and a string. This is no accident since the model represents communication as the transmission of information in much the same way as signals are electronically relayed over telephone lines. Accordingly, the elements of communication are represented as the encoder-channel-decoder, or as the sender-message-receiver.

One of the problems with this model is that it regards communication (and information) as an end in itself rather than as a means toward some end. Pauly (1977) suggests that this obsession with information per se is the heritage of classical liberal and Enlightenment thought, espoused most notably by Locke, who held that, through reason, the human mind "could perceive truth and understand the immutable laws of nature" (p. 12). Based upon a faith in science as reason's gateway to truth and nature, "the transmission model measures all communication (and all knowledge about the world) by the criteria of science" (p. 16). It aims, Pauly notes, "to study communication as a chemist studies molecules" (p. 19).

According to this model, the measure of effective communication is the clarity and precision of the message. As Britton (1975) asserts:

> The primary, though certainly not the sole, characteristic of technical and scientific writing lies in the effort of the author to convey one meaning and only one meaning in what he says . . . the reader must be given no choice of meanings; he must not be allowed to interpret a passage in any way but that intended by the writer. Insofar as the reader may derive more than one meaning from a passage, technical writing is bad; insofar as he can derive only one meaning from the writing, it is good. (p. 10)

While it would seem that the problems inherent in such a view of language and communication would be apparent to anyone who uses words to speak or write, the transmission model continues to influence much of the current research on writing.

It has spawned a host of studies that attempt to account for either how writers encode ideas into texts or how readers decode ideas from texts. One of the byproducts of the latter research has been the tremendous emphasis in recent years upon readability formulas (for example, Gunning's Fog Index) that presumably measure the effectiveness of written texts by such things as the mean number of words per sentence. The corollary in composition studies, as was discussed in Chapter 2, has been the attempt to quantify the quality of essays by the number of T-units, clauses, propositions, or cohesive devices.

Given the traditional definition of technical writing as the objective rendering of an objective reality, it is easy to see why the transmission model of communication has had such appeal and why technical writers are so often enamored of readability formulas that purport to provide a seemingly scientific way of assessing the effectiveness of communication. Furthermore, to think of writing in terms of the packaging, shipping, and receiving of information has a high-tech, industrial appeal, evoking images of conveyor belts and impressions of efficiency and productivity.

The main limitation of the transmission model of communication, as well as the studies alluded to in Chapter 2 and the definitions of technical writing quoted above, is the failure to account for the contexts within which texts are created, comprehended, and used. A message, however potentially clear and readable, has no meaning apart from the text that transports it and the situation in which it is transported. To speak of a message being *encoded* assumes, further, that the message has a pre-textual existence—that, for example, there is a mental language (*mentalese*) that is different from the natural language into which the message is encoded and from which the message is decoded.

REALITY, LANGUAGE, AND KNOWING

As many have pointed out (for example, Halloran, 1978; Miller, 1979; and Dobrin, 1983), the traditional view of technical writing, as well as the transmission model of communication, is based primarily upon positivist assumptions about the nature of reality, assumptions rooted in Cartesian rationalism and reflected in the universalist, *windowpane* theory of language. Briefly, and simply put, this theory, as described by Dobrin (1983, pp. 234–35), holds that (a) there exists a world out there independent of the human mind, (b) that reality is logical, systematic, and governed by natural laws and, hence, that it is knowable, (c) thus, by properly applying our minds we can know the world, and (d) through the precise use of language we can accurately represent the objective reality of the world.

This separation of reality, knowing, and language, each of which supposedly exists independently but which together ideally mirror each other, has been challenged on several grounds. Some of the major criticisms of this view were discussed in Chapter 3, which examined social theories of communication. The following extends that discussion by focusing on science.

Reality and the Mind

First, many philosophers, sociologists, and historians of science—most notably Fleck (1979), Kuhn (1970, 1977), Lakatos (1978), and Rorty (1979)—have emphasized the highly conceptual, consensual, and contextual nature of truth and reality. Hanson (1958), for example, has aptly illustrated the conceptual nature of facts in science by comparing how Kepler and Brahe each considered "the same" phenome*non* quite different phenome*na*. Although Kepler and Brahe were stimulated by the same "optical sensibilia," each perceived quite different "facts" as they watched the sunrise. Accordingly, Hanson contends that theories of science are nothing more than conceptual gestalts. To Fleck (1979), conceptual gestalts are thought styles (*Denkkollektiv*), and he interestingly demonstrates how the thought style of the seventeenth century influenced anatomical illustrations that distorted reality. To Kuhn (1970), the conceptual gestalts of a science are paradigms, or as he later called them, disciplinary matrixes—a set of shared theories and methods that for a time govern how scientists perceive and interpret the world. When enough anomalies challenge the accepted paradigm, that is, when other theories seem to explain the world better, a gestalt switch occurs and scientists turn to gathering other facts to support the emerging paradigm. Such gestalt switches, according to Kuhn, are at the heart of scientific revolutions.

Similarly, Lakatos (1978, p. 2) contends that "there can be no valid derivation of a law of nature from any finite number of facts," and that theories, contrary to accepted scientific lore, do not support facts but vice versa: We look for, and indeed create, facts to support our theories. Thus, facts, like perception, are theory-laden.

That facts are manufactured to sanction our currently accepted view of reality is inherent in the derivation of the word *fact*. Knorr-Cetina (1981) observes that "the etymology of the word 'fact' reveals a fact as 'that which has been made,' in accord with its root in the Latin *facere*, to make. Yet we tend to think of scientific facts as given entities and not as fabrications" (p. 3).

This faith in facts as objective entities is fostered by our faith in the scientific method and in scientific reasoning as the only route to truth. As Lakatos (1978, p. 2) points out, however, scientific experiments can be constructed to prove almost anything. As an example, he cites the vast seventeenth-century literature on witchcraft, "full of reports of careful observations and sworn evidence—even of experiments." Lakatos further notes that "Glanvill, the house philosopher of the early Royal Society, regarded witchcraft as the paradigm of experimental reasoning."

Language and Reality

Similar to this spurious one-to-one correspondence between a fact and our cognition of that fact is what Steiner (1975) calls the universalist view of language in which words have fixed, precise meanings apart from the context within which words are uttered. In reference to technical writing, Miller (1979) calls this the windowpane theory of language, a theory that claims for language a transparent, objective view to reality. Britton's one-word/one-meaning criteria for technical writing, as quoted earlier, is the popularized version of this theory.

In criticism of this theory, Dobrin (1983), points out, as have many linguists before him, that "language is not information. The image of language as discrete units comes from our picture of the dictionary in which each word has 'n' meanings" (p. 233). To treat a sentence as though it were a mathematical equation of concatenated dictionary definitions, as some developers of artificial languages have attempted to do, simply does not work. The same word, sentence, or entire discourse, when uttered in different situations and to different individuals can mean quite different things. Thus, the humor in the cartoon that depicts a drowning man calling to the person on shore, "Give me a hand!" and the person on shore responding by applauding. In an operating room, the same imperative sentence uttered by a surgeon who is reattaching a limb would have quite a different meaning, and still another meaning at a poker table when uttered by a losing player to the dealer as he is passing out the cards. Meaning is indeterminate without context. Though this is part of the tacit knowledge that people have about language use—for otherwise they could not communicate—the idea of a univocal language still persists, especially among technical writers.

The notion that writers or speakers search for words to fit their knowledge—just as their knowledge in turn is fit to reality—assumes that knowledge and ideas, like reality, have a pre-existent, nonverbal life of their own. This view has been challenged on the grounds that knowledge, thought, and language are inseparable and that, if anything, language gives rise to ideas, rather than the other way around.

Language and Knowing

In his book *Thought and Language*, Vygotsky (1962) contends that "Thought is not merely expressed in words; it comes into existence through them" (p. 125). Lewis (1977, p. 24) points out that many writers, including Mallarme, Proust, Joyce, and Kafka, "have powerfully demonstrated that their thought takes form only as they are writing, that their art is fully conceived only at the moment when it receives verbal formulation."

Even Humbolt, the father of linguistics, recognized the reciprocity of language and knowing. As Steiner (1975) summarizes his ideas: "Language does not convey a pre-established or separately extant content, as a cable conveys telegraph messages. The content is created through the dynamics of statement" (p. 82). Interestingly, though he was writing long before the transmission model of communication was developed by Shannon and Weaver, Humbolt, in attacking such a view of communication, uses the same metaphor upon which the model was later based.

Other linguists, notably Sapir and Whorf, have further suggested that the language of a particular culture governs the perception and thought of its members. In Whorf's famous example of the Hopi Indians, he contends that because of their language, the Hopi do not think of time as past, present, and future but as time-distance. Whorf's conclusion, as explained by Steiner (1975, p. 88), is that "There is, so far as human consciousness goes, no such entity as a universally objective physical reality"; rather, that, in Whorf's words, "We dissect nature along lines laid down by our native language." The syntax and the lexicon of a language determine modes of perception, thought, and response—*thought worlds*, according to Whorf— which may be quite different from those of groups using different language systems. Whorf's idea that "different linguistic communities literally inhabit and traverse different landscapes of conscious being" (Steiner, p. 89) is similar to Kuhn's idea that scientists of different paradigms (different thought worlds), though they may use a common language, seldom understand one another.

Finally, two studies have demonstrated how the terminology used to describe phenomena can sometimes lead scientists to false assumptions and theories about the phenomena. Fleck (1935), in his analysis of the development of the Wasserman test, discusses how, for a long time, the different terms for syphilis prevented an understanding of the disease and led researchers down blind alleys. Similarly, Bazerman (1983, p. 167) refers to a study by Zuckerman (1975) in which the misnaming of bacteria as *schizomycetes* (that is, bacteria that reproduce only through asexual splitting) severely retarded research in that area.

As suggested in the foregoing discussion, the conventional view of technical writing as objective is based upon isomorphic conceptions of reality, knowing, and language. Reduced to its simplest, most naive form, this view holds that reality is refracted upon the mind, and that the mind in turn reflects that reality through language. The aim of the technical writer, thus, is to minimize distortion of perception and presentation, or, as the transmission model of communication represents it, to reduce the *noise*. Ideally this is accomplished by purging from writing of all traces of human intervention, through avoiding, for instance, the active voice and connotative words. It is accomplished especially by eschewing anything resembling "rhetoric."

SCIENCE AND RHETORIC

With the aim of communication as the conveyance of objective, factual information, it is little wonder that technical writing is often considered a-rhetorical. For, if facts speak for themselves, what need is there for persuasion? Accordingly, rhetoric is usually regarded as anathema to technical writers—at best deception and puffery; at worst effusive self-indulgence. Listen, for example, to MacIntosh (1973), who claims for technical writing the typical virtues of "clarity, conciseness, precision, and logic," virtues, which he adds, are "not the qualities evident in devotees of orgasmic rhetoric and ejaculatory style" (p. 28). While Cox and Roland (1973) admit that rhetoric cannot be totally avoided, they find it equally repugnant:

> Rhetoric is defined as language designed to persuade or impress; the word may be considered a euphemism for loaded language. . . . Anyone who is convinced that only facts should persuade must, logically, condemn such rhetoric in scientific literature. Realistically, of course, rhetoric cannot be eliminated entirely. But its use can be constricted significantly, and both readers and writers should be on guard against this violation of scientific principles. . . . Since scientists agree that their observations and conclusions should be presented as objectively as possible, rhetoric should be avoided assiduously in scientific writing. (p. 140)

This dichotomy between science and rhetoric is also evident among rhetoricians such as Kinneavy (1971), who, in his scheme of discourse aims—the expressive, referential, literary, and persuasive—relegates scientific, informative, and exploratory discourse to the referential category. As many have noted (for example, Miller, 1979; Weimer, 1977; Halloran, 1978; and Bazerman, 1983), the aim of science has traditionally been truth, while the aim of rhetoric has been persuasion. Miller (1985) explains that scientific discourse was excluded from classical rhetoric because its aim—demonstrable truth—was viewed as quite different from that of rhetoric—matters of probability and opinion. Halloran (1978) traces the separation of science and rhetoric to Aristotle, who maintained that rhetoric was the discovery of the available means of persuasion used in public oratory to address ordinary citizens. These means of persuasion were universal and common *topoi* available to and understood by anyone. In contrast, Aristotle held that the sciences used specialized or esoteric propositions—"special *topoi*"—to address expert practitioners in a particular field of knowledge.

With the development of modern science during the Renaissance, the gulf between science and rhetoric widened further as science became the method of discerning truth by the demonstration of logical proofs, and rhetoric became the influence of minds by the ornamental use of language.

According to Weimer (1977), the view of science as the accumulation of truths proven by logic or dialectic is an extension of the classical belief that geometry was the highest, most perfect form of knowledge. He suggests that "Compared to the beauty and perfection of eternally valid and certain Euclidean systems, mere empirical knowledge seemed flawed and degraded" (p. 2). For the Greeks, science was mathematics and mathematics was certain knowledge. Weimer proposes that this fusion has since dominated Western epistemology so that science has become equated with mathematical derivation, and knowledge has become identified with proof and certainty.

Today, more than ever, social, moral, and political issues are debated upon scientific grounds and in highly technical language. The public's faith in scientific evidence as the touchstone of knowledge has not waned a bit and statistics still sway, whether it is a matter of strategic weapons or toothpaste. The apparent invincibility of facts and the scientific aura of technical jargon have become themselves a mode of discourse and a means of persuasion. As Connors (1983) notes, even in composition studies, a field he contends does not lend itself to strict scientific study and quantification, many researchers have become so enamored with quasi-scientific means for describing the composing processes of writers and for measuring the quality of texts that they have become blinded by their own assumptions and methodologies.

That science itself is a mode of rhetoric is a view that has become increasingly popular among scholars of science. Overington (1977) suggests that science as a knowledge-producing activity is essentially rhetorical "*because* the construction of scientific knowledge involves argumentation before an audience" (p. 144). Ziman (1968) and Polanyi (1964) similarly contend that scientific research is not a quest for truth but a quest for agreement. An important point for Ziman is that publication makes research public and thereby available to scrutiny by the "invisible college" of scientific scholars upon whom acceptance and consensus depend. Publication itself does not turn research into knowledge.

For Popper (1962), science is criticism. Overington (1977), summarizing Popper's thesis, states that "Science is one among many forms of human myth-making that is distinguished from all other traditions of myth production by a second order tradition, that of critically discussing the myths" (p. 151). But upon what basis do scientists critically evaluate scientific myths? Upon what grounds do they accept or reject theories? What is the initiation rite for membership into the invisible college? In short, what are the rhetorical means of persuasion in science?

Zappen (1983) contends that all theories of rhetoric for science are object-oriented, that is, that all of them have as their aim the reconstruction of the objective world, but that rhetorical theories of science can be classified by the different ways in which they attempt to validate its reconstruction. He proposes the following three rhetorical categories: symbol-oriented (language-oriented) rhetoric, speaker- or writer-oriented rhetoric, and listener- or reader-oriented rhetoric. Since Zappen's work is one of the few to provide a systematic way of conceptualizing the issues surrounding science and rhetoric, the following will examine his framework more closely.

Language-oriented Rhetoric

The first, language-oriented rhetoric, is represented by Korzybski (1958), who, influenced by the new mathematical physics of Einstein, Minkowski, and others, attempted to establish a universal mathematical language for science and society. The ambitious aim of such a language, according to Korzybski, was "to match our verbal structures, often called theories, with empirical structures, and see if our verbal predictions are fulfilled empirically or not, thus indicating that the two structures are either similar or dissimilar" (p. 63). In essence, this is the windowpane theory of language discussed earlier in which words are presumed to have definite referents to external realities. Similarly, Korzybski's notion of a universal language free of ambiguity or misinterpretation is similar to Britton's one-word/one-meaning criterion for technical writing. As Zappen points out, apart from the impossibility of constructing a universal language, the problems with this theory are, first, that some theories, like Einstein's theory of relativity, for example, cannot be confirmed; and, second, even if words could objectively symbolize empirical phenomena, it does not follow that our theories about that phenomena are therefore correct.

Speaker- or Writer-oriented Rhetoric

Zappen uses Polanyi's work to represent the second category of rhetorical theories, speaker- or writer-oriented rhetoric. To Polanyi (1962), the criteria for the evaluation and acceptance of scientific theories are essentially matters of personal commitment to "universal intellectual standards" (p. 303) regarding facts, knowledge, proof, reality, and the like. As Polanyi insists, these "universal standards" are "impersonally" established by the consensus of scientists, but for the individual they exist as matters of personal faith: "Unless ye believe, ye shall not understand" (p. 266). One problem with this view is that standards may be only relatively "universal"; that is, they may only appear to be "universal" because, at a certain time and place within the history of the world, the scientific community has sanctioned them as such. Another difficulty with such a rhetorical theory for science, as Zappen points out and as Polanyi himself admits, is that without an established community of believers (without Ziman's invisible college), the theory leads to controversies that can be resolved only by the persuasive powers of the individual scientist. In other words, science is another form of rhetoric.

Audience-oriented, or Context-oriented, Rhetoric

Audience-oriented rhetorics reject the personal standard of judgment in favor of standards that reside within the collective audiences, or contexts, of science or technology. Zappen examines three versions of context-oriented rhetoric as represented by Popper (1962), Kuhn (1970), and Toulmin (1972). Although all three locate the criteria of evaluation and acceptance within the scientific community, each differs with regard to the nature of these criteria and the nature of the scientific community.

To Popper, "the criterion of the scientific status of a theory is its falsifiability, or refutability, or testability" (Popper, p. 37). This criterion, for Popper, is based upon a scientific method common to all scientific communities. Lakatos (1978), however, claims that theories cannot be proved or disproved, and that "exactly the most admired scientific theories simply fail to forbid any observable state of affairs" (p. 16). He illustrates this with an imaginary case of planetary behavior, which I will quote here in its entirety since it amusingly depicts a course of scientific research that, on a smaller scale, may represent what occurs in R&D programs when scientists assume the validity of accepted theories.

A physicist of the pre-Einsteinian era takes Newton's mechanics and his law of gravitation, (*N*), the accepted initial conditions, *I*, and calculates, with their help, the path of a newly discovered small planet, *p*. But the planet deviates from the calculated path. Does our Newtonian physicist consider that the deviation was forbidden by Newton's theory and therefore that, once established, it refutes the theory *N*? No. He suggests that there must be a hitherto unknown planet *p'* which perturbs the path of *p*. He calculates the mass, orbit, etc., of this hypothetical planet and then asks an experimental astronomer to test his hypothesis. The planet *p'* is so small that even the biggest available telescopes cannot possibly observe it: the experimental astronomer applies for a research grant to build yet a bigger one. In three years' time the new telescope is ready. Were the unknown planet *p'* to be discovered, it would be hailed as a new victory of Newtonian science. But it is not. Does our scientist abandon Newton's theory and his ideas of the perturbing planet? No. He suggests that a cloud of cosmic dust hides the planet from us. He calculates the location and properties of this cloud and asks for a research grant to send up a satellite to test his calculations. Were the satellite's instruments (possibly new ones, based on a little-tested theory) to record the existence of the conjectural cloud, the result would be hailed as an outstanding victory for Newtonian science. But the cloud is not found. Does our scientist abandon Newton's theory, together with the idea of the perturbing planet and the idea of the cloud which hides it? No. He suggests that there is some magnetic field in that region of the universe which disturbed the instruments of the satellite. A new satellite is sent up. Were the magnetic field to be found, Newtonians would celebrate a sensational victory. But it is not. Is this regarded as a refutation of Newtonian science? No. Either yet another ingenious auxiliary hypothesis is proposed or. . . the whole story is buried in the dusty volumes of periodicals and the story never mentioned again. (pp. 16–17)

The tenacity with which scientists cling to their theories is also a central idea in Kuhn's work. Unlike Popper, Kuhn locates the criteria of a scientific theory within the particular paradigm of a particular scientific community. Since competing paradigms are based upon competing criteria, this leads to what Kuhn (1970) calls "the incommensurability of standards of competing paradigms" (p. 149), or the lack of any absolute criteria by which to evaluate either the standards or the paradigms. To Kuhn, "As in political revolutions, so in paradigm choice—there is no standard higher than the assent of the relevant community" (p. 94).

Finally, Toulmin (1972), unlike Kuhn, argues that there are continuous, general standards of judgment and that these are located not, as suggested by Popper, in all scientific communities, but in specific disciplines of science and technology. These standards of judgment vary from discipline to discipline, each with its own scientific concepts, goals, problems, and methodologies.

Zappen recommends Toulmin's brand of context-oriented rhetoric for research in sciences and technologies, but he suggests that the theory needs to be expanded to account for the various other audiences and real-world contexts that practitioners of science and technology have to consider. These are the audiences and contexts of the intellectual discipline; the business, industrial, or military organization; the government regulatory agency; and the private or government funding agency. Each of these, according to Zappen, has its own criteria and standards of acceptability that determine conventions of discourse and means of persuasion that may be quite different from those of science.

Zappen, however, does not discuss in any detail the context of the business, industrial, or military organization except to say that researchers in these organizations must address "diverse goals, current capacities, problems, and criteria of evaluation that derive from and operate within the organization. These may include reasonable cost and ease of manufacture, limits of liability, employee safety and satisfaction, public health and safety, and protection of the environment" (p. 132).

Seemingly, these pragmatic criteria have little to do with the intellectual criteria of science. However, as will be discussed shortly, practical considerations often influence the research activities of an organization. When, as in the case of an R&D organization, those activities are both scientific and technological, researchers may find it difficult to determine which set of criteria—the pragmatic or the intellectual—governs their work and the evaluation of that work as presented in technical reports.

As I will suggest later in Part Three when discussing the findings of my own study, Zappen's three categories of rhetoric may provide a way of distinguishing the different criteria that readers and writers of progress reports use to evaluate the importance of the information contained in the reports: whether they point to criteria that are language-oriented (for example, the clarity and precision of the information), criteria that are writer-oriented (for example, personal belief in the significance of the information), or criteria that are audience-oriented (for example, information that satisfies the needs of the readers and the goals of the organization).

For now, let us turn to another theoretical distinction that has implications for the activities of an R&D organization and for notions of progress that may subtly influence the informational content of progress reports: the distinction between science and technology.

SCIENCE AND TECHNOLOGY

In theory at least, science and technology can be distinguished by their audience, aims, means of persuasion, and products. In practice, however, there is often a symbiotic relationship between the two, especially in an R&D organization.

Zappen (1983) suggests that the philosophical distinction between science and technology "derives ultimately from Aristotle's distinction among three kinds of science—theoretic, practical, and productive—or sciences of knowing, doing, and making" (McKeon, 1973). To the sciences of knowing belonged metaphysics, mathematics, and physics; to the sciences of doing belonged politics and ethics; and to the sciences of making belonged such arts and crafts as medicine, architecture, cobbling, and rhetoric. Since Aristotle's time, the first, knowing, has been equated with science, and the third, making, with technology.

Toulmin, for instance, notes that the goals of science are explanatory, while those of technology are practical. Similarly, Skolimowski (1966) suggests that both the aims and means of science and technology are different: "Science aims at enlarging our knowledge through devising better and better theories; technology aims at creating new artifacts through devising means of increasing effectiveness" (p. 376). As Skolimowski points out, in technology, problems are investigated *not* with an eye to increasing knowledge but with an eye to a solution of a technical problem. An important difference between the two, then, is that whereas science *investigates* the reality that is given, technology *creates* a reality according to human designs. One of the products of technology, according to Dobrin (1983), is technical writing itself—for example, manuals and instructions that accommodate technology to the user.

The criteria used to evaluate the products of science and technology are also different. In science, the critical issue is whether something is true; in technology it is whether something is useful, faster, more durable, more reliable, more sensitive, or some combination of these. As Skolimowski notes, however, in technology these criteria are often weighed against two other criteria that are based upon sheer business economics: reduced time and cost of production. These differing criteria of science and technology further imply different concepts of progress. Whereas scientific progress is commonly viewed as the advancement of knowledge, technological progress is commonly measured by effectiveness of product and efficiency of production.

A common assumption is that scientific progress provides the basis for technological progress, that in research programs there is a continual progression from basic science to applied science to development. This same idea of "progress" as the accretion of knowledge which is later put to practical use also characterizes the views of many composition theorists, such as Gieselman (1986), who contends that academic theories of writing ought to inform the practice of writing. In response to charges that researchers of writing are too biased in the direction of theory alone, Gieselman counters, "My answer is that it is impossible to be too theoretical! Yes, the academy is a 'theory factory.' That's what we academicians are being paid to produce. That's how knowledge is created and disseminated. Without it, the profession would rapidly stultify; soon, it would wither and die" (p. 10). There is little doubt that the state of composition research has advanced since 1963 when, as quoted in the epigram to this chapter, an NCTE report found it in the same state as "chemical research as it emerged from the period of alchemy." However, whether that progress can be attributed to academic theories of writing is doubtful; rather, as discussed throughout Part One of this volume, that progress seems to have come *despite* academic theories and research, and largely as a reaction *against* academic notions of good writing.

In the field of science, too, the assumption that theory guides practice (rather than vice versa) appears to lack foundation either in the historical accounts of science and technology or in the practices of R&D organizations. Allen (1977, p. 48) notes that "it is becoming generally accepted that technology builds upon itself and advances quite independently of any link with the scientific frontier, and often without any necessity for an understanding of the basic science which underlies it." Allen further contends that entire civilizations have often emphasized science or technology to the exclusion of the other. He cites as examples the Greeks, who were very active in science but relatively unconcerned with the practical applications or implications of their discoveries, and the Romans, who developed a highly technological civilization more concerned with the practical physical and social environment than with theoretical sciences. Allen further contends that these independent paths can be traced through history to the present time.

Supporting evidence that refutes the idea of technology as something "growing out of" science is presented by Price (1965), who, upon the basis of his investigations of citation patterns in scientific and technological journals, concludes that science and technology progress quite independently of one another. Other studies of specific technological achievements (Sherwin & Isenson, 1967; IIT Research Institute, 1968; Battelle Memorial Institute, 1973) have found that the advancement of technology is not precipitated by scientific theories or discoveries. In fact, Morton (1965), upon the basis of his studies of electronics and microwaves, proposes that the reverse is quite often the case—that technology defines for science important problems for investigation.

Science often has to play catch-up to technological innovations in order to provide the basic research to support some new product or process. In many cases, technological discoveries can redirect the course of a corporation or revolutionize an entire industry. A good example of the former is the accidental discovery of NutraSweet™ by a researcher at G. D. Searle, a pharmaceutical company that subsequently developed an extensive research program geared toward supporting the company's new nonpharmaceutical venture and that led to a multibillion enterprise larger than that of the parent company. An example of the latter—a technological discovery that revolutionizes an entire industry—is the invention of the computer, which has generated new avenues of scientific research in medicine, education, and aerospace, to name but a few.

SCIENTISTS AND ENGINEERS

Given the different aims of science and technology, it is not surprising that the literature reveals that scientists and engineers often have quite different educational backgrounds, perspectives, goals, and even personalities. As reported by Allen (1977), in their study of engineering and science undergraduates Krulee and Nadler (1960) found that students majoring in science placed a greater value on independence and education for its own sake, while students majoring in engineering valued education as a means to a career. In the same vein, Ritti (1971) found a sharp contrast between the work goals of engineers and those of scientists after graduation. Whereas the engineers are more concerned with the internal goals of a company, such as meeting schedules and developing products, scientists, though they are also concerned with career development, more often tie their professional advancement to the reputation they establish outside the company. For Ph.D. scientists, publication of results and professional autonomy are clearly valued goals, but for baccalaureate engineers these goals are the least valued. Allen suggests that level of education is the most crucial difference between scientists and engineers in research organizations. Scientists, he claims, are almost always expected to have a doctorate, whereas the majority of engineers have only a bachelor's degree, a few the master's, and some no college at all. Furthermore, an article in *Chemical and Engineering News* (1982) reports that, compared with chemists, chemical engineers are less verbal and tend to have poorer communication skills. The same article, however, contends that chemical engineers, since they are more gregarious, aggressive, and quick to make practical decisions, make better managers than do chemists, who tend to work alone or who supervise only a small group of people in a laboratory.

Allen (p. 35) notes that in studies of the activities of scientists and engineers the usual practice is to combine the two groups and call them all *scientists*. "This approach," explains Allen, "totally neglects the vast differences between the two professions," and is "especially self-defeating in information use studies because confusion over the characteristics of the sample has led at times to what would appear to be conflicting results."

To my knowledge, studies of written reports in research organizations have not distinguished between the reports written by scientists and those written by engineers. Rather, most of the studies have been of the published reports of research scientists. One variable, then, that my study in Part Three will examine is what differences, if any, there are in the types of information contained in the progress reports written by engineers versus those written by scientists.

SCIENTISTS AND MANAGERS

Research suggests that the differences between scientists and managers may be even greater than the differences between scientists and engineers. Kornhauser (1963) and McLeod (1978) propose that the issue of basic versus applied research is central to the communication problem between professional scientists on the one hand, and business or industrial management on the other. Professional science tends to favor contributions to knowledge per se rather than profits; and long-term, high-quality research rather than short-term, low-cost research. These differences, as suggested previously, breed conflict of values and goals—a conflict that has been examined by several other researchers in addition to Kornhauser and McLeod (for example, Marcson, 1960; Evan, 1965; Pelz & Andrews, 1966; Smith, 1970; and House, Filley, & Kerr, 1971).

McLeod (1978) summarizes the communication problem between scientists and managers as follows:

> Management is naturally and understandably interested in speedy, low-cost production of a marketable product, but is often uncertain how to communicate to its research scientists its need for essentially applied rather than theoretical research. On the other hand, the scientist often fails to persuade management that his research budget should not be cut, and that his work cannot be subjected to the same type of cost-effectiveness studies or manufacturing standards that are applicable to production departments. (p. 28)

One of the issues I therefore sought to investigate in my own study is whether or not researchers and their supervisors and directors would value the same type of information in progress reports. If scientists are indeed more concerned with the results of their research than with the practical implications of those results for the company, their progress reports may lack the type of information that management needs to determine the potential benefit of their work. However, there is another reason that their reports may seldom contain such information. Although progress reports are written frequently during the course of a project, scientists, particularly those engaged in long-range exploratory research, may not be able to determine the practical significance of their work until late in the project. Their early progress reports, therefore, may not contain anything more than information on what was done, how it was done, and why it was done. In addition, if, as suggested previously, scientists tend to withhold judgment until all the facts are in, they may be reluctant to draw tentative conclusions in their progress reports, even though this may be the very type of information that their readers expect and need.

Toward A Conceptual Framework for the Present Study

Writing in organizations differs from that done in the classroom in that, as initially experienced by the writer, the organizational context is unknown. . . . The information, arguments, and justifications that will be considered relevant and persuasive may not be logical or intuitive. Finally, the style of organizational documents may be idiosyncratic and may, in fact, be dictated by informal rules in the organization.

Harrison (1987, p. 17)

As discussed in the previous chapter, the traditional view of technical writing as the scientific and objective representation of an objective reality, and the corresponding model of communication as the clear transmission of information, have recently been criticized on both theoretical and practical grounds. This chapter briefly describes some recent definitions of technical writing and models of communication that have begun to challenge, though by no means replace, the conventional ones. These will provide a working framework from which to examine progress reports as generally defined and as specifically used within the particular context of the present study. As Harrison notes in the above epigram to this chapter, the conventions governing reports within organizations are usually context-dependent, that is, influenced by local expectations and constraints characteristic of a particular organization's culture and community. A basic tenet of the study reported in Part Three is that good writers, as opposed to poor writers, have a better understanding of organizational context insofar as they know what types of information their readers expect and need in progress reports.

EMERGING DEFINITIONS OF TECHNICAL WRITING

The main limitation of the traditional definitions of technical writing discussed previously is their emphasis upon the subject matter and style of technical writing apart from its particular purposes, audiences, and contexts. More recent attempts to distinguish technical writing from other types of written discourse often emphasize its pragmatic functions for specific and often highly specialized audiences.

For some theorists, such as Dobrin (1983), the functional element of technical writing is based upon the different aims and criteria of science and technology, as discussed in the previous chapter, with the aim of science as knowledge itself and its criterion of truth, in contrast with the aim of technology as the application of knowledge and its criterion of use. Thus, Dobrin distinguishes technical writing from scientific writing by focusing upon the productive aim of technology.

At first glance, Dobrin's definition of technical writing as "writing that accommodates technology to the user" (p. 242) seems too narrow to include scientific writing produced for eventual technological applications. The rare examples he uses to illustrate his points concern only consumer manuals or simplistic instructions of the "Fit-nut-A-to-bolt-B" variety. Although Dobrin admits that science and technology often overlap, and although he suggests that technology includes administrative systems and strategies, he offers no insight into that overlap nor does he discuss technical writing within the context of administrative systems. Thus, while Dobrin's definition clearly encompasses writing that *results* in making technology usable, it does not account for the written results—research reports and their "technological" uses within an organization.

Some modification of Dobrin's consumer-oriented definition of technical writing is necessary in order to include the creators and users of technology within a research organization. Perhaps a better, more inclusive definition of technical writing is that technical writing is writing that accommodates scientific research and technology to users of technology—where "users" refers to both those within and outside the research organization. Such a definition would include both the internal reports written for specialized audiences and the external manuals written for general audiences. At the same time, the definition would exclude purely scientific writing, such as that published in professional journals, which does not have specific audiences beyond the scholars of a given discipline and which is generated more for intellectual aims than for technological ends. Also excluded in the definition would be scholarly technological articles, for, though they treat technological subjects, they are written to professional audiences at large in order to advance technological knowledge rather than to turn that knowledge to practical use within a specific context.

A growing number of technical writing textbooks have begun to stress the pragmatic purpose of technical writing. Stratton (1984), for example, begins his textbook, *Technical Writing: Process and Product*, by defining technical writing as "a pragmatic sort of writing designed to generate some observable response on the part of its readers. It is writing designed to get people to do things" (p. 3). This definition, however, would seem to allow for a wide variety of written texts that normally would not be considered scientific or technical writing, from stop signs to notes to the milkman, or rather nowadays notes to the Hinckley & Schmitt delivery person.

Other definitions, such as the following, broaden the traditional definition of technical writing to include purpose, subject, and audience:

> Technical communication is the use of effective language to express a *commercial, industrial,* or *scientific* message to achieve a predetermined purpose. (Dagher, 1978, p. 2)

> In technical writing you report factual information objectively for the practical use of your readers. This information is usually specialized and directed toward a specific group of people. (Lannon, 1982, p.3)

> Technical writing is writing that tries to inform people about a complex and specialized subject so that they can perform their own complex and specialized jobs more effectively. (Sandman, Klompus, & Yarrison, 1985, p. 3)

Perhaps the best definition to date, and the one best suited to the present study, is the definition proposed by Mathes and Stevenson (1976), who assert that "the technical report is an act of communication by a professional in an organizational system to transfer information necessary for the system to continue to function" (p. 3). The definition, though restricted to technical reports, is comprehensive enough to include all elements of technical communication within an organization—the writer, text, reader, and context—as well as all types of technical reports—for instance, laboratory notebooks, proposals, progress reports, memoranda, and formal reports. The definition is also appealing in that, unlike the traditional definition of technical writing, which is based upon the criterion of objectivity, Mathes and Stevenson's definition specifies a criterion based upon the pragmatic needs of the system. Thus, what makes a technical report effective is not simply that it conveys information clearly, accurately, and objectively or even that it conveys factual information, but that it conveys information *necessary* for the organization to function effectively. Whereas the traditional definition of technical writing emphasizes the content and style of a report, Mathes and Stevenson's definition emphasizes both the audience and purpose of a report. It is a definition in which, to use the architectural adage alluded to in Chapter 2, form follows function.

For technical writers, the fundamental question, then, is not how to make reports more readable (though this is important and also must be of eventual concern) but, first and foremost, what information the intended readers need in the report. My experiences with technical writers suggest, however, that many of them are more concerned with improving the readability of their reports and the presentation of technical information than with whether or not that information serves their readers' purposes and the goals of the organization.

This tendency of writers to focus upon the surface features of reports and to overlook or assume the report's audience and purpose may be attributable to lingering notions of the traditional view of technical writing. But, as suggested in Chapter 2, it may also be attributable to the nature of academic writing that the researchers initially learned as undergraduate and graduate students and that, as professionals of the scientific community, they still read and perhaps write. Indeed, the very format of technical reports historically evolved from the organization and content of academic and professional scientific papers, so that to this day most company technical reports reflect the organizational components common in scientific articles: for example, *Introduction, Theoretical Background, Method, Results and Discussion,* and *Conclusions.* These sections imply a certain order, type, and coverage of information that, while it may meet the requirements of academic audiences, may or may not serve the needs of organizational audiences. For writers, this blurring of scientific writing and technical writing may further blur the different aims and criteria of science and technology, as explained in the preceding chapter. Thus, writers may assume that, since the conventions of technical report writing appear to look the same as those of scientific academic writing, their readers (for instance, supervisors and directors) are engaged in the same kind of knowledge-and-truth-seeking enterprise as is the scientific community of scholars. In short, writers may assume that function follows form.

At the time it was written over a decade ago, Mathes and Stevenson's textbook, *Designing Technical Reports,* was different from most other technical writing textbooks in that its emphasis is not upon the formats for various types of technical reports (that is, upon technical writing as product) but upon the decisions regarding audience and purpose that writers must make in designing reports (that is, upon technical writing as process). Although the present study investigates the products of writers (specifically their progress reports), the objective is not to characterize the ideal progress report (as most textbooks attempt to do) but to analyze the informational content of reports to reveal the writer's implicit assumptions about the report's audience and purpose and to compare these assumptions with both the writer's stated intentions and the intended reader's stated expectations. Thus, the study is an attempt to make Mathes and Stevenson's definition of technical writing operational by examining what information writers and readers regard as necessary to effect the goals of their organization. Such a definition of technical writing is based upon a view of communication quite different from the transmission model of communication.

EMERGING MODELS OF COMMUNICATION

While the focus of the transmission model of communication is upon the message, the focus of some recent models of communication is upon the intended effect of a message upon its intended listener or reader. This shift from *what* and *how* information is conveyed to *why* and *with what results* information is communicated entails a corresponding shift in the criteria for effective communication. In the traditional model, effectiveness is judged by how clearly messages are transmitted and received; in more recent models, effectiveness is judged by how well a speaker's or a writer's intention, as realized in the discourse or text, matches his intended listener's or reader's needs and expectations.

Like most recent definitions of technical writing, most emerging models of communication are based upon the pragmatic goals of communication. Since no research organization, or other corporate organization for that matter, is in the business of communication for its own sake, the transmission model of communication is inadequate in that it excludes the specific aims and contexts for communication. Even when the purpose of a technical report is to convey information, something must eventually be done with that information. Companies do not encourage report writing merely to record and stockpile information. At some point, that information is used to make decisions, and those decisions are based upon more than simply how clear the reports are. Readers may have no difficulty comprehending a report but may regard it as ineffective for a number of reasons, one of which may be that the report does not contain the kind of information that the reader needs to assess the potential practical value of the research for the organization.

Although no model of communication, to my knowledge, has been proposed that specifically addresses technical communication in organizations, there exist a plethora of communication models from the field of business communication. Many of them (for example, those described by Schramm, 1954; Berlo, 1960; Campbell & Level, 1985; and Lewis, 1987) are but sophisticated variations of the Shannon and Weaver transmission model of communication. As Targowski and Bowman (1988) point out, even the best of these models, which attempt to account for the various things that can go wrong within a specific context for communication, focus primarily on the external text—on "the bits of information encoded by a sender and passed along a channel to a receiver for decoding" (p. 6). As an alternative to these models, Targowski and Bowman propose their own model of communication, which the authors themselves christen as a "new paradigm," a model that attempts to meet the needs of "an information intensive culture, one that explicitly addresses the issue of the relationship between the information supplied by the sender—the message—and that supplied by the receiver as he or she receives the information" (p. 6). The Targowski/ Bowman model is too intricate to discuss in detail here; moreover, the assumptions and metaphors upon which it is based have little relevance to my present study. Still and all, it is of passing interest because it represents the trend in business communication, similar to the trend in composition research which was discussed in Chapter 2, to build models of communication based on a hybrid of cognitive psychology and computer science.

If you have ever removed the cover of your computer's operating unit and looked inside at all the rows of microchips, you have a good idea of the Targowski/Bowman model of communication. In essence, they attempt to represent communication as a "system" comprised of a "Cognitive Management Apparatus" and a network of ten "layer-based links" (physical links, systems links, audience links, session links, environmental links, functions/role links, symbol links, behavior links, values links, and storage/retrieval links), that connect through seven "multipaths." The main idea, as Targowski and Bowman explain it, is that "as information flows along the paths and through the ten links, the sender and receiver add to and subtract from the 'bits' of information included in the actual message according to their own perceptions of each other, the situation, the environment, and the message" (p. 17). Just how senders and receivers do so, however, is not clearly explained or illustrated by reference to real-world examples; rather, we are given several mathematical formulas for calculating the effectiveness of communication.

Apart from the fact that you have to be a computer programmer to fully understand this model and that we are given no user-friendly manuals to help us wade through the morass of cognitive-computerese, there remains the dubious assumption that communication can be so neatly configured and represented—that is, reduced to formulas, bits and bites, digital thinking, electronic pathways, and mathematical certainty. The idea that information is an interplay of triggering mechanisms and automatic responses along a binary relay-system grossly oversimplifies the intricacies of human communication. For example, what does it mean when Targowski and Bowman explain that miscommunication occurs when "sender and receiver exchange only subsets of reflecting information and messages, whose compensating subsets have been lost in the symbol link L7 during the coding process" (p. 21)," as represented by the following formula:

$$F_{rj} \neq F_{sj}, \ R_{rj} \subset R_{sj} \text{ and } M_{rj} \subset M_{sj}$$

While it would be great to be able to tell a client, as my computer technicians tell me when I bring in a down computer, "Well, we've run our diagnostics on your text, and you've got a weak L7 link in the motherboard. That'll be $105 to repair; delivery is extra," I can't imagine ever doing so. Less facetiously, even as a theoretical (as opposed to a practical) model of communication, Targowski and Bowman's model strikes me as but a more elaborate, quasi-scientific model of the windowpane theory of language discussed in Chapter 5. Here, the notion of one-word/one-meaning is extended to include the notion of one-stimulus/one-response, or one information-input/one information-output. Furthermore, in the final analysis, despite many cross arrows, links, and pathways between the sender and receiver megaboxes, the Targowski/Bowman model is not, after all, so very different from the Shannon and Weaver transportation model of communication.

Other theorists have developed goal-oriented models of business communication, which are seemingly more relevant to my present study. Herbert (1977), for example, suggests a behavioristic model, which he calls a "pragmatic goal- and results-oriented model," that focuses communication upon the receiver's response to a message-stimulus. Effective communication, or writing in this case, becomes a matter of how well the reader's behavioral response to the text—for example, a change in opinion, perception, relationship, or behavior—matches the writer's desired response.

Upon the surface, Herbert's model appears applicable to the present study's investigation of the match between a writer's intentions and text, and the intended reader's expectations. However, upon closer examination, it becomes apparent that Herbert's model has more relevance to business communications that typically involve downward or crossward communication than to internal technical communications that seldom involve downward communication. Because the two contexts imply different relationships between readers and writers—different rhetorical stances—the nature of the stimulus and response may also be quite different in the two situations. In business, the messages communicated by managers serve as stimulus for response not simply by virtue of the messages themselves but also because the writers command a position of authority within the organizational hierarchy, a position that is itself a powerful stimulus for the response of readers. In contrast, a much neglected characteristic of technical communication in organizations is that it is almost always upward communication. Technical reports, of whatever sort, typically are written by subordinates to their supervisory or managerial superiors. Thus, the message (the report) is not so much stimulus for reader response as it is the writer's response to reader-induced stimuli.

To use the Pavlovian analogy, with Herbert's model the writer rings the bell and the reader salivates. In technical communication, the situation is quite often the reverse: The writer salivates (produces the technical report) in response to the reader's ringing a bell (the need for certain information). Of course the report may also further serve as stimulus for change in the reader's perceptions or actions, and these may in turn trigger greater changes in the course of the organization's research activities and goals. But the important point is that the report is a stimulus for response only insofar as writers perceive and produce the report in response to the organizational needs (or stimuli) conveyed by management to researchers. One of the main premises of the present study is that the extent to which the researchers, as writers, understand these needs influences the extent to which the researchers' reports contain the type of information that the organization requires to continue to function effectively.

SPEECH-ACT THEORY

The model of communication that comes the closest to representing this interrelationship of writer intentions, texts, and reader expectations is the speech-act theory of communication initially expounded by Austin (1962), further developed by Searle (1969, 1979), a student of Austin's, and later elaborated by Bach and Harnish (1979). Although speech-act theory, as explained by these individuals, is based upon oral communication, Steinmann (1982) has demonstrated its application to written communication and Hamermesh (1981) has suggested its pedagogical adaptation to the teaching of technical writing.

Speech-act theory is appealing for two reasons: First, it explains effective communication as a function of both how clear a message is to an intended audience and how well that intended audience comprehends the communicative intent of the speaker or writer; second, and more important for my present purposes, it accounts for the particular context within which communication occurs, especially the dynamic role of the speaker's (or writer's) and the listener's (or reader's) mutual contextual beliefs in shaping what is said and how it is interpreted, as well as what other intentional or unintentional effects these two—the what and how—may have upon the listener's (or reader's) beliefs or behavior.

Briefly, speech-act theory, as summarized by Steinmann (1982), holds that "linguistic communication is more than merely saying something; it is saying something in a certain context, with certain intentions, and with the reader's (or listener's) recognition both of what is said and of these intentions" (p. 297). When, for instance, a writer writes something, he performs two acts:

1. The *locutionary act* of intentionally saying something to the reader, with the expectation that the reader will comprehend the communicative intent (that is, will understand not only the words and propositions, but also their reference to the particular situation and to the mutual contextual beliefs of the writer and reader).

2. The *illocutionary act* of intending, through the locutionary act, to, among other things, assert, ask, greet, promise, or apologize, again with the expectation that the reader will recognize this intent.

In addition, the writer may also perform a *perlocutionary act* in which he intends to produce in the reader some other effect beyond communication, as for instance, influencing the reader to believe or do something.

Since the focus of the present study is upon neither the locutionary nor the perlocutionary effectiveness of technical reports, but more so upon their illocutionary effectiveness, especially as governed by the writers and readers' mutual contextual beliefs, let us examine the latter—illocutionary intentions and mutual contextual beliefs—in greater detail.

In general, the illocutionary intent of most writers of progress reports is to inform. According to speech-act theory, communication is complete when the intended reader realizes that the writer intends that the reader realize the writer's intention to inform. For example, let us say that, by submitting a progress report to his supervisor that details the procedure the researcher used to analyze compound X, the researcher-writer intends that his supervisor be informed of that procedure. In reading the report, the supervisor realizes that the writer intends that the supervisor be informed of the procedure. The illocutionary act is done; the reader is informed and knows what the writer wanted him to know. But has the communication been effective? Is the information in the report what the reader wanted? Here is where the concept of mutual contextual beliefs becomes important.

In general, mutual contextual beliefs (MCBs) are the assumptions, knowledge, and beliefs that the writers and readers share. Within the particular context of an R&D organization, the MCBs related to progress reports may include such things as the reader's knowledge of the research project, the format and organization of progress reports, assumptions about what constitutes *progress*, the purpose and importance of progress reports, the type of information desired, and the degree of specificity appropriate. Such MCBs shape the intentions of writers and the expectations of readers; they furthermore determine the criteria by which progress reports are evaluated and by which communication is judged effective.

As mentioned previously in this volume, my experiences in teaching technical writing in R&D organizations suggest that the expectations concerning technical reports are seldom made explicit except for occasional guidelines regarding format. Examining just how mutual are the contextual beliefs of writers and readers may reveal that problems in communication are due more to poorly defined or conflicting assumptions and expectations than to poorly written reports. The present study, therefore, extends speech-act theory from a model for examining specific instances of linguistic communication to a model for examining the MCBs that underlie communication. The topic of investigation is not how texts promote the reader's understanding of the writer's intentions, but rather how the writer's understanding of reader expectations influences the writer's intentions and texts. Since the focus of this study is the informational content of progress reports, a brief overview of the general nature of technical progress reports and the nature of information is necessary before turning at last to the study itself.

THE GENERAL NATURE OF PROGRESS REPORTS

Whatever they are called in textbooks or in organizations—interim reports, status reports, periodic reports, progress reports, quarterly reports, monthly reports, or semimonthly reports—progress reports, as described in most textbooks on technical writing, are distinguished from other types of technical reports by their scope, purpose, and organization.

Typically, the main objective of the progress report, according to Mills and Walter (1986), is "to present information about work done on a particular project during a particular period of time" (p. 280). They point out that the information may serve one or both of the following aims:

1. To keep management "informed about various projects under their supervision [so that they can] decide intelligently whether the work should be continued, given new direction or emphasis, or discontinued."
2. "To assure those in charge that satisfactory progress is being made—that workers are earning their keep." (p. 280)

In addition, as Mills and Walter further note, the progress report has value as a record for future reference.

As I will suggest later, these three quite different functions of the progress report—as input into managerial decision making, as evidence of the researcher's job performance, and as documentation of a project—may imply different sorts of information or emphasis. Rarely, however, do textbooks discuss in any detail the informational content of progress reports. Instead, content is usually dismissed as a matter of organization. The commonly prescribed format, as outlined by Mills and Walter (1986), Ulman and Gould (1972), Pauley (1979), Andrews and Bickle (1982), and Stratton (1984), follows a narrative account of what the report is about, what work has been done, and what work remains to be done. While such distinctions easily lend themselves to the section headings typical in progress reports—for example, *Work Accomplished - Work Scheduled*; or, as in many of the reports examined in this study, *Objective - Results - Future*—the distinctions are often little help to writers in determining the exact nature of information that ought to be included in these sections.

Furthermore, these distinctions, since they are based solely upon time, encourage reports that are seldom more than diaries or timesheets that chronicle the researcher's activities during a given period. Recognizing this potential pitfall, Mills and Walter warn writers to "remember that the report is not a personal record for the writer, but information for some particular reader or readers about the work done. If you keep this in mind, you should have little trouble" (p. 281).

Little trouble? Over the last 10 years, the majority of the more than 800 researchers with whom I have consulted indicate that the greatest difficulty they have is in determining what information to include in their reports. The range and variation of the information contained in their progress reports vary considerably, depending upon such things as what they regard as the primary purpose of progress reports, how they define *information*, and what type of information they think their readers want.

THE NATURE OF INFORMATION

Although *information* is a key term in nearly every definition of technical writing, seldom is it defined or discussed. As suggested in the Introduction and Chapter 5, while most writers and readers agree that the purpose of a technical report is to convey information, what they mean by *information* may vary considerably. Introduction, theoretical background, methods, procedures, data, facts, observations, results, explanations, speculations, conclusions, recommendations—all of these are used as referents for *information*. Since it is difficult to think of what would not qualify as information, it is little wonder that writers have trouble deciding what to include in their reports.

Dictionary definitions of *information* confirm the vagueness of the term. According to *Webster's Ninth New Collegiate Dictionary*, the most common definition is the "communication or reception of knowledge or intelligence." Interestingly, the emphasis here is upon information as a communicative act—as the sending or receiving of knowledge. Information is not *what* is sent or received (the knowledge) but rather the *sending* or *receiving* itself. Information *is* communication, if by communication one has in mind the transmission model of communication, a model that is, in turn, based upon information theory.

Webster's second definition for *information* is "knowledge obtained from investigation, study, or instruction." Here, *information* is not a process of transmitting or receiving knowledge but rather the knowledge (the *what*) itself. In addition to *knowledge*, the synonyms listed for *information* are *facts* and *data*. In true dictionary fashion, the definitions for these terms employ the word *information*: *data* is "factual information," a *fact* is "a piece of information presented as having objective reality," and *knowledge* is "the fact or condition of having information." An important point to note about these definitions is the exclusion of terms such as *opinion, speculation, conclusion,* or *recommendation.*

Let me suggest at this point how the dictionary definitions of *information* are related to the foregoing discussion of speech-act theory as applied to progress reports. If *information* is the communication of knowledge, then in effect what writers are communicating is information about the states of their minds—knowledge about what they think are the facts. The intention, thus, is not to inform the reader of the facts but of the fact that the writer thinks these are the facts. That is, the intent is not simply "I want you to know X," but rather "I want you to know that I know X," and, beyond that, "that I think X means Y."

Similarly, Rescher (1970) talks about the difference between *explanation* and *justification,* between giving reasons for why X is true as opposed to giving reasons for why we say X is true. This medieval distinction between a *ratio essendi* ("reason for being") and a *ratio cognoscendi* ("reason for knowing") is a key to understanding the subtleties of the seemingly simple illocutionary intent of writers to inform their readers of the facts.

In an R&D organization consisting of several ongoing research projects, it seems unlikely that supervisors, much less managers, would read progress reports in order to fully comprehend information about the research in progress. First, they do not have the time. Second, even if they did, they do not have the specialized expertise in the various disciplines represented by the multitude of research projects—expertise that they would need in order to understand the work in any detail. And, third, it is not their job to know everything their researchers know but to put that knowledge to use.

Rather, it seems more likely that readers would want to know to what extent the writers know what the research means. If that is the case—and the present study suggests that it is, at least for the one R&D organization examined—then perhaps what readers want primarily is not information (insofar as it is defined in dictionaries) but rather reasoned judgments about the significance of that information. They may want to know what the researchers *think*—a *ratio cognoscendi*—more than what the researchers did, why they did it, how they did it, or what they found.

If readers expect only the latter types of information in a progress report, or if writers think that their readers expect only the latter types of information, the writers' progress reports are likely to be filled with only observations, methods, procedures, facts, and data—or what the dictionary lists as the second meaning of *information.* If so, readers are then confronted with the problem of having to make sense of information based upon research, which the readers—the higher their position and thus the more removed they are from the laboratory—cannot hope to understand.

For writers, the rhetorical situation becomes extremely complex when the same progress report is written to heterogeneous audiences—for example, to co-workers, immediate supervisors, directors, the vice president of R&D, and corporate business managers—each of whom may have a different purpose in reading the report and who therefore may need different types of information. Complicating the situation further is that the writers and readers may have quite different notions of *information*. Some may think of *information* in the same way that dictionaries define it—as strictly objective facts and data—whereas others may think of *information* as the results, implications, or conclusions drawn from the data and facts.

Whether or not the writers and readers of progress reports use the word *information* in the same way as the dictionary defines it is probably not important. What is important, however, is that the writers and readers have similar notions about the information that ought to be contained in the reports.

The present study is an attempt to analyze and classify the types of information that researchers (scientists and engineers) include in their reports, in order to examine to what extent these types of information reflect the intentions of writers and the expectations of readers (mainly the researcher's immediate supervisor and director).

It should be noted that future references to *information* in this study are not based upon the way in which dictionaries narrowly define the term but upon the various ways in which the writers and readers in this study used the term. Thus, *information* will be used to refer to both unprocessed information and processed information, and accordingly will encompass not only facts and data but also such things as results, explanations, speculations, and conclusions. Admittedly, such a working definition, since it includes anything that conceivably might be contained in a progress report, makes the term *information* so vague as to be almost useless. Such, however, is the nature of the problem that initially motivated my inquiry. Indeed, one of the goals of the present study is to discover the range and variation of information included in progress reports and to use this knowledge as the basis for developing a scheme for classifying information. This scheme is presented in Chapter 10 during the discussion of Phase 2 of this study.

III
A Study of Progress Reports in an R&D Organization: Writer Intentions, Texts, and Reader Expectations

8
Overview of the Study

The study that is reported in the next three chapters is an examination of the informational content of technical progress reports in a corporate R&D organization. It compares the types of information that researchers (scientists and engineers) *intend* to include in their reports, the information actually *contained* in their reports, and the information their intended supervisor readers *expect* in these reports. The study involved nearly 50 subjects at all levels of the R&D organization—from the vice president of R&D to the secretarial staff—and was conducted in three phases over a year's time. The main subjects of this study, however, are the researcher-writers and their supervisor-readers.

During Phase 1, which consisted of interviews and surveys, the context within which progress reports are written, read, and used was studied; in addition, the supervisors identified the poor-writer and the good-writer subjects, and the writers' and the reader's preferences for different kinds of information were compared. During Phase 2, a method for classifying types of information was developed and used to analyze the researchers' progress reports that were collected during Phase 1. During Phase 3, two context-based experimental tasks, which were based upon these reports, were designed and conducted to compare the types of information identified as most important or as least important by the researcher-writers and their intended supervisor-readers and to determine the extent to which these subjects had similar notions of the terms they themselves commonly use to refer to information: namely, *data*, *result*, and *conclusion*. In addition, Phase 3 included interviews that asked the subjects to explain their definitions of these terms.

Among the study's major findings are that, with respect to the informational content of progress reports, the good writers, as compared with the poor writers, have intentions that more closely match their intended supervisor-readers' expectations; their progress reports contain a significantly lower percentage of unprocessed information and a higher percentage of processed information; and the good writers more closely agree with their respective supervisors about the types of information that are most important and least important to include in progress reports. Also, the findings suggest that the poor writers, while they know what is *not* desired or expected in a progress report, have difficulty determining what *is* desired or expected.

Analysis of other variables indicates that such differences between the good writers and the poor writers cannot be explained by educational degree, major field of study, prior coursework in writing, years' work experience, years at the company, or years working for their respective supervisors. In fact, for all of these variables, as reported in Phase 1, the poor writers outscored the good writers. (This is not to say, however, that in another study involving a greater number of subjects such variables might not prove significant.) As possible explanations for this study's findings, it is suggested that the differences between the two groups may be due to their different composing strategies, different concepts about the nature of communication and progress, and different assumptions about the purpose and audience of progress reports.

PURPOSE OF THE STUDY

The main purpose of this study was to examine the extent to which the writers and readers of progress reports within an R&D organization share similar ideas about the types of information that should or should not be included in these reports. A major assumption underlying this study is that good writing is largely a matter of successfully meeting the needs and expectations of the writers' intended readers. Thus, one criterion of an effective report is the extent to which there is a match among the writer's *intentions*, the writer's *text*, and the readers' *expectations*.

In the Introduction to this volume and in Chapter 5, I explained the situation that motivated my inquiry into the nature of progress reports in an R&D organization and that shaped the study reported in the following chapters. To review briefly, during my experiences in teaching technical writing at an R&D organization, I observed that the researcher–writers of progress reports had unclear and conflicting ideas about the information that should or should not be included in their progress reports. Later, when I discussed this with the researchers' supervisors and directors, I discovered that they too seemed to have differing opinions. At issue, it seemed to me, were several questions about the functions progress reports served within the organization and the larger company, as well as the writers' and the readers' concepts of "progress," and how these concepts reflected and shaped organizational goals. One of the most fundamental questions, and that one that initially guided my research, was simply "What makes a good progress report within this organization?"

RESEARCH DESIGN

In order to investigate that question, I realized that I had to find ways of uncovering the criteria that the individuals in this organization were using as they wrote, read, and used progress reports—even though they themselves apparently were not consciously aware of those criteria. This is what concerned me most at the initial phase of my study. While many studies of writing are carefully predesigned and constructed to test a particular hypothesis according to some preconceived methodology and known statistical test(s)—where the data is gathered to fit form—I began primarily with questions. I did not worry much at first about where those questions might lead, what I might find, or the potential problems I might later have in analyzing my data. (Though indeed there later were problems and still perhaps may be some problems.) I was not concerned, that is, with the means of my study so much as with its goals; to use Thoreau's phrase, I set out mainly with the desire of "seeing what I could see." With the possible exception of ethnographic studies, in most traditional, "scholarly," academic research, the convention seems to be that researchers ought to know beforehand where they are headed, how they are going to get there, and what they are likely to find once there. Or if they don't have all of this figured out beforehand, at least to give that impression in the final, published version of their study. I intentionally chose not to follow that path for I thought that doing so would thwart the very purposes of my investigation and divert me from other potentially fruitful sources of inquiry.

As was discussed in Chapter 1, the research on real-world business and technical writing is as yet in its infancy, and as such requires more innovative, exploratory research than what we have become accustomed to doing. By imposing upon the study of real-world writing the same assumptions, criteria, and methodologies we use to study academic writing in school settings, we run the risk of ignoring the importance of context in influencing what, why, and how texts are produced and used in nonacademic, organizational settings. The danger is that, while we may produce highly sophisticated studies that yield significant findings according to our own predetermined standards, if those standards are not the same as those of our research subjects, we may unwittingly be led astray by our own research findings. Like the blind men and the elephant in the Ogden Nash poem, we may think we have an understanding of the animal by examining only one of its parts. In the long run, however, such premature closure only retards progress in the field of business and technical writing, for we end up chasing down blind alleys and creating models and theories of the nature of some mythical beast that may have little resemblance to reality.

At the same time, however, I wish to point out that I did not approach my research as a "free fall," nor was I motivated by the kind of subjective, expressive urges that, as discussed in Chapter 2, some devotees of the process school of writing embrace. I did not begin, as it were, in a bog of total chaos and darkness out of which I hoped some glimmerings of meaning might emerge. No researcher embarks upon a study without some assumptions, however loose they may be. At the onset of this study, I made some key assumptions that influenced the design and direction of my study. Perhaps my main assumption was that, contrary to traditional models of business and technical writing, good communication is more than conveying information clearly. With respect to progress reports in particular, I assumed that "good" writing, beyond being clear and well organized, is largely a matter of shared writer and reader assumptions, or mutual contextual beliefs, about the purpose and content of those reports. I further speculated that one measure of an effective progress report would be the extent to which there was a match among writer intentions, their texts, and their reader expectations, and that this match would be closer for the writers of progress reports judged superior by their intended supervisor-readers than for the writers of progress reports judged inferior by their intended supervisor-readers.

Were I to use two adjectives to describe the research design for this study, they would be "organic" and "integrative." First, the study is organic insofar as the results of one phase of the study influenced the design of the next phase. At the onset of the study, I knew that, rather than I, the intended readers of progress reports within this organization were in the best position to judge what characterized a "good" progress report. It was upon the basis of their determinations that the two main groups of this study—the poor writers and the good writers—were identified. The results of my Phase 1 interviews with these writers, as well as with the intended readers of their reports (their immediate supervisors and directors) in turn shaped the design of Phase 2 of this study, which examined the informational content of the progress reports according to a scheme of types of information that evolved from my Phase 1 interviews with the writers and readers of progress reports. Upon the basis of the results of Phase 2, I then designed, for Phase 3, two context-based experimental studies to investigate (a) whether the subjects' *stated* preferences for certain types of information (the results from Phase 1) conformed to their *actual* preferences when, given actual progress reports, the writers and readers of these reports were asked to identify the most important and least important information in these reports, and (b) whether, when presented with the same progress report, the writers of the progress reports and the intended supervisor-readers of these reports would similarly identify information as either *data, results,* or *conclusions.*

The study is also integrative insofar as it employs several different research methodologies—both those descriptive and qualitative and those experimental and quantitative—to explore the match among writer intentions, writer texts, and intended reader expectations. Phase 1, for instance, employs interviews and surveys to explore the particular context within which progress reports are written, read, and used at this specific R&D organization. Upon the basis of the Phase 1 findings, Phase 2 involves text analysis—specifically a schema for analyzing the informational content of progress reports. And, upon the basis of the Phase 2 findings, Phase 3 employs a combination of discourse-based interviews and two context-based experiments that examine the match between writer versus reader preferences for certain types of information in progress reports.

The following briefly describes the company at which I conducted my research, the subjects for this study, and its main phases.

RESEARCH SETTING

This study was conducted at the R&D center of an international corporation involved in what the company calls *agribusiness*. The company's R&D work is devoted to researching the processes and products that convert agricultural raw materials into a wide range of end-products for numerous food and nonfood industries. Research activities include developing better or new manufacturing processes, exploring biochemical properties and processes for potential development, and providing analytical services related to methods, instrumentation, and quality assurance.

SUBJECTS

The study involved nearly 50 people from all levels of R&D, including the vice president and his executive assistants, the 4 directors of the organization's research departments, all 12 of the supervisors in those departments, and 24 of these supervisors' researchers. In addition, the first phase of the study included interviews with the personnel manager and with support staff from the Information Services Department, from the manager of this department to the secretaries who typed the progress reports. The main subjects of the study, however, were the supervisors and their researchers.

PHASES OF THE STUDY

This study was divided into three phases. Though interrelated, each of these phases had its own objectives and methodology.

Phase 1

The purpose of Phase 1, which consisted of one-hour interviews with 48 people at all levels of the R&D organization, was to gather background information about the subjects and about the context within which progress reports are written, read and used. During Phase 1 the researcher-writer subjects were identified by their supervisors, samples of their reports were collected, and key issues for later investigation were identified. Most important for the remainder of the study, during Phase 1 the researcher-writers indicated to what extent they intended to include certain types of information in their progress reports, and the intended readers of these reports (supervisors and directors) indicated to what extent they expected certain types of information in the reports.

Phase 2

During Phase 2 a scheme for classifying the informational content of technical reports was developed and used to analyze 44 of the researchers' progress reports that had been collected during Phase 1. This classification scheme evolved out of the distinctions that the writer-researchers and their reader-supervisors themselves made while discussing the informational content of progress reports during Phase 1; it was not a system that had been transported from theoretical models in the literature nor was it a system that had been designed prior to the study. This analytical scheme was used to measure the extent to which the types of information that the writers *said* they intended to include in their reports and that the readers *said* they expected in their researchers' reports (as indicated by Phase 1) were *actually* contained in the reports.

Phase 3

Phase 3 was the experimental portion of the study. It consisted of task-oriented interviews with each of the directors, supervisors, and researchers initially interviewed during Phase 1. Whereas Phase 1 examined the subjects' stated preferences for types of information, in this phase the subjects were presented with the progress reports that had been collected during Phase 1 and analyzed during Phase 2 and were asked to make certain distinctions and judgments regarding the nature and importance of the informational content of the reports.

As part of Phase 3, following this experimental task, the subjects were asked to explain their choices and to give informal definitions of terms commonly used to describe types of information—namely, *data, result*, and *conclusion*. Researchers were asked to point to examples of these types of information in their reports and, later, supervisors and directors were asked to identify these examples as either *data, result, conclusion* or *something else*.

In summary, then, this study examines the type of information that the readers and writers of progress reports *said* they thought ought to be included in the reports (Phase 1), the type of information that was actually *contained* in the progress reports (Phase 2), and the type of information that readers and writers, when presented with their reports, *selected* as most important and least important (Phase 3).

ANALYSIS OF RESULTS

The key question this study attempted to answer was whether or not the writers of the good progress reports, as compared with the writers of the poorer progress reports, had a better understanding of the type of information their intended supervisor readers wanted and whether the type of information contained in their progress reports came closer to supervisor expectations than did the information contained in the progress reports of the poorer writers. Cross-comparisons of the results from all three phases provided a means of assessing the three-way match among writer intentions, texts, and reader expectations.

Results from each phase were analyzed according to several variables in addition to the good-writer/poor-writer variable. These other variables included department, position, experience, and scientist/engineer distinctions. The specific objectives, methodologies, and results of each phase are discussed in Chapters 9, 10, and 11, with a summary of the study's major findings and implications in Chapter 12.

9

Phase 1: Interviews with Writers and Readers

OBJECTIVES

The main objectives of Phase 1 were as follows:

1. To become familiar with the nature of progress reports as written, read, and used at the particular R&D organization that was the focus of this study.
2. To examine writer- and reader-stated preferences for certain types of information in progress reports.
3. To collect progress reports for later analysis in Phase 2 of the study and for use in the experimental tasks in Phase 3.

SUBJECTS

Phase 1 involved 46 people from all levels of the R&D organization, including the vice president of R&D and his executive assistant; the personnel manager; three individuals from the Information Services Department (including the manager, assistant, and a secretary); the 4 directors of the organization's research departments; all 12 of the supervisors in those research departments; and 24 of these supervisors' researchers (including scientists and engineers)—or, two researchers per supervisor.

Of this initial sample, the readers of the reports were (a) the vice president and his executive assistant; (b) the 4 directors of the research departments; and (c) the 12 supervisors. The writers of the reports were the 24 researchers. However, because of changes in personnel after Phase 1 of the study was conducted, only 11 of the 12 supervisor-reader subjects and only 22 of the 24 researcher-writer subjects participated in all three phases of the study. Therefore, the main subjects of the entire study are the 11 supervisors (as readers of the progress reports) and their 22 researchers (as writers of the progress reports). This latter group of 22 researcher-writers consisted of two researcher-writers per supervisor, one that the supervisor had identified as a poor writer and the other that the supervisor had identified as a good writer.

METHOD

Approximately one-hour interviews were held with each of the 46 subjects described above. These interviews were based upon a seven-page questionnaire consisting of multiple-choice and open-ended questions, as well as over 30 items that used a Likert scale of agreement/disagreement to measure the subjects' attitudes toward such things as their job, writing tasks, and their readers' expectations concerning written reports. (See Appendix 9-A for the questionnaire used for the researcher-writer subjects. The same basic questionnaire was also used for the reader subjects—the supervisors, directors, and the vice president—except the wording of some questions was modified slightly to reflect their role as readers versus writers. For example, whereas one of the questions for the writers is worded, "I am clear about my section leader's [herein called *supervisor's*] expectations regarding semimonthly reports [herein called *progress reports*]," the same question on the supervisor's survey is worded, "My researchers are clear about what I expect in a semimonthly report.")

Subjects were assured of the confidentiality of these interviews and all materials they submitted to me. Also, they were informed at the onset of the interviews of the general nature of the study: that it involved an analysis of the type of information contained in progress reports. They were further assured that my objective as a researcher was not to evaluate the quality of their reports but simply to describe the context within which those reports were written, read, and used. Since the subjects knew that my field was English, it was important to set them at ease at the very beginning by dispelling any notions they might have that there were right or wrong answers to my questions or that I was approaching my investigation with any preconceived English-teacher criteria of effective writing.

The researcher subjects were selected in the following manner. Prior to the interviews, each supervisor was asked to select two progress reports written by two different researchers in his group—one progress report that the supervisor considered superior and the other that the supervisor considered inferior—and to have these ready to submit to me at the interview. The writers of these reports then became the researcher-subjects of the study, with half of this group representing the good progress-report writers and the other half representing the poor progress-report writers. (It should be noted here that some of the supervisors, especially those who were in the smaller works units and who therefore had fewer researchers, were reluctant to describe their researchers' reports as "inferior"; the reports, as some of these supervisors explained, were only "less good" by comparison with the better reports.) At no point during the study were the researchers told upon what basis they were selected for the study. Insofar as they knew, they had been selected at random.

It should be noted here, too, that during the first-round interviews with upper management (directors and above), it became apparent that what are called *progress reports* in this R&D organization are not what I, authors of most technical writing textbooks, or those within most other companies would call *progress reports*. Within this organization, the term *progress report*, as I soon discovered, refers to long (approximately 15–40 page) formal reports that cover several months or more of research (what most organizations would call a formal technical report), whereas short, periodic reports of progress (what elsewhere are commonly referred to as *progress reports*) are called *semimonthly reports*. Since the researchers' reports that were submitted to me during my initial interviews with the supervisors were not this organization's semimonthly reports but rather the researchers' longer, more formal reports, the researcher subjects were instructed to bring to their interviews with me their last three semimonthly reports.

Prior to these interviews, I recontacted the supervisors to make sure that the poor report/good report selections they had made earlier still applied since it was the semimonthly reports and not the long formal reports that I was interested in using as the basis for my study. In all cases, the supervisors indicated that the writers whose progress reports they had previously identified as inferior also typically wrote the more inferior semimonthly reports and that the writers whose progress reports they had previously identified as superior also typically wrote the more superior semimonthly reports. Thus, although the purpose of this study was not to examine whether the criteria used to evaluate reports are genre-specific, this incidental finding suggests that, at this organization at least, whatever criteria the supervisors are using to distinguish poor reports from good reports appear to extend to both the short, periodic reports and to the long formal research reports.

It should be noted, then, that the progress reports referred to in this study—the ones that are discussed during Phase 1, that were analyzed during Phase 2, and that formed the basis of the task experiments in Phase 3—are actually this organization's semimonthly reports. Hereafter, within this chapter and all succeeding chapters, the term *progress report* refers to these semimonthly reports.

ANALYSIS AND REPORTING OF DATA FROM THE PHASE 1 INTERVIEWS

Data obtained from the first-phase interviews were analyzed by the Chi-square test to determine any significant differences between the attitudes, practices, and perceived expectations on the part of the poor writers versus the good writers. For ease of reference, most of the data concerning differences between these two groups' education, experience, attitudes, and perceived expectations are contained in the Tables 9.1 - 9.13 of Appendix 9-B. These data are reported as percentages. Where survey items required subjects to respond according to a Likert scale, the means for the poor writers and good writers are also indicated. The tables further indicate the couple of instances in which the Chi-square test revealed a statistically significant difference at the .05 level.

Data concerning the reader and writer preferences for types of information in progress reports (also along the Likert scale) are reported within the main text of this chapter, as are the subjects' responses to open-ended questions. As for the latter, the subjects' responses to the open-ended questions were examined in order to try to find recurrent themes. In those instances in which the responses could be grouped into several categories, tables are provided within the body of this chapter. In other instances, however, in which either the responses were so diverse as to defy classification or the responses were clustered around a dominant theme, no tables are provided and the data were not subjected to statistical testing. Instead, the results are simply presented in narrative form, with percentages reported wherever possible.

Finally, I wish to remind my readers of the discrepancies in terms alluded to in the previous section. To avoid confusion especially when looking at the survey questions in Appendix 9-A and the tables in Appendix 9-B, it is important to keep in mind that certain terms used in the survey and in these tables are specific to the organization at which this study was conducted— namely, the terms *semimonthly report, progress report,* and *section leader*—and that throughout this chapter and all other chapters of this volume I have used other, more generic terms to refer to the same entities. One way to avoid potential confusion for my readers, I realize, would have been to revise the wording of the survey and some of the tables, substituting my terms for those of my subjects' terms. Doing so, however, would have meant tampering with the survey as originally used in Phase 1 and thereby compromising the authenticity of the research context for the sake of my own readers. Instead, I chose to preserve the integrity of the research context by not changing the wording of the appended survey and tables. In the hopes of minimizing confusion on the part of my readers, I offer the following key, which lists the terms used by my subjects and the equivalent terms used by me within the main body of this volume:

Research Subjects' Term	*Equivalent Generic Term*
as Used in Appendixes 9-A & 9-B	*as Used in This Volume*
semimonthly report	progress report
progress report	formal research report
section leader	supervisor

DISTINCTIONS BETWEEN POOR WRITERS VS. GOOD WRITERS

Background and Experience

Chi-square analysis of the data from the survey revealed no significant differences between the poor writers and the good writers with respect to educational degree, total number of years' work experience in their field, number of years working at the company, number of years in their present position, or number of years working for their present supervisor. (See Appendix 9-B for tables.) Nor was there any significant difference between the percentage of poor writers who are scientists or engineers versus the percentage of good writers who are scientists or engineers. Of the poor writers, 64 percent are scientists and 36 percent are engineers; of the good writers, 82 percent are scientists and 18 percent are engineers. Poor writers and good writers have had approximately the same educational training in composition and technical writing, and both groups spend about the same amount of time on the job reading and writing.

Because only 18 percent of the total number of researcher subjects are female, it was not possible to determine whether sex was a significant variable. However, since three of the four female subjects were in the good-writer group, this may be a variable that needs further investigation.

Given the small number of subjects involved (11 poor writers and 11 good writers), the Chi-square test may not have revealed what might have been significant differences between these two groups had a larger sample been used. In the event that this may be the case, the following discusses some apparent and unexpected differences between the two groups based upon the cross tabulations of percentages reported in the tables in Appendix 9-B.

First, while it might seem logical to expect that the good writers as opposed to the poor writers might have had more education, more college coursework in writing, more years of professional experience, and more tenure in their current position at the company, such is not the case. (See Tables 9.1–9.3 of Appendix 9-B.) In fact, 63 percent of the poor writers, as opposed to only 36 percent of the good writers, have advanced degrees, that is, either MS or Ph.D degrees (see Table 9.1). Also, whereas 54 percent of the poor writers have had a total of 14 or more years total professional experience, only 27 percent of the good writers can claim the same. Another anomaly concerns the number of years that the poor writers versus the good writers have been at this company. While common sense would suggest that the longer one has been with a company, the more familiarity one would have with the company's expectations and therefore the better their reports, as revealed by Table 9.2, apparently this is not the case at this organization. Of the poor writers, 46 percent have been with the company only 1–4 years, as compared with 73 percent of the good writers. Furthermore, the most experienced employees are the poor writers, not the good writers. For example, again in reference to Table 9.2, 54 percent of the poor writers have been with the company 14–35 years, whereas only 27 percent of the good writers have been with the company 14–20 years. (None of the good writers have been with the company more than 20 years.) As for the total number of years each group (the poor writers vs. the good writers) has spent in their current position and the number of years each group has worked for their current supervisor, there appear to be no appreciable differences. As revealed in Table 9.2, 63 percent of both the poor writers and the good writers have been in their current position two years or less. Furthermore, as also revealed by Table 9.2, the same percentage of both the poor writers and the good writers (45 percent) have worked for their present supervisors for one year. However, when one takes a closer look at this percentage and breaks it down according to the number of poor writers versus good writers who have worked for their present supervisors for six months or less, the figures suggest a different picture. While only one good writer (9 percent of all good writers) has worked for his supervisor six months or less, three poor writers (27 percent of all poor writers) have worked for their supervisors six months or less. What do these findings mean? Perhaps, as Paradis, Dobrin, and Miller (1985) found in their study at Exxon ITD, writers may need more than six months—and sometimes as long as three years—to become socialized within the organizational culture and to realize what is expected of them as writers.

The data reported in Table 9.3 also reveal another anomaly. Though a higher percentage of good writers (64 percent) than poor writers (55 percent) have taken college composition courses, a much lower percentage of good writers (27 percent) than poor writers (55 percent) have taken college courses in technical writing. Also, the groups disagreed about how well these courses prepared them for their present job-related writing (see Table 9.4). The vast majority of the poor writers who had taken a composition course (83 percent) said it was ineffective, while about half as many good writers (43 percent) said their composition course was ineffective. None of the poor writers but 29 percent of the good writers said their composition courses were "very effective." In evaluating the effectiveness of their college technical writing courses in preparing them for their current job-related responsibilities, the poor writers (50 percent of that group) were more inclined than were the good writers (only 33 percent of that group) to indicate that such courses helped them in their job-related writing. One possible explanation for this apparent anomaly, as indicated in Table 9.3, may be the small number of subjects in this study who have had a course in technical writing (only 6 individuals within the poor-writer group and only 3 writers within the good-writer group). Such numbers are too small upon which to base solid conclusions.

Attitudes

Chi-square analysis of the data also revealed that for the vast majority of the 36 survey items pertaining to the writers' attitudes toward the company, job, superiors, and writing, and to their perceived expectations regarding writing, the two groups—the poor writers and the good writers—did not differ significantly. (See Tables 9.5 - 9.10 in Appendix 9-B.) With respect to their attitudes toward the company, their jobs, and their supervisors, both groups expressed a generally high degree of satisfaction. However, when compared with the poor writers, the good writers indicated a higher degree of satisfaction with their jobs and more highly rated their working relationships with their supervisors and their directors. As indicated in Table 9.5, 91 percent of the good writers as opposed to 73 percent of the poor writers agreed or strongly agreed that they are happy with their jobs. Also, as indicated in Table 9.6, while 27 percent of the good writers and 27 percent of the poor writers agreed that their relationship with their supervisor is good, 73 percent of the good writers but only 36 percent *strongly* agreed. That is, 100 percent of the good writers indicated a good relationship with their supervisor, as compared with only 63 percent of the poor writers. When compared with poor writers, the good writers also indicated a better relationship with their respective director, as shown in Table 9.6. Of the good writers, 90 percent agreed or strongly agreed that their relationship with their director is good, as compared with 73 percent of the poor writers.

As for what these findings may mean, it is difficult to say. Perhaps the good writers, as compared with the poor writers, are happier with their jobs and have better rapport with their supervisors and directors because they are more successful and confident as writers. Perhaps, too, the good writers, as opposed to poor writers, are good writers because they are better at intuiting their readers' expectations. This speculation is supported by the facts that the good writers, when compared with the poor writers, have had fewer total years job experience, fewer years experience working at this particular company, and fewer college courses in technical writing. Despite their educational level, training, and experience, there are evidently some things that good writers of progress reports think, know, do, or feel that the poor writers of progress reports do not.

One thing may be the importance that good writers versus poor writers attach to their writing. For instance, as shown in Table 9.7, good writers as opposed to poor writers are more likely to think of their writing as a significant factor in the evaluation of their job performance and to believe that the quality of their progress reports reflects not only upon themselves as writers but also upon their immediate supervisors. Also, as further shown in Table 9.7, all of the good writers, 100 percent, as opposed to only 60 percent of the poor writers, either strongly disagreed or disagreed with the statement that "If I am only sitting at my desk composing a report, it looks to my section leader [supervisor] as if I am doing nothing." That is, more than the poor writers, the good writers believe that their supervisors understand that writing is a normal part of the researcher's job responsibilities. As will be discussed shortly, a significant difference between the poor writers and the good writers is that the poor writers think they are expected to do some of their job-related writing at home rather than at work.

With respect to their attitudes toward writing, the good writers, as opposed to the poor writers, expressed more confidence in their writing abilities and indicated a greater liking for writing. As shown in Table 9.8, whereas more than half of the good writers (55 percent) agreed or strongly agreed that they like to write, only two of the poor writers (18 percent) claimed the same. Conversely, while only 18 percent of the good writers said they disliked writing, 45 percent of the poor writers said they disliked writing.

Though the above findings are interesting and seemingly significant, Chi-square analysis of the data did not reveal statistically significant differences at the .05 level between the responses of the poor writers and those of the good writers. This is not to say, however, that in a study involving a larger sample that such differences may not prove statistically significant.

Even with the small number of subjects in this study, however, chi-square analysis did reveal two significant differences between the poor writers and the good writers.

The first statistically significant difference ($p < .015$) between the two groups involves their perceptions of how satisfied their respective supervisors are with the quality of their reports. As shown in Table 9.9, while 100 percent of the good writers either agreed or strongly agreed that they thought their supervisors are satisfied with their reports, only 45 percent of the poor writers expressed such agreement. A greater percentage of the poor writers either were unsure of their supervisors' estimate of their writing (36 percent) or were convinced that their supervisors were dissatisfied with their writing (18 percent).

Perceived Expectations

Before discussing the other statistically significant difference between the two groups, let us examine some of the other findings from Table 9.9 relating to the writers' perceptions of their readers' expectations regarding writing in general and more specifically formal technical reports and progress reports. On all such survey items, the good writers, more than the poor writers, indicated that they were clear about their supervisors' expectations. When asked whether they thought that they and their supervisors shared similar notions about what constitutes a good report, 100 percent of the good writers as opposed to 70 percent of the poor writers said that they thought that they and their supervisors held similar views (survey item 5). With respect to their formal technical reports, the majority of both the poor writers (64 percent) and the good writers (72 percent) agreed that they are clear about what their supervisor expects in these reports (survey item 8). However, while 45 percent of the good writers strongly agreed, none of the poor writers did so. Similar results were obtained when the writers were asked whether they were clear about what their supervisors expect in a progress report (survey item 22). Of the good writers, 36 percent strongly agreed that such expectations were clear, while of the poor writers, only 9 percent strongly agreed.

Table 9.9 also contains the results of other survey items that asked the writers about the extent to which they thought their supervisor's expectations for writing are similar to those of other supervisors' (survey item 26), and the extent to which they thought their supervisor's expectations for formal technical reports and for progress reports are similar to those of their director's (survey items 13 and 12, respectively). Interestingly, except for item 26, the poor writers were slightly more inclined than were the good writers to think that their supervisor's expectations matched those of their director. As for whether or not the poor writers' perceptions are accurate is something that will be discussed later when we examine the directors' and the supervisors' stated and actual preferences for certain types of information in progress reports.

The other statistically significant difference ($p < .007$) concerns whether the writers felt that they were expected to do some of their job writing at home. As shown in Table 9.10 (survey item 14), while none of the good writers said they thought this is an expectation, 54 percent of the poor writers agreed or strongly agreed that it is an expectation. Interestingly, however, there was no significant difference between the two groups with regard to whether or not they actually *do* some of their job writing at home (survey item 16). Nevertheless, the results do reveal that 54 percent of the poor writers, as opposed to 27 percent of the good writers, agreed or strongly agreed that they do some of their job writing at home.

Composing Strategies and Revision Practices

Finally, other close-ended survey items requiring the subject's response along a Likert scale of agreement/disagreement concerned the writers' composing practices and the extent to which others revised their reports. As for the former, their composing practices, the results from the few items on the survey, reported in Table 9.11, while hardly a sufficient basis upon which to draw conclusions about how these writers *actually* do compose, suggest that the good writers may take more care with their writing than do the poor writers, and that they be more critical of their writing than are the poor writers. For instance, while both the good writers (100 percent) and the poor writers (91 percent) agreed or strongly agreed that they think through their main points before they write (survey item 15), a higher percentage of the good writers (72 percent) than the poor writers (63 percent) agreed or strongly agreed that they follow a systematic procedure when writing their reports (survey item 20); a higher percentage of the good writers (54 percent) than the poor writers (36 percent) agreed or strongly agreed that they make several false starts when writing (survey item 27); and a higher percentage of the good writers (92 percent) than the poor writers (63 percent) agreed or strongly agreed that they frequently change word choices and sentences as they compose (survey item 18). A better indication of the writers' composing strategies, however, are their responses to the survey's open-ended questions. These results, which include all subjects (supervisors and directors, as well as writers), and which also concern the subjects' criteria for reports, are discussed in the next section.

If, as indicated previously, the poor writers, as compared with the good writers, feel less confident about their writing, are less clear about their supervisor's expectations, and are less inclined to think that their supervisors are satisfied with their reports, then one indication of the quality of their reports may be the extent to which they undergo revision, as well as who is doing these revisions. The results of the remaining survey items reported in Table 9.12 suggest some differences between the two groups of writers in these areas. First, in response to survey item 7, 82 percent of the good writers, as opposed to only 45 percent of the poor writers, agreed or strongly agreed that they revise quite a bit when they write. Second, while about half of both groups of writers agreed or strongly agreed that their supervisors and directors revise their formal technical reports (survey items 30 and 36), none of the good writers but 45 percent of the poor writers agreed or strongly agreed that their supervisors revise their progress reports (survey item 10).

The above findings correlate well with the other findings reported earlier, which suggest that the good writers, as compared with the poor writers, more clearly understand their supervisor's expectations, are more confident about their writing, and are more convinced that their supervisors are satisfied with the quality of their reports. As a result, the supervisors (at least according to these writers) seldom revise the progress reports written by the good writers whereas they frequently revise those written by the poor writers. A contributing factor here, too, appears to be the fact that the good writers are more likely than are the poor writers to make extensive revisions to their own reports before they submit them to their supervisors. An even greater factor, however, may be that the good writers spend more time writing than do the poor writers. As shown in Table 9.13, the good writers spend an average of 20 percent of their job-related time writing, whereas poor writers spend an average of only 14 percent of their time writing. Furthermore, of the good writers, more than half (54 percent) spend 25–35 percent of their time writing, as compared with only one-fourth (18 percent) of the poor writers.

WRITING CRITERIA, WEAKNESSES, AND COMPOSING STRATEGIES

During the interviews, the supervisors and the researchers were asked to describe the criteria they use to evaluate their own writing, the weaknesses they think they have in writing, and the procedure they typically use to write their reports.

The subjects were first asked what criteria they use to evaluate their own writing—that is, how they determine whether their reports are "good." Responses were later classified into four types of criteria, the first three based upon the categories of rhetoric proposed by Zappen (1983) and previously discussed in Chapter 6.

1. *Language-oriented criteria* includes references to the conciseness, clarity, or continuity of the report.
2. *Audience-oriented criteria* includes references to the readers' purpose for reading the report, references to assuming the point of view of the intended reader in order to determine content, and references to feedback from readers.
3. *Writer-related criteria* includes one subject's reference to how the report "sounded" to him and another subject's reference to whether the report "felt right" to him.
4. *Research-related criteria* includes references to the accuracy or logic of the research results.

Finally, a fifth category, *Don't know*, was added to account for the one subject who said he had no way of knowing whether or not what he writes is effective.

The results, shown in Table 9.14, indicate that for the supervisors, the poor writers, and the good writers, the audience-oriented criteria are most important, the language-oriented criteria are next most important, and the

Table 9.14. Criteria Supervisors and Researchers Use to Evaluate Their Own Reports.

Criteria Categories	% Supervisors (n = 11)	Researchers (n = 22)	
		% Poor Writers (n = 11)	% Good Writers (n = 11)
Language-oriented	32	23	17
Audience-oriented	59	36	71
Writer-oriented	0	14	0
Research-oriented	9	18	12
Don't know	0	9	0

writer-oriented criteria are least important (excluding the one researcher who said he did not know what criteria he used).

The results further reveal that nearly three-fourths of the good writers, twice as many as the poor writers, use audience-oriented criteria to evaluate their own reports. This suggests that the good researcher–writers, more than the poor researcher–writers and more than even their supervisors, keep in mind the needs of their readers as they plan and write their reports.

When the subjects were asked how they arrived at their criteria, the majority (76 percent) cited experience: The longer they were at the company and the longer they had worked for a particular supervisor, the more reports they had written and the more feedback they had received. About half of the supervisors (45 percent) explained that their criteria for writing were based upon their experiences in reading numerous reports. Of the good writers, 27 percent indicated that their criteria were derived from either good teachers or from a previous boss who had instilled in them certain principles of effective writing. By contrast, none of the poor writers, as well as none of the supervisors, referred to having been influenced by a mentor. Only the poor writers (27 percent) could not explain the reasons for their criteria. Interestingly, no one from any of the three groups said that their criteria came from textbooks or from other written guidelines for reports.

The responses that the subjects gave to the question "What do you feel are your main weaknesses in writing?" were sorted into the categories shown in Table 9.15.

Results show that approximately one-fourth of the writers in each group think that the main problem with their reports is stylistic—that, for instance, the report is too technically worded, too concise, or too wordy. One-half of the poor writers attribute their weaknesses to problems in

Table 9.15. Writer-Identified Weaknesses in Writing.

Response Categories	% Supervisors (n = 11)	Researchers (n = 22)	
		% Poor Writers (n = 11)	% Good Writers (n = 11)
Content	14	18	27
Grammar	9	27	0
Style	27	23	27
Organization	14	14	9
Slow writing process	27	0	27
Timeliness of report	0	9	0
None or Don't know	9	9	9

either grammar or style. Although none of the good writers point to gram-matical weaknesses, they report about the same percentage of difficulty with style as do the poor writers and the supervisors.

One of the notable differences among the groups is that, whereas 27 percent of the supervisors and 27 percent of the good researcher-writers said that their main problem as a writer (or perhaps their main virtue) is that they spend too much time writing, none of the poor writers said they have a similar problem. Whether this means that poor writers do not spend as much time writing as do the good writers and the supervisors cannot be determined from this data. However, as discussed previously, other data (see Table 9.13, Appendix 9-B) indicate that the good researcher-writers spend an average of six percent more time on their job writing than do poor researcher-writers (an average of 20 percent for the good writers and 14 percent for the poor writers).

But perhaps the most important difference between the good writers and the poor writers is in the way the two groups reportedly approach their writing tasks. When the researchers were asked to describe how they nor-mally go about composing reports, they indicated quite different planning, organizing, and revising strategies, as revealed in Table 9.16.

First, with regard to planning strategies, poor writers are seven times more likely than good writers to use a parts-to-whole, or inductive, ap-proach. That is, by their own accounts, they tend to begin by immersing themselves in the particulars of their work—first assembling all of their data, graphs, and tables, and then either beginning to write a narrative, chronological account of their research or attempting to draw some conclu-sions from the particulars. This approach is best described by one of the poor-writer researchers: "I get all of my information (tables, etc.) gathered

Table 9.16.   Composing Strategies of Poor Writers and Good Writers.

	% Poor Writers (n = 11)	% Good Writers (n = 11)
Planning Strategies		
Parts-to-whole approach	64	9
Whole-to-parts approach	36	91
Organizing Strategies		
Uses no outline or plan	36	0
Uses a written outline	27	73
Outlines mentally	27	9
(Does not mention outlining)	9	18
Revising Strategies		
Revises while writing	18	23
Revises after 1st draft	27	59
Does not revise	9	9
(Does not mention revising)	45	9

together. I usually never make an outline. I sit down and think of why I'm writing, start there and tell the story: I did this and then this happened." On several occasions, the poor writers, like this writer, referred to their reports as "stories."

By contrast, over 90 percent of the good writers said that they use a whole-to-parts, or deductive, approach in planning their reports. That is, they begin by thinking of the major conclusions and points they want to emphasize and only then turn to the supporting data and details.

Not surprisingly, as shown in Table 9.16, over three times the number of good writers as compared with poor writers begin by constructing a written outline. Whereas none of the good writers denied using an outline or plan for their reports, 36 percent of the poor writers said they never use an outline or plan, either written or mental.

The revising strategies of the good writers versus the poor writers are also noteworthy. Compared with 27 percent of the poor writers, over twice as many of the good writers, 59 percent, said that they leave revising to the end, that is until after they have written a first draft. Although more good writers than poor writers indicated that they revise as they are writing the first draft, 45 percent of the poor writers never mentioned revising at all as part of their composing process, as compared with only 9 percent of the good writers. In short, the good writers are five times more likely to revise than are the poor writers. This finding corroborates previously reported results in which the good writers, more than the poor writers, reported that they "revise quite a bit."

THE NATURE OF PROGRESS REPORTS

Within this organization, the researchers write progress reports on a semi-monthly basis. These reports are submitted to their immediate supervisors and the director of the department, as well as distributed site-wide to those in the other departments, to top management and to select individuals (primarily business managers) at the corporation's international headquarters located in another state.

Characteristics of the Progress Reports

In total, 44 progress reports were collected from the 22 researchers (two reports from each researcher). In general, the progress reports are about one page, with a mean length of 20 lines. The t test revealed no statistically significant difference at the .05 level of probability in the length of the reports written by the poor writers ($M = 21$ lines) and those written by the good writers ($M = 19$ lines), ($p < .483$, $df = 20$). However, there is a statistically significant difference ($p < .051$, $df = 20$) in the length of the reports written by the scientist researchers ($M = 22$ lines) and those written by the engineer researchers ($M = 14$ lines).

About half (46 percent) of the progress reports have no appended tables or graphs, 27 percent have one, 18 percent have two, and 9 percent have three. With the exception of the analytical services department, which uses no prescribed format, most of the progress reports are organized according to an *Objective-Results-Future* format.

According to the subjects interviewed, in theory the reports are expected to be the informal, unpolished, and unedited work of the researchers. This was especially the unanimous consensus of the vice president and directors. Other subjects, however, confided that in practice some of the supervisors and occasionally the directors revise the reports before they are distributed. Most of these revisions were reportedly stylistic rather than substantive. Also, while most of those in upper management stressed that they did not expect that the results contained in the progress reports be totally validated—"people," as one director said, "aren't held responsible for their conjectures"—, many of the supervisor and researcher subjects either were not aware or were not convinced that this was the expectation. For various reasons that will be discussed later, the subjects were often reluctant to include speculations or opinions in their progress reports.

Basis for Expectations

When asked whether they knew of any explicit company or department guidelines for writing technical reports, the overwhelming majority of the supervisor and researcher subjects (85 percent) indicated that they were unaware of any explicit guidelines for semimonthly progress reports, though a few individuals vaguely recalled a memorandum that the vice president of R&D had issued a couple of years earlier concerning the format for formal technical reports. A small minority (9 percent) indicated that occasionally the minutes of staff meetings included suggestions for technical reports and that these minutes sometimes had model reports attached. For the most part, however, the subjects said that the guidelines are informal and left up to the individual directors, supervisors, and researchers. This was especially the case where the semimonthly progress reports are concerned.

When the same subjects were asked to rate, on a scale of 1 to 5 (with 1 least effective and 5 most effective), the present system of employee training in the area of written communication, the supervisors gave it a mean rating of 2.8; the poor writers, a mean rating of 2.2; and the good writers, a mean rating of 1.9. This indicates that, while all of them think that the system for training is below average, the supervisors are more content with it than are their researchers and that, of the researchers, the poorer writers are slightly more satisfied with the system than are the better writers.

Using the same 1–5 scale (1 = very inconsistent; 5 = very consistent), the subjects were asked to assess how consistent they think the expectations for reports are, both across research departments and within their own department. Not surprisingly, the results, shown in Table 9.17, reveal that all three groups perceive a greater consistency of expectations within their own departments than across departments. Both groups, supervisors and researchers, think that the expectations within their own departments are highly consistent but that the expectations across departments are only somewhat consistent. Interestingly, once again, the lowest ratings across the board were given by the good writers. It may be that the good writers, since they are more confident of their writing abilities, may feel freer to express criticism than the poor writers, who, during the interviews, seemed much more defensive and diffident about their capabilities as writers and in

Table 9.17. Means for Perceived Consistency of Expectations Within and Across Departments: Supervisors and Researchers.

| | | Researchers (n = 22) | |
	Supervisors (n = 11)	Poor Writers (n = 11)	Good Writers (n = 11)
Consistency of Expectations			
Within department	4.5	4.4	3.5
Across departments	3.0	3.3	2.7

general less inclined to make critical statements of any sort. It may be, too, that the good writers are simply more critical thinkers or that their standards are higher, perhaps even higher than those of their own supervisors.

As Table 9.18 reveals, the vast majority of good writers (63 percent) and poor writers (91 percent) said they learned expectations regarding progress reports by sheer experience—by "trial and error," as many of them said. Although the supervisors also said they relied primarily on trial and error, 27 percent indicated that they inferred expectations upon the basis of reading their co-workers' progress reports, whereas only 18 percent of the good writers and none of the poor writers said they did so.

Table 9.18. Basis for Reader and Writer Expectations Concerning Progress Reports.

		Researchers (n = 22)	
Response Categories	% Supervisors (n = 11)	% Poor Writers (n = 11)	% Good Writers (n = 11)
Trial & error	36	91	63
Reports of co-workers	27	0	18
Developed own	10	0	0
Supervisor guidelines	0	9	9
Director guidelines	15	0	9
Technical writing course	5	0	0

Later, during Phase 3, the subjects were again interviewed, only this time the questions pertained specifically to the researchers' progress reports (that is, their semimonthly reports) that had been analyzed during Phase 2 according to the different types of information contained in them. Since many of the open-ended questions in these second-round interviews concerned the subjects' perceptions of the importance, audience, and purpose of progress reports, I will report the results of these findings within this chapter instead of Chapter 11, which concerns Phase 3. (For the questionnaire that was used for the researcher-writer subjects in Phase 3, Experimental Task 1, see Appendix 11-A in Chapter 11. Once again, similar questionnaires were also used for the reader subjects, with slight changes in wording to reflect their role as the readers rather than the writers of the reports.) The following discussion is based on results from these round-two interviews (Phase 3), as well as further results from the round-one interviews.

Perceived Importance of Progress Reports to Various Audiences

The directors, supervisors, and researchers were asked to rate on a scale from 1 (not at all important) to 5 (very important) how important the progress reports were to themselves and how important they thought the progress reports were to their various audiences. Table 9.19 gives the mean ratings for each group. The following ranks each group's means in order from the audience that the group thinks values the progress reports the most to the audience that the group thinks values the reports the least.

Directors	*Supervisors*	*All Researchers*	*Poor Writers*	*Good Writers*
Director	Director	Res. & Dir.	Director	Res. & Sup.
Supervisor	VP of R&D	Supervisor	Researcher	Director
VP of R&D	Supervisor	VP of R&D	Supervisor	VP of R&D
Corp. Hdqtrs	Corp. Hdqtrs	Corp. Hdqtrs	VP of R&D	Corp. Hdqtrs
			Corp. Hdqtrs	

All three groups think that progress reports are not very important to the readers at corporate headquarters but that they are very important to the directors—in fact, slightly more important to the directors than to the supervisors, with the exception of the good writers, who think the reports are are more important to the supervisors than to the directors. Also, both the poor-writer researchers and the good-writer researchers feel that their progress reports are very important to themselves ($M = 4.0$). However, while the directors and supervisors regard the progress reports as very important to the vice president ($M = 3.9$), the researchers—both the poor writers and the good writers—regard the reports as only slightly above moderate importance ($M = 3.2$) to the vice president. Results therefore suggest that the researchers do not realize how important their progress reports may be to the vice president of R&D. If this is the case, they may be gearing the informational content of their reports to audiences within their own depart-

Table 9.19.   Means for Subjects' Perceived Importance of Progress Reports to Various Audiences.

	Subjects' Mean Ratings				
	Directors (n = 4)	**Supervisors** (n = 11)	**All Researchers** (n = 22)	**Pr Wtrs** (n = 11)	**Gd Wtrs** (n = 11)
Perceived Audiences					
Researcher	—*	—*	4.0	4.0	4.0
Supervisor	4.0	3.8	3.9	3.6	4.0
Director	4.3	4.3	4.0	4.3	3.7
VP of R&D	3.9	3.9	3.2	3.2	3.2
Corp Hdqtrs	2.1	2.7	2.8	3.0	2.6

*Inadvertently not asked due to an oversight when the second-round questionnaires were revised for each group of subjects.

ments (themselves, their supervisors, and their directors)—audiences that they assume are more knowledgeable about their research projects than may be the audiences outside the departments.

As will be discussed shortly, the more remote the readers, the less sure researchers are about how readers are using their progress reports or whether they are reading them at all. One supervisor suggested that the progress report is the only means of direct access that researchers have to those in upper management, and that, similarly, upper management regards the progress report as their direct line to the unfiltered, unedited work and thinking of the researchers. Evidently, however, the researchers do not recognize this channel of communication; or, if they do, they do not think it as important as the inside channels of communication leading to their immediate supervisors and directors.

General Purposes of Progress Reports

Although the progress reports serve various purposes depending upon the specific audience, most subjects at all levels indicated that the primary purpose of the progress report is to inform. The vice president said that the director and the supervisors of a department use the progress reports to make decisions regarding the following two weeks' research. The comments of the subjects, however, seldom revealed whether or not the reports are used in this manner. While three of the supervisors (27 percent) explicitly said that they use the reports for short-term decision making, the other 73 percent did not indicate whether or not they use the reports to make decisions. More interesting is the fact that two of the good writers (18 percent) but none of the poor writers said that they thought the reports are used for decision making. Conversely, although two of the poor writers (18 percent) said they did not think that the reports are used for decision making, only one of the good writers indicated as much, saying, "I'd like to think that they're used in decision making but they're not at any level. Personal communication and politics is what gets things done." These results, though based on low percentages of a small sample suggest that good writers, more than poor writers, may be more aware of upper management's expectation that progress reports be used as a basis for decision making.

When the supervisor and researcher subjects were asked to explain the specific purposes that they think the progress reports serve for various readers, in general the subjects made the following distinctions:

Supervisors, the subjects said, use the reports

1.   To keep abreast of the status of current work.

2. To have documentation of the work for use at staff meetings or for use in preparing weekly highlights or quarterly reports.
3. To evaluate the researcher's performance.

Directors, the subjects said, probably read the reports for similar reasons. Many subjects, however, indicated that the directors are usually not as interested in the details of the research as are the supervisors, but rather are more interested in the overall picture, direction, and value of the various research projects within the department. The directors, more than the supervisors, need backup information to convince top management of the progress and, thus, the value of the department's projects.

Most of the supervisor and researcher subjects said that they were convinced that the vice president does indeed read all or most of the progress reports issued every two weeks. Several guessed that he reads them in order to keep informed of and monitor the various research projects or to justify or promote R&D programs to both corporate headquarters and subsidiaries abroad. A few of the researchers said that they thought his main purpose in reading the reports is to assess the effectiveness of the researchers themselves. A few other researchers, however, doubted whether the vice president reads the reports at all.

While all of the supervisors were aware that specific individuals at corporate headquarters read the progress reports, about one fourth of the good-writer researchers and nearly one half of the poor-writer researchers said either that they were not aware that people at corporate headquarters receive or read the reports, or that they did not know why corporate headquarters was receiving the reports or how they were using them. Most of the supervisors and researchers, however, indicated that individuals at corporate headquarters are probably reading the reports to "watchdog" specific projects under their budgetary jurisdiction in order to allocate funding or to identify promising avenues for long-term investment. Once again, the better writers seem more aware than the poorer writers of their remote readers and the reasons why these readers needed their progress reports.

A few of the supervisor subjects and the good-writer subjects who were sensitive to the long-distance, economic interest of corporate headquarters suggested that perhaps corporate headquarters should not be receiving the semimonthly progress reports since this audience often does not realize that the reports' speculations and conclusions, whether positive or negative, are simply tentative and subject to change in the following weeks' progress reports. Some researchers said that, while R&D management encouraged them to speculate about the significance of their short-term research results, those at corporate headquarters were often too eager to assume that these results meant long-term success. In a similar vein, some researchers expressed anxiety about reporting negative short-term results or setbacks for fear these might discourage corporate support and prematurely abort a project that, if allowed to continue, could eventually yield positive results. As indicated previously, however, both the supervisors and the researchers regard readers at corporate headquarters as the least important audience for progress reports.

Purposes of Progress Reports for Supervisor Readers and Researcher Writers

Since the primary purpose of the progress report is apparently to inform, and since the primary readers are the supervisors and directors, it important to examine, first, how informative (or news-bearing) the readers think that the reports are, as compared with how informative the writers of the reports think that their readers think the reports are; and, second, the ways in which readers—here, specifically, supervisors—use the information in progress reports, as compared with how the writers think that these readers use the information in their reports. In addition, as indicated above, since the researchers said that their reports are of equal or greater importance to themselves as to their readers, it is important to examine what purposes the reports are serving for the writers.

When the supervisors and researchers were asked whether they thought the information contained in progress reports came as news to their respective directors, 91 percent of the supervisors, 73 percent of the poor-writer researchers, and 67 percent of the good-writer researchers said they thought that most of the information in the progress reports would be news to their directors. Since the supervisors rather than the researchers are in daily contact with their respective director, the supervisors are probably in the best position to judge how much their director knows about a given project.

While the progress reports are news-bearing to directors, according to the supervisors, they are not news-bearing to themselves. When the supervisors were asked whether the information contained in their researchers' progress reports was generally news to them as readers, only 18 percent of the supervisors said that the information came as news; the other 72 percent said that through verbal communication with their researchers they usually knew most of the information by the time the progress reports were submitted to them. Interestingly, when the researchers were asked whether they thought that the information contained in their progress reports was news to their supervisors, the same percentage of good writers as supervisors (18 percent) said that they did not think that the information was news to their supervisors. By contrast, 45 percent of the poor writers— three times as many as the good writers—said that they *did* think that the information in their reports was news to their supervisors.

When, during Phase 3, the data were further examined to determine the match between individual supervisors and their researchers, results revealed that 86 percent of the good writers correctly judged whether or not their respective supervisors regarded the information in their progress reports as news, whereas only 36 percent of the poor writers correctly judged whether the information in their reports was news to their respective supervisors. This misjudgment on the part of the poorer writers suggests that, compared with the better writers, they are much less aware of what their supervisors know and need to know. The better writers, both as a group and individually, more accurately assess their supervisor readers' knowledge of the work in progress than do the poorer writers. In short, to use speech-act terminology, compared with the poor writers and their supervisors, the good writers and their supervisors have mutual contextual beliefs or assumptions about the news value of progress reports.

These results also suggest that, contrary to the popular notion that the aim of progress reports is to inform, at this company the progress reports do not have an informative purpose for the vast majority of the supervisor readers. This being the case, then what other purposes do the .progress reports serve for these readers? Table 9.20 categorizes the responses that the subjects gave when the supervisors were asked how they use their researchers' progress reports and when the researchers were asked how they thought that their supervisors use their progress reports.

First, it is interesting to note that for over one-fourth of the supervisors the progress reports serve no purpose. The remaining three-fourths, however, do use the reports either to get an overview of the project's progress and thus to make decisions or to provide them with the documentation they need to further report information to their superiors. While over one-third of the poor writers assume that the supervisors use their progress reports either to check the accuracy of the researchers' results or to give the re-

Table 9.20. Purposes of Progress Reports for Supervisors.

		Researchers (n = 22)	
	% Supervisors (n = 11)	% Poor Writers (n = 11)	% Good Writers (n = 11)
Response Categories			
No purpose	27	27	18
Information to determine progress or to make decisions	36	9	27
Reference or documentation	36	27	45
Check accuracy; give researcher direction	0	36	9

searcher direction, none of the supervisors indicate this as their purpose for reading the reports. The one good-writer researcher who did cite this as a purpose took a different slant: he said that his supervisor screened the report not so much for its accuracy as for its political tone and implications.

The results also indicate that the good writers are three times as likely as the poor writers to realize that one of the main reasons that the supervisors read the reports is to evaluate the progress of the project and not, as some of the poor writers assume, to evaluate either the research or the researcher. Also, nearly half of the good writers—about twice as many as the poor writers—realize that the supervisors' other main purpose in reading the reports is to have the information as reference.

These findings suggest that, compared with the poor writers, the good writers have not only a better understanding of the knowledge of their supervisor-readers but also a better understanding of how their supervisors actually use the information in their progress reports. This is the case both when comparing group against group responses (those of the poor writers and good writers versus those of their supervisors) and when comparing the matches between individual writers and their supervisors.

In addition, although both groups of researchers—the poor writers and the good writers—regard their progress reports as very important to themselves, the two groups value the progress report for quite different reasons. Table 9.21 categorizes the reasons the researchers gave when they were asked why their progress reports are important to them, as well as the reasons that their supervisors gave for why they think the progress reports are (or ought to be) important to the researchers.

Table 9.21. Purposes of Progress Reports for the Researcher Writers.

		Researchers (n = 22)	
	% Supervisors (n = 11)	% Poor Writers (n = 11)	% Good Writers (n = 11)
Response Categories			
Helps to write formal reports; keeps data organized	9	55	23
Helps to plan the next two weeks' work	0	27	0
Helps to think through results, discover significance of research	64	18	68
Chance to communicate with management	18	0	9
No purpose	9	0	0

The first two categories listed above describe essentially instrumental functions of the progress reports. In the first response category the progress report is used to help researchers later write their longer, more formal reports; in the second response category, the report is used to help researchers schedule their work. In the third response category, however, it is not so much the report itself but rather the *writing* of the report that is important to the researcher. As many of the good writers attested, having to write a progress report forces them "to figure out the meaning of the data," "to crystallize results," "to clarify the significance of the research," — in short, "to think." Writing thus serves a primarily heuristic function for the better progress-report writers.

The results in Table 9.21 indicate that the good writers are over three times as likely as the poor writers to value progress reports, or rather progress report writing, as a means of generating ideas and critically evaluating their work. Conversely, the poor writers are over three times as likely as the good writers to value the progress reports as a means of planning either future reports or future work (categories one and two combined). Unlike the good writers, the poorer writers do not tend to view their progress reports as having value in and of themselves but rather as a means toward some practical, task-oriented ends in the future. The majority of supervisors, on the other hand, think that the progress reports are of value to the researchers primarily because of their heuristic function. Many of them explicitly stated that this was the main reason for and biggest benefit of the reports—that the reports forced the researchers to think about the meaning and significance of what they were doing. Only one supervisor said that he thought that the progress reports served a primarily utilitarian function for the researchers (that is, to help them write their formal reports).

Again, the intentions of the good writers and the expectations of supervisors are in closer agreement than those of the poor writers and supervisors. The extent to which the good writers value progress reports for their heuristic importance (68 percent) closely matches the extent to which the supervisors think that the researchers value, or ought to value, the reports for this purpose (64 percent).

Weaknesses in Progress Reports

When asked what they perceived as the main weaknesses in progress reports, the majority of the subjects—both the writers and the readers of the reports—indicated that the reports are often too technical. Some pointed out that in many instances the technical jargon is unavoidable, given the esoteric nature of much of the research, and that it is unrealistic to expect anyone but those directly involved in a project to comprehend the nature of the work, much less the report. This, they said, is especially the case when the research is of a highly exploratory nature, demanding very specialized and advanced knowledge in, for instance, microbiology, biochemistry, or genetics.

But by far the most common complaint regarding progress reports was that they contain too many details and too few conclusions. Often, data or results, the subjects said, are presented as though their significance is self-evident. The failure to draw conclusions, however tentative, was attributed to several causes, which can be reduced to these three: (a) the periodic nature of the reports, (b) the heterogeneous audience for the reports, and (c) the writers themselves.

First, several subjects noted that the progress reports are written by the calendar rather than by the need to report research results. Because of the scope and duration of some of the projects, some felt that it may simply be impossible at the initial stages of a project to report anything more than, say, the details of the method, sample preparation, or raw data. Significant results, in short, do not present themselves like clockwork in two-week intervals.

Second, because the progress reports are distributed to a heterogeneous audience—an audience including one's immediate co-workers, supervisor, and director; the researchers, supervisors, and directors of other research departments on site; upper management of R&D; and business managers at corporate headquarters—many subjects indicated that it is difficult in one report to provide the kind and degree of information that each of these audiences needs since their degree of knowledge about and interest in the project varies. Whereas, for instance, supporting details and data may be of importance to the project supervisor, who has to monitor and evaluate the quality of the research, that same information may be extraneous, if not confusing and distracting, to those who, for budgetary or planning pur-poses, may be interested in simply whether or not something works or looks promising. If, as was suggested earlier, the writers of the progress reports view the reports as being most important to themselves and their immediate supervisor and director, they may gear the content of their re-ports to those closest to their research and thus may emphasize specifics that their other, secondary audiences may not comprehend, need, or appreciate.

Most of the subjects interviewed, however, attributed the preponderance of details and lack of conclusions in the progress reports to the writers themselves. Despite the difficulties inherent in meeting the needs of diverse audiences, many subjects suggested that the writers simply fail to consider their audience at all when writing their progress reports—that they write for themselves rather than for their intended readers. Others surmised that the writers are hesitant to speculate about the significance of their findings for fear that such speculations might later be proven wrong and thus might reflect upon them poorly as researchers.

In a related vein, when the supervisors were asked whether they thought that their researchers felt any anxiety about reporting negative results or news (that is, information that suggested the project might not be as promising as had been hoped), 78 percent of the supervisors said that they thought their researchers definitely felt such anxiety. One supervisor said that "a lot of editing goes on if the result is negative. Even a negative can be couched in the positive"; another said that "some [researcher writers] tend to whitewash the project or avoid reporting negative results at all"; and another suggested that the pressure to avoid bad news comes from the director and those higher up: "I can think of examples where he [the director] has said 'We aren't going to publish this' and the results were cast in a more favorable light." One supervisor explained that whether or not people felt or ought to feel anxiety was due primarily to the quality of their research itself: "Sometimes you get bad results from good experimental work; if so, there's no anxiety. But if a poor experimental design leads to negative results, then there is anxiety. And the worst case scenario of all is when a bad experimental design produces positive results." Finally, another supervisor indicated that, although he thought some researchers felt anxiety, "it is the section leader's [supervisor's] job to assure them that they shouldn't—that they are not going to be held personally responsible. We want to know these things [problems, negative results] early."

Despite the anxiety that the supervisors think that their researchers have about reporting bad news, only a few of the researchers said they actually felt such anxiety. One said, "I tend to support the negative with the positive until I'm ready to say 'This is a dog' because these guys [people in upper management] tend to take any negative news as a sign of failure." Similarly, another researcher said, "If you want a project to go, you have to put positive results in. Negative results will kill it." The majority of researchers (70 percent of the poor writers and 75 percent of the good writers), however, said that they feel no anxiety about reporting negative results when they write their progress reports. As one researcher put it, "It's in the best interests of the company that we let them know early on if something isn't going well. This way we can save the company a lot of money in the long run."

Some of the subjects also suggested that writers may be intentionally loading their progress reports with uninterpreted data and observations in order to make their work appear more complex and inscrutable than it is or to make themselves appear industrious and scientific. Some explained this as "job security": if it appeared that no one else but the researcher himself could comprehend the complexities of the work reported, then the researcher might be viewed as indispensable. Still others explained the tendency toward obscure and excessive detail as a carryover of the writers' experiences with school writing in which their teachers, so it seemed, evaluated papers by how long and belabored they were.

PREFERENCES FOR TYPES OF INFORMATION IN PROGRESS REPORTS

One of the main objectives of Phase 1 was to examine the extent to which the readers and writers of the progress reports thought that certain types of information ought or ought not be included in progress reports. To assess their preferences, the subjects were asked to rate on a scale of 1 to 5 the degree to which they thought that the types of information listed in the following tables belong in a progress report (1 = not at all; 5 = most definitely). Table 9.22 gives the preferences, in rank order, of all 39 of the writers and readers of the progress reports who participated in this study.

Table 9.22. Total Subjects' Overall Mean Preferences for Types of Information in Progress Reports.

Type of Information	All Subjects (n = 39)	
	Mean	SD
Facts, observations	3.92	1.13
General conclusions	3.64	1.27
Explanations, discussion	3.23	1.11
Detailed data	2.49	1.23
Opinions	2.43	1.29
Recommendations	2.33	1.42
Procedure, experimental	2.02	1.36
Historical background	1.90	1.07
Context of project	1.88	1.08

As indicated above, the results for the entire sample reveal that writers and readers most prefer facts and observations, with conclusions a close second, and furthermore that these subjects least prefer information about the historical background or context of the project. These data then were sorted according to the preferences of various subpopulations (that is, the director and supervisor readers versus those of the researcher-writers; the poor writers versus the good writers; the scientist-researchers versus the engineer-researchers; and those writers in the organization's four departments). For the paired groups, the two-tailed *t* test (pooled variance) and for the four departments the one-way analysis of variance test were chosen as the appropriate tests for these data. For the most part, the mean preferences of these various subgroups for various types of information do not vary significantly from those indicated in Table 9.22 and therefore these data are not reported here. There is, however, one notable exception.

As shown in Table 9.23, there is a statistically significant difference (p <.05) between the readers (directors and supervisors) and writers (researchers) of the progress reports, with regard to the two groups' preference for facts. The readers, though they think that facts are important (M = 3.53), do not place nearly as much importance upon them as do the writers (M = 4.23). Furthermore, whereas the readers prefer facts only slightly more than conclusions, the writers prefer facts much more than conclusions.

Table 9.23.   Mean Preferences of Readers (Directors and Supervisors) vs. Writers (Researchers) for Various Kinds of Information in Progress Reports.

Type of Information	Readers (Directors & Supervisors) (n = 15)		Writers (Researchers) (n = 22)	
	Mean	SD	Mean	SD
Facts	3.53*	1.46	4.23*	0.69
Conclusions	3.40	1.40	3.82	1.22
Explanations	3.20	1.21	3.36	1.00
Data	2.73	1.33	2.41	1.18
Opinions	2.53	1.51	2.32	1.21
Recommendations	2.33	1.45	2.27	1.49
Procedure	1.93	1.16	2.09	1.15
Background	1.87	1.13	2.00	1.07
Context	2.07	1.22	1.72	0.99

$*p < .05$ $t = -1.95$ $df = 35$ (pooled variance)

Reorganization of Data by Phase 2 Classification of Information

Following Phase 1, the types of information listed in Tables 9.22 and 9.23 were reorganized and grouped to reflect the five types of information that were used during Phase 2 to classify the information in the researchers' progress reports. This was done so that comparisons between the types of information preferred and the types of information actually contained in the progress reports could later be made. Since the five types of information are described in detail in the next chapter, the following identifies only the labels of the five types of information and lists only how the various types of information listed in Tables 9.22 and 9.23 were later resorted according to the Phase 2 scheme of classification.

Phase 2	*Types of Information*	*Tables 9.22 & 9.23 Information*
1	(What I did)	historical background; context of project
2	(How I did it)	procedure, experimental
3	(What I got)	detailed data; facts, observations
4	(What it means)	explanation, discussion; opinions
5	(What it's good for)	general conclusions; recommendations

To derive the data concerning the subjects' mean preferences for Types 1, 2, 3, 4, and 5 information, the subjects' original mean scores for the various kinds of corresponding information listed in the right column were added and averaged. For example, to obtain the poor writers' mean preference for Type 3 information, their mean preferences for detailed data, facts, and observations were combined and averaged.

Group Preferences for Types 1, 2, 3, 4, 5 Information

The new data were sorted and analyzed to determine whether there were any significant differences between the following groups in their preferences for Types 1, 2, 3, 4, and 5 information:

1. departments 1, 2, 3, and 4
2. readers and writers
   2.1 directors and supervisors versus researchers
   2.2 supervisors versus poor writers; supervisors versus good writers
3. writers
   3.1 poor writers versus good writers
   3.2 scientist writers versus engineer writers

Tables 9.24–9.27 give the mean preferences of each of these groups for the five types of information. In general, the groups least prefer Types 1 and

Table 9.24. Means of Department Preferences for Types 1, 2, 3, 4, 5 Information.

Info	Dept. 1 (n = 10)		Dept. 2 (n = 7)		Dept. 3 (n = 13)		Dept. 4 (n = 7)	
	Mean	SD	Mean	SD	Mean	SD	Mean	SD
Type 1	2.35	0.97	1.86	0.63	1.85	0.92	1.57	0.73
Type 2	1.40	0.97	2.57	1.13	2.23	1.17	2.00	1.15
Type 3	2.75	0.83	2.93	1.17	3.62	0.94	3.43	0.84
Type 4	2.40	0.46	2.79	1.04	3.08	1.17	3.00	1.29
Type 5	2.90	1.51	2.76	1.22	2.81	0.99	3.64	1.18

*Means are not significant at .05 level of probability.

Table 9.25. Means of Director- and Supervisor-Reader and Researcher-Writer Preferences for Types 1, 2, 3, 4, 5 Information.

Information	Directors & Supervisors (n = 15)		Researchers (n = 22)	
	Mean	SD	Mean	SD
Type 1	1.93	0.93	1.89	0.84
Type 2	2.00	1.16	2.09	1.15
Type 3	3.13	1.30	3.27	0.73
Type 4	2.80	1.19	2.84	0.92
Type 5	2.90	1.35	3.05	1.43

*Means are not significant at .05 level of probability.

2 information and most prefer Type 3 information, followed closely by Type 5 information and next by Type 4 information. The exceptions are departments 1 and 4 (Table 9.24) and the supervisors (Table 9.26), all of whom most prefer Type 5 information.

Analysis of the results by the two-tailed t test, and for the departments by the one-way analysis of variance test, revealed no significant differences at the .05 level of probability among the four departments (Table 9.24) or between the director and supervisor readers and the researcher writers (Table 9.25) in their preferences for the five types of information.

The lack of significant differences in the means of these groups suggests that the expectations of the four departments are similar. That is, each department prefers the same type of information to approximately the same extent, and the director and the supervisor readers and the researcher writers prefer the same type of information to approximately the same extent.

The results shown in Table 9.26 further indicate no statistically significant difference at the .05 level of probability between the mean preferences of the supervisors and the poor writers or between the mean preferences of the supervisors and the good writers. In other words, both groups of writers tend to prefer the same type of information as do the supervisors. However, as shown in 9.26, for all types information except Type 2, the mean preferences of the good writers are closer to their supervisors' mean preferences than are the mean preferences of the poor writers and those of their supervisors.

Next, the data were resorted and analyzed to determine whether there were any significant differences between the writers in their preferences for Types 1, 2, 3, 4, and 5 information. Table 9.27 shows the mean preferences of the poor writers versus the good writers and the mean preferences of the scientist writers versus the engineer writers. Analysis of the data by the

Table 9.26. Means of Supervisor and Poor Writer vs. Good Writer Preferences for Types 1, 2, 3, 4, 5 Information.

Information	Supervisors (n = 11)		Researchers (n = 22)			
			Poor Writers (n = 11)		Good Writers (n = 11)	
	Mean	SD	Mean	SD	Mean	SD
Type 1	2.09	1.07	1.50	0.71	2.27	0.82
Type 2	1.90	1.22	1.73	0.91	2.46	1.29
Type 3	3.09	1.04	3.27	0.47	3.27	0.91
Type 4	2.64	1.21	3.05	0.99	2.64	0.84
Type 5	3.14	1.12	2.91	0.97	3.18	1.32

*Means are not significant at the .05 level of probability.

two-tailed t test (pooled variance) revealed that for most types of information there is no statistically significant difference between the writers' preferences.

As these tables reveal, however, there is a significant ($p < .02$) difference between the poor writers and the good writers in their preference for Type 1 information (description of what they did and why), with the good writers placing more importance on this type of information than do the poor writers. Also, there is a significant difference ($p < .04$) between the scientist

Table 9.27. Means of Writer Preferences for Types 1, 2, 3, 4, 5 Information.

Information	Poor Writers (n = 11)	SD	Good Writers (n = 11)	SD
Type 1	1.50*	0.71	2.27*	0.82
Type 2	1.73	0.91	2.46	1.29
Type 3	3.27	0.47	3.27	0.91
Type 4	3.05	0.99	2.64	0.84
Type 5	2.90	0.29	3.18	0.40

Information	Scientist Writers (n = 16)	SD	Engineer Writers (n = 6)	SD
Type 1	2.06	0.79	1.42	0.86
Type 2	2.25	1.18	1.67	1.03
Type 3	3.09**	0.69	3.75**	0.52
Type 4	2.72	0.89	3.17	0.98
Type 5	3.03	1.10	3.08	1.36

*$p < .02$ $t = -2.37$ $df = 20$ (pooled variance)
**$p < .04$ $t = -2.10$ $df = 20$ (pooled variance)

writers and the engineer writers with respect to their degree of preference for Type 3 information (facts, data, and observations), with the engineers preferring this type of information to a greater extent than do the scientists. Quite frankly, I am not sure what to make of this finding, especially since it seems to run counter to the prevailing notions about scientists versus engineers, as discussed in Chapter 5, and counter to my own experiences in working with the reports of scientists versus those of engineers. One possible explanation is that the lopsided distribution of the number of scientist writers (16) versus the much smaller number of engineer writers (only 6) may have skewed the data.

PERCEIVED INFLUENCE OF STAGE OF PROJECT UPON INFORMATIONAL CONTENT OF PROGRESS REPORTS

When the subjects were asked whether they thought that the stage of a research project affects the type of information contained in a progress report, 36 percent of the supervisors, 40 percent of the good writers, and 80 percent of the poor writers said that they thought that the type of information would be the same regardless of whether the report was written toward the beginning, middle, or end of the entire research project. Most of those who thought that the stage of the project was a variable suggested that the initial progress reports would contain more background and explanation of what was done; that the reports written toward the middle would contain more data and results; and that the reports written toward the end of the project would contain more conclusions, implications, and recommendations.

A few of the subjects, however, suggested that the earlier the stage of the research project, the more likely a report would contain opinion, "hype," and recommendations and that the data and results would come only toward the end of the project. Still a couple of others suggested that what determined the type of information included in the progress report was not the stage of the research project so much as the nature of the specific research project or the nature of the research done within a particular department.

CONCLUSIONS

The most notable differences between the poor writers and the good writers are that, to a greater extent than the poor writers, the good writers express the following:

1. More positive working relationships with their respective supervisors and directors.
2. A greater confidence in their writing.
3. A greater awareness of their supervisor's expectations concerning progress reports.
4. A greater belief that their own notions about what constitutes a good report closely match those of their supervisors.
5. A greater belief that their supervisors are satisfied with the quality of their reports.
6. A greater amount of time on the job spent writing.
7. A greater amount of time spent revising their reports.
8. A greater tendency to use audience-oriented criteria to evaluate their reports.
9. A greater tendency to use a deductive versus an inductive strategy when planning their reports, as well as a greater tendency to use outlines.
10. A greater tendency to value as most important in their progress reports the same types of information that their supervisors most value.

In addition, with respect to progress reports, the good writers, in contrast with the poor writers, are more aware of their supervisors' prior knowledge about the work reported and more accurate in their assumptions about the ways in which the supervisors use the information contained in progress reports.

The results of this phase also suggest that the planning strategies of the two groups of writers may be different. The poor writers tend to view their progress reports as narratives and to use a chronological, parts-to-whole planning strategy when composing their reports. In addition, the reasons that the poor writers gave for why progress reports are important to them indicate that they view the progress report as a link in the chain of events leading to some future action they will perform (either writing a formal report or scheduling the next two weeks' work).

By contrast, the results reported thus far suggest that the planning strategies of the better writers may be governed more by logical, rather than temporal, relationships. They generally do not plan their reports by reviewing what they did and in what order, as do many of the poor writers, but rather by thinking of the overall conclusions and significance of their work. Interestingly, unlike several of the poorer writers, none of the better writers referred to their progress reports as "stories." The better writers tend to view their progress reports as opportunities for conceptualizing the significance of their work, whereas for the poorer writers the reports are opportunities for chronicling the events of their work.

At this R&D organization, no explicit guidelines for progress reports exist; rather, expectations are learned on a trial and error basis. The reports are read by a diverse audience that extends from one's co-workers to business managers. For some, the progress report is informative (for instance, for directors and the vice president of R&D); for others, the report serves primarily as reference or as a guide to short-term decision making. The writers regard themselves, their directors, and their supervisors as the most important audiences for the progress reports, and corporate headquarters as the least important. Subjects said that the main weaknesses of progress reports are that they are written at too technical a level and do not contain enough interpretation of the data, observations, or results.

Readers and writers tend to most prefer the same type of information—namely, facts, conclusions, and explanations—and to least prefer the same type of information—namely, background and context of the project. However, writers prefer facts to a significantly greater degree than do the readers (directors and supervisors). This might be explained by the writers' greater involvement in the research and by the readers' greater need to know what the facts signify rather than to know the facts themselves.

When the subjects' preferences were translated into the types of information used in Phase 2 to analyze the reports, it was found that most groups tend to most prefer Type 3 information (facts, data, observations), followed closely by either Type 4 information (what the Type 3 information means) or Type 5 information (how the Type 4 information can be applied). The supervisors, however, most prefer Type 5 information.

Analyses revealed no significant differences among the preferences of the four departments or between the readers and writers of the progress reports. The former suggests that the nature of research done within the different departments does not affect the departments' preferences for Types 1, 2, 3, 4, or 5 information. The latter suggests that the readers and writers have mutual contextual beliefs about the type of information most and least desirable in progress reports. However, the preferences of the good writers and the supervisors reveal a closer match than do the preferences of the poor writers and the supervisors.

When the preferences of the writers were compared, it was found that the good writers prefer Type 1 information (description of what was done and why) to a significantly greater extent than do the poor writers. Also, the engineer writers prefer Type 3 information to a significantly greater extent than do the scientist writers. For the most part, however, the preferences of the writers—poor writers and good writers, and scientist writers and engineer writers—are about the same.

APPENDIX 9-A
SAMPLE SURVEY USED FOR PHASE 1 INTERVIEWS

Phase 1 Survey & Interviews with Researcher-Writer Subjects

Name_____ Position_____

1. Number of years with this company_____
   a) 1–3 b) 4–8 c) 9–15 d) 16–25 e) over 25

2. Number of years in your present position_____
   a) 0–3 b) 4–6 c) 7–10 d) 11–15 e) over 15

3. Total number of years experience in this field_____
   a) 1–5 b) 6–10 c) 11–20 d) 20–30 e) over 30
   [the field: _____]

4. Highest degree held_____ Major_____
   a) BS b) MS c) MBA d) Ph.D. e) other

5. What formal training in writing have you had either in college or within this or another corporation? How effective was that training in preparing you for the type of on-the-job writing you currently do?

	Low			High	
a) college composition or rhetoric	1	2	3	4	5
b) business writing undergrad	1	2	3	4	5
c) " " grad	1	2	3	4	5
d) technical writing undergrad	1	2	3	4	5
e) " " grad	1	2	3	4	5
f) other_____	1	2	3	4	5

6. Approximately what percentage of your time on the job entails writing?
   _____

7. Describe the following regarding your own writing:

   Type   Length   Frequency   Audience   % of Total Wtg

8. Approximately what percentage of your time on the job is spent reading letters, memos, or reports sent to you? (Include reports that are not directed to you but which are circulated to you.)

   Total %_____ (letters: _____% memos_____%
   reports: _____% other_____%)

INDIVIDUAL INTENTIONS

9. What criteria do you use to evaluate the effectiveness of your own writing? (How do you know whether what you're writing is good?)

10. How did you arrive at that criteria?

11. What criteria do the following use to evaluate your reports?
    a. your section leader—

    b. your director—

12. What do you think are the strengths of your writing?

13. What do you think are the weaknesses of your writing?

14. Briefly describe how you normally go about composing a letter, memo, or report.

15. What do you consider the main weaknesses in the semimonthly reports written by researchers? What do you think are the main reasons for those weaknesses? Approximately what percentage of the total number of semimonthly reports you read contain those weaknesses?

    Weakness   *Cause*   *Frequency*

16. What do you consider the main weaknesses in the progress reports written by researchers? Who do you think are the reasons for those weaknesses? Approximately what percentage of the total number of progress reports you read contain those weaknesses?

    Weakness   *Cause*   *Frequency*

COMPANY/DEPARTMENT/SECTION EXPECTATIONS
CONCERNING WRITTEN COMMUNICATION

17. Describe how you learned the department's expectations concerning semimonthly and progress reports.

18. Do you know of any explicit or implicit guidelines regarding the general style, format, organization, or content of written reports? If so, at what level(s) of the company do they exist, how were they developed, and how are they conveyed to personnel?

19. How would you rate the present system of employee training in the area of written communication?

    Low   High
    1   2   3   4   5

20. Describe the distinctions, if any, between the semimonthly report and the progress report, with respect to the following:

    Semimonthly   *Progress*
    a) style

  b) organization
  c) content (type of info.)
  d) format
  e) purpose

21. Within the R&D organization, to what extent are the above expectations consistent across departments of R&D?

<table>
<tr><td></td><td colspan="5">Not at all   Highly</td></tr>
<tr><td></td><td>1</td><td>2</td><td>3</td><td>4</td><td>5</td></tr>
</table>

22. To what extent are these expectations consistent within the department you are in?

       1   2   3   4   5

23. To what extent does your section leader expect you to include the following types of information in a semimonthly report and in a progress report (1=not at all; 5=most definitely)

	Semimonthly	*Progress*
	1 2 3 4 5	1 2 3 4 5

  a) detailed data
  b) facts, observations
  c) explanations, discussion
  d) general conclusions
  e) background (historical context of project)
  f) references to previous reports on the same project
  g) recommendations
  h) opinions
  i) description of procedure (experimental)

24. Explain what happens once you submit a semimonthly report to your section leader.

25. Explain the way in which progress reports are written in your section.

26. How, if at all, does the type of information in a semimonthly report or a progress report change depending upon the stage of the research project, the nature of the particular research, or any other variables?

SURVEY OF ATTITUDES

Strongly Disagree	Disagree	Neutral	Agree	Strongly Agree
1	2	3	4	5

  1. I feel confident about my writing.   1 2 3 4 5

2. Expectations regarding written reports are pretty much the same across sections.   1 2 3 4 5

3. I am generally happy with my job.   1 2 3 4 5

4. The ability to write well is a significant factor in evaluation of job performance.   1 2 3 4 5

5. My section leader and I have similar notions about what a good report is.   1 2 3 4 5

6. My section leader is satisfied with the quality of my reports.   1 2 3 4 5

7. I revise quite a bit when I write.   1 2 3 4 5

8. I am clear about what my section leader expects in a semimonthly report.   1 2 3 4 5

9. The ability to write well is important in promotion decisions.   1 2 3 4 5

10. My section leader normally revises my semimonthly reports.   1 2 3 4 5

11. I like to write.   1 2 3 4 5

12. My section leader and my director have similar expectations regarding progress reports.   1 2 3 4 5

13. My section leader and my director have similar expectations regarding semimonthly reports.   1 2 3 4 5

14. I am expected to do some of my job writing at home.   1 2 3 4 5

15. When I plan a report, I usually think through the main points before I begin to write the actual report.   1 2 3 4 5

16. I usually do some job writing at home.   1 2 3 4 5

17. The amount of writing associated with my job is realistic.   1 2 3 4 5

18. When I write, I frequently change word choices and sentences as I am composing.   1 2 3 4 5

19. My working relationship with my section leader is good.   1 2 3 4 5

20. I have a systematic procedure that I follow when I write my reports.   1 2 3 4 5

21. If I am only sitting at my desk composing a report, it looks to my section leader as if I am doing nothing.   1 2 3 4 5

22. I am clear about what my section leader expects in a progress report.   1 2 3 4 5

23. My section leader likes to see most data in a table appended to the report.   1 2 3 4 5

24. I try to avoid references to myself (e.g., the use of "I") when I write.   1 2 3 4 5

25. My director normally revises my semimonthly reports.   1 2 3 4 5

26. My section leader's expectations regarding reports are similar to other section leaders' expectations.   1 2 3 4 5

27. I usually make several false starts when I write.   1 2 3 4 5

28. I would recommend this company highly to someone looking for a job similar to mine.   1 2 3 4 5

29. My relationship with my director is good.   1 2 3 4 5

30. My section leader usually revises my progress reports.   1 2 3 4 5

31. Were I to write a poor semimonthly report, it would reflect poorly upon my section leader.   1 2 3 4 5

32. I do most of the writing of the progress reports.   1 2 3 4 5

33. I am clear about what my director expects in a progress report.   1 2 3 4 5

34. Researchers are too overburdened with writing responsibilities.   1 2 3 4 5

35. Section leaders are too overburdened with writing responsibilities.   1 2 3 4 5

36. My director normally revises my progress reports.   1 2 3 4 5

APPENDIX 9-B
SUPPLEMENTARY TABLES

Table 9.1.   Educational Background of Poor Writers vs. Good Writers.

	Percent of Poor Writers (n = 11)	Percent of Good Writers (n = 11)
Degree		
BS	36	64
MS	36	9
Ph.D	27	27
Major field		
Science	64	82
Engineering	36	18

Table 9.2. Professional Experience of Poor Writers vs. Good Writers.

	Percent of Poor Writers (n = 11)	Percent of Good Writers (n = 11)
Years experience (at this company and elsewhere)		
1–3 yrs	36	46
4–5 yrs	0	0
6–10 yrs	9	27
11–13 yrs	0	0
14–22 yrs	36	18
23–24 yrs	0	0
26–35 yrs	18	9
Years at this company		
1–2 yrs	46	27
3–4 yrs	0	46
5–13 yrs	0	0
14–20 yrs	36	27
21–29 yrs	0	0
30–35 yrs	18	0
Years in current position		
1 yr or less	36	36
2 yrs	27	27
3–5 yrs	27	27
6–9 yrs	0	0
10 yrs	9	0
10–15 yrs	0	0
16 yrs	0	9
Years working for present supervisor		
0–6 mos	27	9
6–12 mos	18	36
1–2 yrs	36	36
3–5 yrs	0	9
over 5 yrs	18	9

Table 9.3. Previous College Coursework in Writing Taken by Poor Writers vs. Good Writers.

	Percent of Poor Writers (n = 11)	Percent of Good Writers (n = 11)
Composition course		
Have not taken	45	36
Have taken	55	64
Technical writing course		
Have not taken	45	73
Have taken	55	27

Table 9.4. Poor Writers' vs. Good Writers' Evaluation of Their College Coursework in Writing.

I. **Effectiveness of composition course in preparing individual for current job-related writing**

	Percent of Poor Writers (n = 6)	Percent of Good Writers (n = 7)
Very ineffective	33	29
Ineffective	50	14
Somewhat effective	0	14
Effective	17	14
Very effective	0	29

II. **Effectiveness of technical writing course in preparing individual for current job-related writing**

	Percent of Poor Writers (n = 6)	Percent of Good Writers (n = 3)
Very ineffective	0	0
Ineffective	33	33
Somewhat effective	17	33
Effective	33	0
Very effective	17	33

Table 9.5. Attitudes of Poor Writers vs. Good Writers Toward Company and Job.

Survey item 28: "I would recommend this company to someone seeking a job similar to mine."

	Percent of Poor Writers (n = 11)	Percent of Good Writers (n = 11)
1 = Strongly Disagree	0	0
2 = Disagree	9	0
3 = Neutral	18	27
4 = Agree	45	36
5 = Strongly Agree	27	36
	(M rating = 3.9)	(M rating = 3.8)

Chi-square = 1.45, df = 3, $p < .693$ (ns)

Survey item 3: "I am generally happy with my job."

	Percent of Poor Writers (n = 11)	Percent of Good Writers (n = 11)
1 = Strongly Disagree	0	0
2 = Disagree	9	0
3 = Neutral	18	9
4 = Agree	18	55
5 = Strongly Agree	55	36
	(M rating = 4.2)	(M rating = 4.3)

Chi-square = 3.73, df = 3, $p < .291$ (ns)

Table 9.6. Poor Writer vs. Good Writer Perceptions of Their Relationships with Their Supervisors and Directors.

Survey item 19: "My working relationship with my section leader is good."

	Percent of Poor Writers *(n = 11)*	*Percent of Good Writers* *(n = 11)*
1 = Strongly Disagree	0	0
2 = Disagree	18	0
3 = Neutral	18	0
4 = Agree	27	27
5 = Strongly Agree	36	73
	(M rating = 3.6)	*(M rating = 4.7)*

Chi-square = 5.33, *df* = 3, $p<.149$ (ns)

Survey item 29: "My relationship with my director is good."

	Percent of Poor Writers *(n = 11)*	*Percent of Good Writers* *(n = 11)*
1 = Strongly Disagree	0	0
2 = Disagree	0	9
3 = Neutral	27	0
4 = Agree	55	45
5 = Strongly Agree	18	45
	(M rating = 3.9)	*(M rating = 4.2)*

Chi-square = 5.37, *df* = 3, $p<.146$ (ns)

Table 9.7. Poor Writer vs. Good Writer Perceptions of the Importance of Their Writing.

Survey item 4: "The ability to write well is a significant factor in evaluation of job performance."

	Percent of Poor Writers (n = 11)	Percent of Good Writers (n = 11)
1 = Strongly Disagree	9	0
2 = Disagree	0	9
3 = Neutral	27	9
4 = Agree	45	45
5 = Strongly Agree	18	36
	(M rating = 3.6)	(M rating = 4.0)

Chi-square = 3.66, df = 4, p<.453 (ns)

Survey item 9: "The ability to write well is important in promotion decisions."

	Percent of Poor Writers (n = 11)	Percent of Good Writers (n = 10)*
1 = Strongly Disagree	0	0
2 = Disagree	9	30
3 = Neutral	18	10
4 = Agree	55	30
5 = Strongly Agree	18	30
	(M rating = 3.8)	(M rating = 3.6)

Chi-square = 2.49, df = 3, p<.096 (ns)

Survey item 31: "Were I to write a poor semimonthly report, it would reflect poorly upon my supervisor."

	Percent of Poor Writers (n = 11)	Percent of Good Writers (n = 11)
1 = Strongly Disagree	9	0
2 = Disagree	9	0
3 = Neutral	27	27
4 = Agree	45	27
5 = Strongly Agree	9	45
	(M rating = 3.4)	(M rating = 4.2)

Chi-square = 5.17, df = 4, p<.270 (ns)

Survey item 21: "If I am only sitting at my desk composing a report, it looks to my section leader as if I am doing nothing."

	Percent of Poor Writers (n = 10)*	Percent of Good Writers (n = 11)
1 = Strongly Disagree	30	36
2 = Disagree	30	65
3 = Neutral	10	0
4 = Agree	20	0
5 = Strongly Agree	10	0
	(M rating = 2.5)	(M rating = 1.6)

Chi-square = 5.71, df = 4, p<.222 (ns)

*One subject indicated he did not know.

Table 9.8. Poor Writer vs. Good Writer Attitudes Toward Their Own Writing.

Survey item 1: "I feel confident about my writing."

	Percent of Poor Writers (n = 11)	*Percent of Good Writers (n = 11)*
1 = Strongly Disagree	9	0
2 = Disagree	9	0
3 = Neutral	36	0
4 = Agree	18	45
5 = Strongly Agree	27	55
	(M rating = 3.5)	*(M rating = 4.5)*

Chi-square = 8.29, *df* = 4, *p*<.081 (ns)

Survey item 11: "I like to write."

	Percent of Poor Writers (n = 11)	*Percent of Good Writers (n = 11)*
1 = Strongly Disagree	0	0
2 = Disagree	45	18
3 = Neutral	36	27
4 = Agree	9	36
5 = Strongly Agree	9	18
	(M rating = 2.8)	*(M rating = 3.5)*

Chi-square = 3.56, *df* = 3, *p*<.313 (ns)

Table 9.9.   Poor Writer vs. Good Writer Perceptions of Their Readers' Expectations Regarding Writing.

I. Writing in General

Survey item 6: "My section leader is satisfied with the quality of my reports."

	Percent of Poor Writers (n = 11)	Percent of Good Writers (n = 11)
1 = Strongly Disagree	0	0
2 = Disagree	18	0
3 = Neutral	36	0
4 = Agree	36	36
5 = Strongly Agree	9	64
	(M rating = 3.4)	(M rating = 4.6)

Chi-square = 10.50, df = 3, p<.015

Survey item 5: "My section leader and I have similar notions about what a good report is."

	Percent of Poor Writers (n = 10)*	Percent of Good Writers (n = 10)*
1 = Strongly Disagree	0	0
2 = Disagree	10	0
3 = Neutral	20	0
4 = Agree	60	50
5 = Strongly Agree	10	50
	(M rating = 3.7)	(M rating = 4.5)

Chi-square = 5.76, df = 3, p<.124 (ns)

Survey item 2: "Expectations regarding writing are pretty much the same across sections."

	Percent of Poor Writers (n = 11)	Percent of Good Writers (n = 11)
1 = Strongly Disagree	0	9
2 = Disagree	27	18
3 = Neutral	36	36
4 = Agree	27	36
5 = Strongly Agree	9	0
	(M rating = 3.0)	(M rating = 3.0)

Chi-square = 2.34, df = 4, p<.673 (ns)

Survey item 26: "My section leader's expectations regarding reports are similar to other section leaders' expectations."

	Percent of Poor Writers (n = 11)	Percent of Good Writers (n = 9)**
1 = Strongly Disagree	27	0
2 = Disagree	0	11
3 = Neutral	27	44
4 = Agree	45	44
5 = Strongly Agree	0	0
	(M rating = 2.9)	(M rating = 3.2)

Chi-square = 4.09, df = 3, p<.251 (ns)

Table 9.9. *(Continued)*

II. Progress Reports (i.e., formal reports in this organization)

Survey item 8: "I am clear about what my section leader expects in a progress report."

	Percent of Poor Writers (n = 11)	Percent of Good Writers (n = 11)
1 = Strongly Disagree	9	0
2 = Disagree	9	0
3 = Neutral	18	27
4 = Agree	64	27
5 = Strongly Agree	0	45
	(*M* rating = 3.4)	(*M* rating = 4.1)

Chi-square = 8.80, *df* = 4, *p*<.066 (ns)

Survey item 33: "I am clear about what my director expects in a progress report."

	Percent of Poor Writers (n = 11)	Percent of Good Writers (n = 11)
1 = Strongly Disagree	9	0
2 = Disagree	9	0
3 = Neutral	36	27
4 = Agree	27	64
5 = Strongly Agree	18	9
	(*M* rating = 3.4)	(*M* rating = 3.8)

Chi-square = 4.08, *df* = 4, *p*<.396 (ns)

Survey item 13: "My section leader and my director have similar expectations regarding progress reports."

	Percent of Poor Writers (n = 10)*	Percent of Good Writers (n = 11)
1 = Strongly Disagree	0	0
2 = Disagree	10	9
3 = Neutral	10	27
4 = Agree	70	55
5 = Strongly Agree	10	9
	(*M* rating = 3.8)	(*M* rating = 3.6)

Chi-square = 1.03, *df* = 3, *p*<.793 (ns)

III. Semimonthly Reports (i.e., what are referred to as "progress reports" in this study)

Survey item 22: "I am clear about what my section leader expects in a semimonthly report."

	Percent of Poor Writers (n = 11)	Percent of Good Writers (n = 11)
1 = Strongly Disagree	0	0
2 = Disagree	9	0
3 = Neutral	9	18
4 = Agree	73	45
5 = Strongly Agree	9	36
	(*M* rating = 3.8)	(*M* rating = 4.2)

Chi-square = 3.83, *df* = 3, *p*<.281 (ns)

Table 9.9. (*Continued*)

III. **Semimonthly Reports (i.e., what are referred to as "progress reports" in this study)**

Survey item 22: "I am clear about what my section leader expects in a semimonthly report."

	Percent of Poor Writers (n = 11)	Percent of Good Writers (n = 11)
1 = Strongly Disagree	0	0
2 = Disagree	9	0
3 = Neutral	9	18
4 = Agree	· 73	45
5 = Strongly Agree	9	36
	(M rating = 3.8)	(M rating = 4.2)

Chi-square = 3.83, df = 3, p<.281 (ns)

Survey item 12: "My section leader and my director have similar expectations regarding semimonthly reports."

	Percent of Poor Writers (n = 9)**	Percent of Good Writers (n = 10)*
1 = Strongly Disagree	0	0
2 = Disagree	0	0
3 = Neutral	22	30
4 = Agree	44	50
5 = Strongly Agree	33	20
	(M rating = 4.1)	(M rating = 3.9)

Chi-square = 0.46, df = 2, p<.795 (ns)

*One subject indicated that he did not know.
**Two subjects indicated that they did not know.

Table 9.10. Poor Writer vs. Good Writer Practices and Perceived Expectations Regarding Their Writing.

Survey item 14: "I am expected to do some of my job writing at home."

	Percent of Poor Writers (n = 11)	Percent of Good Writers (n = 11)
1 = Strongly Disagree	36	27
2 = Disagree	0	65
3 = Neutral	9	0
4 = Agree	36	0
5 = Strongly Agree	18	0
	(M rating = 3.0)	(M rating = 1.7)

Chi-square = 14.13, df = 4, p<.007

Survey item 16: "I usually do some job writing at home."

	Percent of Poor Writers (n = 11)	Percent of Good Writers (n = 11)
1 = Strongly Disagree	27	36
2 = Disagree	9	45
3 = Neutral	9	0
4 = Agree	27	18
5 = Strongly Agree	27	9
	(M rating = 3.2)	(M rating = 2.4)

Chi-square = 4.87, df = 4, p<.301 (ns)

Survey item 17: "The amount of writing associated with my job is realistic."

	Percent of Poor Writers (n = 11)	Percent of Good Writers (n = 11)
1 = Strongly Disagree	0	0
2 = Disagree	0	0
3 = Neutral	9	9
4 = Agree	64	55
5 = Strongly Agree	27	36
	(M rating = 4.2)	(M rating = 4.3)

Chi-square = 0.22, df = 2, p<.896 (ns)

Survey item 32: "I do most of the writing of the progress reports."

	Percent of Poor Writers (n = 11)	Percent of Good Writers (n = 11)
1 = Strongly Disagree	0	0
2 = Disagree	9	0
3 = Neutral	0	0
4 = Agree	36	9
5 = Strongly Agree	55	91
	(M rating = 4.4)	(M rating = 4.9)

Chi-square = 3.80, df = 2, p<.149 (ns)

Table 9.11.   Composing Strategies as Described by Poor Writers vs. Good Writers.

Survey item 15: "When I plan a report, I usually think through the main points before I begin to write the report."

	Percent of Poor Writers (n = 11)	Percent of Good Writers (n = 11)
1 = Strongly Disagree	0	0
2 = Disagree	0	0
3 = Neutral	9	0
4 = Agree	36	36
5 = Strongly Agree	55	64
	(*M* rating = 4.5)	(*M* rating = 4.6)

Chi-square = 1.07, *df* = 2, *p*<.583 (ns)

Survey item 20: "I have a systematic procedure that I follow when I write my reports."

	Percent of Poor Writers (n = 11)	Percent of Good Writers (n = 11)
1 = Strongly Disagree	0	0
2 = Disagree	18	0
3 = Neutral	18	27
4 = Agree	45	36
5 = Strongly Agree	18	36
	(*M* rating = 3.6)	(*M* rating = 4.1)

Chi-square = 2.98, *df* = 3, *p*<.395 (ns)

Survey item 27: "I usually make several false starts when I write."

	Percent of Poor Writers (n = 11)	Percent of Good Writers (n = 11)
1 = Strongly Disagree	9	9
2 = Disagree	45	27
3 = Neutral	9	9
4 = Agree	27	45
5 = Strongly Agree	9	9
	(*M* rating = 2.8)	(*M* rating = 3.2)

Chi-square = 1.00, *df* = 4, *p*<.909 (ns)

Survey item 18: "When I write, I frequently change word choices and sentences as I am composing."

	Percent of Poor Writers (n = 11)	Percent of Good Writers (n = 11)
1 = Strongly Disagree	0	0
2 = Disagree	18	0
3 = Neutral	18	9
4 = Agree	36	18
5 = Strongly Agree	27	73
	(*M* rating = 3.7)	(*M* rating = 4.6)

Chi-square = 5.27, *df* = 3, *p*<.153 (ns)

Table 9.12. Revision Practices as Described by Poor Writers vs. Good Writers

Survey item 7: "I revise quite a bit when I write."

	Percent of Poor Writers (n=11)	Percent of Good Writers (n=11)
1 = Strongly Disagree	9	0
2 = Disagree	18	9
3 = Neutral	27	18
4 = Agree	27	45
5 = Strongly Agree	18	27
	(*M* rating = 3.3)	(*M* rating = 3.1)

Chi-square = 2.23, *df* = 4, *p*<.693

Survey item 10: "My section leader normally revises my semimonthly reports."

	Percent of Poor Writers (n=11)	Percent of Good Writers (n=11)
1 = Strongly Disagree	9	45
2 = Disagree	18	27
3 = Neutral	27	27
4 = Agree	18	0
5 = Strongly Agree	27	0
	(*M* rating = 3.7)	(*M* rating = 1.8)

Chi-square = 7.87, *df* = 4, *p*<.097 (ns)

Survey item 30: "My section leader usually revises my progress reports."

	Percent of Poor Writers (n=10)*	Percent of Good Writers (n=10)*
1 = Strongly Disagree	10	0
2 = Disagree	10	20
3 = Neutral	20	20
4 = Agree	20	30
5 = Strongly Agree	40	30
	(*M* rating = 3.4)	(*M* rating = 3.4)

Chi-square = 1.67, *df* = 4, *p*<.795 (ns)

Survey item 36: "My director normally revises my progress reports."

	Percent of Poor Writers (n=10)*	Percent of Good Writers (n=8)**
1 = Strongly Disagree	20	13
2 = Disagree	20	38
3 = Neutral	10	13
4 = Agree	30	13
5 = Strongly Agree	20	25
	(*M* rating = 3.1)	(*M* rating = 3.0)

Chi-square = 1.33, *df* = 4, *p*<.857 (ns)

*One individual from each group indicated he did not know.
**Some individuals indicated that they did not know.

Table 9.13. Percentage of Time Poor Writers vs. Good Writers Spend Writing.

Percent of total time spent writing	*Percent of Poor Writers (n = 11)*	*Percent of Good Writers (n = 11)*
3–5	9	18
10	46	18
12–13	18	0
15	0	9
20	9	0
25	0	9
30	18	36
35	0	9
Mean percent of time spent writing for poor writers: 14%		
Mean percent of time spent writing for good writers: 20%		

10
Phase 2: The Informational Content of Progress Reports

OBJECTIVE

The main objective of Phase 2 was to analyze the researchers' progress reports collected during Phase 1 in order to determine the types of information contained in them. These results were then compared with the writers' intentions and readers' (supervisors' and directors') expectations as revealed through the Phase 1 interviews and as reported in Chapter 9.

SAMPLE

Prior to the Phase 1 interviews, the 22 researcher subjects were asked to make copies of their last three semimonthly progress reports. These 66 reports were collected at the end of the Phase 1 interviews. Because of some unexpected variances in the collected samples (for instance, some reports were co-authored and others were trip reports rather than research reports), only two of each researcher's three progress reports were selected for analysis. In all, 44 reports were analyzed (two from each of the 22 researchers).

METHOD OF ANALYSIS

Several methods have been used to analyze various features of written texts. For example, Halliday and Hasan (1976) have developed a scheme for analyzing the cohesive elements of texts; Christensen (1967) has suggested a means of charting basic patterns of development in paragraphs; Pitkin (1977a, 1977b) has proposed a way of classifying logical relationships among sentences; and Meyer (1975) has developed hierarchical tree structures for analyzing the organization of texts according to their superordinate and subordinate ideas. Useful as these methods may be for examining the lexico-syntactic, semantic, and propositional features of texts, these methods were not considered directly applicable to this study. The main reason is that these methods are based upon predetermined features of texts *qua* texts rather than upon those features and criteria of texts that the readers and writers within a particular context themselves consider important. Also, unlike these other studies, this study was not concerned with *how* sentences, paragraphs, or whole texts are structured or with the cohesive devices that make texts cohere, but rather with *what* types of information are contained in texts. Furthermore, studies that have been concerned with content analysis, such as van Dijk's (1983) examination of the superstructure of news stories and Lasswell's (Lasswell, Leites, & Associates, 1965; Lasswell, Lerner, & Pool, 1952) analysis of propaganda strategies, most often focus upon the discourse of mass media. Although content analysis, as Carney (1972) notes, has been applied to various disciplines, including communications, sociology, anthropology, social anthropology, psychology, and literature, its use as a research tool is limited primarily to quantitative and qualitative analyses of texts apart from the contexts within which they are produced and used. For these reasons, it was necessary in this study to develop a method of analysis that would distinguish among the various types of information contained in technical progress reports and that would also be adaptable to a comparative analysis of the intentions, expectations, and preferences of the writers and the readers of the progress reports.

The greatest challenge in developing such a method was to find a classification scheme that would (a) include all possible types of information that might be contained in a progress report, (b) be based upon a single classifying principle, and (c) be based upon distinctions that the writers and readers of the reports themselves regard as important. Subsequent to my research, I learned of a classification scheme that Latour and Woolgar (1979) had used to differentiate between the types of information contained in written scientific discourse aimed at the public versus that aimed at scientists. In their taxonomy, Latour and Woolgar distinguished among five types of information along a continuum with, at one end, statements expressing facticity, objectivity, or certainty, and at the other end, statements expressing speculativeness, subjectivity, or uncertainty. They applied this scheme to show how the certainty or uncertainty of statements in scientific texts changes to suit different genres of scientific discourse aimed at different audiences. Their main finding is that the information contained in accommodated scientific writing, such as that found in popularized articles written for the public, expresses a higher degree of certainty than when the same research appears in scientific journals or research reports intended for knowledgeable peers. In the latter, claims are weakened by the use of hedge words and qualifiers. One of the limitations of Latour and Woolgar's study, as Fahnestock (1986) points out, is that they examined only the statements of texts and not how the intended readers of these texts actually interpreted such statements. As a result, Fahnestock further suggests that "Latour and

Woolgar's scale may. . . introduce a specious rigor into the investigation of what happens to 'information' as it travels from limited to larger audiences. After all, the degree of certainty conveyed by a statement may depend more on context as it does on wording" (pp. 289–290).

While the scheme I developed for use in this study is similar to Latour and Woolgar's insofar as it is also based upon a continuum of five types of information, it differs from theirs in two important ways. First, the classifying principle I used evolved out of the context itself; it was not something I had predetermined beforehand. Second, the principle is based not so much upon the degree of a statement's certainty (as in Latour and Woolgar's scheme), but, as explained below, upon the extent to which information is "unprocessed" or "processed." Finally, this study differs from Latour and Woolgar's in that the scheme used to analyze the informational content of texts was further used (in Phase 3) to examine the extent to which the writers and readers of these texts similarly identified the five types of information as most important or least important.

Classifying Principle

Among the classification schemes that I initially considered but later rejected were the categories of information that I had developed prior to the Phase 1 interviews and that I had used during those interviews to have subjects indicate their degree of preference for various kinds of information in progress reports (detailed data; facts, observations; explanations, discussion; general conclusions; historical background; context of project; recommendations; opinions; and procedure or method) and the categories commonly used to organize sections of technical reports—categories such as *Objectives, Introduction, Method, Results, Discussion, Conclusions,* and *Recommendations.* I rejected these categories as a means for analyzing the reports when it became apparent during the study that the information contained in these categories often overlapped and that, as revealed during the round-one interviews with the subjects in Phase 1, and as confirmed in Phase 3 by the second-round interviews and by the results of the second task experiment, the subjects often disagreed about the meaning of terms such as *data, result,* and *conclusion.*

The basis for the classification scheme that was used to analyze the progress reports in this study evolved out of the distinctions the writers and readers of these reports themselves made when discussing the types of information contained in them. Frequently, the subjects talked about the degree to which information was either "raw," "unfiltered," "undigested," or "unprocessed," as opposed to information that was "chewed," "sifted," "digested," or "processed." These distinctions suggested to me a classifying principle based upon the degree to which the writer had mentally manipulated the information—a classification scheme based upon qualitatively different cognitive processes.

The classifying principle underlying the method of analysis used in this study can be expressed as a continuum of mental activities that at one end represents the objective recording of phenomena (selective but unprocessed information), that at the middle of the continuum represents the interpretation of that phenomena (digested information), and that at the other end represents the subjective implications of that interpretation (processed information). Figure 10.1 illustrates this continuum, along which are also plotted some suggested synonymous relationships derived from various metaphors that have been used to distinguish cognitive processes. Figure 10.1 also includes the related, specific types of information that were used to classify the information in the researchers' progress reports.

These categories of information were proposed to me by one of the researchers. He suggested that the information contained in progress reports generally falls into one of four categories: *What I did, What I got, What it means,* and *What it's good for.* To these four categories I added a fifth in between the first and second categories—*How I did it.*

The first three types of information—What I did, How I did it, and What I got—involve description or narration—relatively low-level cognitive operations that require simply the presentation of factual-type information. Thus, on Figure 10.1 these three types of information are to the left of the continuum. The fourth and fifth types of information—What it means and What it's good for—involve comparatively high-level cognitive operations and therefore are placed to the right of the continuum, with the fourth type

PRINCIPLE FOR CLASSIFYING INFORMATION

←—————————————————————————————————→

unprocessed information	digested information	processed information
record player	synthesizer	conductor
comprehension	assimilation	accommodation
description, narration	analysis evaluation	recommendation
information	belief	action

CORRESPONDING CATEGORIES OF INFORMATION

What I did   How I did it   What I got   What it means   What it's good for

←—————————————————————————————————→

Figure 10.1. Continuum Illustrating the Principle for Classifying Information and the Categories of Information Along the Continuum.

of information toward the three-quarters mark of the continuum and the fifth toward the far right.

An important point to note about this classification scheme is that it makes no attempt to distinguish explanations or discussion since both of these cut across all of the other categories; that is, a researcher might explain why the project was undertaken, why a certain procedure was used, why he concluded this or that, or why he is making a particular recommendation. Therefore, in this study, any such explanations or discussion were subsumed within the five categories of information.

Categories of Information

The following explains the range and variation of information contained within each category and gives examples drawn from several of the progress reports analyzed in Phase 2.

Type 1 Information: What I Did. This category includes references not only to what was done during the period covered by the report but also to what had been done in the past and what is going to be done in the future. Also included are the following:

> objectives of the research
> background or context of the research
> statements of the problem
> references to literature or previous reports
> conclusions of previous research
> what was analyzed and why
> parameters of acceptability or repeatability
> criteria for evaluation

Examples of Type 1 Information:

1. Due to the new dual fermentation research for acetone butanol and ethanol, two new fermentation by-products, methanol and caproic acid, are being formed.
2. Aqueous extracts from the tissue of 12 callus cultures of *P. somniferum* were examined with the RIA. These cultures were chosen because the presence of thebaine had been confirmed previously via high press liquid chromatography (HPLC).
3. Dry-milled fiber is difficult to handle in bulk. In order to be pumpable the dry substance of the fiber slurry must be ~ 15% or less. Since the starch content of fiber runs around 30%, even if 100% of the starch could be recovered in the filtrate the dry substance would only be 4.5%

In an effort to increase the dry substance of the fiber hydrolyzate the filtrate was used in a recycle process.
4. Data for normal operating conditions (i.e., with air sweep) is being collected and will be analyzed for comparison purposes.

Type 2 Information: How I Did It. This category includes all references to methodology, including

> description of method
> use and limitations of method
> description of equipment and materials
> samples, medium, or batches used
> sample preparation
> stages of procedure
> operating conditions and parameters
> formulas and calculations

Examples of Type 2 Information:

1. A method using Comassie Blue G 250 dye reagent is carried out in micro-wells designed for Enzyme Linked Immunosorbent Assay (ELISA). The dyed protein is measured directly in the micro-well using the MICRO ELISA™ minireader MR590. The range of the method is about 2–30 ppm using bovine serum albumin.
2. After the SO_2 level dropped below 500 ppm the steep was inoculated with plant light steepwater to provide a healthy lactic acid bacteria culture. Additional process consisted of a 24 hr incubation and evaporation at 120°F to produce a concentrated product.

Type 3 Information: What I Got. This category includes the immediate output of the research experiment—the raw data (numbers) and observations—as well as generalized data, results, or findings (for example, that X was found to be larger than Y).

Examples of Type 3 Information:

1. Cells which were resuspended in medium without added glucose and containing 9 g/liter acetate pH 5.5 had an intracellular acetate concentration of 7.36 + 2.4 g/liter. Aerobic cells in medium containing 15 g/liter glucose, 9 g/liter acetate, pH 5.5 had an internal acetate level of 7.2 + 0.96 g/liter. These values are 83% and 80%, respectively, of the external acetate concentrations.
2. Some cultures contain no detectable alkaloids or related compounds (2, 11 and 12), some contain detectable but low levels while others accumulate relatively high levels (3 and 10).

Type 4 Information: What It Means. This category includes all attempts to make sense of the data, results, findings, or observations (the Type 3 information). The category includes such things as speculation, opinion, hypothesis, assessment, and evaluation. It also includes comparisons of results from the same research project or from the present research project and previous projects or studies, as well as comparisons of research methods when the aim of the research was to find a new or better method.

Examples of Type 4 Information:

1. This high chloride content was probably due to residual material from previous tests.
2. The precision of the slurry Karl Fischer method is evident in the standard deviations for each sample, especially for the smaller particle size samples, such as milo and wheat. The larger standard deviations for the corn samples indicate a sampling problem (only 5 g or kernels of corn is used).
3. Recent endosperm slurry steep-fiber separation, milling and washing test results indicate there may be a problem with Rotex screen blinding in the fine fiber separation and washing steps.

Type 5 Information: What It's Good For. Information in this category goes one step beyond Type 4 information in that it interprets the significance of the findings within the context of the research project's objectives. Type 5 information may further include recommendations for future consideration or action and suggested remedies to problems. Management often views this type of information as "the bottom line." In general, this information is the answer to the "so what?" of the research.

Examples of Type 5 Information:

1. This fluorescence may not be from the enzyme at all, but it might serve as a diagnostic tool even so.
2. The problem of low clarity levels in the pilot plant has not been fully resolved to date.
3. Using this RIA, hundreds of samples can now be rapidly screened and those having no or low levels of alkaloids discarded.

I should note here that my categorization of the above sentences is based upon a reading of the entire reports from which these sentences were drawn. I wish to stress that, without the complete text, it difficult to determine whether an isolated sentence is unprocessed or processed information. For instance, any of the above sentences illustrating Type 5 information could conceivably be unprocessed information in another report, one in which such statements were reported as part of the project's context or background—that is, established, or known, information rather than, as in the case of the reports from which these sentences were excerpted, speculations, opinions, or conclusions unknown to the readers. For the sake of brevity and confidentiality, I have cited only sentence-level examples. In the following section, I will illustrate longer examples of text. In the meantime, I wish to reiterate what I hope was made clear in previous chapters: that meaning is indeterminate apart from context.

PROCEDURE

Although various units of measurement have been used to segment written texts—for example, T-units, clauses per sentence, and propositions per statement—these units were considered too cumbersome and unnecessarily sophisticated for the present study. More importantly, the purposes for which these units are used in other studies have little to do with the purposes of this study. For example, while counting the number of syntactic units within a sentence (whether T-units, clauses, or chunks) may be an appropriate means for measuring readability or syntactic fluency, and while counting and categorizing propositions may be an appropriate means of analyzing such things as the level of generality or specificity of statements and generic means of development (for example, comparison/contrast, generalization/example, cause/effect), this study was not concerned with any of these matters. The sentence as a basic unit of measurement was also rejected because of the great variability in the length of sentences in the researchers' progress reports. For instance, a report might contain three sentences of Type 2 information but those sentences might be very long, whereas another report might contain six sentences of Type 2 information but those sentences might be very short. Thus, to simply count the number or percentage of sentences for each type of information in a report would not accurately reflect the extent to which the report emphasized a given type of information nor the extent to which different reports contained different types of information.

The unit of measurement that was eventually decided upon was simply the number of typewritten lines devoted to each type of information. Since all of the reports were typed by the same secretarial pool, the layout of each of the reports was the same; that is, the margins, spacing, and typeface were identical for all reports.

For each of the 44 progress reports, the name of the writer was masked. The reports were then shuffled and analyzed in random order according to the following procedure.

First, the lines were numbered consecutively along the margin. Then each line was identified as either Type 1, 2, 3, 4, or 5 information, using the category distinctions described above. In those instances in which the type of information shifted within the same line—as, for example, when a new sentence was begun in mid-line that contained a different type of information—the line was counted as that type of information that occupied the greater share of the line. The lines of internal tables were counted as Type 3 information; however, tables or graphs appended to the report were not counted. The following is an illustration of the procedure, using a portion of one of the reports analyzed. This particular paragraph was selected because it contains four of the five different types of information. In this respect, it is not typical of most of the reports, the paragraphs of which usually contained one or two, and sometimes three, types of information.

	Line #	Info #
A pH-stat was set up to obtain a culture of *Lactobacillus acidophilus*	3	1
with increased free lactic acid tolerance. The fermentor is currently	4	1
operating at pH 4.45, 40–42°C, 2.65% lactic acid with a very slow	5	3
dilution rate (i.e. < 0.03 hr^{-1}). It had been expected that product	6	4
inhibition would not occur until a much higher concentration of product	7	4
had been reached. However, a basic *C. thermoaceticum* medium was used.	8	2
Unlike most *Lactobacillus* media, it contained no Tween 80, no citrate or	9	3
acetate and 50% of the tryptone concentration. Therefore, the culture	10	4
may be nutrient limited.		

The Type 4 information in line 10 refers to the sentence beginning with "Therefore" and continuing onto the next line. Had that line run beyond the mid-line point, it would have been line 11, and line 10 would have been identified as Type 3 information and line 11 as Type 4 information. (Something similar occurs in lines 3–5 in which the shift in information occurs at the sentence break in line 4; in this case, line 4 is counted as a continuation of Type 1 information begun in line 3, and the beginning of Type 3 information ("The fermentor. . ."), since it is less than half of the line, is carried over to and identified in line 5 as Type 3 information.) As can be seen from the example, a shift in type of information normally occurs at sentence boundaries; the unit of measurement, however, remains the number of lines, not the number of sentences.

For each report, the percentage of lines devoted to each type of information was calculated in the following way: The total number of lines for each type of information was divided by the total number of lines in the entire report. Thus, it was possible to determine the extent to which the researcher's reports emphasized the various types of information.

Prior to using this procedure to identify the types of information contained in the researchers' 44 progress reports and the percentage of each of the five types of information contained in each report, I met with two researchers and two supervisors from this organization and explained to them the scheme I intended to use as a basis for distinguishing between the types of information in progress reports. After a few preliminary dry-runs in which they used the scheme to identify the various types of information in progress reports, the five of us individually used the scheme to identify the types of information contained in five of the reports used in this study. Nine times out of ten we similarly identified the type of information contained in the reports, resulting in an interrater reliability of 90 percent.

RESULTS

Once the informational content of the entire sample (all 44 of the researchers' reports) was determined, the data were further sorted according to the following variables: poor writers versus good writers; scientists versus engineers; departments; and stage of research project.

Total Sample

As shown in Table 10.1, of the five types of information, the progress reports primarily contain information about what was done (40 percent), followed next by what was gotten (the observations, data, or results) and what it means. To a lesser extent, the reports contain information about how the research was conducted, and least of all, what the research results are good for.

Another way of viewing these results is to consider how much of the information contained in the reports is unprocessed information (to the left of the continuum in Figure 10.1) and how much is processed information (to the right of the continuum in Figure 10.1). When the percentages are

Table 10.1.   Mean Percentages of Each Type of Information in All Progress Reports.

Type of Information	Mean Percentage of Type of Information in All Reports (n = 44)
1 (What I did)	40
2 (How I did it)	13
3 (What I got)	21
4 (What it means)	18
5 (What it's good for)	9

(Note: In this table and others reporting percentages, the total percentage may not equal 100 percent because individual percentages were rounded off to the nearest decimal.)

grouped in this manner, Types 1, 2, and 3 information (the unprocessed) represent a combined average of 74 percent of the information in all reports, and Types 4 and 5 information (the processed) represent a combined average of 27 percent. This clearly indicates that the vast majority of information in the progress reports is strictly reportive in nature, involving primarily description or narration rather than analysis or evaluation.

Poor Writers Versus Good Writers

Next, the reports were grouped by those written by the poor writers and those written by the good writers in order to analyze whether there were any differences between the two groups in the type of information emphasized in their reports. (Recall that the poor-writer/good-writer distinctions were made by the researchers' supervisors prior to Phase 1 of the study.) The results are shown in Table 10.2.

Analysis of the results by the two-tailed t test indicate significant differences between the poor writers and the good writers with respect to the percentages of Type 1 and Type 5 information contained in their progress reports. The poor writers' reports contain a significantly greater percentage of Type 1 information than do the good writers' reports ($p <.05$). Of even greater significance ($p <.006$), however, is that the good writers' reports, when compared with the poor writers' reports, contain three and a half times as much Type 5 information. Since the mean percentages of Types 2, 3, and 4 information are close for the two groups, the higher percentage of Type 5 information in the reports of the good writers can be explained by their correspondingly lower percentage of Type 1 information. Whereas the good writers' reports contain 34 percent (about a third) of Type 1 informa-

Table 10.2. Mean Percentage of Types of Information in Progress Reports: Poor Writers vs. Good Writers.

Type of Information	Reports of Poor Writers (n rpts = 22)		Reports of Good Writers (n rpts = 22)		
	Mean %	SD	Mean %	SD	t
1 (What I did)	45*	22.57	34*	17.17	1.96*
2 (How I did it)	15	15.94	14	18.40	0.25
3 (What I got)	22	16.40	21	21.31	0.18
4 (What it means)	15	11.20	19	13.56	−1.04
5 (What it's good for)	3**	4.96	13**	15.33	−2.88**

*$p <.05$ $df = 42$ (pooled variance)
**$p <.006$ $df = 42$ (pooled variance)

tion, the poor writers' reports contain 45 percent (almost half) of Type 1 information.

When these results are interpreted in light of the principle that was used to classify information (Figure 10.1), it becomes apparent that an important distinction between the progress reports of the poor writers and those of the good writers is the amount of unprocessed versus processed information. Whereas the good writers' reports contain an average of 32 percent processed information (Types 4 and 5 information), the poor writers' reports contain only 18 percent. In other words, compared with the poor writers, the good writers are more than twice as likely to emphasize the type of information that, as revealed in Chapter 9, their supervisor readers say they most prefer.

Scientists Versus Engineers

Table 10.3 shows the results when the same progress reports were grouped according to whether they were written by scientist researchers or engineer researchers. Analysis of the results by the two-tailed *t* test revealed no significant differences between the types of information contained in the progress reports written by the scientist researchers and those written by the engineer researchers. The results do indicate, however, that the engineers (48 percent) are more likely to emphasize Type 1 information in their reports than are the scientists (37 percent), whereas the scientists (39 percent) are slightly more likely to emphasize Types 4 and 5 information (processed information) than are the engineers (23 percent).

These results run counter to popular notions about the distinctions between scientists and engineers, as discussed toward the end of Chapter 6 where I also speculated that the engineers' reports might contain more

Table 10.3. Mean Percentage of Types of Information in Progress Reports: Scientist-Researcher Writers vs. Engineer-Researcher Writers.

	Reports of Scientist Writers (n = 32)		Reports of Engineer Writers (n = 12)		
	Mean %	SD	Mean %	SD	*t*
Type of Information					
1 (What I did)	37	16.24	48	25.88	−1.21
2 (How I did it)	13	11.19	13	12.19	0.09
3 (What I got)	22	14.57	18	16.14	0.64
4 (What it means)	19	8.61	16	13.40	0.65
5 (What it's good for)	10	9.67	7	9.41	0.61

df = 20   (Findings not significant at .05 level of probability.)

processed information than the scientists' reports because engineers, according to the stereotype, are more concerned with the application of research results than with the results themselves. In Chapter 9, where I noted a similar anomaly in the stated preferences of the engineers and the scientists for Type 3 information (with the engineers preferring facts and data to a greater extent than the scientists did), I suggested that the small number of engineer-writer subjects in this study, as compared with the larger number of scientist-writer subjects, may have distorted this study's findings. Here, too, perhaps the comparatively small number of engineers' reports (12), as compared with the larger number of scientists' reports (32), may have skewed the results. Another possible explanation, however, is that the scientist-engineer distinction is not as valid a variable as I initially thought it might be. The engineers in this study are not typical of engineers employed by engineering companies where the work consists of finding solutions to immediate problems. Rather, the engineers in this study, because they are chemical engineers and work in an R&D environment, may have more in common with scientists than with civil, mechanical, or electrical engineers. (See Lipson, 1988, pp. 15–17, for a defense of this view.)

Departments

The same progress reports were also grouped according to the department to which each researcher belonged. Table 10.4 shows the mean percentage of each type of information contained in the reports of the four departments. Analysis of variance indicated no significant differences among the departments.

Table 10.4. Mean Percentage of Types of Information in Progress Reports: By Department.

| | Reports by Department (n=44) | | | | | | | | |
| | Dept. 1 (n = 12) | | Dept. 2 (n = 8) | | Dept. 3 (n = 16) | | Dept. 4 (n = 8) | | |
	%	SD	%	SD	%	SD	%	SD	f
Type of Information									
1 (What I did)	48	15.78	41	11.56	32	15.73	44	33.78	0.91
2 (How I did it)	11	11.34	13	12.89	18	10.69	6	9.52	1.10
3 (What I got)	17	11.58	16	10.08	28	17.91	21	16.09	0.87
4 (What it means)	19	6.32	24	5.68	14	9.86	21	16.15	0.99
5 (What it's good for)	6	8.28	9	5.18	10	6.63	10	19.00	0.21

$df = 3$ (Findings not significant at the .05 level of probability.)

Phase of Research Project

Finally, the reports were analyzed to determine whether the type of information contained in the reports varied according to whether the report was written toward the beginning, middle, or end of the entire research project. During the second-round interviews of Phase 3, the researchers located each of their reports along a time line representing the duration of the entire project:

Very beginning		*Middle*		*Very end*
1	2	3	4	5

Table 10.5 shows the percentages of Types 1, 2, 3, 4, and 5 information contained in the reports written at each of the above five stages of the project. Analysis of variance revealed no significant relationship between the stage of the research project and the type of information contained in the progress reports.

Table 10.5.   Mean Percentage of Types of Information in Progress Reports: By Stage of Research Project.

| | Reports by Stage of Research Project (total n=44) | | | | | | | | | |
| | Beginning 1 (n = 11) | | 2 (n = 8) | | Middle 3 (n = 10) | | 4 (n = 8) | | End 5 (n = 7) | | |
	%	SD	%	SD	%	SD	%	SD	%	SD	f
Type of Info											
1	50	19.58	43	14.34	37	18.91	25	17.24	39	28.17	1.97
2	22	21.86	8	17.26	9	13.56	19	8.83	11	17.64	1.36
3	11	11.33	18	19.71	24	19.12	32	14.43	26	25.77	1.88
4	12	10.42	27	18.60	15	8.46	16	8.05	18	12.39	2.00
5	5	13.80	5	7.05	16	18.20	8	6.90	7	5.81	1.30

$df = 4$ (Findings not significant at the .05 level of probability.)

CONCLUSIONS

The findings from Phase 2 indicate that the vast majority of the information in the researchers' progress reports (74 percent) is unprocessed information of a reportive nature, that is, information primarily about what was done; how it was done; and what data, observations, and results were obtained (Types 1, 2, and 3 information, respectively). Only about a quarter of the information contained in the reports (27 percent) is processed information of a speculative or evaluative nature, that is, interpreted information that indicates what the findings mean and how the results can be applied (Types 4 and 5 information, respectively).

Analyses revealed that, of the variables examined, the only significant variable affecting the type of information contained in the progress reports is whether the report was written by a poor writer or a good writer. Contrary to previous speculations, the differing nature of research conducted within the four departments does not appear to influence the type of information contained in the researchers' progress reports. For example, the progress reports written in the department engaged in primarily scientific, exploratory research contain approximately the same proportion of a given type of information as do the reports written by the department engaged in engineering research. In accordance with this finding is the finding that the reports written by the scientist writers and those written by the engineer writers do not differ significantly in their respective percentages of Types 1, 2, 3, 4, or 5 information.

In addition, contrary to the speculations of the majority of the subjects (as reported in Chapter 9), the stage of the research project at which the progress report is written appears to have no effect upon which type of information is most or least emphasized in the report. That is, reports written at either the beginning, middle, or end of the research project are just as likely to contain a certain type of information.

The results of Phase 2, however, do reveal that there are significant differences between the reports of poor writers and those of good writers with respect to both Type 1 and Type 5 information. The poor writers' reports contain a higher percentage (45 percent) of Type 1 information (what was done) than do the reports of the good writers (34 percent). Conversely, at the other end of the continuum of types of information, the good writers' reports contain a significantly higher percentage (13 percent) of Type 5 information (what the results are good for) than do the reports of the poor writers (3 percent).

Possible explanations for these findings are the differences, reported in Chapter 9, between the two groups' planning strategies and their assumptions about how much their supervisors know about the research reported and about how those readers are using the information contained in the researchers' progress reports.

First, it may be that the poor writers' tendency to emphasize Type 1 information is due to the inductive, narrative approach they use to compose their reports, an approach that is conducive to the what-I-did Type 1 information. By contrast, it may be that the good writers' significantly lower percentage of Type 1 information and, conversely, their significantly higher percentage of Type 5 information are due to the deductive approach that the good writers use to compose their reports, an approach that is more conducive to the "so-what?" or "bottom-line" Type 5 information.

Second, since the poor writers falsely assume that the main reason their supervisors read the progress reports is to become informed about the research and to check up on the researchers' work, it makes sense that their reports would emphasize Type 1 information. Since the good writers, on the other hand, correctly assume that their supervisors already know the results of the research before they read the progress report, it makes sense that they (the good writers) would not emphasize Type 1 information as much as do the poor writers. Also, since the good writers are far more likely than are the poor writers to realize that the supervisors use the reports to evaluate the work in progress and thus to make decisions, it makes sense that the good writers' reports would contain a higher percentage of Type 5 (as well as Type 4) information than would the reports of the poor writers.

In short, it appears from the Phase 2 results that both the poor writers and the good writers are capable of translating their intentions into text. That is, in their progress reports each group is providing their supervisors with the type of information that they, the writers, *think* their supervisors want and need. The important difference is that, compared with the intentions of the poor writers, the intentions of the good writers more accurately match their supervisors' expectations.

The question, then, is why the good writers are more aware of their supervisors' expectations than are the poor writers. As reported in Chapter 9, the two groups—the poor writers and the good writers—do not differ significantly in degree of education, major, total years' of experience, years at company, or years working for their present supervisor. In fact, when compared with the poor writers, the good writers have had *less* education and experience. Since, in this case, background and situational context cannot explain the differences between the two groups of writers, we must look elsewhere for possible explanations.

My hunch, though it cannot be proven from this study, is that the two groups may have different conceptions of communication. The poor writers, I would venture, think of communication as the transmittal of objective facts (the old transmission model of communication upon which traditional definitions of technical writing are based): communication for the sake of communication. By contrast, the good writers, I think, view communication as a response to the needs of readers and as a means of furthering the goals of the department and organization (the newer goal-oriented model of communication upon which more recent definitions of technical writing are based): communication as a means toward some end. This hypothesis is supported by the finding, reported in Chapter 9 (Table 9.14) that the vast majority of good writers (71 percent), as compared with poor writers (36 percent), use audience-oriented criteria to plan and evaluate their own reports. Good writers, that is, approach their writing tasks not by asking "What did I do?" but rather by asking "What do my intended readers need to know?"

Flower (1979) has similarly found that an important distinction between the composing processes and essays of poor student writers and those of good student writers is that, while the former tend to create "writer-based" texts, the latter tend to create "reader-based" texts. Although this study does not examine the actual planning strategies of the researcher writers but only what the writers say are their planning strategies, the findings do suggest that the same egocentrism that Flower found among poor student writers and evidenced in their texts may be characteristic of poor adult writers and their texts—specifically, in this case, poor writer-researchers and their progress reports.

Finally, some preliminary conclusions can be made at this point regarding how the preferences of readers and writers for certain types of information contained in progress reports (Phase 1) compare with the actual types of information contained in the reports (Phase 2).

First, it appears that the subjects' complaint that the major weakness in progress reports is the preponderance of uninterpreted technical information is justified since the progress reports contain 74 percent of unprocessed information (Types 1, 2, and 3) and only 27 percent of processed information. Although there is no way of determining an optimum percentage of each type of information, what is clear from the Phase 2 results is that the good writers' reports contain a lower percentage of unprocessed information and a higher percentage of processed information when compared with the poor writers' reports.

Second, comparisons of the results from Phase 1 and Phase 2 would seem to indicate that the preferences of the readers and the writers for certain types of information are in direct opposition to the types of information actually contained in the progress reports. For instance, while all of the subjects say they least prefer Type 1 information, this is the very type of information most contained in the progress reports (40 percent). On the other hand, while the supervisor readers say they most prefer Type 5 information, this is the very type of information least contained in the progress reports (9 percent).

Upon closer examination, one realizes that this apparent discrepancy between preference and performance is based upon the assumption that quantitative indices of preference can be quantitatively compared with quantitative indices of performance. As Chomsky and others have pointed out, this is a false assumption underlying much of the research involving content analysis. The problem is best illustrated by Chomsky (1959) in his criticism of Skinner's work. Chomsky presents the hypothetical case of two women, each of whom receives a luxurious bouquet of flowers. The first woman, upon seeing the flowers, immediately exclaims "Beautiful! Beautiful! Beautiful! Beautiful! Beautiful!" at the top of her lungs. The second woman, upon seeing the flowers, pauses for 10 seconds, and then quietly whispers "Beautiful." The point is that there is not necessarily a direct correlation between measures of intensity of attitudes and measures of frequency of performance.

Similarly, one must exercise caution when comparing the expectations of readers and the performance of writers. While the supervisors may say they least prefer Type 1 information and most prefer Type 5 information, this does not necessarily mean that they want reports that contain the lowest percentage of Type 1 information and the highest percentage of Type 5 information. Thus, all that can be concluded at this stage of the study is that the good writers, when compared with the poor writers, are more likely to recognize the preferences of their supervisors and more likely to give them the type of information they want and need. This, perhaps, is not surprising since, at the onset of this study, it was the supervisors themselves who identified the poor-writer and the good-writer subjects upon the basis of their reports. At the same time, however, since the supervisors were given no criteria upon which to select their researchers' good reports and their researchers' poor reports, the findings reported thus far support the fundamental premise of this study: that the informational content of progress reports is an important criterion supervisors use when assessing the quality of their researchers' progress reports. Whether this criterion is more or less important to them than other criteria, such as the clarity (readability) or organization of information is beyond the scope of this study and is a topic I leave for other researchers to investigate.

11
Phase 3: Identification and Evaluation of Information in Progress Reports

Thus far, this study has focused upon (a) the types of information that writers intend to include in their progress reports and the types of information that their readers expect (Phase 1), and (b) the types of information actually contained in the researchers' progress reports (Phase 2). Like Phase 1, Phase 3 examines the subjects' preferences for types of information in progress reports, except this time, the subjects, instead of being asked to what extent they preferred various types of information (as in Phase 1), were presented with the actual progress reports and asked to select the information they considered most important and least important. In addition, Phase 3 examines the subjects' selections and definitions of the three types of information most frequently referred to in conjunction with technical reports: data, results, and conclusions.

The subjects for Phase 3 were the 4 directors, the 11 supervisors, and the 22 researchers. Phase 3 consisted of two experimental tasks, both of which were carried out during a second round of interviews with each of the subjects. Each second-round interview was approximately one hour. The interviews were conducted in the following order: researchers, supervisors, and directors. The reports used for both experimental tasks were the same 44 progress reports collected during Phase 1 and analyzed during Phase 2. Because it was not feasible for the directors, as a group, to carry out the experimental tasks using all 44 reports, and because this group represents a small portion of the entire population of subjects, in most cases the data generated from the directors' second-round interviews are not included in the analysis of results. Rather, the focus of Phase 3 is upon the supervisors and the researchers since each of these groups did use all 44 progress reports in the two experimental tasks. The objectives, methods, analytical procedures, and results of each of these experimental tasks are discussed below.

EXPERIMENTAL TASK 1: IDENTIFICATION OF MOST IMPORTANT AND LEAST IMPORTANT INFORMATION IN PROGRESS REPORTS

Objectives

The objectives of the first experimental task were as follows:

1. To examine the types of information that the various groups select as most important (MIMP) and least important (LIMP) in progress reports.
2. To determine whether there are any significant differences between the groups in the types of information they select as MIMP and LIMP.
3. To determine whether there are any significant differences in the degree of match between the MIMP and LIMP selections of the paired poor writers and their respective supervisor-readers and the MIMP and LIMP selections of the paired good writers and their respective supervisor-readers.

Method

During the second-round interviews with the researchers, each researcher was presented with the two progress reports that he had written and was asked to identify, by line number, what he thought was the most important information (MIMP) and the least important information (LIMP) in each report. The subjects were allowed up to three lines for their MIMP selections and up to three lines for their LIMP selections. These line numbers, the subjects were informed, did not have to be consecutive; the three MIMP lines, for instance, could be selected from different portions of the report. (In the few cases in which the report ran only a paragraph, the subject was asked to restrict his choice to only a line or two for MIMP's and for LIMP's.) When a sentence began or ended within a line, the line was counted as a MIMP or LIMP choice only if the information occupied more than half of the line. Following these selections, the researcher was asked to explain his choices.

During the second-round interviews with the supervisors, each supervisor was presented with the four progress reports written by his two researchers: two written by the poor writer; two written by the good writer. These were the same reports that the researcher writers had used for their MIMP and LIMP selections. However, the supervisors were not told what information the writers had selected as MIMP and LIMP, nor were they even told that the writers had previously performed the same task. The experimental task was carried out in the same manner as described above for the researchers.

During their second-round interviews, the directors also performed the same experimental task. However, because of the inordinate amount of time it would have taken for each director to analyze all of the progress reports written by the researchers in his respective department, each director was given only a select sample of four progress reports written by four different researchers in his department: two reports written by two of the poor writers; two reports written by two of the good writers. The directors, however, did not know upon what basis the reports had been selected or that earlier in the study the supervisors had identified the poor-writer and good-writer subjects. The directors carried out the experimental task in the same manner as did the supervisors and researchers.

See Appendix 11-A for the instrument that was used for experimental task 1 to record the researcher-writer subjects' MIMP and LIMP choices and to gather additional information regarding the audiences, purposes, and importance of progress (semimonthly) reports. For the reader subjects a similar form was used.

Analytical Procedure

First, the data were analyzed to examine the types of information that the subjects identified as MIMP and LIMP. For each report, the line numbers that a subject identified as MIMP or LIMP were translated into the categories of information used to analyze the reports in Phase 2; that is, Types 1, 2, 3, 4, and 5 information. Since the number of lines selected by the subjects was not held constant, each subject's number of MIMP choices by type of information was divided by the subject's total number of MIMP choices in order to arrive at the breakdown percentages of Types 1, 2, 3, 4, and 5 information. The same method of calculation was used to determine the breakdown percentages of LIMP choices for the various types of information. Thus, for example, if, as was most frequently the case, a subject selected three MIMP lines and if two of those lines were Type 4 information and one of the lines was Type 3 information, then the subject had 66 percent Type 4 MIMP and 33 percent Type 3 MIMP.

Next, the data were also analyzed to determine the extent to which various groups (for example, directors, supervisors, and researchers; and poor writers and their supervisors versus good writers and their supervisors) similarly identified the same type of information in the researchers' reports as MIMP or LIMP. The group data were calculated upon the basis of the total percentage of matches between two groups—for instance, the percentage of times the supervisors and the good writers similarly identified the same lines in the researchers' progress report as MIMP or LIMP. These matches were then translated into the five types of information.

Finally, the data were also analyzed to determine the MIMP and LIMP matches, again by type of information, of a specific writer and his respective supervisor reader. The pairs examined were the poor writers and their supervisors and the good writers and their supervisors. For each of the paired subjects, the following were calculated:

1. The total percentage of MIMP matches and the total percentage of LIMP matches by type of information (that is, the number of times that the pair similarly identified the same type of information as MIMP or LIMP divided by the total number of lines that the pair identified).
2. Breakdown percentages of matches by Types 1, 2, 3, 4, and 5 information that accounted for the total percentage of MIMPs and the total percentage of LIMPs.

Results

MIMP and LIMP Selections of Directors, Supervisors, and Researchers. Table 11.1 shows the mean breakdown percentages of Types 1, 2, 3, 4, and 5 information for the directors', the supervisors', and the researchers' total mean MIMP and total mean LIMP selections.

As the table reveals, in general, the groups vary little in the types of information that they selected as most important or as least important. All groups most frequently selected Type 3 information (what was found: data, observations, results) as the most important information. In addition, all groups most frequently selected Type 1 information (explanation of what was done) as the least important information. Specifically, the groups selected Type 3 information (what was found) and Type 4 information (what the results mean) as most important an average of 58 percent of the time and selected Type 1 information as least important an average of 50 percent of the time.

For the most part, these results corroborate the results from Phase 1 (reported in Chapter 9) in which the same groups indicated a high degree of preference for Types 3 and 4 information and a low degree of preference for Type 1 information. It would appear, therefore, that there is little discrepancy between the type of information that the groups *say* they most or least prefer (Phase 1) and the type of information that, when presented with the reports, they *actually* prefer (Phase 3).

The only notable exception regarding the preferences reported in Phase 1 and the selections reported here concerns Type 5 information (what the results are good for—for example, speculations, implications, conclusions,

Table 11.1. **Mean Percentages of MIMP and LIMP Selections by Type of Information: Directors, Supervisors, Researchers**

I. **Mean Percentages of Total MIMP Selections by Type of Information**

Type of Information	Directors (n = 4) (reports = 16)	Supervisors (n = 11) (reports = 22)	Researchers (n = 22) (reports = 44)
1 (What was done)	15	18	19
2 (How it was done)	10	4	7
3 (What was found)	32	28	24
4 (What it means)	30	28	31
5 (What it's good for)	13	21	20

II. **Mean Percentages of Total LIMP Selections by Type of Information**

Type of Information	Directors (n = 4) (reports = 16)	Supervisors (n = 11) (reports = 22)	Researchers (n = 22) (reports = 44)
1 (What was done)	42	50	58
2 (How it was done)	27	20	14
3 (What was found)	19	16	18
4 (What it means)	8	9	8
5 (What it's good for)	4	6	3

recommendations). Whereas the results of Phase 1 indicate that the groups say they prefer this type of information more than Type 4 information (with the supervisors preferring Type 5 more than any other type of information), the results in Table 11.1 suggest that, of the MIMP percentages, Type 5 information ranks only third among the groups' preferences.

One possible explanation for this is that the subjects had much less of a chance of selecting Type 5 information because the reports themselves contained a much lower percentage of this type of information as compared with the percentages of other types of information. As reported in Chapter 9, the progress reports contained only 9 percent of Type 5 information; yet, despite this small percentage, the subjects in Phase 3 selected Type 5 information as being most important an average of 18 percent of the time.

Similarly, comparisons between the percentages of unprocessed information (Types 1, 2, and 3) and processed information (Types 4 and 5) in the reports and the percentages of times the groups selected unprocessed and processed information as most and least important reveal that the subjects' preferences are not random; that is, the percentage of information contained in the report is not a predictor of the likelihood that a subject will select that information as most important or as least important. Although the reports, as analyzed in Phase 2, contained only 27 percent of processed information, the subjects selected processed information as most important an average of 46 percent of the time and as least important an average of only 13 percent of the time. Conversely, although the reports contained 73 percent of unprocessed information, the subjects selected unprocessed information as most important an average of only 18 percent of the time and as least important an average of 88 percent of the time. Such comparisons underscore the deliberate nature of the subjects' choices of information and reveal, as in the example just cited, that processed information is of great importance to the subjects despite so few instances of it within the reports.

MIMP and LIMP Selections of Scientist Writers Versus Engineer Writers. As shown in Table 11.2, while the scientist writers and the engineer writers do not differ significantly in their selections of most important information, analysis by the two-tailed *t*-test (pooled variance) reveals a significant difference between the groups ($p < .04$) in the percentage of times they selected Type 1 information as least important. The engineer writers are nearly twice as likely as are the scientist writers to select Type 1 information as least important (80 percent of the time for the engineer writers; 47 percent of the time for the scientist writers).

Since the two groups do not vary significantly in their Phase 1 preference

Table 11.2. Mean Percentages of MIMP and LIMP Selections by Type of Information: Scientist Writers vs. Engineer Writers.

I. Mean Percentages of Total MIMP Selections by Type of Information

Type of Information	Scientists (n = 16) (reports = 32)	Engineers (n = 6) (reports = 12)	t	df	p
1 (What was done)	18	20	−0.13	41	.897
2 (How it was done)	9	0	1.12	41	.271
3 (What was found)	23	26	−0.20	41	.845
4 (What it means)	28	39	−0.83	41	.411
5 (What it's good for)	22	15	0.52	41	.604

II. Mean Percentages of Total LIMP Selections by Type of Information

Type of Information	Scientists (n = 16) (reports = 32)	Engineers (n = 6) (reports = 12)	t	df	p
1 (What was done)	47*	80*	−2.09	36	*.044
2 (How it was done)	18	6	1.09	36	.281
3 (What was found)	24	4	1.63	36	.111
4 (What it means)	7	10	−0.42	36	.680
5 (What it's good for)	4	0	0.67	36	.504

*Significant at <.05 level of probability.

for Type 1 information, and since the two groups' reports do not contain a significantly different percentage of Type 1 information, this finding remains an anomaly, especially in view of their similar MIMP percentages for Type 1 information. Since, as suggested previously, it may be that the small number of engineer subjects in this study, as compared with the relatively large number of scientist subjects, may have skewed the data, no other variables regarding these two groups will be examined in this section. Rather, the following will concentrate upon the groups that are the focus of this study: the poor writers and the good writers and their supervisors.

MIMP and LIMP Selections of Poor Writers Versus Good Writers. The data regarding the researchers' MIMP and LIMP selections were analyzed by the two-tailed *t* test (pooled variance) to determine any significant differences between the types of information selected by the poor writers and the types of information selected by the good writers.

As shown in Table 11.3, while there are no significant differences between the groups in their LIMP choices, there are significant differences at the .05 level of probability between them in their MIMP choices.

First, the poor writers are four times as likely as the good writers to select Type 3 information as most important (p <.008). Whereas the poor writers selected Type 3 information as most important 38 percent of the time, the good writers selected it as most important only 9 percent of the time. Second, there is a significant difference (*p* <.003) between the groups with regard to the percentage of times they selected Type 5 information as most important. Compared with the poor writers, the good writers are over seven times as likely to select Type 5 information (5 percent for the poor writers; 37 percent for the good writers). In fact, as Table 11.3 shows, the good writers are as likely to select Type 5 information as most important as are the poor writers to select Type 3 information as most important.

With regard to Type 3 information, the significant difference between the two groups cannot be explained by differences in either the Phase 1 preferences of the two groups for certain types of information or the percentage of Type 3 information contained in the two groups' reports (22 percent for the poor writers' reports; 21 percent for the good writers' reports).

Also, the significant difference between the two groups in their MIMP selections of Type 5 information cannot be explained by differences between the two groups' stated preferences for Type 5 information since the Phase 1 analysis revealed no significant differences between the two groups' degree of preference. On the other hand, since the Phase 2 analysis did indicate that the good writers' reports contain a significantly greater percentage of Type 5 information than do the reports of the poor writers, it could be argued that the poor writers, when compared with the good writers, were not as likely to select Type 5 information as most important

Table 11.3. Mean Percentages of MIMP and LIMP Selections by Type of Information: Poor Writers vs. Good Writers.

I. **Mean Percentages of Total MIMP Selections by Type of Information**

Type of Information	Poor Writers (n = 11) (reports = 22)	Good Writers (n = 11) (reports = 22)	t	df	p
1 (What was done)	17	21	-0.41	41	.687
2 (How it was done)	9	5	0.55	41	.587
3 (What was found)	38*	9*	2.81	41	*.008
4 (What it means)	32	29	0.21	41	.845
5 (What it's good for)	5*	37*	-3.17	41	*.003

II. **Mean Percentages of Total LIMP Selections by Type of Information**

Type of Information	Poor Writers (n = 11) (reports = 22)	Good Writers (n = 11) (reports = 22)	t	df	p
1 (What was done)	52	62	-0.62	36	.540
2 (How it was done)	18	11	0.61	36	.545
3 (What was found)	16	19	-0.29	36	.773
4 (What it means)	14	3	1.50	36	.143
5 (What it's good for)	0	5	-0.90	36	.375

*Significant at <.05 level of probability.

simply because their reports contained a significantly lower percentage of Type 5 information. This line of reasoning, however, is weakened by the fact that, although the reports of the two groups were significantly different in their percentages of Type 1 information (see Table 10.2, Chapter 10), there was not a correspondingly significant difference between the poor writers and the good writers in the percentage of times that they selected Type 1 information as either most important or least important.

One possible explanation for the differences between the poor writers' and the good writers' MIMP selections of Type 3 and Type 5 information concerns the different criteria these groups use to evaluate their reports and the different perceptions these two groups have about how their supervisor readers use their progress reports. As revealed in Phase 1 (and reported in Chapter 9), the good writers are twice as likely as the poor writers to use audience-oriented criteria to evaluate their reports. In addition, the good writers, when compared with the poor writers, have a better understanding of the ways in which the supervisors actually use the progress reports. Since the poor writers incorrectly assume that their supervisors use the information in their progress reports to check the accuracy of their research, and since Type 3 information would be most appropriate for that purpose, this may explain why the poor writers choose Type 3 information as most important. Conversely, since the good writers correctly assume that their supervisors use the progress reports to evaluate the progress of the project and to make decisions, and since Type 5 information would be most appropriate for these purposes, this may explain why the good writers choose Type 5 information as most important.

This hypothesis is further supported by comparisons between the two groups' MIMP selections of unprocessed information (Types 1, 2, and 3 information) versus processed information (Types 4 and 5 information). When the percentages in Table 11.3 are totalled in this manner, it becomes apparent that, while both groups agree about what information is least important, they disagree about what information is most important. Table 11.4 shows the mean percentages of their MIMP and LIMP selections according to processed information versus unprocessed information.

With respect to their LIMP selections, there is little difference between the poor writers and the good writers. Both groups overwhelmingly selected unprocessed information as least important and rarely selected processed information. With respect to the groups' MIMP selections, however,

Table 11.4. Mean Percentages of MIMP and LIMP Selections by Processed Information vs. Unprocessed Information: Poor Writers vs. Good Writers.

I. Percentage of Total MIMP Selections	Poor Writers (n = 11) (reports = 22)	Good Writers (n = 11) (reports = 22)
Unprocessed Info (Types 1,2, & 3)	64	35
Processed Info (Types 4 & 5)	37	66

II. Percentage of Total LIMP Selections	Poor Writers (n = 11) (reports = 22)	Good Writers (n = 11) (reports = 22)
Unprocessed Info (Types 1,2, & 3)	86	92
Processed Info (Types 4 & 5)	14	8

there is a marked difference between the poor writers and the good writers. Whereas the poor writers are more apt to select unprocessed information as most important (64 percent of the time), the good writers are more apt to select processed information as most important (66 percent of the time). These findings suggest that the poor writers know what is *not* important information to their readers, but that they have more difficulty than do the good writers in accurately assessing what is the most important information to include in their progress reports. By contrast, the good writers seem to know both what is least important and most important to include in their progress reports, especially with respect to their intended readers' stated preferences as reported in Chapter 9, Phase 1. This speculation is further supported by data concerning the matched preferences for MIMPs and LIMPs between individual researcher-writers and their respective supervisor-readers.

MIMP and LIMP Matches of Poor Writers and Their Supervisors Versus Matches of Good Writers and Their Supervisors. Next the data were analyzed in order to determine how often a writer and his intended supervisor reader, when presented with the same two progress reports written by the researcher, selected the same type of information as most important or least important. Of particular interest was whether there were any appreciable differences between the MIMP and LIMP matches of the poor writers and their respective supervisors and the MIMP and LIMP matches of the good writers and their respective supervisors. Table 11.5 shows the total mean percentages of MIMP and LIMP matches for each pair group, as well as the mean percentages of matches by type of information.

Comparison of the mean percentages of total MIMP matches for the two pair groups indicates no difference between the two groups. That is, 47 percent of the time the MIMP selections of the poor writers matched those of their respective supervisors, and 47 percent of the time the MIMP selections of the good writers matched those of their respective supervisors. However, comparison of the two groups' total mean percentage of LIMP matches indicates that the good writers and their supervisors have a higher percentage of overall LIMP matches (42 percent) than do the poor writers and their supervisors (32 percent).

Furthermore, although the two pair groups have the same mean percentage of total MIMP matches, a comparison of the mean percentages by type of information reveals a notable difference between the two groups with respect to Type 5 information. Whereas the poor writers and their respective supervisors similarly selected Type 5 information an average of only 8 percent of the time, the good writers and their respective supervisors similarly selected Type 5 information an average of 26 percent of the time.

Although attempts were made to analyze the statistical significance of the MIMP and LIMP matches of the two pair groups, such attempts were

Table 11.5.   Mean Percentages of MIMP and LIMP Matches by Type of Information: Paired Poor Writers and Their Supervisors vs. Paired Good Writers and Their Supervisors.

I.   Mean Percentage of MIMP Matches

	Poor Writer/Supervisor Pairs (n pairs = 11) (reports = 22)	Good Writer/Supervisor Pairs (n pairs = 11) (reports = 22)
Total *M* % Match	47	47
M % of Match by Type of Info		
1 (What was done)	11	3
2 (How it was done)	3	0
3 (What was found)	17	10
4 (What it means)	15	14
5 (What it's good for)	8	26

II.   Mean Percentage of LIMP Matches

	Poor Writer/Supervisor Pairs (n pairs = 11) (reports = 22)	Good Writer/Supervisor Pairs (n pairs = 11) (reports = 22)
Total *M* % Match	32	42
M % of Match by Type of Info		
1 (What was done)	18	23
2 (How it was done)	0	9
3 (What was found)	6	0
4 (What it means)	5	0
5 (What it's good for)	0	0

Note: When totaled, the individual percentages for the MIMPs and for the LIMPs by type of information do not equal the total MIMP or LIMP percentage because all of these percentages are means.

confounded by the complex nature of the data as originally collected and as later calculated. As a result, none of the available tests of significance were considered appropriate for this part of the Phase 3 study. Thus, all that can be concluded from the percentages reported above is that, of all types of information, the good writers and their supervisors are more likely to select Type 5 information as most important to a much greater extent than are the poor writers and their supervisors. While such a finding further supports the speculations and results discussed previously, the finding cannot be upgraded to a conclusion until further research is conducted, research that would entail redesigning Experimental Task 1 to build in greater controls, as for instance holding constant the number of MIMP and LIMP selections and somehow standardizing the length of the reports examined.

EXPERIMENTAL TASK 2: SELECTION AND DEFINITION OF DATA, RESULTS, AND CONCLUSIONS

It was noted in the Introduction and Chapter 5 of this volume that this study was motivated in part by the seemingly inconsistent ways in which those in R&D organizations refer to the types of information contained in technical reports. Part of the problem, as explained in Chapter 5, is that the word *information*, both as defined in dictionaries and as commonly used, encompasses a wide range of meanings. Furthermore, as also illustrated in Chapter 5, there is considerable overlap between dictionary definitions of *fact* and *data*, as well as between definitions of *result* and *conclusion*.

To a large extent, the match between writers' intentions and readers' expectations concerning the informational content of progress reports necessitates a mutual understanding and use of the terms that the researchers and their supervisors typically use to refer to types of information. Thus, the purpose of Experimental Task 2 was to examine the extent to which the writers and readers of progress reports have similar definitions of the three most common terms used to describe information: *data*, *result*, and *conclusion*.

Objectives

The objectives of this experimental task were as follows:

1. To examine whether the examples that a researcher identifies as data, result, and conclusion in his own reports are similarly identified by his respective supervisor.
2. To analyze whether there are significant differences between the paired poor writers and their supervisors and the paired good writers and their supervisors in their identification of data, result, and conclusion.

Method

Experimental Task 2 was conducted during the last part of the subjects' second-round interviews. First, each researcher was presented with his two progress reports and asked to point to examples of data, result, and conclusion. The researchers were asked to identify their choices by simply the line numbers in the margin of their reports. Following their selections of these examples, each researcher was asked to give his definitions of the terms *data*, *result*, and *conclusion*.

Next, during the second-round interviews with the supervisors, each supervisor was given four progress reports: the two written by his poor-writer researcher and the two written by his good-writer researcher. In each report, the supervisor was directed to the line numbers of the report that his researcher-writer of the report had previously identified as containing an example of either data, result, or conclusion. The supervisors, however, were not told how their researchers (the writers of these reports) had previously identified the same information, nor were they even told that their researchers had done so. Next, the supervisor was asked what he would call the information in that particular line: Data? Result? Conclusion? Or something else? As with the researchers, the supervisors were then asked to give their definitions of *data, result,* and *conclusion.*

Finally, the directors, during their second-round interviews, were given the same experimental task as described above for the supervisors. However, because of the inordinate amount of time it would have taken each director to analyze all of the progress reports written by the researchers within his respective department, each director was given only a select sample of four progress reports written by four different researchers in his department: two reports written by two of the poor writer-researchers and two reports written by two of the good writer-researchers. Experimental Task 2 was then carried out in the same manner as described above for the supervisor subjects.

Analytical Procedure

To determine the extent to which the paired subjects similarly identified the same lines as data, result, or conclusion, the number of total matches was divided by the total number of lines identified by the pair. Breakdown percentages of this total match were calculated to determine the percentage of times the pair similarly identified the information as either data, result, or conclusion. Since the subjects' definitions of these terms could not be analyzed quantitatively, the range of their responses is simply described and reported later in this chapter.

In the results presented below, the director subjects have been excluded from the analysis of data because there were so few of them (only four directors) and because, unlike the supervisors, they did not evaluate the total sample of reports.

Results

Identification of Data, Results, and Conclusions. The percentages of matches and mismatches by type of information (that is, data, result, conclusion, or something else) for each of the following pair groups are shown in Tables 11.6–11.8:

Table 11.6: All Researchers and Their Supervisors
Table 11.7: Poor-Writer Researchers and Their Supervisors
Table 11.8: Good-Writer Researchers and Their Supervisors

Table 11.6. Mean Percentages of Matches and Mismatches (44 Progress Reports) by Type of Information: Paired Researchers and Supervisors.

Supervisors (n = 11)	Researchers (n = 22)			
Type of Info:	Data	Result	Concl.	Other
Data	12	4	0	1
Result	6	15	6	1
Concl.	4	11	14	2
Other	2	1	4	9

Comparisons of all three tables reveal that all three groups of paired subjects have approximately the same total percentage of matches and mismatches in their overall identification of data, results, and conclusions: a 50 percent match for researchers and supervisors; a 50 percent match for poor writers and their supervisors; and a 48 percent match for good writers and their supervisors. Furthermore, for all three pair groups the likelihood of a match or mismatch is about the same.

Whether or not a batting average of .500 is high, low, or average in this situation cannot be determined since this is one case study of one R&D organization. The results do indicate, however, that, contrary to the results from Phase 1 that revealed a closer overall agreement between the preferences of the good writers and those of their supervisors than between the preferences of the poor writers and those of their supervisors, the good writers and their supervisors do not have more similar notions about what

Table 11.7. Mean Percentages of Matches and Mismatches (44 Progress Reports) by Type of Information: Paired Poor Writers and Their Supervisors.

Supervisors (n = 11)	Poor Writers (n = 11)			
Type of Info:	Data	Result	Concl.	Other
Data	9	4	0	1
Result	8	17	9	0
Concl.	4	4	15	3
Other	1	2	0	9

Table 11.8. Mean Percentages of Matches and Mismatches (44 Progress Reports) by Type of Information: Paired Good Writers and Their Supervisors.

Supervisors (n = 11)	Good Writers (n = 11)			
Type of Info:	Data	Result	Concl.	Other
Data	12	3	0	0
Result	4	13	3	1
Concl.	4	17	14	1
Other	4	0	9	9

constitutes data, results, and conclusions than do the poor writers and their supervisors.

On Tables 11.6–11.8, the specific areas of match are in the boxes that run diagonally from the upper left box to the lower right box. The specific areas of mismatch are found along the intersecting row and column boxes (excluding the box along the diagonal) for each type of information.

Comparisons of the percentages in Tables 11.7 and 11.8 reveal that the specific areas of match are similar for both the poor writers and their supervisors and for the good writers and their supervisors. In both cases, the highest percentages of matches are for results and conclusions (17 percent and 15 percent, respectively, for the poor writer/supervisor group; 13 percent and 14 percent, respectively, for the good writer/supervisor group). However, while the good writer/supervisor group's percentage of match for data (12 percent) is close to their percentages of match for results and conclusions, the poor writer/supervisor group's percentage of match for data (9 percent) is considerably lower than their percentage of match for results (17 percent) and for conclusions (15 percent).

Of more interest and potential significance than the areas of match, however, are the areas of disagreement or mismatch within and between the two pair groups. Comparisons of Tables 11.7 an 11.8 reveal that, while there is relatively little disagreement over data and conclusions, there is some disagreement over data and results, and considerable disagreement over results and conclusions. With regard to the latter, the source of disagreement or mismatch is quite different for the two groups.

For the poor writer/supervisor group, 12 percent of the time data and results are mismatched. What 8 percent of the time the supervisors identify as a result, the poor writers identify as data; and what 4 percent of the time what the supervisors identity as data, the poor writers identify as a result. To a similar extent (13 percent of the time), this group also disagrees about results and conclusions. What 9 percent of the time the supervisors call a result, the poor writers call a conclusion; and what 4 percent of the time the supervisors call a conclusion, the poor writers call a result.

Compared with the poor writer/supervisor group, the good writers and their supervisors are more in agreement about what data and results mean. Only 7 percent of the time did this group reveal a mismatch. To a much greater extent than the poor writer/supervisor group, however, the good writers and their supervisors disagree about results and conclusions (20 percent mismatch). The nature of that disagreement, however, is not the same as for the poor writer/supervisor group. Whereas the supervisors were more likely to regard as a result information that the poor writers identified as a conclusion, here the situation is quite the reverse. What 17 percent of the time the supervisors call a conclusion, the good writers call a result. These comparisons suggest that in the progress reports of the good writers the supervisors may be inflating (or the good writers may be deflating) the meaning of *results*. That is, what the good writers regard as only a result, their supervisors are more likely to regard as a conclusion. Conversely, the above comparisons suggest that in the progress reports of the poor writers the supervisors may be deflating (or the poor writers may be inflating) the meaning of *conclusions*. That is, what the poor writers regard as a conclusion, their supervisors may regard as only a result.

If this is indeed the case, then it is the poor writers, rather than the good writers, who stand to lose in the semantic showdown. The poor writers may not realize that, with respect to their progress reports, their intentions are falling short of their supervisors reader's expectations, not because they do not share their supervisors' expectations but because they do not share the same meaning of *conclusion*. The poor writers, that is, may actually *think* that they are giving their supervisors conclusions—that they are reporting "progress"—when in fact those "conclusions" are registering as only results to their supervisors.

By comparison, the good writers' mismatches may actually be working to their advantage. Although they may *think* that in their progress reports they are giving their supervisors only results, they may in fact be giving the supervisors what the supervisors regard as conclusions—the very sort of information that in Phase 1 the supervisors said they most prefer in a progress report.

Subjects' Definitions of Data, Result, and Conclusion. As noted in the above discussion, the subjects' identification of information reveals that the main areas of disagreement or confusion concern data and results, and results and conclusions. In order to further explore the nature of these differences of opinion, the subjects were asked to give their definitions of *data*, *result*, and *conclusion*. The following is a cross sample of the subjects' definitions:

Data.

figures, graphs, or tables
raw numbers in any form
the numbers or results the work generates
the information obtained from the experiment—always numbers
actual physical results
only the output numbers, not the numerical operating conditions or
    parameters
numbers and observations

Results.

selective data
an analysis of the data
an evaluation of the data
massaging the data
a combination of results and conclusion
an interpretation of the data
a conclusion
the conclusions and recommendations pulled out of the data
same thing as data but with some discussion
a conclusion drawn from the data
data in sentence form
a summary of the data; could be in table form

Conclusions.

taking a result and inserting it into the overall project
a result
the "so what" of the data
summary of the work done
the final interpretation of one or more experiments as it relates to the
    project
an extended result; a bigger leap; your neck on the block
a synthesis from the analysis; some interpretation; some underlying
    significance; reducing it to practice
the importance of the results; could also be a recommendation
generalizing the results
bottom line; implications of results
an assumption, conclusion or decision based on results
a definite result

> fitting results into your model or changing the model to fit the results
> how the results affect us or how we can utilize them

The above cross sample points to inconsistencies within the definitions for each of the terms, as well as some overlap between the definitions of *data* and *result* and between the definitions of *result* and *conclusion*.

First, for some subjects *data* refers to only numbers, but to other subjects *data* further includes non-numerical observations. Also, those who think of *data* as only raw numbers disagree about whether those numbers refer to only the data generated from the research or whether those numbers include both the input data (for example, the operating conditions) as well as the output data. Other subjects define *data* simply by its format—that is, graphs, figures, or tables. Finally, some use the term *results* as a synonym for the term *data*.

Second, *results* is defined as either the verbal, rather than the numerical, presentation of data; a summary of the data; or an analysis or interpretation of the data. In the first of these definitions, the terms *results* and *data* are often used interchangably; and, in the last of these definitions, the terms *result* and *conclusion* are often used interchangeably.

Third, definitions of *conclusion* range from a summary of the results to interpretation of the results, to the significance of the results to the project's goals. Each of these definitions of *conclusion* implies a different mode of thinking on the part of the writer and results in a different kind of information for the reader, ranging from Type 3 to Type 4 to Type 5 information, as described in Chapter 9.

Finally, some subjects indicated that in progress reports especially, the results and conclusions are often synonymous since the progress reports cover only two weeks of work and since the conclusions of the entire research project are later included in the longer, more formal report.

The subjects' confusion over the terms *data*, *result*, and *conclusion*, as demonstrated by both their identification and definition of these terms, may be attributable in part to this organization's format for the progress reports. Under the headings *Objectives*, *Results*, and *Future*, one finds a wide range of information. For instance, numerical data, speculations, and procedure appear under any of these headings. And what appears under the heading of *Results* is as likely to be data, results, or conclusions, depending upon one's definition.

If the supervisor readers of the progress reports are not getting as much of the information they most prefer (Type 5, which includes conclusions), perhaps one of the reasons is that the format of the progress report does not encourage conclusions, however tentative. While there is a definite section that calls for results, there is not a section that calls for conclusions. Since, as we have seen, the writers of the reports may regard *results* to mean anything from data to conclusions, it is not surprising that the "Results" section contains such diverse information.

CONCLUSIONS

In general, the information that the readers and writers in their first-round interviews of Phase 1 said that they most and least prefer in progress reports is the same type of information that in their second-round experimental-task interviews of Phase 3 they selected as most important and as least important in the progress reports.

Both the readers and writers most often preferred and selected Type 3 information (what was obtained—data, observations, and results) and Type 4 information (what the results mean) as most important, and they least preferred and most often selected as least important Type 1 information (what was done).

Results from Experimental Task 1 indicate that, although there are no significant differences between the poor writers and the good writers with respect to the information they selected as least important in their reports, there are significant differences with respect to the information they selected as most important. Whereas the poor writers selected Type 3 information as most important in their progress reports an average of 38 percent of the time, the good writers selected it as most important an average of only 9 percent of the time. With respect to Type 5 information (what the results are good for), the situation is quite the reverse. Whereas the good writers selected Type 5 information as most important an average of 37 percent of the time, the poor writers selected it as most important an average of only 5 percent of the time.

As explained in this chapter, the differences between these groups cannot be explained either by significant differences in their Phase 1 stated preferences for Types 3 and 5 information or by Phase 2 differences in the percentages of these types of information contained in their progress reports. Thus, it was suggested that the differences may be attributable to the different criteria that the poor writers and the good writers use to evaluate their own reports and the different conceptions that the two groups of writers have about both the purpose of progress reports in general and the ways in which their supervisors use the reports. Since the good writers are more likely to use audience-oriented criteria and to realize that their supervisor-readers most prefer information that helps them evaluate the project's progress, the good writers are more likely than the poor writers to prefer, select, and include in their progress reports Type 5 information.

This hypothesis is further supported by the considerably higher percentage of match between the paired good writers and their supervisors than between the paired poor writers and their supervisors with respect to their identification of Type 5 information. Although both groups have about a 50 percent overall match in the information they select as most important, the good writer/supervisor group is over three times as likely as the poor writer/supervisor group to similarly identify Type 5 information as most important. In addition, the good writers and their supervisors, when compared with the poor writers and their supervisors, are more likely to agree about the information that is least important in the progress reports.

With respect to Experimental Task 2, the subjects' identifications and definitions of *data*, *result*, and *conclusion* revealed considerable overlap in the terms *data* and *result* and in the terms *result* and *conclusion*. The writers and readers of the progress reports similarly identified information as data, result, or conclusion about 50 percent of the time. For the poor writers and their supervisors, the areas of mismatch concerned data and results, as well as results and conclusions. For the good writers and their supervisors, most of the mismatch concerned results and conclusions.

With respect to the nature of the mismatch of results and conclusions, however, the two pair groups are notably different. In general, what the poor writers identified as a conclusion, their supervisors identified as a result; and what the good writers identified as a result, their supervisors identified as a conclusion. These findings suggest that the poor writers may not be getting as much mileage out of their "conclusions" as they may think they are, and, conversely, that the good writers may be getting more mileage out of their "results" than they may think they are.

APPENDIX 11-A
SAMPLE OF INSTRUMENT USED FOR EXPERIMENTAL TASK 1

Phase 3 Second-Round Interviews with Researcher-Writer Subjects
(Experimental Task 1)

Name_____

Semimonthly #1: MIMP News? To Whom? Why Imp/not Imp? To Whom?
(line #s)   _____
                _____
                _____
                LIMP
(line #s)   _____
                _____
                _____

Semimonthly #2: MIMP
(line #s)   _____
                _____
                _____
                LIMP
(line #s)   _____
                _____
                _____

1. What is your criterion for "important"?

2. How are the semimonthly reports used? (What is their purpose?)
    use/purpose to you:
    use/purpose to your section leader:
    use/purpose to your director:
    use/purpose to the VP of R&D:
    use/purpose to those at corporate headquarters:

3. How important are the semimonthly reports (and why are they important)?

	not at all	not much	somewhat	important	very imp
	1	2	3	4	5
to you?					
your section leader?					
your director?					
VP of R&D?					
corp hdqtrs?					

4. How often, if at all, do you read the semimonthly reports written by other researchers in your section?

	never	seldom	sometimes	often	very freq.
	1	2	3	4	5

5. Do you feel any anxiety about reporting negative results (or "failure") in your semimonthly reports? If so, why?

definitely   somewhat   no

12
Conclusions

Given the confusion over the term *conclusions*, as discussed in the last chapter, perhaps a better title for this chapter is "Type 5 Information," for this chapter addresses, at last, the "bottom line" or "so-what?" of the findings reported in the previous three chapters. To return to the distinctions between the aims of science and the aims of technology made earlier in Chapter 7, the following is an attempt to summarize and synthesize the contributions that this study may make to the science of technical writing (to knowledge about technical writing, and about progress reports in particular) and the implications of this study's findings for the technology of technical writing (for the pragmatic use of that knowledge for practitioners, teachers, and researchers of technical writing).

First, however, it may be useful to summarize the main findings. Because of this study's scope and the many variables examined, it is not possible in this chapter to review all of the results from Phases 1, 2, and 3 without reiterating everything that has already been covered in the conclusion sections of Chapters 9, 10, and 11. The following is, therefore, a summary of only the main highlights.

SUMMARY

With respect to the type of information preferred in progress reports, Phase 1 of the study found that the subjects most prefer the following types of information: Type 3 (data, observations, and results), Type 4 (interpretation of the results), and Type 5 (the significance or "so what?" of the results); and that they least prefer the following types of information: Type 1 (the background or context of the research), and Type 2 (how the research was done).

In general, Phase 3 found that the subjects' selections of most important and least important information in the progress reports corresponded to the above Phase 1 stated preferences for types of information. That is, the subjects most often selected Types 3, 4, and 5 information as most important and most often selected Types 1 and 2 information as least important.

Interestingly, the Phase 2 analysis of the types of information contained in the researchers' progress reports revealed that they overwhelmingly contain the very type of information that the subjects said they least prefer and that they least selected as most important: Type 1 information. Also, the reports contain the least amount of the type of information that the subjects said they highly prefer and that they frequently selected as most important: Type 5 information. While this appears to indicate a discrepancy between preference and practice, such quantitative comparisons, as explained in Chapter 10, may not be appropriate for the simple reason that there is not necessarily a one-to-one correlation between one's degree of preference for a type of information and the amount of that type of information actually contained in one's progress report.

More important than these general findings, which are based upon all writer and reader subjects and all researchers' reports, are the findings that point to significant differences between the writers of the good progress reports and the writers of the poor progress reports. Briefly, this study supports the hypothesis that, with respect to the informational content of progress reports, there is a closer match between the intentions and texts of the good writers and the expectations of their supervisors than there is between the intentions and texts of the poor writers and the expectations of their supervisors. To use speech-act terminology, the mutual contextual beliefs of the good writers and their supervisors are more mutual than are the mutual contextual beliefs of the poor writers and their supervisors. Specifically, this study found that, compared with the poor writers, the good writers of progress reports

1. Have a better understanding of the ways in which their supervisor readers use the researchers' progress reports.
2. Have a better understanding of the type of information that their supervisor readers most prefer in a progress report (that is, Type 5 information).
3. More closely agree with their supervisors about the types of information that they most and least prefer in progress reports.
4. Have in their progress reports a significantly greater percentage of the type of information (Type 5) that their supervisors most prefer, and a significantly smaller percentage of the type of information (Type 1) that their supervisors least prefer.
5. In their own progress reports, are more likely to select as most important the same type of information that their supervisors select as most important (Type 5 information).

As suggested previously, these findings are probably not that surprising since the good-writer and the poor-writer subjects were initially identified by the supervisors themselves. However, since the supervisors were given no criteria upon which to base their selections, these findings do help explain what it is that, from the supervisors' perspective at least, distinguishes the good progress reports (and the good progress report writers) from the poor progress reports (and the poor progress report writers). As indicated by the above results, the most important distinction concerns Type 5 information.

In view of some of the speculations made previously, it should be noted here that this study also disclosed some unexpected findings. Among these are:

1. Despite the research that indicates substantial differences between engineers and scientists in their academic orientations, research interests, career goals, and personalities, there appears to be no significant difference between them in either the types of information contained in their progress reports or the types of information they select as most important in their progress reports.
2. The type of research conducted within a particular department (whether, for instance, it is oriented more toward science or more toward engineering) appears to have no significant effect upon the type of information contained in a progress report.
3. The stage of the project at which a progress report is written appears to have no significant effect upon the type of information contained in the progress report.

This is not to suggest, however (as implied by all of the "appear's"), that these variables may not be significant when another research design is employed or when another context is investigated. Indeed, it should be pointed out that even the significant differences found between the good writers and the poor writers pertain only to this one large case study of this one R&D organization. Furthermore, this study employed statistical tests—namely, the t test—for a relatively small group of subjects and texts. In another study, one involving a larger sample, other statistically significant differences might emerge. And finally, further research is needed in order to determine whether the results of this study extend to writers, texts, and readers in other R&D organizations.

These, then, are the major findings of this study. Whatever interest these findings may have, however, the findings by themselves are more "results" than "conclusions"—more unprocessed information than processed information. What is needed at this point is the very type of information that the supervisors, as well as the good writers, value most in progress reports: some indication of the significance and practical applications of this study's results.

THE SCIENCE OF TECHNICAL WRITING

Since technical writing, like all other kinds of writing, is largely a creative act, incapable of being reduced to hard-and-fast rules, formulas, or algorithms, it may be argued that, strictly speaking, there can be no "science" of technical writing, any more than there can be a science of poetry or painting. Thus, the term *science* is used here in its most general sense to refer only to a state of knowledge within a particular discipline.

Even in this sense of the word, however, there is scarcely a science of technical writing since most of what is known about the subject is based primarily upon textbook descriptions (and prescriptions), anecdotal articles, and pedagogical testimonies. With rare exceptions, the field of composition research is concerned with the academic writing of students. Although a few recent studies have begun to examine real-world writing, the area of real-world technical writing remains virtually unexplored. Outside the field of composition research, there exist a few studies of the technical communication within R&D organizations; however, as discussed in Chapter 5, these studies focus primarily upon either the evolution of research ideas and projects or the discrepancies between the research as conducted within the laboratory and the research as reported in published scientific papers.

The present study represents what may be the first study of technical writing within an organizational context to examine the interrelationship among all three aspects of written communication: the writer, the text, and the reader. Specifically, this study contributes to our understanding of the type of technical report most commonly written, read, and used within an R&D organization, but which has been the least investigated: the progress report. These contributions are in three related areas:

1. The purposes of progress reports to both writers and readers.
2. The different meanings of *progress* that are related to these purposes.
3. The different types of information that are in turn implied by the different meanings of *progress*.

Although, as discussed previously, many textbooks on technical writing acknowledge the importance of progress reports and the various purposes they serve within an organization, the textbooks do not discuss what implications those various purposes have for the type of information to be contained in a progress report or for the meaning of *progress*. If anything, the *Work Accomplished, Work Scheduled* format typically prescribed in most technical writing textbooks encourages progress reports that contain information that is little more than a log or timesheet of what was done and what remains to be done (in other words, essentially unprocessed information). Furthermore, such a format implies a concept of progress that is based solely upon how much one has accomplished during a given period of time rather than upon the potential significance of what one has accomplished (or, in other words, processed information).

The findings of the present study suggest that what writers regard as the primary purpose of a progress report influences both the type of information that they include in their progress reports and the way in which they interpret *progress*. The interrelationship of all of these—purpose, progress, and information—shape the intentions and texts of the writers of progress reports and help explain the differences found in this study between the poor progress reports and their writers and the good progress reports and their writers.

Purposes of Progress Reports

In general, this study confirms that the main purposes of progress reports are the same as those commonly described in technical writing textbooks. In order of priority, these purposes are as follows:

1. To keep management informed about the status of the various research projects so that they can make decisions regarding the value and direction of those projects, as well the implications that the research may have for any new projects.
2. To document the work in progress.
3. To assess the effectiveness of the researchers themselves; to assure management that, to use Mills and Walters' phrase, the "workers are earning their keep" (1986, p. 280).

This study revealed that at this particular organization the readers of the progress reports are most concerned with the first purpose; that is, they use the progress reports primarily as a means of assessing the significance of the research reported and thereby making decisions to direct the course of the project. While the good writers are likely to realize that this is the main reason their supervisors read their progress reports, the poor writers are more likely to mistakenly assume that the main reason their supervisors read their progress reports is to check up on the accuracy of the researcher's work.

The study furthermore revealed another important purpose of progress reports, one that is often overlooked in textbook discussions: the value of the actual writing for the researchers themselves. The findings of this study indicate that the poor writers and the good writers value progress reports, or progress report writing, for quite different reasons. The majority of the poor writers view their progress reports as a means of helping them to later write their longer, more formal reports or as a means of planning their next two weeks' work. The good writers, on the other hand, view their progress reports as a means of helping them to discover the significance of their results. Thus, the purpose that the progress reports serve for the good writers corresponds well with the purpose for which the supervisors read the progress reports. According to many of the supervisors, the real value in having the researchers write progress reports is the heuristic function they serve in helping the researchers to think about the meaning of their work.

Concepts of Progress

While it seems obvious that any discussion of progress reports ought to consider the meaning of *progress* itself, textbooks on technical writing rarely delve into this matter. Rather, the common assumption is that *progress* means accomplishing work over a given period of time. While this is one concept of progress, there are other, more subtle and complex ones that are related to both the different purposes of progress reports, as described above, and the types of information contained in progress reports, as will be discussed in the next section.

Etymologically, *progress* means "to advance or go forth." However, depending upon what it is that one regards as advancing or going forth, progress reports may be based on different notions of *progress*. The present study suggests that the poor writers and the good writers of the progress reports may have different conceptions of *progress*.

First, *progress* may mean no more than that one has done an additional amount of work during the present two-week period; that, in other words, one has been busy doing something during that time, whether it is running three more tests, analyzing two more samples, inspecting the spectrographs of the tests conducted during the previous period, or completing an inspection of a hydrocarbon analyzer. For someone writing an academic research paper, it may mean that 20 more pages have been written. Here, progress is measured by the apparent industriousness of the workers: first, whether work is being accomplished and, second, whether that work is on schedule, moving forward in time.

Second, *progress* may mean that one now knows more during the present two-week period than one knew during the last two-week period; that, for instance, one is closer to understanding the nature of a chemical reaction or the reasons that the filter line of the reactor is plugged. For someone writing an academic research paper, it may mean finally figuring out that the statistical data either confirms or rejects one's initial hypothesis. Here, progress is not necessarily measured by either time or industriousness (for one can work diligently for days or months and still know no more than when the project began) but rather by a gain in knowledge. Furthermore, that gain in knowledge is itself "success," whether or not that knowledge may be construed by others in the R&D organization as a failure because it does not, as anticipated, lead to the development of a better process or product but rather leads to the cancellation of the entire project and the loss of hundreds of thousands of dollars. As discussed in Chapter 7, this concept of progress as strictly the advancement of knowledge is the same as that of science. Whether that knowledge confirms the prevailing construct or paradigm of reality or whether it rejects that construct and perhaps in the process erects a new one makes little difference: either way, progress has been made.

Finally, *progress* may mean that one has successfully solved a problem, gotten closer toward developing a better (for example, a faster, cheaper, simpler, more reliable, or more profitable) process or product, or has made significant strides toward the successful adaptation of scientific knowledge to a technological application. It may mean finding a way of unplugging the filter line of the reactor, improving the process for removing the particle fines in syncrudes in order to produce synfuels, or discovering a way to grow synthetic protein for commercial use. For someone writing an academic research paper, it may mean extrapolating from the results of the research some practical implications or applications. In any event, the criterion is usefulness. As discussed in Chapter 2, this concept of progress is similar to that of technology where progress implies success—a success defined by pragmatics. Such technological progress, although it often comes in the wake of scientific progress or knowledge, can be made without scientific knowledge and may, in fact, open up new avenues of scientific research and progress.

Concepts of Progress and Types of Information in Progress Reports

Each of the above concepts of progress in turn implies a different focus of information in technical progress reports. The first concept of progress—that based on the amount work of work accomplished in a given period—leads to Type 1 and Type 2 information, an emphasis upon what was done and how it was done. The implicit aim of such a report is to convince the reader that the researcher is busy doing the work for which he is paid and that whatever work the previous period's progress report had indicated would be done during the present period has in fact been done: in other words, that the research and the researcher are proceeding on schedule.

Such a view of progress and the types of information it implies naturally lend themselves to the *Work Accomplished—Work Scheduled* type of progress report. The present study indicates that this may be the notion of progress held by the poor writers of the progress reports since (a) they perceive the purpose of the progress report in this manner, and (b) their progress reports, compared to those of the good writers, contain a significantly higher percentage of Type 1 information (what was done).

The second view of progress—that based upon a gain in knowledge—leads to either Type 3 information or Type 4 information, depending upon one's definition of *knowledge*. When *knowledge* is defined, as in the dictionary, as factual information, then the emphasis in a progress report is most likely to be upon Type 3 information—data, facts, observations, and results. When, however, *knowledge* is defined as the interpretation of facts, then the emphasis is most likely to be upon Type 4 information, that is, the significance of the Type 3 information within some larger frame of reference (for example, some theory, model, or paradigm).

Here, it is difficult to say whether it is the poor writers or the good writers who most have this concept of progress since their progress reports contain approximately the same percentages of Type 3 and Type 4 information. However, since in their progress reports the poor writers selected Type 3 information as most important a significantly greater percentage of the time than did the good writers in their progress reports, it would appear that the poor writers are more likely than the good writers to interpret progress as the accumulation of factual knowledge.

Finally, the third concept of progress—that based upon the practical significance of one's research results—leads to Type 5 information, an emphasis upon how the results might actually be used. Here, it is quite clear from the findings of this study that it is the good writers (as well as their supervisor readers) rather than the poor writers who most hold this concept of progress. This is evidenced by (a) the significantly greater percentage of Type 5 information in the progress reports of the good writers than in those of the poor writers, and (b) the higher percentage of matches between the paired good writers and their supervisors than between the paired poor writers and their supervisors in their identification of Type 5 information as most important in the progress reports.

Concepts of Information

Finally, this study may further our understanding of the informational content of progress reports in that it provides a conceptual framework for distinguishing between different types of information. Perhaps no single word is more often used in definitions of technical writing and discussions of technical reports than is the word *information*. Rarely, however, does one find in the textbooks and articles on technical writing any explanation of the wide range in types of information; rather, *information* is used as a catchall to refer to anything that might conceivably be included in a technical report.

Furthermore, as revealed in Phase 3 of this study, even the more specific terms that are commonly used to refer to different types of information, terms such as *data, result,* and *conclusion,* often blur and overlap and may mean different things to different people. Since such terms, especially *results* and *conclusions,* often appear as subject headings in technical reports, one might expect that textbooks would contain explanations and examples of the differences between these terms; such, however, is seldom the case.

This is not to suggest, however, that there ought to be definitive definitions of *information, data, results,* and *conclusions,* for such attempts, like the attempts of those who advocate a universalist language, are doomed to failure because of the nature of language itself. What is needed, and what this study attempts to do, is to provide some classifying principle on which to base theoretical distinctions between the types of information.

The classifying principle proposed in this study, as described in Chapter 10, and used to analyze the types of information in progress reports, is one that is based upon the extent to which the writer has mentally manipulated the knowledge gained from his research work. Simply put, information, it is suggested, can be represented along a continuum that at one end is essentially unprocessed information—that is, information that simply provides a record of experience as perceived—and at the other end is essentially processed information—that is, information that provides some interpretation of experience or, beyond that, suggests the significance of that experience for guiding or creating future work.

Unprocessed information, as discussed in Chapter 10, consists primarily of three types of information: what was done, how it was done, and what was observed or obtained from the work done (Types 1, 2, and 3 information, respectively). Processed information consists primarily of two types of information: what the observations or results obtained mean and how what they mean has practical significance for future decisions or action (Types 4 and 5 information, respectively).

This theoretical framework is useful because it avoids the ambiguity of terms such as *results* and *conclusions.* Furthermore, it helps to explain the connections between different modes of thinking (and reporting) and the different types of information that these modes engender. Unprocessed information is the result mainly of describing and narrating, of simply selecting and recording that which exists. Processed information is the result of analyzing, deducing, interpreting, and evaluating that which exists, and speculating about that which can, may, should, or should not exist. The first, unprocessed information, serves primarily as documentation of experience, as history. The second, processed information, has the predictive and creative power to alter theory, direct the course of experience, and pave new paths for future research—to create history.

Finally, this theoretical framework for information is also associated with the different purposes of progress reports and the different concepts of progress as discussed earlier. When researchers view the main purpose of progress reports as simply informing their readers about what they have done during the time period, and when they view progress as the amount of work they have done within that period, the result is likely to be a progress report containing mostly unprocessed information. When, however, the researchers view the main purpose of progress reports as informing their readers about the significance of the work they have done during the time period so that the readers are better able to make decisions about the value and direction of that work, and when researchers view progress as a gain in knowledge or as the practical application of that knowledge, the result is likely to be a progress report that contains a greater emphasis on processed information ("greater," that is, than the progress reports of those researchers who have the other views of purpose and progress).

These, then, are the main contributions that this study makes to our understanding of the nature of technical writing and the types of information contained in progress reports. The study reveals how the traditional definition of *technical writing*, and its corresponding model of communication—as the transmission of objective, factual information—oversimplifies, distorts, and neglects the complex purposes that technical information serves within the context of a research organization. Although further work is needed to build a more accurate model of technical communication, the relationships suggested above among the different concepts of purpose, progress, and information may help lay the groundwork for future models.

THE TECHNOLOGY OF TECHNICAL WRITING

This section will at last conclude this study with some of the practical implications that the findings may have for R&D departments of corporations, teachers of technical writing, and researchers interested in further investigating the nature of real-world technical writing.

Technical Reports in R&D Organizations

A common assumption of managers within R&D organizations is that their researchers, because they have advanced degrees, ought to know how to write. What is often overlooked, however, is that the problems their researchers may have in writing effective technical reports may not be due to lack of writing skills (for example, problems in constructing clear, grammatically correct sentences) but rather to a lack of knowledge about the expectations at that particular company (for example, problems in determining the nature and amount of information that ought to be included in a progress report). While the first problem can be blamed in part upon the schools' failure to assure that their graduates have adequate writing skills, the second problem is more the failure of the organization itself to provide their employees with adequate training. As was pointed out earlier, academic writing is quite different from organizational writing; a technical report written for a course or a journal has different conventions and purposes than a technical report written for in-company communication.

Although the present study investigated only progress reports, there appear to be some factors that influence the intentions of writers regardless of the type of report they are writing. An awareness of the bases of writer intentions can help managers identify the possible sources of confusion and therefore guide them in their training programs. The present study suggests that the intentions of writers are shaped by the following:

1. General conceptions about the nature of communication, the aim of technical writing, and the criteria for effective technical reports.
2. Notions about what constitutes *data*, *result*, and *conclusion*.
3. Awareness of general company expectations concerning technical reports.
4. Awareness of one's immediate director's and supervisor's expectations concerning technical reports.

While the first two can be attributed to beliefs that the researcher has upon coming to an organization (beliefs that, in turn, may have been nurtured by schools or by other organizations), the second two are clearly the result of the researcher's experiences at that particular organization. Although research organizations may not see themselves in the role of educators, part of their responsibility in job training is to assure that employees know how to use the skills they have to do the work expected and, when the employees lack the necessary skills, to meet those needs through instruction. When it comes to applying, or even developing, research skills necessary for on-the-job training, most companies readily acknowledge the need. However, when it comes to the writing associated with the researcher's job, companies often overlook the need to make explicit their expectations regarding the written work associated with the researcher's job. The following are, thus, some suggestions for how companies can help improve the quality of technical reports within their organizations by making their expectations more explicit.

First, there is a need for company or department guidelines for writing technical reports. The findings of this study, as well as my experiences at other R&D organizations, indicate that most often the researchers learn company expectations by sheer trial and error. Where guidelines exist, they are often simply a brief description of the company's prescribed formats for different reports—guidelines that may be more useful for secretaries than for researchers. What writers need, but what companies rarely provide, are guidelines that explain the audience, purpose, content, organization, and style of the various reports within that particular organization. These guidelines might also include model reports and illustrations of the common pitfalls of the various reports.

This implies, of course, that the company has figured out its expectations. I would guess, however, that in most companies those expectations are not the result of deliberation (or, if so, that the deliberation probably occurred years before most people can remember) but rather the result of evolution or accretion: that is, the types of reports written, as well as their content and organization, exist simply because, as far as anyone recalls, that is the way they have always been done or because every now and then a manager, disturbed about the quality of reports, rummages through his files to find a good report and issues it as a model for others to follow.

My second suggestion, then, which is really my first since it is the logical precursor to the development of guidelines, is for managers to consider the types of information they need from researchers in order for the organization to function most effectively and efficiently, and, then, upon the basis of identified needs, to determine the nature, frequency, organization, and content of the reports that would best fulfill those needs. Having developed an "ideal-case" scenario based upon the pragmatics of their current situation—as well as upon speculations about future needs, such as the ways in which computer storage and retrieval of reports may affect their content, organization, and use—managers can access how well present documentation practices and expectations are serving the organization and thereby make appropriate changes.

Third, once expectations have been determined and guidelines formulated, companies can do several things to ensure that those expectations are consistently carried out and reinforced. A common complaint of managerial personnel is the great amount of time and effort expended in shuttling reports back and forth between readers and writers for numerous revisions. Once expectations are made clearer, the problem will be avoided to a great extent. However, directors and supervisors can insure that guidelines do not gather dust in file cabinets if they occasionally make writing the topic of their department or section meetings.

At the organization that was the subject of this study, some of the supervisors volunteered some of the ways they periodically reinforce their expectations for written reports. One supervisor reported that he takes a poorly written report, does a revision, and distributes the before and after versions to his group, explaining to his researchers the nature of and reasons for his changes. Another supervisor reported doing the same sort of demonstration but followed with an application exercise in which all of the researchers revised another report and then discussed their revisions. In both cases, the supervisors said that the ideas they most often tried to get across to their researchers were the need to interpret results, to make complex technical information clear to nonspecialists (mainly managerial readers), and to put important information in emphatic positions within the report.

These, then, are only a few of the ways in which R&D organizations can help ensure that the reports written by their researchers contain the sort of information that the readers most need in order to carry on the business of the company. The better writers, as suggested by this study, seem better able to intuit the expectations of their readers even though they have received the same training as the poorer writers. (In fact, in some cases, the standards of the better writers seem higher than those of their supervisors, as evidenced by their tendency to call a result what their supervisors call a conclusion.) The point, however, is that, because of the importance of technical reports to the on-going efforts of an R&D organization, the researchers should not have to second guess their readers' expectations. To do so is not in the best interests of either the researcher or the organization for the progress of the latter depends upon the progress of the former. And the progress of both depends upon clear distinctions between the various types of progress reported.

Teaching Technical Writing

In academe, technical writing is often taught in the same way as are other composition courses (primarily because in most universities the teachers of the technical writing courses are the composition teachers). The focus, therefore (as in the majority of technical writing textbooks), is most often upon patterns of organization and modes of development, with attention to some generic formats for technical reports. While such skill development and awareness of technical formats are necessary, these remain only ways of communicating information; whether or not the information communicated is appropriate or sufficient for a given audience and purpose is quite another matter, and one that can be determined only by the contextual exigencies of a particular real-world situation.

Thus, the problem confronted by most teachers of technical writing is the same as that of teachers of other composition courses: given no real-world audience and purpose for writing (other than the teacher), how can students learn to adapt content, organization, and style to achieve different purposes and to meet the needs of different readers? In other words, how can they practice communication as a means toward some real end (beyond a grade) rather than an end it itself? How can they practice communication rather than practice writing skills?

This is a dilemma that has yet to be solved satisfactorily. More recent textbooks on technical writing, like recent composition textbooks, have begun to include chapters on planning—chapters that advise students of the importance of considering their specific audience and purpose before beginning to write. A few textbooks, usually the better ones, further include exercises that describe hypothetical real-world situations that stipulate a particular problem, audience, and purpose—a donnee—for writers to use as a basis for generating and evaluating reports. For the most part, however, these exercises are afterthoughts, appendices to chapters rather than integral extensions of the material discussed and illustrated in the chapters.

Compared with the pedagogical methods and materials of business communication, those of technical communication have lagged behind in the articulation of what goes on in the real world and what goes on in the classroom. The reason, perhaps, is that business communication is often taught by business schools rather than by English departments. The use of case studies and simulation exercises has long been a tradition in business schools. Most notably, the Harvard School of Business has built its curriculum around case studies. Moreover, those teaching business communication, especially at the graduate level, often have first-hand experience and continuing ties with those in the business world. In the case of technical communication, academic courses in technical writing are often left to the English departments, and until very recently rarely have the English teachers had either the experience or inclination to venture outside academe into the alien world of corporate R&D organizations where the real-world technical writing occurs. Furthermore, I have had many English teachers tell me that they majored in English (which until recently was synonymous with literature) partially because they did not have an interest in or aptitude for the sciences.

Part of the problem, then, in preparing students for real-world technical writing is not only the artificiality of academic writing as compared with real-world writing but also the unpreparedness or unfamiliarity of the teachers themselves with the nonacademic purposes that technical reports serve within the corporate context. That English teachers have begun to take a greater theoretical and practical interest in technical writing beyond the classroom is evidenced by the increasing emphasis upon this field, as witnessed by the growing number of journal articles, affiliate subgroups of professional organizations, and convention workshops and presentations.

It is only a matter of time before this interest is translated into better textbooks and teaching methodologies. In the meantime, the following are some practical, classroom implications of the present study.

First, in order to familiarize themselves with the ways in which technical reports are actually written, read, and used within research organizations, and at the same time to give them real-world problems and samples of technical writing to be used within the classroom, teachers can solicit from technical organizations examples of real reports. As well as the examples themselves, the teachers can request from the organizations descriptions of the actual constraints governing a particular report—the problem, purpose, and audience. Such reports (negative as well as positive) and the specific situations prompting the reports can be used for discussion and assignment purposes.

Second, teachers can arrange for guest speakers from R&D organizations (the writers or the readers of technical reports) to share their perspectives on how students can best prepare themselves for the type of technical writing they will have to do in conjunction with their careers.

Third, so that students can themselves gain first-hand experience in the ways in which technical reports are written, read, and used in real-world contexts, teachers might investigate the possibility of work-study arrangements with corporations. This would be especially appropriate in a graduate level technical writing course and might be orchestrated in consort with the university's science or engineering departments.

Fourth, and more directly related to the concerns of the present study, teachers can develop lessons and exercises on those topics which, although (and probably because) they are least treated in textbooks on technical writing, are of primary importance to real-world writers and readers. These, as suggested by the present study and outlined below, concern the need for writers to become more well versed in the range and variation of information contained in technical reports and to become more versatile in adapting the content of a report to meet various purposes and diverse audiences. Specifically, there is a need for lessons and exercises that focus upon the following:

1. Distinctions between different types of information (for example, unprocessed versus processed information, or results versus conclusions) and the different purposes and audiences each might serve in hypothetical contexts for technical reports.
2. The level of specificity and technicality with which information is presented in a report.
3. The degree of objectivity or subjectivity with which information is presented in a report.
4. How, keeping the topic and the audience the same but varying purpose (for example, to inform, to convince, to instruct, to recommend), the informational content, organization, and style of a report change.
5. How, keeping the topic and the purpose the same but varying the audience (for example, technical versus nontechnical readers, or fellow-researcher readers versus management readers), the informational content, organization, and style of a report change.

These, then, are only a few of the ways that teachers of technical writing can help create contexts for writing that reflect the challenges of real-world technical writers. Perhaps the most difficult yet useful skill that the student of technical writing needs to acquire is the ability to select and present the kind of information appropriate for various audiences and purposes. In academic technical reports, whether they are written in science, engineering, or English courses, the audience and purpose are typically confined to the teachers or scholars of a discipline and to the aims of scientific knowledge (that is, to the pursuit of truth, or at least better truths). Since, in business, knowledge and truth are not ends but means toward the practical and profitable application of knowledge, students need practice in addressing the kinds of situations and audiences that await them beyond the classroom. They need to know that in the real world progress is measured by yardsticks that may have little to do with the criteria upon which teachers may give an *A* to a technical report. They need to know, too, that the yardsticks may change from organization to organization, and even within organizations, depending upon the particular type of report or the particular supervisor. They need to know how to become versatile not only in such things as syntactic structures, patterns of organization, and modes of development—the things most frequently emphasized in writing courses—but also in such things as contextual and "contentual" flexibility. They need to know, in short, how to read and analyze an organization's culture and community—and how to accurately judge what constitutes "good" writing within that organizational setting.

Researching Technical Writing

The history of research in composition suggests that experience directs areas of needed investigation, that need stimulates inquiry, and that inquiry motivates research—research that in turn may shape experience, and experience that in turn may further direct areas of research, and so on. So it is that much of the earlier research in composition has evolved, and so it is that research in other fields normally evolves. The symbiotic relationship between experience, knowledge, and action is essentially the same as the interrelationship between reality, science, and technology discussed previously in Chapter 6, and the same as that of the distinctions drawn in this study between unprocessed information (Types 1, 2, and 3) and processed information (Types 4 and 5).

The impetus for the present study, as explained in the Introduction and Chapter 5, arose out of my experiences in teaching technical writing in real-world settings. The research led to knowledge that, as suggested in the preceding section, may have practical implications for the teaching of technical writing in academic settings. The research, however, also has implications for further research, research that may lead to greater knowledge of technical writing (its science) as well as to better applications of that knowledge (its technology) within business or academe.

Because of the scope of the present study, which encompasses the writers, texts, and readers of technical progress reports, it was not possible to examine any one of these aspects in detail. This study thus raises many more questions than it answers. However, in an attempt to chart the territory that others may wish to explore, I propose the following areas of research:

The Composing Strategies of Technical Writers. In the present study, the writers of the good progress reports indicated that they use deductive planning strategies, whereas the writers of the poor progress reports indicated that they use inductive planning strategies. Whether or not they in fact do approach a writing task differently needs further investigation.

In a pilot study that used protocol analysis to investigate the planning strategies of supervisors and their researchers, each of whom had been given the same writing task, Barabas (1982) found that the supervisors began by generating a superstructure of main ideas and then upon the basis of this superstructure thought about more specific details and examples to support and explain the main ideas. The researchers, on the other hand, began by generating very specific, diverse ideas and only eventually drew some generalizations from the particulars and then attempted to create some general framework for those particulars. The accounts given by the writers in the present study suggest that the good writers use an approach similar to that of the supervisors just described—that is, a whole-to-parts strategy—and that the poor writers in the present study use an approach similar to that of the researchers just described—that is, a parts-to-whole strategy.

If, in the progress reports of the poor writers, the intended readers are not getting the type of information that they need, then perhaps the reason is due in part to the planning strategies of the poor writers. To a greater extent than the good writers, the poor writers may be emphasizing unprocessed information in their reports because they begin planning their reports by thinking about what they did, how they did it, and what results they got (Types 1, 2, and 3 information, respectively)—a temporally-ordered generation of ideas that focuses upon the specifics and events central to the writer and his research. Conversely, to a greater extent than the poor writers, the good writers may be emphasizing processed information in their reports because they begin planning their reports by thinking about the main conclusions of their research and its significance for future work (Types 4 and 5 information, respectively)—a logically-ordered generation of ideas that focuses upon the generalizations and implications important to the reader and organization.

The possible distinctions between the composing strategies of supervisors and those of their researchers, and between the composing strategies of the good-writer researchers and those of the poor-writer researchers, are but two areas that need further investigation. Other questions that await research are the following:

1. Do scientists and engineers use different planning strategies?
2. What effect do various report purposes (whether, for instance, the report is written to inform or to persuade) have upon the writer's planning strategies?
3. What effect do various audiences (whether, for instance, the report is written for technical specialists or managerial nonspecialists) have upon the writer's planning strategies?
4. What effects do different planning strategies have upon such things as
   4.1 the type of information contained in the report
   4.2 the organization of information in the report
   4.3 the level of specificity or generality of the information contained within the report
   4.4 the effectiveness of the report as judged by its intended reader(s)?
5. Given a typical college-essay assignment and a real-world technical-report assignment, will real-world technical writers use the same planning strategies for both writing tasks?

As discussed previously, in Chapter 2, many studies in composition have begun to investigate the composing strategies of student writers as they plan essays. However, whether the results of those studies have anything to do with the ways in which real-world writers plan technical reports cannot be determined until more research is conducted within the field of technical writing.

Features of Technical Reports. In addition to studies that explore the composing strategies of real-world writers, there is a need for studies that examine various features of the reports themselves. While the present study examined only the types of information contained in progress reports, there remain several other related issues that need to be explored. Among these are the following:

1. Beyond differences in the types of information contained in the progress reports of good writers versus those of poor writers, are there any other significant differences between the two groups' reports in
   1.1 the order in which the types of information are presented
   1.2 the degree of objectivity or subjectivity with which the information is presented
   1.3 the amount of explanation devoted to clarifying, supporting, or justifying the statements made with respect to the various types of information?

2. With respect to the above variables, are there any significant differences
    2.1 between the reports of scientists and those of engineers
    2.2 between types of reports (for example, progress reports, pro-
        posals, and formal reports that document a project)?
3. What patterns of organization are used in progress reports? (For exam-
    ple, is information arranged inductively—from specifics toward
    generalizations—or deductively—from generalizations toward specif-
    ics? To what extent do the reports employ natural patterns, such as
    time, or logical patterns, such as cause-effect, comparison-contrast, and
    classification?)
    3.1 Are certain types of patterns more common in certain types of
        reports?
    3.2 Are there significant differences between good writers and poor
        writers or between scientist writers and engineer writers in the
        types of patterns they use in their reports?
    3.3 Are there any connections between certain types of information
        and certain patterns of organization?

Effects of Technical Reports upon Readers. Any examination of the features of technical reports should also consider their effects upon readers
since, unlike academic student writing, the aim of reports in R&D organizations is not to practice communication skills or to show comprehension of a
subject but rather to help readers comprehend a subject (or a project) and,
beyond that, to provide them with information that they need to assess the
direction of the project. In addition to further studies that examine the kinds
of information that readers most and least prefer in particular types of
technical reports, other studies might investigate the following:

1. What effects do the various organizational features of technical reports,
    such as those listed in the section above, have upon readers? (For exam-
    ple, do readers prefer reports that are deductively or inductively orga-
    nized? What effect do stylistic variables, such as the specificity or objec-
    tivity with which information is presented, have upon readers?)
2. To what extent do readers evaluate reports by content, organization, or
    style?
3. Do readers at different levels of the organization use the same criteria to
    evaluate technical reports?
4. Given unfamiliar reports or excerpts from reports, how would the
    subjects identify the information within the reports? (Are there some
    context-independent bases for distinguishing between types of infor-
    mation, such as data, result, and conclusion?)
5. Apart from how the readers say they use the information contained in
    the researchers' reports, how do they in fact use the information?

Although this section contains suggestions for research that focuses upon the writer, or the text, or the reader, there is a need for research that examines, as does the present study, the interrelationships of these elements within actual contexts of communication. Because of their breadth, such integrative, context-based studies may not be able to achieve the degree of depth typical of the more traditional studies that examine in detail some narrow aspect of only one of the elements (the writer, text, or reader). The advantage of integrative, context-based studies, however, is that they can reveal connections among the process, product, and effect of written communication that are otherwise overlooked and unapparent in the more traditional studies.

Finally, with respect to research methodology, this study demonstrates how researchers can use a combination of methods in order to conduct integrative, context-based studies. This study, for example, is partially descriptive and partially experimental. Unlike most experimental studies, however, it does not begin with a set of assumptions and hypotheses or with a predesigned experiment to test those hypotheses. Furthermore, unlike most discourse analysis studies, it does not begin with a preconceived scheme for analyzing texts. In this sense, the study is organic: Out of the findings from the first phase of the study—which employed methods of survey, interview, observation, and collection—the hypotheses evolved, the discourse analysis scheme was developed, and context-based experiments were designed.

MAKING CONNECTIONS, MAKING PROGRESS

> It's like trying to put together a puzzle without having the picture on the box and without being sure you even have all the pieces. Over time, you begin to discover how some pieces connect, you discover meaning, you begin to create a picture, a picture that itself may change as you find more pieces.
> —a researcher discussing progress reports

Whether we are researchers in R&D organizations or whether we are researchers in academe, we are engaged in the same process of making sense of experience, of trying to make the pieces fit. Progress reports in R&D organizations are one means by which the researchers provide their readers with an ongoing account of their attempts to make meaning from experience and from that meaning to shape future experience. In making such connections, researchers are making progress. They are creating pictures that their readers can use to make decisions, pictures without which the R&D organization cannot continue to function.

In the field of technical writing, the picture is just beginning to take shape. This study examined only the nature of some of the pieces—the types of information contained in progress reports, and the importance of those pieces to the writers and readers of progress reports. There remain several more pieces that have yet to be examined and connected before we can truly say we are making progress toward understanding the nature of real-world technical writing and the practical implications of this knowledge for researchers, whether the researchers be in academe and or in R&D organizations.

References

Allen, T. J. (1977). *Managing the flow of technology: Technology transfer and the dissemination of technological information within the R&D organization.* Cambridge, MA: MIT Press.

Anderson, J. E. (1986). A comment on "territoriality" in rhetoric. *College English, 48,* 736–737.

Anderson, P. V. (1985). What survey research tells us about writing at work. In L. Odell & D. Goswami (Eds.), *Writing in nonacademic settings.* New York: Guilford Press.

Anderson, P. V., Brockmann, R. J., & Miller, C. R. (Eds.). (1983). *New essays in technical and scientific communication: Theory, research, and practice.* Farmingdale, NY: Baywood.

Anderson, R. C., Reynolds, R. E., Schallert, D. L., & Goetz, E. T. (1977). Frameworks for comprehending discourse. *American Educational Research Journal, 14,* 367–381.

Andrews, D. C., & Bickle, M. D. (1982). *Technical writing* (2nd ed.). New York: Macmillan.

Andrews, J. D., & Sigband, N. B. (1984). How effectively does the "new" accountant communicate? Perceptions by practioners and academics. *Journal of Business Communication, 21,* 15–24.

Applebee, A. (1986). Musings. . . Principled practice. *Research in the Teaching of English, 20,* 5–7.

Austin, J. L. (1962). *How to do things with words.* Oxford, England: Clarendon Press.

Bach, K., & Harnish, R. M. (1979). *Linguistic communication and speech acts.* Cambridge, MA: MIT Press.

Bain, A. (1866). *English composition and rhetoric.* New York: D. Appleton.

Bakhtin, M. M. (1981). Discourse in the novel. In M. Holquist (Ed.), *The dialogic imagination* (Trans. C. Emerson & M. Holquist). Austin, TX: University of Texas Press.

Barabas, C. 1982. *Idea-generation strategies of engineers and their supervisors: A pilot study.* Unpublished manuscript.

Barnett, L. (1968). *The universe and Dr. Einstein* (2nd rev. ed.). New York: Bantam.

Barnum, C. M., & Fischer, R. (1984). Engineering technologists as writers: Results of a survey. *Technical Communication, 31,* 9–11.

Barton, B., & Barton, M. (1981). The nature and treatment of professional engineering problems: The technical writing teacher's responsibility. *Technical Communication: Perspectives for the Eighties* (NASA Conference Publication 2203, Pt. 2), 511–522.

Bataille, R. R. (1982). Writing in the world of work: What our graduates report. *College Composition and Communication, 31,* 9–11.

Battelle Memorial Institute. (1973). *Interactions of science and technology in the innovation process: Some case studies.* Final report to the National Science Foundation (NSF-C667). Columbus, OH: National Science Foundation.

Bazerman, C. (1983). Scientific writing as a social act: A review of the literature of the sociology of science. In P. V. Anderson, R. J. Brockmann, & C. R. Miller (Eds.), *New essays in technical and scientific communication: Theory, research, and practice.* Farmingdale, NY: Baywood.

Beach, R., & Bridwell, L. (Eds.). (1984). *New directions in composition research.* New York: Guilford Press.

Beaugrande, R. A. de. (1977). Information and grammar in technical writing. *College Composition and Communication, 29,* 325–332.

Becker, A. L. (1965). A tagmemic approach to paragraph analysis. *College Composition and Communication, 16,* 237–242.

Belohlov, J. A., Popp, P. O., & Porte, M. S. (1974). Communication: A view from inside of business. *Journal of Business Communication, 11,* 53–59.

Bennett, J. C. (1971). The communication needs of business executives. *Journal of Business Communication, 11,* 53–59.

Bennett, J. C., & Olney, R. J. (1986). Executive priorities for effective communication in an information society. *Journal of Business Communication, 23,* 13–22.

Berlin, J. (1982). Contemporary compositon: The major pedagogical theories. *College English, 44,* 765–777.

Berlo, D. K. (1960). *The process of communication.* New York: Holt, Rinehart, and Winston.

Berthoff, A. E. (1982). *Forming, thinking, writing: The composing imagination.* Upper Montclair, NJ: Boynton.

Bitzer, L. (1968). The rhetorical situation. *Philosophy and Rhetoric, 1,* 1–14.

Bizzell, P. (1982). Cognition, convention, and certainty: What we need to know about writing. *Pre/Text, 3,* 213–43.

Blundell, W. E. (1980, August). Confused, overstuffed corporate writing often costs firms much time—and money. *Wall Street Journal, 28,* 21.

Blyler, N. R. (1986). The heuristics of pedagogy: Approaches to teaching technical writing. *The Technical Writing Teacher, 8,* 101–111.

Bogdanowicz, M. (1983). *Who should be the judge of successful communication?* Paper presented at the Conference on College Composition and Communication.

Bohannan, L. (1980). Shakespeare in the bush. In J. McCuen & A. C. Winkler (Eds.), *Readings for writers* (3rd ed.). New York: Harcourt Brace Jovanovich.

Boice, R. (1985). The neglected third factor in writing: Productivity. *College Composition and Communication, 36,* 472- 490.

Bower, M. (1966). *The will to manage.* New York: McGraw-Hill.

Brandt, D. (1986). Toward an understanding of context in composition. *Written Communication, 3,* 139–157.

Britton, J., Burgess, T., Martin, N., McLeod, A., & Rosen, H. (1975). *The development of writing abilities (11–18).* London, England: Macmillan Education.

Britton, W. E. (1965). What is technical writing? *College Composition and Communication, 16,* 113–116.

Britton, W. E. (1975). What is technical writing? A redefinition. In D. H. Cunningham & H. A. Estrin (Eds.), *The teaching of technical writing.* Urbana, IL: National Council of Teachers of English.

Broadhead, G. J., & Freed, R. C. (1986). *The variables of composition: Process and product in a business setting.* NCTE Studies in Writing and Rhetoric. Carbondale, IL: Southern Illinois University Press.

Brown, J. S. (1985, September). The impact of the information age on the conduct and communication of science. *Science Policy Hearings, 10,* 198–216.

Bruffee, K. A. (1986). Social construction, language, and the authority of knowledge: A bibliographic essay. *College English, 48,* 773–790.

Bruner, J. (1977). Right and left hands. In M. Nystrand (Ed.), *Language as a way of knowing: A book of readings.* Toronto, Canada: The Ontario Institute for Studies in Education.

Brusaw, C. T., Alred, G. J., & Oliu, W. E. (1976). *Handbook of technical writing.* New York: St. Martin's Press.

Burke, J. (1978). *Connections.* London, England: Macmillan.

Burke, K. (1986, February 23). Letter to D. B. Smith. (Cited in D. B. Smith, 1986).

Campbell, D., & Level, D. (1985). A black box model of communications. *Journal of Business Communication, 22,* 37–47.

Carney, T. F. (1972). *Content analysis.* Winnipeg, Canada: University of Manitoba Press.

Carr, W. K., & Francke, A. W. (1976). Culture and the development of vision. *Journal of the American Optometric Association, 47,* 14–41.

Chemical Engineering News. (1982, October 18). Pp. 38–42.

Chomsky, N. (1959). Review of B. F. Skinner, *Verbal behavior. Language, 35,* 26–58.

Christensen, F. (1965). A generative rhetoric of the paragraph. *College Composition and Communication, 16,* 144–156.

Christensen, F. (1967). *Notes toward a new rhetoric.* New York: Harper & Row.

Christensen, F., & Christensen, B. (1976). *A new rhetoric.* New York: Harper & Row.

Clark, E., & Clark, H. (1977). *Psychology and language: An introduction to psycholinguistics.* New York: Harcourt Brace Jovanovich.

Coles, W., Jr. (1969). Freshman composition: The circle of unbelief. *College English, 31,* 134–142.

Collins, J. L., & Williamson, M. M. (1984). Assigned rhetorical context and semantic abbreviation in writing. In R. B. Beach & L. S. Bridwell (Eds.), *New directions in composition research.* New York: Guilford Press.

Coney, M. B., Ramey, J. A., & Souther, J. W. (1984). Technical writing in the English department: An outside perspective. *ADE (Association of Departments of English) Bulletin, 79,* 40–42.

Connors, R. J. (1983). Composition studies and science. *College English, 45,* 1–20.

Connors, R. J. (1985). The rhetoric of explanation. *Written Communication, 2,* 49–72.

Cooper, C. R., with Cherry, R., Copley, B. Fleischer, S., Pollard, R., & Sartisky, M. (1984). Studying the writing abilities of a university freshman class: Strategies from a case study. In R. Beach & L. Bridwell (Eds.), *New directions in composition research.* New York: Guilford Press.

Cooper, M. M. (1986). The ecology of writing. *College English, 48,* 364–75.

Corbett, E. P. J. (1987). Teaching composition: Where we've been and where we're going. *College Composition and Communication, 38*(4), 444–452.

Couture, B., & Goldstein, J. R. (1984). *Cases for Technical and Professional Writing.* NY: Little, Brown.

Cox, B. G., & Roland, C. G. (1973). How rhetoric confuses scientific issues. *IEEE Transactions on Professional Communication, PC–16,* 140–142.

Cox, H. L. (1976). The voices of experience: The business communication alumnus reports. *Journal of Business Communication, 6,* 3–12.

Dagher, J. P. (1978). *Technical communication.* Englewood Cliffs, NJ: Prentice-Hall.

Daiker, D., Kerek, A., & Morenberg, M. (1978). Sentence combining and syntactic maturity in freshman English. *College Composition and Communication, 29,* 36–41.

D'Angelo, F. (1975). *A conceptual theory of rhetoric.* Cambridge, MA: Winthrop.

D'Angelo, F. (1976). The modes. In G. Tate (Ed.), *Teaching composition: Ten bibliographial essays.* TX: Texas Christian University Press.

D'Angelo, F. (1984). Nineteenth-century forms/modes of discourse: A critical inquiry. *College Composition and Communication, 35,* 31- 42.

Davis, R. M. (1968). The way we write it makes a difference— sometimes: An experiment in the effects of non-standard expression. *Journal of Business Communication, 6,* 15–22.

Davis, R. M. (1977). How important is technical writing? A survey of the opinions of successful engineers. *The Technical Writing Teacher, 4,* 83–88.

Deal, T. E., & Kennedy, A. A. (1982). *Corporate culture: The rites and rituals of corporate life.* Menlo Park, CA: Addison-Wesley.

Deal, T. E., & Kennedy, A. A. (1983). Culture: A new look through old lenses. *Journal of Applied Behavioral Science, 19,* 497–506.

Debs, M. B. (1985). *Collaboration and collaborative writing: A study of technical writing in the computer industry.* Unpublished doctoral dissertation. Troy, New York: Rensselaer Polytechnic Institute.

Denton, L. W. (1979). In-house training in written communication: A status report. *Journal of Business Communication, 16,* 3–14.

Diederich, P. B. (1974). *Measuring growth in writing.* Urbana, IL: National Council of Teachers of English.

Dijk, T. A. van. (1983). Discourse analysis: Its development and application to the structure of news. *Journal of Communication, 33,* 20–43.

Dillon, G. L. (1981). *Constructing texts: Elements of a theory of composition and style.* Bloomington, IN: Indiana University Press.

Dobrin, D. N. (1983). What's technical about technical writing? In P. V. Anderson, R. J. Brockmann, & C. R. Miller (Eds.), *New essays in technical and scientific communication: Theory, research, and practice.* Farmingdale, NY: Baywood.

Dobrin, D. N. (1985). What's the purpose of teaching technical communication? *Technical Writing Teacher, 12,* 146–160.

Dobrin, D. N. (1987). Writing without discipline(s). *Iowa State Journal of Business and Technical Communication, 1,* 5–8.

Document Design Project (1981). *Guidelines for document designers.* Washington, DC: American Institutes for Research.

Doheny-Farina, S. (1986). Writing in an emerging organization. *Written Communication, 3,* 15–185.

Doheny-Farina, S. (1984). *Writing in an entrepreneurial business setting: An ethnographic study.* Unpublished dissertation. Troy, New York: Rensselaer Polytechnic Institute.

Doheny-Farina, S., & Odell, L. (1985). Ethnographic research on writing: Assumptions and methodology. In L. Odell & D. Goswami (Eds.), *Writing in nonacademic settings.* New York: Guilford Press.

Dowd, A. R. (1986, September 15). What managers can learn from manager Reagan. *Fortune,* pp. 32–41.

Driskill, L. P., & Goldstein, J. R. (1986). Uncertainty: Theory and practice in organizational communication. *Journal of Business Communication, 23,* 41–56.

Eco, U. (1976). *A theory of semiotics.* Bloomington, IN: Indiana University Press.

Elbow, P. (1973). *Writing without teachers.* New York: Oxford University Press.

Emerson, F. B. (1987). *Technical writing.* Boston, MA: Houghton Mifflin.

Emig, J. (1967). On teaching composition: Some hypotheses as definitions. *Research in the Teaching of English, 1,* 127–35.

Emig, J. (1971). *The composing processes of twelfth graders* (NCTE Research Report No. 13). Urbana, IL: National Council of Teachers of English.

Eschholtz, P. A., Rosa, A. F., & Clark, V. P. (Eds.). (1974). *Language awareness.* New York: St. Martin's Press.

Eurich, N. (1985). *Corporate classrooms: The learning business.* Princeton, NJ: The Carnegie Foundation for the Advancement of Learning and the Princeton University Press.

Evan, W. M. (1965, June). Superior-subordinate conflict in research laboratories. *Administrative Science Quarterly,* pp. 55–63.

Evered, R. (1983). The language of organizations: The case of the Navy. In L. R. Pondy, P. J. Frost, G. Morgan, & T. C. Dandridge (Eds.), *Organizational symbolism.* Greenwich, CT: JAI.

Fahnestock, J. (1986). Accommodating science: The rhetorical life of scientific facts. *Written Communication, 3,* 275–296.

Faigley, L. (1986). Competing theories of process: A critique and proposal. *College English, 48,* 527–542.

Faigley, L., Cherry, R. D., Jolliffe, D. A., & Skinner, A. (1985). *Assessing writers' knowledge and processes of composing.* Norwood, NJ: Ablex.

Faigley, L., Miller, T. P., Meyer, P. R., & Witte, S. P. (1981). *Writing after college: A stratified survey of the writing of college-trained people.* Austin, TX: University of Texas at Austin.

Faigley, L., & Witte, S. (1983). Topical focus in technical writing. In P. V. Anderson, R. J. Brockmann, & C. R. Miller (Eds.), *New essays in technical and scientific communication: Theory, research, and practice.* Farmingdale, New York: Baywood.

Farrell, T. B. (1976). Knowledge, consensus, and rhetorical theory. *Quarterly Journal of Speech, 62,* 1–14.

Fischer, W. A. (1979). The acquisition of technical information by R&D managers for problem solving in nonroutine contingency situations. *IEEE Transactions in Engineering Management, EM–26,* 8–14.

Flatley, M. E. (1982). A comparative analysis of the written communication of managers at various organizational levels in the private business sector. *Journal of Business Communication, 19,* 35–49.

Fleck, L. (1979). *Genesis and development of a scientific fact.* Chicago: University of Chicago.

Flower, L. (1979). Writer-based prose: A cognitive basis for problems in writing. *College English, 41,* 19–37.

Flower, L. S., & Hayes, J. R. (1980a). The cognition of discovery: Defining a rhetorical problem. *College Composition and Communication, 31,* 21–32.

Flower, L. S., & Hayes, J. R. (1980b). The dynamics of composing: Making plans and juggling contraints. In L. W. Gregg & E. Steinberg (Eds.), *Cognitive processes in writing.* Hillsdale, NJ: Lawrence Erlbaum.

Flower, L. S., & Hayes, J. R. (1981). A cognitive process theory of writing. *College Composition and Communication, 32,* 365–387.

Frase, L. T. (1981). Writing, text, and the reader. In C. Frederiksen, & J. F. Dominic (Eds.), *Writing: The nature, development, and teaching of written communication* (Vol. 2). Hillsdale, NJ: Lawrence Erlbaum Associates.

Freed, R. C., & Broadhead, G. J. (1987). Discourse communities, sacred texts, and institutional norms. *College Composition and Communication, 38,* 154–165.

Freedman, S. (1977). *Influences on the evaluators of student writing.* Unpublished doctoral dissertation. Stanford, California: Stanford University.

Freedman, S. (1979a). How characteristics of student essays influence teachers' evaluations. *Journal of Educational Psychology, 71,* 328–338.

Freedman, S. (1979b). Why teachers give the grades they do. *College Composition and Communication, 30,* 161–164.

Freedman, S. W. (1984). The registers of student and professional expository writing: Influences on teachers' responses. In R. Beach & L. S. Bridwell (Eds.), *New directions in composition research.* New York: Guilford Press.

Gieselman, R. D. (1980). Research in business communication: The state of the art. *Journal of Business Communication, 17,* 3–18.

Gieselman, R. D. (1985). Megatrends: The future of business writing, technical writing, and composition. *Bulletin of the Association for Business Communication, 48,* 2–6.

Gieselman, R. D. (1986). A message from the executive director. *Journal of Business Communication, 23,* 9–11.

Gilbert, G. N., & Mulkay, M. (1984). *Opening Pandora's box: A sociological analysis of scientists' discourse.* Cambridge: Cambridge University Press.

Gilsdorf, J. W. (1987). Written corporate communication policy: Extent, coverage, costs, benefits. *Journal of Business Communication, 24,* 35–52.

Glaser, S. R., Zamanou, S., & Hacker, K. (1987). Measuring and interpreting organizational culture. *Management Communication Quarterly, 1,* 173–198.

Goodin, E. H., & Swerdlow, S. (1987, March). The current quality of written correspondence: A statistical analysis of the performance of 13 industry and organizational categories. *Bulletin of the Association for Business Communication, 50,* 12-16.

Goody, J. R. (1977). *The domestication of the savage mind.* Cambridge, England: Cambridge University Press.

Gopnik, M. (1972). *Linguistic structures in scientific texts.* The Hague: Mouton.

Green, M., & Nolan, T. D. (1984). A systematic analysis of the technical communicator's job: A guide for educators. *Technical Communication, 31,* 9–12.

Gregg, R. B. (1984). *Symbolic inducement and knowing.* Columbia: University of South Carolina Press.

Grice, R. A. (1988). Information development as part of product development—not an afterthought. In E. Barnett (Ed.), *Text, context, and hypertext: Writing with and for the computer.* Cambridge, MA: MIT Press.

Hagge, J. (1987). The process religion and business communication. *Journal of Business Communication, 24,* 89–120.

Hairston, M. (1982). The winds of change: Thomas Kuhn and the revolution in the teaching of writing. *College Composition and Communication, 30,* 76–88.

Hairston, M. (1986). Different products, different processes: A theory about writing. *College Composition and Communication, 37,* 442–452.

Halliday, M. A. K., & Hasan, R. (1976). *Cohesion in English.* London: Longman.

Halloran, S. M. (1978). Technical writing and the rhetoric of science. *Journal of Technical Writing and Communication, 8,* 77–88.

Halloran, S. M. (1984). What every department chair should know about scholarship in technical communication. *ADE [Association of Departments of English] Bulletin, 79,* 43–45.

Hamermesh, M. (1981). Sharpening the old saws: Speech-act theory and business communication. *Journal of Business Communication, 18,* 15–22.

Haneda, S., & Shima, H. (1982). Japanese communication behavior as reflected in letter writing. *Journal of Business Communication, 19,* No. 1, 29.

Hanson, N. R. (1958). *Patterns of discovery: An inquiry into the conceptual foundations of science.* Cambridge, England: Cambridge University Press.

Harrison, T. M. (1987). Frameworks for the study of writing in organizational contexts. *Written Communication, 9,* 3–23.

Hayakawa, S. I. (1980). A semantic parable. In J. McCuen & A. C. Winkler (Eds.), *Readings for writers* (3rd ed.). New York: Harcourt Brace Jovanovich.

Hayes, J. R., & Flower, L. (1983). Uncovering cognitive processes in writing: An introduction to protocol analysis. In P. Mosenthal, L. Tamor, & S. Walmsley (Eds.), *Research on writing: Principles and methods.* New York: Longman.

Hays, R. (1984). Political realities in reader/situaion analysis. *Technical Communication, 31,* 16–20.

Heath, S. B. (1981). Toward an ethnohistory of writing in American education. In M. Farr Whiteman (Ed.), *Writing: The nature, development, and teaching of written communication* (Vol. 1). Hillsdale, NJ: Lawrence Erlbaum Associates.

Hellweg, S. A., & Phillips, S. L. (1983, March). *Communication policies and practices in American corporations.* Paper presented at the meeting of the Western Regional Meeting of the American Business Communication Association [Association for Business Communication], Marina del Rey, CA.

Herrington, A. J. (1985). Writing in academic settings: A study of the contexts for writing in two college engineering courses. *Research in the Teaching of English, 19,* 331–359.

Herbert, T. T. (1977). Toward an administrative model of the communication process. *Journal of Business Communication, 14,* 25–36.

Hetherington, M. S. (1982). The importance of oral communication. *College English, 44*, 570–574.

Hildebrandt, H. (1973, July). Communication barriers between German subsidiaries and parent American companies. *Michigan Business Review*, p. 11.

Hildebrandt, H. W., Bond, F. A., Miller, E. L., & Swinyard, A. W. (1982). An executive appraisal of courses which best prepare one for general management. *Journal of Business Communication, 19*, 5–15.

Hirsch, E. D. (1977). *The philosophy of composition.* Chicago: University of Chicago Press.

Hirsch, P. M., & Andrews, J.A.Y. (1983). Ambushes, shootouts, and knights of the roundtable: The language of corporate takeovers. In L. R. Pondy, P. J. Frost, G. Morgan, & T. C. Dandridge (Eds.), *Organizational symbolism*. Greenwich, CT: JAI.

Horner, W. (1979). Speech-act theory and text-act theory: "Theme-ing" in freshman composition. *College Composition and Communication, 30*, 165–169.

Houp, K. W., & Pearsall, T. E. (1984). *Reporting technical information* (5th ed.). New York: Macmillan.

House, R. J., Filley, A. C., & Kerr, S. (1971, March). Relationship of leadership consideration and initiative structure to R and D subordinates' satisfaction. *Administrative Science Quarterly*, pp. 19–30.

Huddleson, R. (1971). *The sentence in written English: A syntactic study based on an analysis of scientific texts.* London: Cambridge University Press.

Huff, A. S. (1983). A rhetorical examination of strategic change. In L. R. Pondy, P. J. Frost, G. Morgan, & T. C. Dandridge (Eds.), *Organizational symbolism*. Greenwich, CT: JAI.

Hunt, K. W. (1970). *Syntactic maturity in schoolchildren and adults.* (Monographs of the Society for Research in Child Development, No. 134.) Chicago, IL: University of Chicago Press.

Ignatieff, M. (1984). *The needs of strangers.* New York: Viking.

IIT Research Institute. (1968). *Technology in retrospect and critical events in science.* Report to the National Science Foundation (NSF-C235).

Johnson, B. M. (1977). *Communication: The process of organizing.* Boston, MA: Allyn & Bacon.

Kellogg, R. T. (1987). Writing performance: Effects of cognitive strategies. *Written Communication, 9*, 269–298.

Kerek, A., Daiker, D., & Morenberg, M. (1979). The effects of intensive sentence combining on the writing ability of college freshmen. In D. McQuade (Ed.), *Linguistics, stylistics, and the teaching of composition*. Akron, OH: L&S Books.

Kerek, A., Daiker, D., & Morenberg, M. (1980). Sentence combining and college composition. *Perception and Motor Skills: Monograph Supplement, 51*, 1059–1157.

Kiesler, S., & Sproull, L. (1982). Managerial response to changing environments: Perspectives on problem sensing from social cognition. *Administrative Science Quarterly, 27*, 548–570.

Kimel, W. R., & Monsees, M. E. (1979). Engineering graduates: How good are they? *Engineering Education, 70*, 210–212.

King, M. L. (1978). Research in composition: A need for theory. *Research in the Teaching of English, 12,* 139–202.

Kinneavy, J. (1971). *A theory of discourse.* Englewood Cliffs, NJ: Prentice-Hall.

Kintsch, W. (1974). *The representation of meaning in memory.* Hillsdale, NJ: Lawrence Erlbaum.

Kjolseth, R. (1971). Making sense: Natural language and shared knowledge in understanding. In J. A. Fishman (Ed.), *Advances in the sociology of language* (Vol. I). The Hague: Mouton.

Knoblauch, C. H., & Brannon, L. (1983). Writing as learning through the curriculum. *College English, 45,* 465–474.

Knoblauch, C. H., & Brannon, L. (1984). *Rhetorical traditions and the teaching of writing.* Upper Montclair, NJ: Boynton/Cook.

Knorr-Cetina, K. D. (1981). *The manufacture of knowledge: An essay on the constructivist and contextual nature of science.* Oxford: Pergamon Press.

Koch, S., & Deetz, S. (1981). Metaphor analysis of social reality in organizations. *Journal of Applied Communication Research, 9,* 1–15.

Kornhauser, W. (1963). *Scientists in industry: Conflict and accommodation.* Berkeley: University of California Press.

Korzybski, A. (1958). *Science and sanity: An introduction to non-Aristotelian systems and general semantics* (4th ed.). Lakeville, CT: Institute of General Semantics.

Kroll, B. M. (1978). Cognitive egocentrism and the problem of audience awareness in written discourse. *Research in the Teaching of English, 12,* 269–281.

Krulee, G. K., & Nadler, E. B. (1960). Studies of education for science and engineering: Student values and curriculum choice. *IEEE Transactions on Engineering Management, 7,* 146–158.

Kuhn, T. B. (1970). *The structure of scientific revolutions* (rev. ed.). Chicago, IL: University of Chicago Press.

Kuhn, T. B. (1977). *The essential tension.* Chicago, IL: University of Chicago Press.

Lakatos, I. (1978). *The methodology of scientific research programmes."* J. Worrall & G. Currie (Eds.). Cambridge, London: Cambridge University Press.

Lannon, J. M. (1982). *Technical writing* (2nd ed.). Boston, MA: Little, Brown and Company.

Lasswell, H. D., Leites, N., & Associates. (1965). *Language of politics: Studies in quantitative semantics.* Cambridge: MIT Press. (Original work published 1949.)

Lasswell, H. D., Lerner, D., & Pool, I. de S. (1952). *The comparative study of symbols.* Hoover Institute Studies, Series C, Number 1. Stanford, CA: Stanford University Press.

Latour, B., & Woolgar, S. (1979). *Laboratory life. The social construction of scientific facts.* Beverley Hills, CA: Sage.

Leslie, S. K. (1986). Practices of internal written communication programs. *Journal of Business Communication, 23,* 51–56.

Lewis, P. E. (1977). Merleau-Ponty and the phenomenology of language. In M. Nystrand (Ed.), *Language as a way of knowing: A book of readings.* Toronto: The Ontario Institute for Studies in Education.

Lewis, P. V. (1987). *Organizational communication: The essence of effective management* (3rd ed.). New York: Wiley.

Lipson, C. (1988). A social view of technical writing. *Iowa State Journal of Business and Technical Communication, 2,* 7–20.

Louis, M. R. (1983). Organizations as culture-bearing milieux. In L. R. Pondy, P. J. Frost, G. Morgan, & T. C. Dandridge (Eds.), *Organizational symbolism.* Greenwich, CT: JAI.

Lunsford, A. (1980). The content of basic writers' essays. *College Composition and Communication, 31,* 278–290.

Luria, A. R. (1976). *Cognitive development: Its cultural and social foundations.* Cambridge, MA: Harvard University Press.

Lutz, J. (1986). The influence of organizations on writers' texts and training. *The Technical Writing Teacher, 12,* 187–190.

Lynn, S. (1987). Reading the writing process: Toward a theory of current pedagogies. *College English, 49,* 902–910.

MacDonald, S. P. (1987). Problem definition in academic writing. *College English, 49,* 315–331.

MacIntosh, F. H. (1973). Teaching writing for the world's work. Paper presented at the annual Southeastern Regional Conference on English in the Two-Year College. In D. H. Cunningham & H. A. Estrin (Eds.), *The teaching of technical writing.* Urbana, IL: National Council of Teachers of English, 1975.

Macrorie, K. (1968). To be read. *English Journal, 57,* 668–692.

Marcson, S. (1960). *The scientist in American industry: Some organizational determinants in manpower utilization.* Princeton, NJ: Princeton University, Industrial Relations Section, Department of Economics.

Manekeller, W. (1980). *So schreibt man Geschaeftsbriefe* (3rd ed.). Muenchen: Taschenbuchverlag Jacobi K. G.

Markel, M. H. (1988). *Technical writing: Situations and strategies* (2nd ed.). New York: St. Martin's Press.

Marshall, T. A. (1987). A comment on "the context of classroom writing." *College English, 49,* 834–836.

Marx, L. (1964). *The machine in the garden: Technology and the pastoral ideal in America.* New York: Oxford University Press.

Mathes, J. C. (1980). Technical communication: The persuasive purpose. *English in Texas, 40,* 81–83.

Mathes, J. C., & Stevenson, D. W. (1976). *Designing technical reports: Writing for audiences in organizations.* Indianapolis: Bobbs-Merrill Educational Publishing.

Matsuhashi, A. (1981). Pausing and planning: The tempo of written discourse production. *Research in the Teaching of English, 15,* 113–134.

Matsuhashi, A. (1982). Explorations in the real-time production of written discourse. In M. Nystrand (Ed.), *What writers know.* New York: Academic Press.

McKeon, R. (1973). General introduction, *Introduction to Aristotle* (2nd ed.). R. McKeon (Ed.). Chicago, IL: University of Chicago Press.

McLeod, M. B. (1978). The communication problems of scientists in business and industry. *Journal of Business Communication, 15,* 27–35.

Medawar, P. B. (1969). *The art of the soluble.* Harmondsworth, Middlesex: Penguin.

Meister, J. E., & Reinsch, N. L., Jr. (1978). Communication training in manufacturing firms. *Communication Education, 27,* 235–244.

Mellon, J. C. (1969). *Transformational sentence-combining* (NCTE Research Report No. 10). Champaign, IL: National Council of Teachers of English.

Meyer, A. D. (1982). How ideologies supplant formal structures and shape responses to environments. *Journal of Management Studies, 19,* 45–61.

Meyer, B. J. F. (1975). Identification of the structure of prose and its implications for the study of reading and memory. *Psychological Review, 85,* 363–94.

Middendorf, W. H. (1980). Academic programs and industrial needs. *Engineering Education, 70,* 835–837.

Miller, C. R. (1979). A humanistic rationale for technical writing. *College English, 40,* 610–617.

Miller, C. R. (1985). Invention in technical and scientific discourse: A prospective survey. In M. G. Moran & D. Journet (Eds.), *Research in technical communication: A bibliographic sourcebook.* Westbrook, CT: Greenwood Press.

Mills, G. H., & Walter, J. A. (1978). *Technical writing* (4th ed.). New York: Holt, Rinehart and Winston.

Mills, G. H., & Walter, J. A. (1986). *Technical writing* (5th ed.). New York: Holt, Rinehart and Winston.

Moffett, J. (1968). *Teaching the universe of discourse.* Boston, MA: Houghton Mifflin.

Morenberg, M. Daiker, D., & Kerek, A. (1978). Sentence combining at the college level: An experimental study. *Research in the Teaching of English, 12,* 245–256.

Morton, J. A. (1965). From physics to function. *IEEE Spectrum, 2,* 62–64.

Murray, D. M. (1978). Internal revision: A process of discovery. In C. R. Cooper & L. Odell (Eds.), *Research on composing: Points of departure.* Urbana, IL: National Council of Teachers of English.

Naisbitt, J. (1984). *Megatrends: Ten new directions transforming our lives.* New York: Warner Books.

Nunberg, G. (1983, December). The decline of grammar. *Atlantic Monthly,* pp. 31–46.

Nystrand, M. (Ed.). (1982). *What writers know.* New York: Academic Press.

Odell, L., & Goswami, D. (1982). Writing in a non-academic setting. *Research in the Teaching of English, 16,* 201–223.

Odell, L., & Goswami, D. (1984). Writing in a non-academic setting. In R. Beach & L. Bridwell (Eds.), *New directions in composition research.* New York: Guilford Press.

Odell, L. (1985). Beyond the text: Relations between writing and social context. In L. Odell & D. Goswami (Eds.), *Writing in nonacademic settings* (pp. 249–280). New York: Guilford Press.

Odell, L., Goswami, D. & Herrington, A. (1983). The discourse-based interview: A procedure for exploring the tacit knowledge of writers in non-academic settings. In P. Mosenthal, L. Tamor, & S. Walmsley (Eds.), *Research on writing.* New York: Longman.

Odell, L., Goswami, D., Herrington, A., & Quick, D. (1983). Studying writing in non-academic settings. In P. V. Anderson, R. J. Brockmann, & C. R. Miller (Eds.), *New essays in scientific and technical communication: Theory, research, and practice.* Farmingdale, New York: Baywood Publishing Company.

Odell, L., & Goswami, D., & Quick, D. (1983). Writing outside the English composition class: Implications for teaching and learning. In R. W. Bailey & R. M. Fosheim (Eds.), *Literacy for life*. New York: Modern Language Association.

O'Hare, F. (1973). *Sentence combining: Improving student writing without formal grammar instruction.* (NCTE Research Report #15.) Urbana, IL: National Council of Teachers of English.

Olson, D. R. (1977). From utterance to text: The bias of language in speech and writing. *Harvard Educational Review, 47*, 257–281.

Overington, M. A. (1977). The scientific community as audience: Toward a rhetorical analysis of science. *Philosophy and Rhetoric, 10*, 143–164.

Paradis, J., Dobrin, D., & Bower, D. (1984). Personal correspondence (Massachusetts Institute of Technology). Reported by P. V. Anderson (1985), What survey research tells us about writing at work. In L. Odell & D. Goswami (Eds.), *Writing in nonacademic settings*. New York: Guilford Press.

Paradis, J., Dobrin, D., & Miller, R. (1985). Writing at Exxon ITD: Notes on the writing environment of an R&D organization. In L. Odell & D. Goswami (Eds.), *Writing in nonacademic settings*. New York: Guilford Press.

Park, D. B. (1986). Analyzing audiences. *College Composition and Communication, 37*, 478–488.

Pauley. S. E. (1979). *Technical report writing today*. Boston, MA: Houghton Mifflin Company.

Pauley, S. E., & Riordan, D. G. (1987). *Technical report writing today* (3rd ed.). Boston, MA: Houghton Mifflin.

Pauly, J. (1977). A case for a new model of business communication. *Journal of Business Communication, 14*, 11–24.

Pearsall, T. E. (1975). *Teaching technical writing: Methods for college English teachers.* Washington, DC: Society for Technical Communication.

Pelz, D. C., & Andrews, F. M. (1966). *Scientists in organizations*. New York: Wiley.

Penrose, J. M. (1976). A survey of the perceived importance of business communication and other business-related abilities. *Journal of Business Communication, 13*, 17–24.

Perl, S. (1979). The composing processes of unskilled college writers. *Research in the Teaching of English, 13*, 317–336.

Perl, S. (1980). Understanding composing. *College Composition and Communication, 31*, 363–369.

Pettigrew, A. (1979). On studying organizational cultures. *Administrative Science Quarterly, 24*, 570–581.

Pfeffer, J. (1981). Management as symbolic action: The creation and maintenance of organizational paradigms. In L. L. Cummings & B. Staw (Eds.), *Research in organizational behavior, I*. Greenwich, CT: JAI.

Pitkin, W. L. (1977a). Hierarchies and the discourse hierarchy. *College English, 38*, 649–659.

Pitkin, W. L. (1977b). X/Y: Some basic strategies of discourse. *College English, 38*, 660–672.

Polanyi, M. (1964). *Personal knowledge: Towards a post-critical philosophy*. New York: Harper & Row.

Popper, K. R. (1962). *Conjectures and refutations: The growth of scientific knowledge.* New York: Harper & Row.

Price, D. J. DeSolla. (1965). Is technology independent of science? *Technology and Culture, 6,* 553–568.

Prince, E. F. (1981). Toward a taxonomy of given-new information. In P. Cole (Ed.), *Radical pragmatics.* New York: Academic Press.

Purves, A. C., & Purves, W. (1986). Viewpoints: Cultures, text models, and the activity of writing. *Research in the Teaching of English, 20,* 174–197.

Rainey, B. G. (1972). Professors and executives appraise business communication education. *Journal of Business Communication, 21,* 53–61.

Reither, J. A. (1985). Writing and knowing: Toward redefining the writing process. *College English, 47,* 620–28.

Report of the Presidential Commission on the Space Shuttle Challenger Accident (Vols I-V). (1986). Washington, DC: U.S. Government Printing Office.

Rescher, N. (1970). *Scientific explanation.* New York: The Free Press.

Rhodes, F. H. (1941). *Technical report writing.* New York: McGraw-Hill.

Ritti, R. R. (1971). *The engineer in the industrial corporation.* New York: Columbia University Press.

Roberts, P. (1980). How to say nothing in five hundred words. In J. R. McCuen & A. C. Winkler (Eds.), *Readings for writers* (3rd ed.). New York: Harcourt Brace Jovanovich.

Robinson, J. L. (1985). Literacy in the department of English. *College English, 47,* 482–498.

Rogoff, R. (1984). Introduction: Thinking and learning in social context. In B. Rogoff, & J. Lave (Eds.), *Everyday cognition: Its development in social context.* Cambridge, MA: Harvard University Press.

Rogoff, R., Gouvain, M., & Ellis, S. (1984). Development viewed in its cultural context. In M. Bornstein, & M. Lamb (Eds.), *Developmental psychology: An advanced textbook.* Hillsdale, NJ: Lawrence Erlbaum Associates.

Rohman, D. G. (1965). Pre-Writing: The stage of discovery in the writing process. *College Composition and Communication, 16,* 106- 112.

Rohman, D. G., & Wlecke, A. O. (1964). Pre-Writing: The construction and application of models for concept formation in writing. U.S. Department of Health, Education, and Welfare Cooperative Research Project No. 2174. East Lansing, MI: Michigan State University.

Rorty, R. (1979). *Philosophy and the mirror of nature.* Princeton, NJ: Princeton University Press.

Rubin, D. L., & Rafoth, B. A. (1986). Social cognitive ability as a predictor of the quality of expository and persuasive writing among college freshmen. *Research in the Teaching of English, 20,* 9–21.

Russell, C., & Russell, W. M. S. (1977). Language and animal signals. In V. P. Clark, P. A. Eschholz, & A. F. Rosa (Eds.), *Language* (2nd ed.). New York: St. Martin's Press.

Saar, D. A. (1986, October). A technical writing teacher becomes a technical writer: Reflections on an IBM experience. *Linking Technology and Users, IEEE Professional Communication Society Conference Record,* Charlotte, NC. New York: The Institute of Electrical and Electronic Engineers, Inc.

Salancik, G., & Pfeffer, J. (1978). A social information processing approach to job attitudes and task design. *Administrative Science Quarterly, 23*, 224–253.

Sandman, P. M., Klompus, C. S., & Yarrison, B. G. (1985). *Scientific and technical writing.* New York: Holt, Rinehart, & Winston.

Sanford, A. J., & Garrod, S. J. (1981). *Understanding written language.* New York: John Wiley.

Schmandt-Besserat, D. (1982). The emergence of recording. *American Anthropologist, 84*, 871–878.

Schramm, W. (1954). *The process and effects of mass communication.* Urbana, IL: University of Illinois Press.

Schultz, A. (1962). *Collected papers: The problem of social reality* (Vol. I). The Hague: Mouton.

Schumacher, G. M. (1986). Reflections on the origins of writing. *Written Communication, 3*, 47–63.

Scribner, S. (1984). Studying working intelligence. In B. Rogoff & J. Lave (Eds.), *Everyday cognition: Its development in social context.* Cambridge, MA: Harvard University Press.

Scribner, S., & Cole, M. (1981). Unpackaging literacy. In M. Farr Whiteman (Ed.), *The nature, development, and teaching of written communication* (Vol. 1). Hillsdale, NJ: Lawrence Erlbaum Associates.

Searle, J. R. (1969). *Speech acts: An essay in the philosophy of language.* Cambridge, MA: Cambridge University Press.

Searle, J. R. (1979). *Expression and meaning: Studies in the theory of speech acts.* Cambridge, MA: Cambridge University Press.

Shannon, C. E., & Weaver, W. (1949). *The mathematical theory of communication.* Urbana, IL: University of Illinois Press.

Sherwin, E. W., & Isenson, R. S. (1967). Project Hindsight. *Science, 157*, 1571–1577.

Shotwell, T. K. (1970, February). Information flow in an industrial research laboratory—A case study. *IEEE Transactions on Engineering Management,* pp. 26–33.

Shuy, R. W. (1981). A holistic view of language. *Research in the Teaching of English, 15*, 101–111.

Sigband, N. B. (1968). Needed: Corporate policies on communications. *S.A.M. Advanced Management Journal, 34*, 61–67.

Silverzweig, S., & Allen, R. (1976, Spring). Changing the corporate culture. *Sloan Management Review,* pp. 33–49.

Simonds, R. H. (1960). Skills businessmen use most. *Nation's Business, 48*, 88.

Skolimowski, H. (1966). The structure of thinking in technology. *Technology and Culture, 7*, 371–383.

Smircich, L. (1981, July). *The concept of culture and organizational analysis.* Paper presented at the Summer Conference on Interpretive Approaches to Organizational Communication.

Smircich, L. (1983). Organizations as shared meanings. In L. Pandy et al. (Eds.), *Organizational symbolism.* Greenwich, CT: JAI Press.

Smith, D. B. (1986). Axioms for English in a technical age. *College English, 48*, 567–579.

Smith, F. (1978). *Understanding reading: A psycholinguistic analysis of reading and learning* (2nd ed.). New York: Holt, Rinehart & Winston.

Smith, G. (1970, June). Consultation and decision processes in the research and development laboratory. *Administrative Science Quarterly*, pp. 203–215.

Smith, W., & Combs, W. (1980). The effects of overt and covert cues on written syntax. *Research in the Teaching of English, 14,* 19–38.

Sommers, N. (1980). Revision strategies of student writers and experienced adult writers. *College Composition and Communication, 31,* 378–388.

Souther, J., & White, M. (1977). *Technical report writing* (2nd ed.). New York: Wiley.

Sperling, M, & Freedman, S. W. (1987). A good girl writes like a good girl: Written response to student writing. *Written Communication, 9,* 343–369.

Spretnak, C. M. (1982). A survey of the frequency and importance of technical communication in an engineering career. *The Technical Writing Teacher, 9,* 133–136.

Staley, R. E. (1984, August 29). The coming revolution in graduate writing programs. *Chronicle of Higher Education, 29,* 80.

Starbuck, W. H. (1982). Congealing oil: Inventing ideologies to justify acting ideologies out. *Journal of Management Studies, 19,* 3–27.

Steiner, G. (1975). *After Babel: Aspects of language and translation.* London: Oxford University Press.

Steinmann, M. (1982). Speech-act theory and writing. In M. Nystrand (Ed.), *What writers know.* New York: Academic Press.

Stewart, D. (1969). Prose with integrity: A primary objective. *College Composition and Communication, 20,* 223–227.

Stine, D., & Skarzenski, D. (1979). Priorities for the business communication classroom: A survey of business and academe. *Journal of Business Communication, 16,* 15–30.

Storms, C. G. (1983). What business school graduates say about the writing they do at work: Implications for the business communication course. *ABCA Bulletin, 46,* 13–18.

Stratton, C. R. (1984). *Technical writing: Process and product.* New York: Holt, Rinehart, Winston.

Szasz, T. (1973). Language. Reprinted in P. A. Eschholtz, A. F. Rosa, & V. P. Clark (Eds.), *Language awareness.* New York: St. Martin's Press, 1974.

Tannen, D. (1982). The myth of orality and literacy. In W. Frawley (Ed.), *Linguistics and literacy.* New York: Plenum.

Targowski, A. S., & Bowman, J. P. (1988). The layer-based, pragmatic model of the communication process. *Journal of Business Communication, 25,* 5–24.

Toffler, A. (1980). *The third wave.* New York: William Morrow & Co.

Toulmin, S. (1972). *Human understanding: The collective use and evolution of concepts.* Princeton, NJ: Princeton University Press.

Tower, J., Muskie, E., & Scowcroft, B. (1987). *The Tower commission report.* New York: Random House.

Ulman, J. N., & Gould, J. R. (1972). *Technical reporting* (3rd ed.). New York: Holt, Rinehart, and Winston.

Van Dyck, B. (1980). *Macrostructures: An interdisciplinary study of global structures in discourse, interaction, and cognition.* Hillsdale, NJ: Erlbaum.

Van Maanen. J., & Barley, S. R. (1984). Occupational communities: Culture and control in organizations. In B. Stern & L. L. Cummings (Eds.), *Research in organizational behavior* (Vol. 6). Greenwich, CT: JAI Press.

Varner, I. I. (1987). Internationalizing business communication courses. *Bulletin of the Association of Business Communication, 50,* 7–11.

Vygotsky, L. (1962). *Thought and language* (E. Hanfmann & G. Vakar, Trans.). Cambridge, MA: MIT Press.

Wason, P., & Johnson-Laird, P. N. (1972). *Psychology of reasoning: Structure and content.* Cambridge, MA: Harvard University Press.

Weick, K. (1979). *The social psychology of organizing* (2nd ed.). Reading, MA: Addison-Wesley.

Weimer, W. B. (1977). Science as a rhetorical transaction: Toward a nonjustificational conception of rhetoric. *Philosophy and Rhetoric, 10,* 1–29.

Why business takes education into own hands. (1979, July 16). *U.S. News and World Report,* p. 70.

Wildavsky, A. (1983). Information as an organizational problem. *Journal of Management Studies, 10,* 29–40.

Winkler, V. (1983). The role of models in technical and scientific writing. In P. V. Anderson, R. J. Brockmann, & C. R. Miller (Eds.), *New essays in scientific and technical communication: Theory, research, and practice.* Farmingdale, NY: Baywood.

Witt, W. (1976). Effects of quantification in scientific writing. *Journal of Business Communication, 26,* 67–69.

Witte, S. P. (1987). Pre-text and composing. *College Composition and Communication, 38,* 397–425.

Witte, S. P., & Faigley, L. (1982). Coherence, cohesion, and writing quality. *College Composition and Communication, 32,* 189–204.

Young, R. (1978). Paradigms and problems: Needed research in rhetorical invention. In C. R. Cooper & L. Odell (Eds.), *Research in Composing: Points of Departure.* Urbana, IL: National Council on Teachers of English.

Young, R., Becker, A., & Pike, K. (1970). *Rhetoric: Discovery and change.* New York: Harcourt Brace Jovanovich.

Zappen, J. P. (1983). A rhetoric for research in sciences and technologies. In P. V. Anderson, R. J. Brockmann, & C. R. Miller (Eds.), *New essays in technical and scientific communication: Theory, research, and practice.* Farmingdale, NY: Baywood.

Ziman, J. (1968). *Public knowledge: The social dimension of science.* Cambridge, London: Cambridge University Press.

Zuckerman, H. (1975). *Cognitive and social processes in scientific discovery: Recombination in bacteria as a prototypical case.* Unpublished manuscript.

Author Index

Subject Index